FOOD BEYOND TERROIR

Food, Nutrition, and Culture

While eating is a biological necessity, the production, distribution, preparation, and consumption of food are all deeply culturally inscribed activities. Taking an anthropological perspective, this book series provides a forum for thought-provoking work on the bio-cultural, cultural, and social aspects of human nutrition and food habits. The books in this series bring timely food-related scholarship intended for researchers, academics, students, and those involved in food policy.

Volume 9
FOOD BEYOND TERROIR
Tasting Place and Placing Taste in Global Perspective
Edited by Anna Colquhoun and Katharina Graf

Volume 8
FOOD AND FAMILIES IN THE MAKING
Knowledge Reproduction and Political Economy of Cooking in Morocco
Katharina Graf

Volume 7
NOURISHING LIFE
Foodways and Humanity in an African Town
Arianna Huhn

Volume 6
THE DANCE OF NURTURE
Negotiating Infant Feeding
Penny Van Esterik and Richard A. O'Connor

Volume 5
THE HERITAGE ARENA
Reinventing Cheese in the Italian Alps
Cristina Grasseni

Volume 4
FROM VIRTUE TO VICE
Negotiating Anorexia
Richard A. O'Connor and Penny Van Esterik

Volume 3
RE-ORIENTING CUISINE
East Asian Foodways in the Twenty-First Century
Edited by Kwang Ok Kim

Volume 2
RECONSTRUCTING OBESITY
The Meaning of Measures and the Measure of Meanings
Edited by Megan McCullough and Jessica Hardin

Volume 1
GREEK WHISKY
The Localization of a Global Commodity
Tryfon Bampilis

Food Beyond Terroir

Tasting Place and Placing Taste in Global Perspective

Edited by
Anna Colquhoun and Katharina Graf

berghahn
NEW YORK • OXFORD
www.berghahnbooks.com

First published in 2026 by
Berghahn Books
www.berghahnbooks.com

Library of Congress Cataloging-in-Publication Data

A C.I.P. cataloging record is available from the Library of Congress
Library of Congress Cataloging in Publication Control Number: 2025026538

British Library Cataloguing in Publication Data

A catalogue record for this book is available from the British Library.

EU GPSR Authorized Representative

LOGOS EUROPE, 9 rue Nicolas Poussin, 17000, LA ROCHELLE, France
Email: Contact@logoseurope.eu

ISBN 978-1-83695-187-2 hardback
ISBN 978-1-83695-188-9 epub
ISBN 978-1-83695-189-6 web pdf

https://doi.org/10.3167/9781836951872

This open access edition has been made available with funding from
MIT Anthro, Goethe University, SOAS University

For all our interlocutors in Croatia and Morocco
who taught us the importance of domaće *and* beldi *food*
and inspired us to create this book.

Contents

Illustrations

Figures

Table

Acknowledgments

This volume has brewed for a long time and benefited from many people's input. The initial idea came from our interlocutors in Croatia and Morocco, who taught us about *domaće* and *beldi* food and insisted we took the terms seriously. As we compared notes, the ideas for this volume emerged: to investigate relations between people, food, and place in cross-cultural comparison, and thereby to decenter *terroir*, the French concept that is so often reached for within such descriptions and analyses.

With tremendous support from Jakob Klein and the SOAS Food Studies Centre, we organized a workshop on this topic in 2022. Then, the following year, with thanks to funding from Goethe University Frankfurt and hosting by the Bolara 60 guesthouse team, we were able to bring a group of us together for a retreat in Croatia to discuss our papers and develop the themes and arguments of this book. We are indebted to the group of scholars who responded so enthusiastically to our call and who have made this project the thoroughly enjoyable and collaborative venture it has been.

Each author in this volume has contributed much more than their own chapter. We thank them for helping us hone our thinking and for giving feedback on others' chapters. Many in our group had already been working on food, taste, and place, some for a long time. This volume builds on their work and insight. Special mention here goes to Harry West, whose critical work on terroir had inspired us both and who generously gave of his time and intellect to help us make sense of the volume and write the introduction. We acknowledge also the very relevant prior work of Melissa Caldwell, Cristina Grasseni, Marion Demossier, Heather Paxson, and Brad Weiss. And we thank, too, Nir Avieli and Gisela Welz, who contributed greatly to our initial meetings and discussions.

We would also like to express our gratitude to the series editors, Jakob Klein and Melissa Caldwell, for their encouragement throughout the process; to Tony Mason, Divjot Kaur, Keara Hagerty, Ryan Masteller, and the whole team at Berghahn who helped create this book; and to our two anonymous reviewers, who gave their time and very constructive suggestions. The open access publication of this book was funded by the Open Access Publication Fund of Goethe University Frankfurt am Main. We would also like to acknowledge further open access funding provided by Heather Paxson at Massachusetts Institute of Technology (MIT) and by Charlotte Sanders at SOAS University of London via the Economic & Social Research Council [grant number ES/J50015X/1].

Finally, we thank our partners for their unwavering patience and support.

Introduction

Anna Colquhoun, Katharina Graf, and Harry G. West

Boycotts and protests, smashed shop windows, and even death threats . . . while wars rage between Russia and Ukraine, and Israel and Palestine, restaurant owners across the world fear for their livelihoods and sometimes their lives, simply because they serve the foods and tastes of their countries of origin.[1] Similarly, Chinese restaurants around the world suffered catastrophic losses of custom, and in some cases vandalism, during the COVID-19 pandemic due to associations some people made between Chinese food, uncleanliness, and the origins of the virus in China.[2] In moments of crisis like these, the linkages between people, food, and place become political and often violent. That peoples and their food tastes are fundamentally connected to their geographical places of origin is a pervasive and resilient idea with considerable visceral power.

While acts like smashing restaurant windows are highly symbolic, they also prompt us to question the meanings, discourses, and practices that people generate around food, taste, and place. Such stark acts may mask the fact that relations between people, place, and food taste are not givens but are rather being constantly made, or indeed unmade. As many Chinese American and British Chinese restaurateurs discovered during the pandemic, while they and their food became associated with the territory of China, their local histories, identities, and belonging in American and British cities were negated. These examples indicate not only how actors shape the ways that place is implicated in creating the taste of food, but also the reverse: how notions and practices of food taste create places, and people. And these configurations can have significant consequences.

This book therefore critically engages with terroir—an idea that suggests that place can be tasted in the foods to which it gives origin. Conventionally, terroir refers to the organoleptic discernment—that is to say, bodily sensing, for example, through taste, sight, and smell—of the physical production site of foods and drinks and asserts a higher-quality product. In English it has been dubbed "the taste of place" (Trubek 2008). Many may associate terroir with fine wines, reflecting the term's French origins and employment within the certification and marketing of specialist foods and drinks, now not only within Europe but also well beyond. Terroir has also been the subject of much scholarly literature, through which we take a brief tour below.[3] The contributors to this volume engage with, extend, and challenge the terroir concept by exploring the diverse and shifting social and material practices through which taste and place are mutually constitutive.

To do this, we shift from taking taste and place as givens, to focus on practices of *making taste* and *making place*. This challenges the reification of taste—as organoleptic, physiological, and passive—and place—as territorial, stable, and enduring—and it necessitates attention to the actors involved, and their interests. Taste and place are thus better thought of as verbs, or processes, than as nouns, or as things. We build on anthropological approaches that interrogate how place and taste are made and experienced in order to explore their complex relationships. In other words, we ask how place is tasted, and how taste is placed.

How taste and place are created and related concerns not only the politics of food in moments of crisis, such as times of war, or the commercial production of elite foods and drinks, such as artisan cheese or fine wines. Taste-place relations also concern the social, economic, moral, cultural, and bodily dimensions of everyday life. In this volume we thus expand our focus to also include the perspectives, and foods, of those producers and consumers often sidelined by the focus on terroir products—for example, domestic cooks, small-scale producers excluded from terroir-based certifications, rural and lower income consumers, and migrant and mixed-heritage populations. We include a diverse range of ethnographic case studies, not only from terroir's traditional stomping grounds—such as French vineyards—but also far beyond, from Russia and Palestine to China and Ghana.

As the restaurant attacks mentioned above highlight, taste-place relations have direct consequences. In contexts of movement and change they can create senses of belonging, or exclusion; they can be mobilized to lay claims to place, or to resist such claims; they can structure and connect multiple temporalities—to remember the past and to make a life in the future. How place and taste are made in relation to each other therefore matters, especially in today's context of ongoing war and displacement, resurgent nationalism, climate crisis, bio-insecurities, and ever-expanding commodification. As the chapters in this volume elaborate, at stake here are the movements and transformations of peoples, foods, and boundaries, responses to the threats and devastation of conflict and climate change, problematic acquisitions of political and economic territory, and the pursuit of more secure futures in the context of a growing worldwide sense of uncertainty.

A crucial part of thinking beyond terroir is the exploration of other frameworks—other languages, values, and scales—through which people relate food to taste and place. A few years ago, a small conversation started among two of us when we compared our own research into the concepts of *domaće* food (in

Croatia) and *beldi* food (in Morocco), which both broadly translate into English as "homemade," "ours," or "local," and are widely considered superior in quality and value to their opposites—generally industrial or imported food, sometimes also certified terroir products (Colquhoun 2019, 2024; Graf 2024). We found that these everyday concepts have very different characteristics to conventional ideas and applications of terroir: they are highly contingent, difficult to define, fix and commodify, and are embedded in subjective, emotional, and bodily experience and knowledge. They are flexibly, sometimes unharmoniously, embedded in bodies, social relations, geographical territories, temporal periods, and production logics. In Croatia and Morocco, at least, they seemed better indices than the lens of terroir for understanding changing local material and social dynamics and their connections to broader political economies of food and taste.

Thus motivated, and in collaboration with the SOAS Food Studies Centre, we brought together a group of scholars, mostly anthropologists, whose research interrogates comparable food concepts elsewhere, including those whose research has engaged with the terroir concept itself. Following an initial two-day workshop to share our research directions, our group decided to produce this edited volume. It has been a collaborative project, including a retreat in Croatia to work on our chapters and to develop the book's main themes and arguments, and an internal peer-review process through which we commented on each other's draft chapters.

The result is a rich collection of comparative ethnographic case studies from around the world that demonstrate the diverse and shifting ways in which people, taste, and place are brought into relation. These include contexts of migration and displacement, colonization and war, poverty, cultural and material movement and mixing, and economic and environmental change. In some cases, the notion of terroir is employed, in others it is contested, and in some it is simply irrelevant. The chapters take us "beyond" terroir by decentering it—encouraging us to pay attention to how else people relate taste to place—and by shifting the focus from taste and place as givens to tasting and placing as acts and processes with far-reaching consequences. This volume therefore challenges narratives of essentialized relationships between people, place, and taste, and we hope it will encourage students, researchers, writers, practitioners, and policymakers to think "beyond terroir."

Terroir

The idea of terroir has risen to prominence in recent decades within Europe—and increasingly elsewhere in the world—in discussions of the relationship between food and place. The term, *terroir*, derives from the Latin *territorium*, referring to the lands surrounding a town (Parker 2015: 5). But terroir denotes a far more substantial phenomenon than mere proximity or location. Contemporary usage of the term has emphasized how the defining characteristics of a particular place are expressed within the products emanating from it. Most notably, terroir discourse has long been prominent in the wine trade. Producers and enthusiasts alike have suggested that wines profoundly reflect the geographical features of the regions—even the individual vineyards, or parcels—upon which the grapes used in their making have been grown, including soil composition, slope, and aspect, as well as patterns of sunshine, precipitation, and temperature (Wilson 1998).

In recent decades the terroir idea has been applied to an ever-expanding number of products—from other alcoholic beverages to fruits, vegetables and herbs, grains, pulses, seeds and nuts, dairy products, meats, and even fish and other products of the sea (with reference to the latter sometimes using the term *merroir*—a mash-up of the French word for sea, *mer*, and *terroir*; see, e.g., Aistara, this volume). The terroir idea has even been adopted to refer to handicrafts associated with particular places, and to precious gems or metals such as gold.

The increased currency of the terroir idea has been driven in part by its close association with geographical indications (GIs). These have a long history. While referring to a foodstuff by reference to where it was or can be made was surely a practice among prehistoric people, and the ancient Egyptians, for example, indicated the origin of grapes on vessels of wine to be consumed by the pharaoh, such references were formally regulated as far back as the ancient Greeks. King Charles VI of France decreed in 1411 that the Roquefort name could only be applied to cheeses aged in the caves of Roquefort-sur-Soulzon, and five centuries later Roquefort was the first product to be granted an *Appellation d'Origine Contrôlée* (AOC).

Other western European countries followed suit, passing similar legislation that reserved the right to use specified place names to producers making these products within strictly delineated borders and adhering to specifications agreed upon by recognized producers. The Lisbon agreement of 1958 led to mutual recognitions among these states of what came to be called *Protected Designations of Origin* (PDO) and *Protected Geographical Indications* (PGI). With the formation of the European Union (EU) in 1992 and its subsequent expansion, this mutual recognition has encompassed an increasing number of states and expanded further still through unilateral agreements with additional non-EU member states. In parallel, the World Trade Organization's (WTO) Agreement of Trade-Related Aspects of Intellectual Property Rights has afforded protection of geographical indications among all its member states, albeit for much more limited categories of products, such as wines and spirits (West 2013a).

As of 2023 there were approximately 65,900 protected GIs worldwide[4] (Crossland-Marr and Krause 2023: 7), including in South America and Asia. This expansion has been driven by the EU, which has lobbied the WTO for international recognition of GIs for its own interests (West 2013a: 225), that is to say, protecting European producers in the context of industrialized and globalized agrifood systems (see also Welz 2013: 268–69). The conceptualization of food-people-place connections through the lens of terroir has also spread in the absence of GIs, being adopted, for example, by American artisan cheesemakers (Paxson 2010, 2013), winemakers (Black 2012), and chefs (Costa and Besio 2011)—a phenomenon that some scholars have encouraged (Trubek 2005, 2008; Trubek and Bowen 2008). And the terroir logic has also been promoted by the Italian-born Slow Food organization, whose founder Carlo Petrini adopted a terroir strategy for his home region of Piedmont and then applied it to Slow Food's work globally (Laudan 2004).

This spread of the terroir concept has attracted scholarly attention. Research demonstrates that terroir's meanings and usages vary across time and space (Trubek and Bowen 2008; Paxson 2010, 2013; Demossier 2011, 2020; Black 2012; Cappeliez 2017; Gyimóthy 2017), prompting us to consider the "terroir of terroir" (West 2013a: 221). As terroir travels beyond its original French homeland, it finds more mixed success, requiring special efforts to find it, explain it, reinterpret it, or even "reverse-engineer" it (Paxson 2010; see also Tregear 2003; Meneley 2011; Black 2012; Belasco 2014; Besky 2014; Jung 2014; Weiss 2016). However, despite terroir's adaptability, at its core remains the assertion of important and enduring links between product, people, and place, which one of us has termed "the terroir triad" (West 2022).

If usage of the term *terroir* has historically been rather unequivocal about the essential relationship between places and their associated products, it has been somewhat more ambivalent with regard to people. French writers in the seventeenth century saw terroir as affecting the inhabitants of a place as much as its bounty—asserting that particular lands influenced the thought, language, and behavior, not to mention the identity and, by some accounts, even the physiological characteristics, of their inhabitants (Parker 2015). In other words, terroir shaped not only agriculture but also human culture. Such usages lent themselves in various contexts both to pejoratives (for example, through paternalistic categorizations of *ethnies*) and to assertions of regional and national pride (Bassett, Blanc-Pamard, and Boutrais 2007).

Recent adaptations of the terroir term have shifted focus away from how lands shape people to ask instead what role people play in the translation of places into particular products. Whereas some proponents of the terroir idea, with a focus on environmental factors, have tended to suggest that places essentially make products—see, for example, Bohmrich's account of *vignerons* who consider themselves mere "stewards of nature" and claim to "let the wine make itself" (Bohmrich 1996: 40)—scholars in the humanities and social sciences have of late asserted a more prominent role for people as the makers even of products profoundly associated with place. To this end they have called attention to the importance of various forms of local knowledge and *savoir-faire* that enable people to craft goods that best express the places of origin in which they live and work (Bérard and Marchenay 1996; Trubek 2008; Trubek, Guy, and Bowen 2010).

Within this cultural turn in terroir discourse, some have highlighted the complex social dynamics at play in the exercise of such forms of situated local knowledge and in the contested claims associated with them. Here it bears reflecting upon how profoundly the terroir idea has become historically entwined with GIs in order to protect the intellectual property of the bearers of such knowledge and to reserve the use of recognized place names for those making products in the places for which these products are named (Barham 2003; West 2013a). How such arrangements work—who benefits from them, and who loses out—are often objects of intense contestation, as many have pointed out (see, e.g., Ulin 1996; Gade 2004; Guy 2007; Bowen 2015; Grasseni 2017; Demossier 2020). Taken together, these contributions have advanced the argument that there can be no terroir products without the active involvement of people as interpreters of the natural environment—that is, that terroir is as much a human construct as it is an environmental one. However, the very terms that Trubek has used to define terroir—"the taste of place"—remain relatively unquestioned within terroir discourse. In short, taste and place continue to be somewhat taken for granted.

We recognize, of course, that Trubek has called attention to the role played by "tastemakers" in the formation of a cuisine (Trubek 2000). But the complex—and sometimes fraught—relationships between producers translating natural factors into place-based foods, for example, and promoters of such foods cultivating demand for them, or various groups of consumers embracing them, is somewhat underscrutinized to date both within terroir discourse and within its critical examination in the literature.

Terroir discourse has also generally taken "place" for granted, treating it as a fixed starting point, not only to be translated into terroir products but also to be recognized and awarded protections. This is unsurprising, as many proponents of terroir have—in the face of ever-greater globalization of the food trade—been fundamentally concerned with challenging the idea that anything can be made by anyone, anywhere. But as one of us has recently argued, the very forces of globalization against which proponents of the terroir idea often orient themselves evince how thoroughly places are themselves constantly being made and remade by human hands—a fundamental element of ever-changing contexts of production with which terroir has yet to fully reckon (West 2022). Examples of this include the place name Gruyère being carried by Swiss dairymen to places like Kars, where it is now an appellation of a "traditional Turkish cheese"; and the reproduction of place-based products such as Parmigiano-Reggiano cheese today depending upon the *savoir-faire* of a workforce composed in significant measure of migrants from north African countries (West 2022).

Tasting Place and Placing Taste

Whereas "the taste of place" implies that taste and place are givens and thus passive, more active forms of tasting place and of emplacing taste remain less explored in terroir conversations (notable openings to this include, e.g., Paxson 2010; Weiss 2011). This volume advances critical engagement with the terroir idea by examining the diverse ways in which people not only make foods and foodways in, and of, particular places, but also, in the process, recreate their tastes as well as the places they inhabit. We therefore build on anthropological approaches to place and taste that foreground their multiple dimensions, their social and material construction, and their contingency.

Place

Since the 1980s, anthropologists have critiqued notions of "a culture," "a people," and "a place," and moreover, the mapping of one onto another (notably, Clifford 1988; Gupta and Ferguson 1992, 1997). Like cultures and peoples, places can be hard to pin down on maps, and their boundaries can be indeterminate and porous. And they are socially and politically imagined while also materially and subjectively experienced (de Certeau 1984; Lefebvre 1991; Basso 1996; Casey 1996). Anthropologists have therefore turned attention to place making. As something always in the making, or unmaking, *place* can be as much a verb as a noun.

Sites are made into meaningful places through acts such as naming, imagining, experiencing, and other ways of attaching meanings to locations (Basso 1996; Aucoin 2017). Such place making may operate on multiple levels: while institutions and structures of power may use "strategies" to generate "proper" places, people in everyday life use "tactics" to negotiate these "rules" in their own ways (de Certeau 1984). Actors have varying interests in shaping material and symbolic geographies, and varying abilities to do so. The success of place-making strategies may require the repressing of some voices, practices, or experiences, while foregrounding others. For example, places such as "the countryside" can be constructed in particular and exclusionary ways, which can be contested (Williams 1973; Murdoch and Pratt 1993; Murdoch and Marsden 1995; Sibley 1995; Holloway and Kneafsey 2004; Domingos, Sobral, and West 2014).

Places are therefore not static and enduring but characterized by movement and change. Today's increasingly globalized world makes this ever more apparent, as global flows of finance, people, products, and ideas impact multiple aspects of daily life as well as our experiences and imaginings of place. Our rapidly changing climate reveals the instability of material place, as dust storms relocate tons of sand, wildfires destroy vast landscapes, and species migrate in new patterns or become extinct (see, e.g., Baer and Singer 2025). Ongoing conflicts and wars, and resulting displacements of people, highlight the impermanence of political borders and the fragility of human connection to place. Meanwhile, commercially and politically motivated attachments of particular cultural products to particular peoples and territories—such as in contexts of tourism or nationalism—rub up against realities of movement and change (see, e.g., Brown 2004; Comaroff and Comaroff 2009; Nyamnjoh 2010; Macdonald 2013; Coombe and Baird 2016; Salazar 2018; Porciani 2019; Cavanaugh 2023).

This begs the questions: What places do people taste in their food? And what places do people *want* to taste?

Foods are often said to express the lands that produced them: soil types detectable in some wines, sun-drenched Mediterranean gardens yielding intensely flavored tomatoes, herb-rich pastures flavoring grazing animals' meat, and milk, and so on (Trubek 2008). The imaginary here is rural and often bucolic. But ecologies of production are complex and, despite the pastoral imagery, often characterized by politics, conflict, and compromise (Ulin 1996; West 2013a; Grasseni 2017; Demossier 2020). Increasingly, we are aware of polluted land and seas. The fact that chemicals such as pesticides seep into our foods is well documented (Pretty 2005; Kalyabina et al. 2021). While second-generation ("non-persistent") pesticides are designed not to persist through to the point of sale, they can be more toxic at the point of application, affecting the health of agricultural workers (Wright 2010). And what of other sites of food production? Globally, more than half of the human population now lives in towns and cities. Much food acquisition, processing, cooking, and eating happens in these urban contexts, as does production with the rise of urban farming (Cockrall-King 2012; de Zeeuw and Drechsel 2015; Rosan and Pearsall 2017). Such urban places can also be tasted (Rhys-Taylor 2017; Edwards, Gerritsen, and Wesser 2021), although these tastes of place are not usually celebrated as terroir.

For many, desired tastes are redolent of home: the comforting taste of homemade food—often considered healthy and especially important for children (Cairns, Johnston, and MacKendrick 2013; Boni 2023)—or of food that reminds one of a past home, or perhaps an imagined one (Seremetakis 1994; Abranches 2014; Aistara 2014; Papacharalampous 2023). For some, however, these tastes of home may be associated with long hours of domestic labor or parental moral anguish, with both burdens notably borne by women, or may conjure memories of conflict or abuse (Charles and Kerr 1988; Paugh and Izquierdo 2009; Bowen, Brenton, and Elliott 2019; Le Moal et al. 2021). For others, this taste may be longed for but hard to achieve, for example, in contexts of migration or displacement (Sutton 2001; Ben-Ze'ev 2004; Abbots 2011; Raman 2011; Meneley, this volume). Sometimes we seek the opposite, the taste of "the Other" or the exotic (Molz 2004; hooks 2014), for example, in restaurants and (other) tourism sites (Heldke 2001; Long 2004; Caldwell 2006). Home is therefore an important place to taste but is far from straightforward. This place may be a particular kin or household group, a domestic or nutritional ideal, a temporal period, or a physically distant territory or community. It may be something we seek to taste, or not.

Similarly, the idea of "local" food is powerful in many contexts. Often imbued with moral and ethical values, food grown or processed "locally" is considered by many fresher, tastier, and healthier (Nabhan 2001; Kingsolver 2007). "Local food" is also often considered "authentic," as a representation of place, being ecologically and/or culturally embedded—qualities that may be tasted (Caldwell 2010; Weiss 2011). However, as with home, this local place is neither a given nor unproblematic. It scales from the smallholding and microregion, via undefined notions of "near here," to the region and nation. At the latter level, food taste becomes important within strategies of "gastronationalism" (DeSoucey 2010) and "gastrodiplomacy" (Rockower 2012; Bestor 2014). At every scale, the "local" we seek to taste is a construct—a choice, often strategic, concerning not only its spatial extent but also its productive, cultural, and social makeup—and thus exclusive, and contestable (Hinrichs 2003; Feagan 2007; Sims 2010; DeLind 2011; Avieli 2013, 2016; Beriss 2019). At every scale, too, it exists in tension with the "global," or translocal—the ongoing movements of peoples, foods, and tastes—which at times may be welcomed and incorporated into the "local" (Watson 1997; Bestor 2001; Caldwell 2004), or considered superior (Jing 2000; Caldwell 2002), while at others resisted, denied, or obfuscated (Zaneri 2013; Cavanaugh 2023; see also Cook and Crang 1996).

Taste

Likewise, we approach the taste of food as something that cannot be taken for granted but instead requires interrogation. By our conception, taste is not merely a constellation of chemicals "out there," waiting to be "naturally" received by the body; it is also something that is conceived, made, and subjectively and socially experienced. Like place, *taste* is as much a verb—tasting—as a noun.

Taste is hard to pin down. On the one hand, it is the most subjective, private, and singular of all bodily senses. Yet on the other, taste is something that connects us to material, social, and ideological worlds, undeniably context-dependent, and able to be communicated and codified (Ferguson 2011; Vercelloni 2016; Counihan and Højlund 2018; Hedegaard 2018). Whereas taste has historically been treated as a lower, more animalistic sense (along with smell and touch)—and therefore a matter of the human body, not of the mind (Korsmeyer 1999)—contemporary social scientists have explored taste beyond a purely physiological response.

Bourdieu (1984) famously elaborated the social and aesthetic foundation and role of taste—the upper classes' taste for fine wines, for example. In this reading, good taste is a marker of social distinction, an ability to discern and appreciate certain tastes, which is learned from one's socially situated upbringing and displayed in order to maintain or improve one's class position (see also Gronow

1997). Others—notably Seremetakis (1994), Korsmeyer (1999) and Sutton (2001, 2011)—have drawn our attention back to the bodily experience of taste, arguing for it to be taken seriously as a cognitive, symbolic, and aesthetic practice, even as a "total social fact," relating to the whole cosmology of a culture (Sutton 2011). Within this work, considerable attention has been given to the relationship between food taste and memory. Taste can stand in for lost times or places (Proust 1913–27; Seremetakis 1994; Sutton 2001; see also Ben-Ze'ev 2004; Caldwell 2006; Dunn 2008). Scholars have also challenged the widespread idea that bodily taste resides solely in the mouth or nose. Tasting can also occur with the fingers, or in the stomach, and it often involves all bodily senses, including a sense of temporality (see, e.g., Sobo 1997; Mann et al. 2011; Graf 2022; Simpson Miller, this volume).

Meanwhile, others have stressed the social and discursive construction of taste. Not only can varying material qualities and tastes be created in food, but how they are recognized, experienced, invested with meaning, and valued by both producers and consumers is down to sociocultural processes. This has been demonstrated through work on, among other things, artisan chocolate (Terrio 2000) and terroir products in France (Trubek 2008), hummus within Arab-Jewish relations (Hirsch 2011), olive oil in Palestine (Meneley 2014), and pork in North Carolina (Weiss 2016). In other words, we learn what and how to taste. Taste is therefore not only historically and culturally specific, it is also shaped by a range of social and material practices—including technologies, languages, and experiences—of tasting (Silverstein 2004; Mol 2009; Everett 2012; Mann and Mol 2019; Graf 2022; Mol 2024).

Food tastes are also intertwined with the political economies of food systems. Tastes and tasting practices are often governed by national and international quality frameworks and technologies that categorize and organize tastes in global hierarchies (Cavanaugh 2007; Grasseni 2011; Welz 2013; West 2013b; Jung 2014; Meneley 2014; Besky 2020). Meanwhile, the sociocultural meanings carried by food qualities and tastes can affect foods' political and economic trajectories. For example, where quality is constructed as assurances of production conditions, such as organic farming, certifiers may capture surplus value, but where "good taste" is constructed as aesthetics and exclusivity, high-end restaurants can do so (Guthman 2002; see also Pratt 2007; Mol 2009). Aesthetic and safety standards also affect movements of foods across political borders and around the world, privileging some producers over others, with far-reaching socioeconomic impact (Freidberg 2003; Dunn 2003; Gille 2016).

As all these scholars, and others, demonstrate, tasting is an active practice. It is learned, requires effort, and creates outcomes. Some have therefore considered tasting to be a form of labor (Spackman and Lahne 2019). People's tasting bodies are implicated in the production of values, be they cultural (Weiss 1996), social (Bourdieu 1984; Weiss 2016), economic (Mintz 1985; Guthman 2002), or political (Caldwell 2002; Hayes-Conroy and Hayes-Conroy 2008). Food taste is thus best thought of not only as the result of food production processes, but also as a co-production, and much else beyond.

In sum, tasting necessarily happens in a particular time and space, and is shaped by actors with particular interests. Even when seemingly abstracted and objectified, taste still relies on people and institutions to locate it. Taste is therefore made in multiple sites: from oceans and fields to factories and domestic kitchens, from socialized bodies to globalized markets, and from nostalgic imaginaries to food standards specifications. And taste operates on multiple scales—organoleptic, emotional, bodily, social, cultural, moral, and political—often simultaneously. Tasting is thus a diverse range of practices bound up with class and distinction, ethnicity and nationalism, community and exclusion, nostalgia and future-making, pleasure and pain, labor and love.

Tasting Place and Placing Taste Beyond Terroir

Although the social science scholarship on taste contains ample references to the necessarily emplaced nature of practices of tasting, beyond explorations of tasting the nation (or "gastronationalism") (see, e.g., Caldwell 2002; Guy 2007; DeSoucey 2010; Monterescu and Handel 2019) it does not systematically engage with the diverse range of relationships between taste and place.

There are a few notable openings. For example, Paxson's study of cheesemakers in the United States highlights how, through crafting artisan cheese and appreciation for it, producers also attempt to craft themselves and the place where they live, both socially and ecologically (Paxson 2013). Weiss's exploration of pastured pork in North Carolina demonstrates how it is the networked social practices of breeding, husbandry, butchery, marketing, and cooking that establish the local taste and authenticity of this pork, revealing how these actors understand and make place (Weiss 2016). This volume builds on these works by bringing together both established and emerging scholarship on the taste-place nexus.

By putting tasting and placing in the gerund form, we shift the emphasis away from essentialized notions of taste and place toward a more complex understanding of taste and place as constituted by (human) practice and thus always in the (re)making. By pairing "tasting place" with "placing taste," we further emphasize how place and taste are dialogically constitutive and thus dynamic constructs. Paxson's and Weiss's ethnographies illustrate that while places and place-making processes can shape tastes and tasting practices, so, too, can tastes and tasting practices produce places in multiple ways. We consider both place and taste as generative: place making and taste making are implicated in each other.

This volume therefore represents a conversation with and around the idea of terroir—the relationship between taste and place. We expand, and thereby challenge, the terroir idea by explicitly moving beyond assumptions of the substantive nature of place and taste and by highlighting their co-constitutive relationship. The volume is therefore not a critique of terroir per se but rather a foray into the breadth of ways in which actors relate place and taste. This allows for a more nuanced understanding of the shifting and contingent relations between taste and place, accommodating, for example, situations of movement and change, or of innovation and destruction.

We take an explicitly comparative approach. By revealing the diversity of ways and sites in which people relate place to taste, we also move beyond terroir by decentering it: while in some contexts actors embrace, or develop, the terroir concept, in others it is simply unused and irrelevant. Furthermore, as terroir narratives increasingly travel around the world, as we sketched above, some actors implicitly or explicitly challenge terroir with other models or interests. This broad comparative approach shifts the focus away from terroir's traditional sites—that of commercial fine food and drink production in western Europe—to include sites, foods, and people often omitted from "taste of place" discussions, such as domestic cooks, degraded seas, conflict zones, and displaced populations. Thinking beyond the conventional terroir model allows researchers to engage with other taste-place languages, practices, and values, and thus attune to diverse situations and dynamics. The inflexible givens of "the taste of place"—not least the kinds of value they often enshrine—do not work in many contexts today, and maybe never did.

The contributors to this book highlight why the taste-place nexus matters and requires critical attention, for it is where and how places and tastes get remade. We pay attention to the range of actors involved—from microbes to international institutions—and what's at stake for whom. Concepts, narratives, and practices linking place and taste matter. Rather than being purely descriptive of a state of affairs, they can have considerable social, economic, legal, and political implications. For example, notions of taste in relation to place may be mobilized by certain actors to include or exclude (peoples and foods); to reaffirm gender, class, or other social relations; to create, dominate, expand, or restrict markets; to further regionalist, nationalist, or imperialist goals; or to resist or challenge such agendas. As the following chapters illustrate, tasting place and placing taste have wide-ranging consequences for human—and other—life.

Organization of the Book

While the theoretical scope of our approach and diversity of case studies included would allow this volume to be structured in multiple ways, we decided to do so by the "sites" in which taste and place are made in relation to each other.

Lands

We might most readily imagine the land as the archetypical siting of the taste of place. Yet the chapters in this section question how land is implicated in tasting place, and they find static, bounded notions of territory inadequate, or problematic. We learn how contingent, contentious, or even irrelevant land can be when relating taste to place.

Anne Meneley asks what happens to the taste of place when territory itself is contested. She describes ways through which Palestinians in Palestine and in the diaspora employ food cultivation, preparation, and knowledge to maintain a sense of belonging and shared identity in the context of forced displacement from their lands. Meneley shows that the nexus between food, taste, and land is vitally important for Palestinians—living on through shared memories and practices—but necessarily resembles something very different to the more conventional, often romanticized notion of terroir. The Palestinian "taste of place" that this chapter depicts is instead fraught with disconnection, destruction, and pollution, and yet it remains resilient as a fundamental element of Palestinian steadfastness.

Simon Pope and Harry West "beat the bounds of terroir" in their chapter on cidermaking in Devon, England. Their research project—a collaboration between an artist and an anthropologist—challenges the institutionalized understanding of terroir as the soil and climate of an area of land by bringing two seemingly opposed scalar perspectives into dialogue: the microbes involved in cidermaking and the folkways through which cider is celebrated. Proposing that these are both crucial elements of cidermaking's ecology of production, and moreover that they both move through space and change over time, Pope and West challenge the focus on bounded territorial place within terroir orthodoxy.

Guntra Aistara challenges the notion of land in another way. Her chapter explores the "taste of place" in smoked flounder in Latvia. While both Soviet and current-day political economic systems have separated and essentialized land and sea identities and livelihoods, with sometimes disastrous consequences, the making of smoked flounder, and its distinctive taste, has long relied on the intertwined features and livelihoods associated with both land and sea. Today its production is highly contingent due to ecological crises in the Baltic Sea, resulting from climate change, overfishing, and pollution, and due to socioeconomic change related to EU regulation, depopulation, and economic crisis. Aistara thus argues for "the taste of place" to incorporate shifting and precarious "amphibious" land-sea relations.

Sarah Czerny considers the apparent placelessness of European vegan cheeses—with their producers, recipes, and ingredients seeming to come from "everywhere and nowhere at the same time." This seems to contrast with the importance of place given to dairy cheeses, not least the terroir of the geolocation of their production. However, Czerny argues that place is in fact also very important to vegan cheesemaking and -eating, and, as with dairy cheeses, makes both the cheeses and their consumers knowable. Rather than giving their cheeses (geo) localized identities, vegan cheesemakers emplace them in "the environment," a broader notion of place founded on ideological commitment. Czerny's chapter demonstrates the malleability of place, with actors foregrounding or obscuring certain aspects of it depending on their interests.

Melissa Caldwell explores what she calls the "terroirism" of *nash* (our) food in Russia. Caldwell takes a historical approach to show how *nash* has been implicated in oppressive political projects of colonialist national expansion, including the recent Russian invasion of Ukraine. Land and soil are central to this process of nashification, as they are felt to impart distinct qualities in foods and consequently in bodies, thus ideologically and viscerally uniting Russian people, Russian national identity, and Russian land. In this case, then, taste is not only implicated in symbolic place making but also in the material, and violent, acquisition of territory.

Laws

While geographical indications such as EU PDOs are presented as legally protecting preexisting taste-place relations, namely the traditional producers of distinctive "tastes of place," the chapters in this section outline how place and taste are brought into relation through social actors' invocations of a broader range of statutory and moral codes. These vary from informal social or individual moralities to formalized (inter)national certifications. We see how some actors attempt to standardize and control how taste and place are coproduced as well as how others (deliberately) work to retain ambiguity or flexibility, with consequences for shifting production methods and food qualities, and for market expansions and exclusions.

Anna Colquhoun's investigation of cured pork in Croatian Istria reveals how its transformation into a legally protected place-named product for an expanded market was at odds with small-scale producers' understandings and practices of making "good" cured pork. While the protected "Istrian ham" is founded on the imported idea of terroir, and territorial notions of place and taste, the latter is based on the concept of *domaće* (homemade) for which the social and moral dimensions of relations of production are more important. While making and appreciating the taste of *domaće* cured pork constitutes a moral critique of, and line of defense against, the political economy surrounding EU GIs, Colquhoun reminds us that informal food quality practices are also subject to social governance.

Marion Demossier demonstrates how the very rules meant to protect the distinctive terroir and wines of Burgundy, France, threaten their existence in the context of environmental change. Here, in the heartland of terroir ideology, while some conventional producers uphold AOC standards and seek to reproduce the expected "taste of place" in their wines, others are adapting to increasing environmental uncertainty through *bricolage*—diverse approaches centered on care for land, plants, and workers—and challenging the rigidity of viticulture and viniculture imposed by the AOCs. These producers assert their wines' true expressions of place as fluid, flexible, and individual, which, Demossier suggests, might constitute a more sustainable and resilient approach to winemaking.

Greg de St. Maurice introduces us to the diversity of place brands in Japan and illustrates how a plethora of both legally defined place-named foods and more "fuzzy" brands for foods—which are not regulated, owned, or managed by a formal or legal entity—coexist and often mutually benefit one another. De St. Maurice thus demonstrates the flexibility with which people make and market relations between taste and place, and he also indicates why rigid "delineated place brands" do not work for some producers and consumers, who prefer instead the flexibility of "fuzzy" or "individual" brands.

Kunbing Xiao's chapter on Chinese black teas introduces the vernacular notion of *fengtu*—which denotes the natural environment and customs of a place—to illustrate the power of narration in creating and regulating taste and place in a globalized market context. Through tracing the development of Lapsang souchong tea in the Tongmu Nature Reserve in the Wuyi Mountains—a region not previously associated with prestigious tea production—Xiao reveals the tea's narrative transformation from a cheap drink produced for foreigners into a highly priced GI product for domestic consumers. Her chapter captures the sometimes accidental steps by which "local imagination" becomes "legalized reality," and her attention to the arising legal conflicts reminds us that the coproduction of taste and place always involves redefinitions and relocations of both.

Bodies

While the existing terroir literature attends to the work and skill of food and drink producers such as vintners and cheesemakers, here we introduce actors rarely associated with terroir discourse, such as low-income consumers and domestic cooks, many of whom are women. The chapters in this section describe not only how these actors use their skilled bodies to create food tastes but also how tasting and placing foods are embodied practices, relating to gender, ethnic, class, and other social relations, and the reproduction of cultural values. We also learn how these deeply personal embodied practices relate to the dynamics of large-scale political economies.

Katharina Graf elaborates on the role of the skilled body in reproducing individual and situated notions of taste and place. Graf introduces the notion of *beldi*—a widely used concept used to place and differentiate people and objects across Morocco and the Arab region—to analyze how poor Marrakshi cooks make sense of and produce foods, tastes, and places in the absence of national quality standards and in the ever-looming presence of food insecurity. *Beldi* shifts attention to the largely hidden work of making taste and place in low-income homes, and thus grounds discussions "beyond terroir" in the context of poverty and increasing uncertainty.

Hanna Garth similarly highlights the role of embodied knowledge in making "Cuban" foods both in Cuban kitchens and in the Cuban diaspora in the United States. Through detailed ethnographic examples, she argues that, although most foods are imported, Cubans still consider their cuisine to have a distinct taste of place, which she locates in the embodied practice of combining ingredients. The ability to mix and create something new—including racial and cultural mixing described as *mestizaje*—has a long history in Cuba and the wider region and shapes the way Cubans relate to food and drink.

James Staples considers the relation of taste to place in India, which now boasts over 350 WTO-recognized GIs for food products, which, as elsewhere, define and protect products according to their geographical place of production. He finds that while these GIs are designed for transnational trade, they had little resonance for his interlocutors in southern India. Although consumers in India may denote regional affiliations through food, Staples argues that for many, foods' links to places are mediated by other concerns, namely ideas about the body, seasonality, gender, caste, and class. In other words, who eats what foods, when, where, and with whom is what matters to his interlocutors. Place is thus both physical and portable, as something embodied in people and carried with them.

Brandi Simpson Miller's historical account of *chop*—proper food—in Ghana demonstrates its past and current relevance to ecological, ethnic, and cosmological relations, and highlights the role of women in making taste, place, and people. Simpson Miller argues that it is women's embodied work of preparing *chop*, for which correct texture is paramount, that creates important social relations and emplaces people. *Chop* thereby emerges as a flexible category that accommodates the movements of peoples and foods across space and time while remaining crucial within people's claims to land, identity, and economic and sexual obligations.

Imaginaries

While conventional notions of terroir tend to stress the past—long-standing traditions honed over generations to suit local conditions—in this section we consider the ways that actors employ multiple imaginaries, and temporalities, in their relating of taste to place. In many cases people are grappling with contexts of movement, change, and uncertainty by combining notions of tradition and modernity, and of "here" and "there." Relating taste to place often becomes an active future-making project rather than an expression of backward-looking nostalgia.

Charlotte Sanders analyzes Sudanese women's everyday food practices in Portsmouth, England, where—in the context of migration and displacement—they seek to recreate familiar tastes of a past home while also creating a new and future home. As border controls have become stricter, importing foods from Sudan has become increasingly difficult and unaffordable. As a result, these women trial new means of food provisioning and processing, and they collaborate across ethnic divides to continue reproducing Sudanese meals. Sanders thus encourages us to see women's domestic food work as powerful future-making and place-making practices.

Jakob Klein argues that British-born Chinese restaurateurs reinvent Chinese cuisine in the UK through what he calls the "politics of authenticity." Against the backdrop of changing patterns of migration from China to Britain over the last century—and of restaurant cuisines along with it—he recounts how second-generation British Chinese who grew up in the catering trade reinvent Chinese restaurant food using very personal visions, experiences, and identities as both British and Chinese. The resulting cuisine is fluidly emplaced in both China and Britain, conjuring both recognition and controversy among their diverse consumers.

Yuson Jung explores how Bulgarian wine professionals are having to engage with globally dominant wine quality standards, namely the terroir ideology that holds that high-quality wines reflect their geographical microregion of production in gustatory terms. Considering the practices and narratives of a range of wine professionals, Jung finds that in Bulgaria terroir wines are not the only "good wine" (*dobro vino*), and that Bulgarian "good wines" reflect diverse social imaginaries of place—from the home and factory to the region and nation—in multiple sensorial terms beyond the gustatory.

Cristina Grasseni focuses on a successful cheese business in Val Taleggio to demonstrate the very deliberate and political ways in which taste and place are coproduced to ensure a viable economic future in this remote region of northern Italy. Key to this strategy is the semantic packaging of cheesemaking, for which keywords such as *territorio*, *tipicità*, *tradition*, and *sustainability* are flexibly used to both sell cheese and assert belonging and sovereignty. In the context of climate change, global market consolidation, and depopulation in mountainous regions, Grasseni argues that while this entrepreneurship is about making money, it is also a reflective, performative, and political act that imagines and creates a future for the local community.

Finally, in their afterword, Heather Paxson and Brad Weiss draw out the range of analytical moves that take us beyond terroir: by detaching place from territory, by approaching borders and boundaries between places as thresholds, and, lastly, by emphasizing foods' capacities to remake the world. They respond to our ongoing conversations by suggesting that we all engage with the "productive ambiguity of terroir"—to embrace it both as an ethnographic category *and* as a generalizable model, or as a quality in a product *and* as a goal toward which (or against which) people aim. Insofar as this volume's collection of case studies reveals how taste and place are made in relation to each other, in diverse and shifting ways, and with far-reaching implications, we hope to have both laid bare some of terroir's most interesting ambiguities and invited further examination of the varied goals that animate people's understanding of and engagement with taste and place—whether through, or "beyond," terroir.

Acknowledgments

We thank all the other contributors to this volume for their enthusiasm and ongoing support, and for our constructive discussions at the initial online workshop and the retreat in Croatia. We would also like to thank the series editors and our two anonymous reviewers for their efforts and time.

Anna Colquhoun is a social anthropologist and Research Associate at the SOAS Food Studies Centre. Her PhD thesis, *Making Local Specialities: Food, Place and Value in Istria*, examined the intersections of making food, place, and value in this rapidly changing borderland region. Her research interests include culinary tourism and the cultural economy, hospitality and cooking, and localized and post-socialist food systems. Anna has a degree in Anthropology and Archaeology from the University of Cambridge and an MA in the Anthropology of Food from SOAS. She has worked in international development, culinary education, food writing, consultancy, and hospitality.

Katharina Graf is a social anthropologist based at Goethe University Frankfurt, Germany. Her research interests range from food, gender, and family to bodily knowledge, generational change, as well as global markets, food security, science and technology, and citizenship. She has recently published *Food and Families in the Making: Knowledge Reproduction and Political Economy of Cooking in Morocco* (Berghahn, 2024). She received her PhD in Anthropology and Sociology from SOAS University of London.

Harry G. West is Professor of Anthropology at the University of Exeter (UK), with expertise in agrarian history and political economy, and food and cultural heritage. His research explores artisan cheesemaking and the cultural economy, including how cheesemakers have embraced and transformed the idea of terroir, and how they have adopted innovative methods while reproducing cheesemaking traditions in changing historical contexts. His publications on these themes include numerous journal articles and book chapters. He is Convener of the Master's in Food Studies, Codirector of the Centre for Rural Policy Research, and Lead of Exeter Food: A University Research Network.

Notes

1. See for example: Pistol 2022; Reiner 2022; Clerkin 2023; Lynn 2023; Haboucha 2024.
2. See for example: Olson and Tang 2020; Ramirez 2020; Williams 2021; Yang 2023.
3. There is now a vast body of literature on and around terroir, so our review here is necessarily partial.
4. This is a World Intellectual Property Organization/Lisbon tally, pertaining to appellations of origin and geographical indications.

References

Abbots, Emma-Jayne. 2011. "It Doesn't Taste as Good from the Pet Shop." *Food, Culture & Society* 14(2): 205–23.

Abranches, Maria. 2014. "Perceptions of the Country Through the Migration of City-Grown Crops: Guinean Food in Bissau and in Lisbon." In *Food between the Country and the City: Ethnographies of a Changing Global Foodscape*, edited by Nuno Domingos, Jose Sobral, and Harry G. West, 127–42. London: Bloomsbury.

Aistara, Guntra A. 2014. "Authentic Anachronisms." *Gastronomica* 14(4): 7–16.

Aucoin, Pauline McKenzie. 2017. "Toward an Anthropological Understanding of Space and Place." In *Place, Space and Hermeneutics*, edited by Bruce B. Janz, 395–412. Cham: Springer International Publishing.

Avieli, Nir. 2013. "What Is 'Local Food?' Dynamic Culinary Heritage in the World Heritage Site of Hoi An, Vietnam." *Journal of Heritage Tourism* 8(2–3): 120–32.

———. 2016. "Local Food, Local Specialities and Local Identity." In *The Handbook of Food and Anthropology*, edited by Jakob A. Klein and James L. Watson, 133–48. London: Bloomsbury.

Baer, Hans A., and Merrill Singer. 2025. *Building the Critical Anthropology of Climate Change: Towards a Socio-ecological Revolution*. London: Routledge.

Barham, Elizabeth. 2003. "Translating Terroir: The Global Challenge of French AOC Labeling." *Journal of Rural Studies* 19(1): 127–38.

Bassett, Thomas, Chantal Blanc-Pamard, and Jean Boutrais. 2007. "Constructing Locality: The Terroir Approach in West Africa." *Africa* 77(1): 104–29.

Basso, Keith. 1996. *Wisdom Sits in Places: Landscape and Language among the Western Apache*. Albuquerque: University of New Mexico Press.

Belasco, Warren. 2014. "Terroir in D.C.? Inventing Food Traditions for the Nation's Capital." In *Edible Identities: Food as Cultural Heritage*, edited by Ronda L. Brulotte and Michael A. Di Giovine. London: Routledge.

Ben-Ze'ev, Efrat. 2004. "Politics of Taste and Smell: Palestinian Rites of Return." In *The Politics of Food*, edited by Marianne E. Lien and Brigitte Nerlich, 141–60. New York: Berg.

Bérard, Laurence, and Philippe Marchenay. 1996. "Tradition, Regulation, and Intellectual Property: Local Agricultural Products and Foodstuffs in France." In *Valuing Local Knowl-*

edge: Indigenous People and Intellectual Property Rights, edited by Stephen B. Brush and Doreen Stabinsky, 230–43. Washington: Island Press.

Beriss, David. 2019. "Food: Location, Location, Location." *Annual Review of Anthropology* 48: 61–75.

Besky, Sarah. 2014. "The Labor of Terroir and the Terroir of Labor: Geographical Indication and Darjeeling Tea Plantations." *Agriculture & Human Values* 31(1): 83–96.

———. 2020. *Tasting Qualities: The Past and Future of Tea*. Berkeley: University of California Press.

Bestor, Theodore. 2001. "Supply-Side Sushi: Commodity, Market and the Global City." *American Anthropologist* 103(1): 76–95.

———. 2014. "Most F(l)avored Nation Status: The Gastrodiplomacy of Japan's Global Promotion of Cuisine." *Gastrodiplomacy* 11: 59–62.

Black, Rachel. 2012. "A Sense of Place." *Boston Hospitality Review* (Fall): 13–17.

Bohmrich, Roger. 1996. "Terroir: Competing Perspectives on the Roles of Soil, Climate and People." *Journal of Wine Research* 7(1): 33–46.

Boni, Zofia A. 2023. *Feeding Anxieties: The Politics of Children's Food in Poland*. New York: Berghahn.

Bourdieu, Pierre. 1984. *Distinction: A Social Critique of the Judgement of Taste*. Cambridge: Harvard University Press.

Bowen, Sarah. 2015. *Divided Spirits: Tequila, Mezcal, and the Politics of Production*. Berkeley: University of California Press.

Bowen, Sarah, Joslyn Brenton, and Sinikka Elliott. 2019. *Pressure Cooker: Why Home Cooking Won't Solve Our Problems and What We Can Do about It*. Oxford: Oxford University Press.

Brown, Michael F. 2004. *Who Owns Native Culture?* Cambridge: Harvard University Press.

Cairns, Kate, Josée Johnston, and Norah MacKendrick. 2013. "Feeding the 'Organic Child': Mothering through Ethical Consumption." *Journal of Consumer Culture* 12(2): 97–118.

Caldwell, Melissa L. 2002. "The Taste of Nationalism: Food Politics in Postsocialist Moscow." *Ethnos* 67(3): 295–319.

———. 2004. "Domesticating the French Fry: McDonald's and Consumerism in Moscow." *Journal of Consumer Culture* 4(1): 5–26.

———. 2006. "Tasting the World of Yesterday and Today: Culinary Tourism and Nostalgia Foods in Post-Soviet Russia." In *Fast Food/Slow Food: The Cultural Economy of the Global Food System*, edited by Richard Wilk, 97–112. Lanham: Altamira Press.

———. 2010. *Dacha Idylls: Living Organically in Russia's Countryside*. Berkeley: University of California Press.

Cappeliez, Sarah. 2017. "How Well Does Terroir Travel? Illuminating Cultural Translation Using a Comparative Wine Case Study." *Poetics* 65 (December): 24–36.

Casey, Edward. 1996. "How to Get from Space to Place in a Fairly Short Stretch of Time: Phenomenological Prolegomena." In *Senses of Place*, ed. Steven Feld and Keith Basso, 13–52. Santa Fe: School of American Research Press.

Cavanaugh, Jillian R. 2007. "Making Salami, Producing Bergamo: The Transformation of Value." *Ethnos* 72(2): 149–72.

———. 2023. "Authenticity and Its Perils: Who Is Left Out When Food Is 'Authentic'?" *Gastronomica* 23(1): 28–37.

Certeau, Michel de. 1984. *The Practice of Everyday Life*. Berkeley: University of California Press.

Charles, Nickie, and Marion Kerr. 1988. *Women, Food, and Families*. Manchester: Manchester University Press.

Clerkin, Ben. 2023. "Antisemitic Mob Targets Jewish Falafel Restaurant in Philadelphia." *The Jewish Chronicle*, 4 December. Retrieved 6 December 2024 from https://www.thejc.com/news/usa/antisemitic-mob-targets-jewish-falafel-restaurant-in-philadelphia-g3xe630y.

Clifford, James. 1988. *The Predicament of Culture*. Cambridge: Harvard University Press.

Cockrall-King, Jennifer. 2012. *Food and the City: Urban Agriculture and the New Food Revolution*. Amherst: Prometheus Books.

Colquhoun, Anna. 2019. "Making Good Meat: From Draft Animal to Local Speciality." *Gastronomica* 19(1): 94–95.

———. 2024. "Making Local Specialities: Food, Place and Value in Istria." PhD diss. London: SOAS University of London.

Comaroff, John L., and Jean Comaroff. 2009. *Ethnicity, Inc.* Chicago: University of Chicago Press.

Cook, Ian, and Philip Crang. 1996. "The World on a Plate: Culinary Culture, Displacement and Geographical Knowledges." *Journal of Material Culture* 1(2): 131–53.

Coombe, Rosemary J., and Melissa Baird. 2016. "The Limits of Heritage: Corporate Interests and Cultural Rights on Resource Frontiers." In *A Companion to Heritage Studies*, edited by William Logan, Mairead Nic Craith, and Ullrich Kockel, 337–54. Hoboken: Wiley & Sons Publishing.

Costa, LeeRay, and Kathryn Besio. 2011. "Eating Hawai'i: Local Foods and Place-Making in Hawai'i Regional Cuisine." *Social & Cultural Geography* 12(8): 839–54.

Counihan, Carole, and Susanne Højlund, eds. 2018. *Making Taste Public: Ethnographies of Food and the Senses*. London: Bloomsbury.

Crossland-Marr, Lauren, and Elizabeth L. Krause. 2023. "Theorizing Authenticity: Introduction to the Special Section." *Gastronomica* 23(1): 5–12.

DeLind, Laura B. 2011. "Are Local Food and the Local Food Movement Taking Us Where We Want to Go? Or Are We Hitching Our Wagons to the Wrong Stars?" *Agriculture & Human Values* 28: 273–83.

Demossier, Marion. 2011. "Beyond Terroir: Territorial Construction, Hegemonic Discourses, and French Wine Culture." *Journal of the Royal Anthropological Institute* 17(4): 685–705.

———. 2020. *Burgundy: A Global Anthropology of Place and Taste*. New York: Berghahn.

DeSoucey, Michaela. 2010. "Gastronationalism: Food Traditions and Authenticity Politics in the European Union." *American Sociological Review* 75(3): 432–55.

Domingos, Nuno, José Manuel Sobral, and Harry G. West, eds. 2014. *Food between the Country and the City: Ethnographies of a Changing Global Foodscape*. London: Bloomsbury.

Dunn, Elizabeth C. 2003. "Trojan Pig: Paradoxes of Food Safety Regulation." *Environment & Planning A: Economy & Space* 35(8): 1493–1511.

———. 2008. "Postsocialist Spores: Disease, Bodies, and the State in the Republic of Georgia." *American Ethnologist* 35(2): 243–58.

Edwards, Ferne, Roos Gerritsen, and Grit Wesser, eds. 2021. *Food, Senses and the City*. London: Routledge.

Everett, Sally. 2012. "Production Places or Consumption Spaces? The Place-Making Agency of Food Tourism in Ireland and Scotland." *Tourism Geographies* 14(4): 535–54.

Feagan, Robert. 2007. "The Place of Food: Mapping Out the 'Local' in Local Food Systems." *Progress in Human Geography* 31(1): 23–42.

Ferguson, Priscilla Parkhurst. 2011. "The Senses of Taste." *American Historical Review* 116(2): 371–84.

Freidberg, Susanne. 2003. "French Beans for the Masses: A Modern Historical Geography of Food in Burkina Faso." *Journal of Historical Geography* 29(3): 445–63.

Gade, Daniel W. 2004. "Tradition, Territory, and Terroir in French Viniculture: Cassis, France, and Appellation Contrôlée." *Annals of the Association of American Geographers* 94(4): 848–67.

Gille, Zsuzsa. 2016. *Paprika, Foie Gras, and Red Mud: The Politics of Materiality in the European Union*. Bloomington: Indiana University Press.

Graf, Katharina. 2022. "Taste Knowledge: Couscous and the Cook's Six Senses." *Journal of the Royal Anthropological Institute* 28(2): 577–94.

———. 2024. *Food and Families in the Making: Knowledge Reproduction and Political Economy of Cooking in Morocco*. New York: Berghahn.

Grasseni, Cristina. 2011. "Re-inventing Food: Alpine Cheese in the Age of Global Heritage." *Anthropology of Food* 8 (May): online. https://doi.org/10.4000/aof.6819.

———. 2017. *The Heritage Arena: Reinventing Cheese in the Italian Alps*. New York: Berghahn.

Gronow, Jukka. 1997. *The Sociology of Taste*. London: Routledge.

Gupta, Akhil, and James Ferguson. 1992. "Beyond 'Culture': Space, Identity, and the Politics of Difference." *Cultural Anthropology* 7(1): 6–23.

———. 1997. "Culture, Power, Place: Ethnography at the End of an Era." In *Culture, Power, Place: Explorations in Critical Anthropology*, edited by Akhil Gupta and James Ferguson, 1–29. Durham: Duke University Press.

Guthman, Julie. 2002. "Commodified Meanings, Meaningful Commodities: Re-Thinking Production-Consumption Links through the Organic System of Provision." *Sociologia Ruralis* 42(4): 295–311.

Guy, Kolleen M. 2007. *When Champagne Became French*. Baltimore: Johns Hopkins University Press.

Gyimóthy, Szilvia. 2017. "The Reinvention of Terroir in Danish Food Place Promotion." *European Planning Studies* 25(7): 1200–1216.

Haboucha, Rebecca. 2024. "Restaurants Outside of Palestine and Israel Are Being Attacked in Protest of War." *The Conversation*, 28 February. Retrieved 6 December 2024 from https://theconversation.com/restaurants-outside-of-palestine-and-israel-are-being-attacked-in-protest-of-the-war-223929.

Hayes-Conroy, Allison, and Jessica Hayes-Conroy. 2008. "Taking Back Taste: Feminism, Food and Visceral Politics." *Gender, Place & Culture* 15(5): 461–73.

Hedegaard, Liselotte. 2018. "(Re)Tasting Places." *Gastronomica* 18(1): 66–75.

Heldke, Lisa. 2001. "'Let's Eat Chinese!' Reflections on Cultural Food Colonialism." *Gastronomica* 1(2): 76–79.

Hinrichs, C. Clare. 2003. "The Practice and Politics of Food System Localization." *Journal of Rural Studies* 19(1): 33–45.

Hirsch, Dafna. 2011. "'Hummus Is Best When It Is Fresh and Made by Arabs': The Gourmetization of Hummus in Israel and the Return of the Repressed Arab." *American Ethnologist* 38(4): 617–30.

Holloway, Lewis, and Moya Kneafsey, eds. 2004. *Geographies of Rural Cultures and Societies*. London: Routledge.

hooks, bell. 2014. "Eating the Other: Desire and Resistance." In *Black Looks: Race and Representation*, 2nd ed., edited by bell hooks. New York: Routledge.

Jing, Jun. 2000. *Feeding China's Little Emperors: Food, Children, and Social Change*. Stanford: Stanford University Press.

Jung, Yuson. 2014. "Tasting and Judging the Unknown Terroir of the Bulgarian Wine: The Political Economy of Sensory Experience." *Food & Foodways* 22(1–2): 24–47.

Kalyabina, Valeriya P., Elena N. Esimbekova, Kseniya V. Kopylova, and Valentina A. Kratasyuk. 2021. "Pesticides: Formulants, Distribution Pathways and Effects on Human Health: A Review." *Toxicology Reports* 8: 1179–92.

Kingsolver, Barbara. 2007. *Animal, Vegetable, Miracle: A Year of Food Life*. New York: HarperCollins.

Korsmeyer, Carolyn. 1999. *Making Sense of Taste: Food and Philosophy*. Ithaca: Cornell University Press.

Laudan, Rachel. 2004. "Slow Food: The French Terroir Strategy, and Culinary Modernism: An Essay Review." *Food, Culture & Society* 7(2): 133–44.

Lefebvre, Henri. 1991. *The Production of Space*. Translated by Donald Nicholson-Smith. Oxford: Wiley-Blackwell.

Le Moal, Fairley, Maxime Michaud, Carol Anne Hartwick-Pflaum, Georgia Middleton, Isabelle Mallon, and John Coveney. 2021. "Beyond the Normative Family Meal Promotion: A Narrative Review of Qualitative Results about Ordinary Domestic Commensality." *International Journal of Environmental Research & Public Health* 18(6): 3186.

Long, Lucy M., ed. 2004. *Culinary Tourism*. Lexington: University Press of Kentucky.

Lynn, Guy. 2023. "Palestinian Takeaway in London Gets Death Threats Every Day." *BBC News*, 20 October. Retrieved 6 December 2024 from https://www.bbc.com/news/uk-england-london-67172707.

Macdonald, Sharon. 2013. *Memorylands: Heritage and Identity in Europe Today*. London: Routledge.

Mann, Anna M., and Annemarie Mol. 2019. "Talking Pleasures, Writing Dialects: Outlining Research on "Schmecka."" *Ethnos* 84(5): 772–88.

Mann, Anna M., Annemarie Mol, Priya Satalkar, Amalinda Savirani, Nasima Selim, Malini Sur, and Emily Yates-Doerr. 2011. "Mixing Methods, Tasting Fingers: Notes on an Ethnographic Experiment." *HAU: The Journal of Ethnographic Theory* 1(1): 221–43.

Meneley, Anne. 2011. "Blood, Sweat and Tears in a Bottle of Palestinian Extra-Virgin Olive Oil." *Food, Culture & Society* 14(2): 275–92.

———. 2014. "Discourses of Distinction in Contemporary Palestinian Extra-Virgin Olive Oil Production." *Food & Foodways* 22(1–2): 48–64.

Mintz, Sidney. 1985. *Sweetness and Power: The Place of Sugar in Modern History*. New York: Viking.

Mol, Annemarie. 2009. "Good Taste: The Embodied Normativity of the Consumer-Citizen." *Journal of Cultural Economy* 2(3): 269–83.

———. 2024. *Eating Is an English Word*. Durham: Duke University Press.

Molz, Jennie Germann. 2004. "Tasting an Imagined Thailand: Authenticity and Culinary Tourism in Thai Restaurants." In *Culinary Tourism*, edited by Lucy M. Long, 53–75. Lexington: The University Press of Kentucky.

Monterescu, Daniel, and Ariel Handel. 2019. "Liquid Indigeneity: Wine, Science, and Colonial Politics in Israel/Palestine." *American Ethnologist* 46(3): 313–27.

Murdoch, Jonathan, and Terry Marsden. 1995. *Reconstituting Rurality*. London: Routledge.

Murdoch, Jonathan, and Andy C. Pratt. 1993. "Rural Studies: Modernism, Postmodernism and the 'Post-rural.'" *Journal of Rural Studies* 9(4): 411–27.

Nabhan, Gary Paul. 2001. *Coming Home to Eat: The Pleasures and Politics of Local Foods*. New York: W. W. Norton & Company.

Nyamnjoh, Francis B. 2010. "Racism, Ethnicity and the Media in Africa: Reflections Inspired by Studies of Xenophobia in Cameroon and South Africa." *Africa Spectrum* 45(1): 57–93.

Olson, Alexandra, and Terry Tang. 2020. "'Chinatown Is Bleeding': Misguided COVID-19 Fears Hit Asian American Businesses." *Global News*, 18 February. Retrieved 6 December 2024 from https://www.nbcnews.com/news/asian-america/pandemic-era-stigma-cost-asian-restaurants-74b-lost-revenue-new-study-rcna67454.

Papacharalampous, Nafsika. 2023. *The Metamorphosis of Greek Cuisine: An Ethnography of Deli Foods, Restaurant Smells and Foodways of Crisis*. London: Routledge.

Parker, Thomas. 2015. *Tasting French Terroir*. Berkeley: University of California Press.

Paugh, Amy, and Carolina Izquierdo. 2009. "Why Is This a Battle Every Night? Negotiating Food and Eating in American Dinnertime Interaction." *Linguistic Anthropology* 19(2): 185–204.

Paxson, Heather. 2010. "Locating Value in Artisan Cheese: Reverse Engineering Terroir for New-World Landscapes." *American Anthropologist* 112(3): 444–57.

———. 2013. *The Life of Cheese: Crafting Food and Value in America*. Berkeley: University of California Press.

Pistol, Rachel. 2022. "Ukraine: How Boycotting Everything Russian—and Blaming Russian Society rather than Putin—Is Xenophobic." *The Conversation*, 23 March. Retrieved 6 December 2024 from https://theconversation.com/ukraine-how-boycotting-everything-russian-and-blaming-russian-society-rather-than-putin-is-xenophobic-179267.

Porciani, Ilaria. 2019. *Food Heritage and Nationalism in Europe*. London: Routledge.

Pratt, Jeff. 2007. "Food Values: The Local and the Authentic." *Critique of Anthropology* 27(3): 285–300.

Pretty, Jules N. 2005. *The Pesticide Detox: Towards a More Sustainable Agriculture*. London: Routledge.

Proust, Marcel. 1913–27. *À la Recherche du Temps Perdu*. Paris: Grasset and Gallimard.

Raman, Parvathi. 2011. "'Me in Place, and the Place in Me': A Migrant's Tale of Food, Home and Belonging." *Food, Culture & Society* 14(2): 165–80.

Ramirez, Rachel. 2020. "How a Chinese Immigrant Neighborhood Is Struggling amid Coronavirus-Related Xenophobia." *Vox*, 14 March. Retrieved 6 December 2024 from https://www.vox.com/identities/2020/3/14/21179019/xenophophia-chinese-community-sunset-park.

Reiner, Adam. 2022. "Many Russian Restaurant Owners in the US Oppose the War on Ukraine. They Still Face Bullying and Shame." *Bon Appétit*, 16 December. Retrieved 6 December 2024 from https://www.bonappetit.com/story/russian-restaurant-owners-ukraine-war.

Rhys-Taylor, Alex. 2017. *Food and Multiculture: A Sensory Ethnography of East London*. London: Routledge.

Rockower, Paul. 2012. "Recipes for Gastrodiplomacy." *Place Branding and Public Diplomacy* 8(3): 235–46.

Rosan, Christina D., and Hamil Pearsall. 2017. *Growing a Sustainable City? The Question of Urban Agriculture*. Toronto: University of Toronto Press.

Salazar, Noel B. 2018. "The Maasai as Paradoxical Icons of Tourism (Im)mobility." In *Indigenous Tourism Movements*, edited by Alexis Celeste Bunten and Nelson Graburn, 56–72. Toronto: University of Toronto Press.

Seremetakis, C. Nadia. 1994. *The Senses Still: Perception and Memory as Material Culture in Modernity*. Boulder, CO: Westview.

Sibley, David. 1995. *Geographies of Exclusion: Society and Difference in the West*. London: Routledge.

Silverstein, Michael. 2004. "'Cultural' Concepts and the Language-Culture Nexus." *Current Anthropology* 45(5): 621–52.

Sims, Rebecca. 2010. "Putting Place on the Menu: The Negotiation of Locality in UK Food Tourism, from Production to Consumption." *Journal of Rural Studies* 26: 105–15.

Sobo, Elisa. 1997. "The Sweetness of Fat: Health, Procreation, and Sociability in Rural Jamaica." In *Many Mirrors: Body Image and Social Relations*, edited by Nicole Landry Sault, 132–54. New Brunswick: Rutgers University Press.

Spackman, Christy, and Jacob Lahne. 2019. "Sensory Labor: Considering the Work of Taste in the Food System." *Food, Culture & Society* 22(2): 142–51.

Sutton, David E. 2001. *Remembrance of Repasts: An Anthropology of Food and Memory*. 2nd ed. Oxford: Berg.

———. 2011. "Memory as Sense: A Gustemological Approach." *Food, Culture & Society* 14(4): 468–74.

Terrio, Susan J. 2000. *Crafting the Culture and History of French Chocolate*. Berkeley: University of California Press.

Tregear, Angela. 2003. "From Stilton to Vimto: Using Food History to Re-think Typical Products in Rural Development." *Sociologia Ruralis* 43(2): 91–107.

Trubek, Amy B. 2000. *Haute Cuisine: How the French Invented the Culinary Profession*. Philadelphia: University of Pennsylvania Press.

———. 2005. "Place Matters." In *The Taste Culture Reader: Experiencing Food and Drink*, edited by Carolyn Korsmeyer, 260–72. New York: Berg.

———. 2008. *The Taste of Place: A Cultural Journey into Terroir*. Berkeley: University of California Press.

Trubek, Amy B., and Sarah Bowen. 2008. "Creating the Taste of Place in the United States: Can We Learn from the French?" *GeoJournal* 73(1): 23–30.

Trubek, Amy B., Kolleen M. Guy, and Sarah Bowen. 2010. "Terroir: A French Conversation with a Transnational Future." *Contemporary French & Francophone Studies* 14(2): 139–48.

Ulin, Robert C. 1996. *Vintages and Traditions: An Ethnohistory of Southwest French Wine Cooperatives*. Washington: Smithsonian.

Vercelloni, Luca. 2016. *The Invention of Taste: A Cultural Account of Desire, Delight and Disgust in Fashion, Food and Art*. London: Routledge.

Watson, James L., ed. 1997. *Golden Arches East: McDonald's in East Asia*. Stanford, CA: Stanford University Press.

Weiss, Brad. 1996. *The Making and Unmaking of the Haya Lived World: Consumption, Commoditization, and Everyday Practice*. Durham: Duke University Press.

———. 2011. "Making Pigs Local: Discerning the Sensory Character of Place." *Cultural Anthropology* 26(3): 438–61.

———. 2016. *Real Pigs: Shifting Values in the Field of Local Pork*. Durham: Duke University Press.

Welz, Gisela. 2013. "Contested Origins: Food Heritage and the European Union's Quality Label Program." *Food, Culture & Society* 16(2): 265–79.

West, Harry G. 2013a. "Appellations and Indications of Origin, Terroir, and the Social Construction and Contestation of Place-Named Foods." In *The Handbook of Food Research*, edited by Anne Murcott, Warren Belasco, and Peter Jackson, 209–28. London: Bloomsbury.

———. 2013b. "Thinking Like a Cheese: Towards an Ecological Understanding of the Reproduction of Knowledge in Contemporary Artisan Cheesemaking." In *Understanding Cultural Transmission in Anthropology: A Critical Synthesis*, edited by Roy Ellen, Stephen J. Lycett, and Sarah E. Johns, 320–45. New York: Berghahn.

———. 2022. "Terroir Products: A Movable Heritage Feast?" *Review of Agricultural, Food & Environmental Studies* 103(1): 1–27.

Williams, Raymond. 1973. *The Country and the City*. Oxford: Chatto & Windus.

Williams, Sophie. 2021. "COVID-19: Chinatowns Fighting Racism and Pandemic to Survive." *BBC News*, 12 February. Retrieved 6 December 2024 from https://www.bbc.com/news/world-55986359.

Wilson, James E. 1998. *Terroir: The Role of Geology, Climate and Culture in the Making of French Wines*. Berkeley: University of California Press.

Wright, Angus. 2010. *The Death of Ramón González: The Modern Agricultural Dilemma*. Austin: University of Texas Press.

Yang, Angela. 2023. "Pandemic-Era Stigma Cost Asian Restaurants $7.4B in Lost Revenue, New Study Finds." *NBC News*, 26 January. Retrieved 6 December 2024 from https://www.nbcnews.com/news/asian-america/pandemic-era-stigma-cost-asian-restaurants-74b-lost-revenue-new-study-rcna67454.

Zaneri, Taylor. 2013. "Tell Me What You Eat, and I Will Tell You Who You Are Not: An Examination of Food, Culture, Ethnicity, and Identity in Italy." In *Food: Expressions and Impressions*, edited by Don Sanderson and Mira Crouch, 71–79. Leiden: Brill.

Zeeuw, Henk de, and Pay Drechsel, eds. 2015. *Cities and Agriculture: Developing Resilient Urban Food Systems*. London: Routledge.

PART I

Lands

CHAPTER 1

Terroir in Contested Territories

Anne Meneley

Introduction

This chapter discusses the idea of terroir in a place, Palestine, where place itself is highly contested. The concept of terroir, the connection between place-people-craft-taste, evokes, inadvertently perhaps, a timeless and unchanging "taste of place." Place is highlighted in Beriss's "Food: Location, Location, Location," which offers an anthropological approach to terroir. He notes how place is at the center of the French notion of terroir: "At the center of these rules is location and the assertion that *place* is essential in the making of the foods protected by geographic indication laws. The idea of *terroir* connecting the regional landscapes, with the craft and culture of French peasants, and the history of the nation became, over the course of the twentieth century, part of a kind of national common sense" (2019: 63, emphasis added).

But what happens to the "taste of place" when place itself is so contested? Along with a plant cultivar or particular animal, and the craft needed to turn the raw product into a foodstuff, a fundamental principle of terroir is "land." Which brings me to my central question: How do you discuss the taste of place for those forcibly displaced from their land? This displacement of Palestinians from their land, their yearning to return to it, and their desire to stay on their beloved land engages with the taste of the land in a different way than many terroir discourses do.

The establishment of the state of Israel seventy-five years ago, what Palestinians call the Nakba (catastrophe), resulted in the fragmentation of the Palestinian population, with at least 750,000 Palestinians displaced as refugees to camps in Syria, Jordan, the Gaza Strip, and various parts of the West Bank. Many Palestinians now refer to their contemporary situation as the "ongoing Nakba," as the displacement of Palestinians from their land continues to the present day with illegal Israeli settlements expanding rapidly into the West Bank. West Bank Palestinians cannot enter Jerusalem, even East Jerusalem or Israel, without a permit.

Since 2006, movement of people and goods, including food, in and out of the Gaza Strip was strictly controlled by Israel. Since 7 October 2023, the movement of food into Gaza has been even more severely limited.

This chapter is based on field research in the West Bank, as well as with Palestinian scholars, chefs, and food activists online, at conferences, and at diasporic events in New York, Washington, and Toronto. With this deliberate fragmentation of the Palestinian population, food and recipes become a means by which some sense of belonging and shared identity is preserved. Food and recipes, like music, literature, poetry, and art, can traverse transnational boundaries with greater ease than people can and have provided the means by which people can inhabit their Palestinianness while in exile, voluntary or not. The food, taste, and place nexus can live on in people, in their embodied memories and knowledge, even—or perhaps especially—in contexts of forced displacement. In fact, the Palestinian case pushes us to reach "beyond terroir" to consider what the taste of place might mean in contexts of involuntary displacement and dispossession (see also Sanders, this volume).

Thinking "beyond terroir" allows us to grasp how the land and belonging to it continue to be so important to people who are prevented from returning to their land. Along with the loss of the land itself is the loss of livelihood and income, and the disruption of the communities themselves. In a moving podcast interview with Truthout (7 December 2023), feminist historian Rana Barakat notes that a central belief for many Palestinians is that they "belong" to the land. This conviction of their belonging continues despite the dispossession and displacement of the Nakba, and the ongoing occupation of the West Bank by Israel which has often served to make Palestinian connection with their beloved land very difficult. As Barakat notes, Palestinians who remain have become an "absent presence" on their own ancestral land. As in other settler colonies like Australia, Canada, and the United States, the settlers assert, despite empirical evidence otherwise, that the land they conquer is empty, ready for the settlers to occupy and "improve." Palestinian land in the West Bank over the past three decades has been increasingly co-opted for checkpoints and illegal Israeli settlements; many West Bank Palestinians have, from a distance, pointed out to me their land, which they can no longer access despite their ownership papers. However, the idea of belonging to this land, memories of the taste of it, continues to feature prominently in Palestinian culinary practices and discussions of them. It is important to note, too, that the use of food and agricultural practices should not necessarily be romanticized as noble resistance; rather, they are part of the myriad practices of steadfastness (*sumud*), essential to keeping a Palestinian presence on their own land.

I begin with a reflection on the early processes of dispossession following the Nakba, drawing on a famous novel by Emile Habiby. I follow with what I learned through my own attempt to encounter the terroir of my own yard, when I began COVID gardening in the spring of 2020 when COVID restrictions prevented me from traveling to Palestine. I then discuss three examples that can be related to a Palestinian terroir (seed saving, foraging, and preserving knowledge), and the terroir of displacement. I end with a brief discussion of how the quality of West Bank agricultural land itself becomes vulnerable as the cement, asphalt, and military waste accumulate.

Who Is Greening the Land?

According to Israeli historian Ilan Pappe (2017), myths about Zionism perpetuate and prop up the Israeli state.[1] Here I examine how some of these myths directly related to agriculture feature in Palestinian literature. I begin with an example from the brilliant 1974 satirical novel *The Secret Life of Saeed: The Pessoptimist* by Emile Habiby. Habiby engages with these two central myths of Zionism: that the land was empty when the Zionists arrived and that it was the Zionists, only, who could make "the desert bloom." Habiby also alludes to the traumatic transformation of Palestinian farmers from owners to laborers on their own land during the early days of Israeli settler colonialism. In the latter half of Habiby's novel the reader joins the protagonist Saeed as he is being taken to prison by an unnamed Israeli whom he calls "big man (short of stature)." The big man lectures Saeed on the Israeli success in "making the desert bloom." Saeed articulates his skepticism: "Feigning ignorance of geopolitics, I commented sarcastically, 'So now we have left the Green Belt and entered the Dust Bowl of the Arabs, who have let their lands go to waste'" (2003: 127).

Toward the end of the novel, Saeed finds himself by accident in a village he calls Salakah, suffering under an Israeli curfew. A villager, Abu Mahmoud, notes that the curfew was lifted by pressure from the nearby kibbutz, where the Palestinians were now laborers on their former lands. Abu Mahmoud explains to Saeed that the lands "yearn for our able hands": "Because they were *our* fields, and it was we who planted them and we do so still. They love us and we love them. The authorities, you see, were unable to confiscate this friendship."

On hearing that the Palestinians are now laborers on their "own" land, now refigured as a kibbutz, Saeed exclaims to the laborers, "So all this greenery is the fruit of 'your' labor, not at all as the big man claimed"! (2003: 143). Habiby highlights this intimate reciprocal relationship between Palestinians and their land, while skewering the claims of the Zionists to have made the desert bloom, by pointing out that it is still the Palestinians who are making the land green and productive. Habiby's characters stress the love between the Palestinians and their land and between them and their plants, something still articulated by many Palestinians, including Rana Barakat, cited above, who articulates it as Palestinians belonging to the land rather than the land belonging to them. The Palestinian terroir is a product of this labor, love, and belonging. Habiby has a gift for saying what many academics have pointed out in our considerably less witty prose: plants, greening, blooming, disputes over rightful ownership, and agricultural laborers have long been at the center of this particular settler colonial encounter. Habiby points us to the question of agency: Who is responsible for the obliteration or production of the planting/greening of Palestine and, by extension, its terroir?

Planthropology

This sentiment of deep love and reciprocity between Palestinians and their land came up in my interviews with Palestinian food and heirloom seed activist and artist Vivien Sansour in the spring of 2018 as I participated in an urban farming workshop with Sansour and Mohammad Saleh, a permaculture practitioner.[2] Along with the other participants, I learned about weeding, the tactics of planting multiple kinds of plants rather than monocropping, and nonchemical fertilizers and insect control. Prevented by COVID travel restrictions from leaving the country in the spring of 2020, I did something I could not have predicted: I began to use Palestinian plant tactics, gleaned from Vivien and Mohammad, in my own front garden, neglected for years, because as soon as our semester was to end in the first week of April, I would get on a plane to conduct research with agro-activists who practice "fertile resistance" to the Israeli occupation. Inspired by my Palestinian friends and teachers, radical plant activists before it became fashionable, who strive for food justice with their unparalleled energy and humor, I found that my amateur greening attempts at home opened up some mental time and space to reflect on Palestine, where I have most often worked in actual fields as a volunteer olive picker and forager. In those contexts, I was very much the laborer who received instructions from farmers or expert foragers. At home, I was branching out alone, determined to overcome what Hartigan calls the "pervasive plant blindness that characterizes modern, urban-bound humans" (2019: 1).

It was with some relief that I realized that there is such a thing as "planthropology," a term coined in 2015 by Danish anthropologist Casper Bruun Jensen. Similarly, John Hartigan notes that while the human-nonhuman relationships have been celebrated in recent scholarship, it is the nonhuman "animal" that anthropologists seem most inclined to embrace, leaving plants out of the "species turn." He also argues that we can do "plant anthropology" (Hartigan 2019). I find my efforts at planthropology resonate with Katharina Graf's (this volume) notion of "participant perception," which inflects her learning Moroccan cooking through doing. Even though land acknowledgments are not always a part of terroir discourses, it makes sense in this particular case, especially to Palestinians and the Indigenous people of Canada, to at least have their stewardship of the land over the centuries recognized. Palestinians are very attentive to land acknowledgments, having experienced their land being confiscated in front of their eyes, a process still ongoing. So as I gardened I acknowledged that the land I cultivate in my yard is in the Indigenous territory of the First Nations of the Wendat, the Haudenosaunee, the Anishinaabe, and the Mississaugas of the Credit, which now host the settler colonial city of Toronto, Canada.

As Hartigan notes, there are difficulties in engaging plants as ethnographic subjects, including the fact that "the vast majority of the socializing that plants do is underground and inaccessible through traditional ethnographic techniques in the field" (2019: 1). It was indeed the underground that provided the first problem for me. After I had to cancel my travel plans, I gazed with new eyes on our long-neglected front yard, trying to evaluate the potential of tasting the terroir of my own land! I began digging. Two hours later, I had cleared a very small part of it from the "natural" weeds. Another two hours passed. Covered in dirt as I toiled, I quickly discovered that doing research with gardeners about their practices was not the same as doing gardening myself. We do not have a large front yard, but after eight hours of digging and planting, it seemed like a vast estate. The next day I could hardly lift a pencil. This effort at making my land productive, or at least a great deal more orderly and greener, made me appreciate the hard work of Palestinian farmers. But I also experienced the pride and pleasure in working the land.

Habiby ironically mocks the contrast of Arab "Dust Bowls" versus Israeli "Green Belts," as Palestine was an agricultural center for centuries. The ancient Palestinian olive trees on carefully crafted terraces are themselves testimonies to the longstanding Palestinian presence and their capacity to make their lands productive. Yet this myth of Israel being responsible for productive agriculture in Palestine/Israel continues to be asserted despite the Israeli state's destruction of cultivable land with rapid expansion of highways and illegal Israeli settlements, which threaten Palestinian olive groves, agricultural land, and lands where Palestinians have traditionally gathered the wild plants. Rarely mentioned in the "make the desert bloom" narrative is the Israeli monopolization of the water aquifers under the Palestinian West Bank. In addition, the Israeli concept of "nature" and the obligation to protect it has serious consequences for Palestinians. Israeli anthropologist and legal scholar Irus Braverman describes the strategic use of the Israeli planting of pine trees to obscure the sites of Palestinian villages whose inhabitants were driven away during the Nakba. These pine trees compete with Palestinian olive groves and are used to create "nature reserves" from which Palestinians are excluded (2009).

Terroir Talk and Olive Oil

The first I heard of an attempt to implement terroir in Palestine involved a tale about a French olive oil expert, perhaps not surprising, given that France is the birthplace of contemporary terroir practices. As Heather Paxson (2013) demonstrates, we need to question the idea of a unitary notion of terroir that is universally meaningful or practical to implement; instead, we need to look to the contexts in which claims of terroir can be made to be persuasive.

In 2007 I spoke with Palestinian olive oil professionals who were updating the local olive presses to facilitate the export of extra-virgin Palestinian olive oil to the EU. They reported that the French olive oil expert proposed creating an *Appellation d'Origine Contrôlée* (AOC) in the Salfit region. He suggested that the AOC designation for their particular olive oil could be used, strategically, to uphold Palestinian claims to their own land. In his view, the AOC could be "reverse-engineered" (in Paxson's formulation) to function as a testimony of long-standing Palestinian presence on the land, and their "right" to be there, and to not have their land annexed for illegal Israeli settlements. This was a different vision of the terroir concept, one that was conceptually appealing, as it used the European elite food concept with a sophisticated cachet to try to keep the land in Palestinian hands. The actual process never panned out, in part because formal terroir certification does depend on considerable legal work. Another factor is that the implementation of geographical indication labeling in the European sense depends very much on the existence of a nation-state. The fact that Palestine does not have a functioning independent state, or anything resembling it, meant that this process did not go anywhere.[3] Even exporting Palestinian products as a "product of Palestine" is itself very difficult, because Palestine does not have a "state slot" for customs officials to fill in on their bureaucratic forms, as I was told by a Canadian importer of Palestinian fair trade olive oil (Robert Massoud, personal communication).

One international label many Palestinian olive farmers did adopt was the label "extra-virgin" (based on a low acidity level determined by a chemical test and an organoleptic taste test) to facilitate the export of their olive oil to the EU and elsewhere. Even fair-trade solidarity olive oil needs to be extra-virgin for effective export. For a low acidity level, the olives need to be pressed as quickly as possible after harvesting; when farmers in cooperatives want to participate in extra-virgin production, to work at scale, they have to press their olives collectively as soon as they are picked. Yet they also hold some of their own olives back for oil for home consumption. Every olive producer in the world seems to think their own oil is the best: they want to taste the oil only made from their own olives, on their own land, ideally picked by known people, and processed at a trusted mill. This is also the kind of olive oil that Palestinians continue to share with their kin in the diaspora. Olive oil was always, and still is, an important gift for their Palestinian

Figure 1.1. Freshly pressed olive oil, green-gold in color. Beit Jala. Palestine, 2018. © Anne Meneley

relatives who had been forced to leave their homeland, allowing them a "taste" of their land, especially those who have difficulty returning, even for a visit.

The famous Cremisan Wine Estate was established in 1885 by the Catholic Salesian Congregation in Beit Jala, next to Bethlehem. But newer Palestinian wine producers, like Sari Khoury and his winery Philokalia, seek to distance themselves from the plonkish reputation of "communion wine." Although his winery was established in 2016, Khoury aims to resurrect the long history of Palestinian winemaking. He notes the number of Palestinian place-names in Palestine deriving from the word for vineyard (*karma*), despite the Israeli winemakers' attempts to erase both ancient and historical Palestinian winemaking traditions. He has revived the tradition of aging wine in dark clay jars inspired by the Canaanites and uses infusions of wild herbs rather than synthetic pesticides to meet the standards of organic production. His white wine "The Grapes of Wrath" has a distinctive story behind it: the vines had been crushed by stone boulders during the building of a road to an illegal Israeli settlement. Yet the vines managed to grow around these rocks, bearing an "exceptional" fruit (Khoury 2021). The "taste of place" here is presented as an example of a very Palestinian kind of planty agency, refusing to be contained by the infrastructures of destruction that facilitate Israeli settlements at the expense of Palestinians and their plants.[4]

Preserving Palestine's Plant Heritage

Khoury mentions other locals working to preserve and extend Palestinian terroir practices, like artist and food activist Vivien Sansour, whom I mentioned above. She has another creative means of getting at distinctive Palestinian terroir without becoming mired in the legal aspect of it. Sansour established the Palestine Heirloom Seed Library in the town of Battir, whose distinctive terraces and water-sharing strategies have facilitated agriculture for centuries.[5] Sansour collects seeds from farmers for distinctive Palestinian vegetables and grains, for future generations who do not want to depend on generic, industrial seeds.[6] These seeds harken back to times before the Israeli occupation of the West Bank, and before the flooding of West Bank markets with Israeli food products. In various media formats, Sansour argues that Palestinians are just as much a part of the land and nature as the food itself, yet they have lost this rich connection between food, taste, and place. Her seed library is an initiative that aims to reconnect Palestinians to the richness of their agricultural past. Sansour makes much of the Ba'al seeds, named after the Canaanite god preceding monotheism. Over centuries, Ba'al seeds were selected as the plant varietals that could live on rainwater alone on Palestinian land. The seeds serve as ambassadors of Palestine's agricultural heritage, providing a distinctive and delicious taste of place.

Sansour's seed library also implicitly contradicts the Zionist narrative's erasure of the long-standing Palestinian presence. Her spin on terroir always highlights the Palestinian "people" and the qualia of the potential plant (the seed) and its long adaptation to the land. Sansour deliberately frames the institution as a "library" rather than a "vault," encouraging farmers to share their seeds.[7] Heirloom seeds are hopeful, little containers of past skill and knowledgeable human cultivators, set to reclaim a bit of Palestinian edible history (see Meneley 2021a for further discussion).

Knowledges, Practices, and Their Preservation

Sansour's seed-sharing project, which focuses on circulating seeds that have been adapted over the centuries to the climate in Palestine, is part of an attempt to retain and reclaim the knowledge of Palestinian farmers. Food knowledge travels more easily than Palestinians themselves, whose physical movement is restricted because of the permit and checkpoint regime in the occupied West Bank. My Palestinian agro-activist and chef friends continue to highlight the distinctive tastes and knowledges of their land even as access becomes more difficult. Wild asparagus and wild mustard flowers are among the tastes I first experienced during Palestine's spring foraging walks, introduced to me by my Palestinian interlocutors, to "taste" the land as we traversed it.

Figure 1.2. Ba'al seeds from the Palestine Heirloom Seed Library, Battir. Palestine, 2019. © Anne Meneley

In the spring of 2019 artist and chef Mirna Bamieh hosted a dinner, designed to highlight the riches of the wild plant world and the special taste of these plants for making Palestinian cuisine distinctive (see Meneley 2021b). Bamieh's Wild Plants Dinner was a beautiful and rollicking sold-out event at the Palestinian Museum in Bir Zeit, with Mirna giving us short lectures—based on interviews she had conducted with the grandmothers (*tetas*) about their practices of foraging, which have become difficult—at the beginning of each course. As artist Jumana Manna notes, Israeli laws focus on prohibiting the foraging of *za'atar* (wild thyme) and *'akkoub* (wild thistle) for "environmental" reasons. The Israeli infrastructure and settlement project have destroyed far more plants than Palestinian foraging practices ever could. Manna argues: "Negotiating the politics of plant extinction with an occupier is always complicated, especially in the context of Palestine, where over the past seventy years *Palestinians themselves have been treated as an invasive species* in urgent need of elimination and control. The protection of one form of life—nonhuman life—has been used as an extra tool to suffocate a people who have survived attempts at cultural erasure and ethnic cleansing" (2020: 11, emphasis added).

While the Israeli restrictions imply that Palestinian foragers aim to clear-cut and destroy the plants, Palestinian foraging has always focused on selective gathering of wild plants, not uprooting or eradicating them, so that the *za'atar* and *'akkoub* could continue to be harvested every year, as they had in the past. This example shows how completely the Israelis discount Palestinian tradition of responsible caretaking of their foraging lands.[8] Indicating another potential of planthropological thinking, many Palestinians I spoke with believe that Israeli concerns about nature and protecting the land are more about controlling (or eliminating) Palestinian movement. The issue of knowledge was also brought up by Mirna as she narrated her Wild Plants Dinner: Palestinians need to learn how to identify the plants correctly while foraging, which is an essential element, and to know how to prepare them correctly according to the knowledge of the *teta*. She gave a powerful example of a plant called *loof*, which is very healthy if prepared correctly but poisonous if not! Both Bamieh and chef and cookbook author Reem Kassis speak of *nafas*, which is the spirit of the *teta* that is embedded with her personal craft and love. This is believed to make the food taste particularly delicious, an unquantifiable spiritual element that can be infused into the food regardless of where it is prepared.

The Terroir of Displacement

Knowledges and sentiments are often passed on not only through families or famous chefs but also in public fora like the Facebook group Mama's Palestinian Kitchen, where group members post photos of and sometimes recipes for their dishes. Whatever the flaws of platforms like Facebook, this particular group hosts complicated, fascinating stories from Palestinians all over the world; from those Palestinians who grew up in the diaspora, yet are proud to learn the cuisine of a land they may never see; from non-Palestinians married to Palestinians and trying to learn how to make pleasing meals for their families; and those from different parts of Palestine comparing notes about how a particular dish may have different qualities depending on the local plants specific to each region, a terroir twist.

In some sense, we could speak of the "terroir of displacement" for those forcibly "unplaced," especially given the number of Palestinians living away from their land or those who have never seen it. While food is often infused with complex emotions like nostalgia, it may take on a particularly acute sensibility of sadness and anger when displacement is involuntary. Most of the talk about the "food of displacement" comes from those forcibly displaced in refugee camps in Palestine or abroad.[9] The organization Afikra is a "global organization that aims to promote intellectualism and the diversity and richness of the Arab world's cultures and histories." They have featured several Palestinian chefs and cookbook authors like Fadi Kattan, Reem Kassis, Joudie Kalla, Reem Assil, and Sami Tamimi on their podcast platform, easily available on YouTube.

Bascunan-Wiley (2019) proposes that Palestinian food consumed in the diaspora can be a way of retaining a connection to their land but also as a form of *sumud* or steadfastness in the diaspora. He offers a wonderful example of the diasporic Palestinian population in Chile. He argues that cuisine and style of preparation are essential to the retention of a sense of cultural belonging in the diaspora. Palestinian movement to Chile began in the 1860s, from the predominantly Christian towns of Beit Sahour, Beit Jala, and Bethlehem, as merchants or traders who kept their ties to the homeland. They continue to express these ties through food. More Palestinians joined this community after the Nakba, and more recently, as some Palestinians living in Syria and Iraq moved to Chile to escape the violence. Through restaurants and recipes, these people try to recreate a taste of Palestine, even though some have not managed to ever visit the land they so strongly identify with. As Bascunan-Wiley argues (2019):

> For Chilean-Palestinians, remembering Palestine through food in Chile is an act of diasporic *sumud*—resistance to the symbolic appropriation and erasure perpetuated by Israel and resistance to forgetting memories of the homeland within the diasporic context. In essence, food memory itself is resistance and a practice of steadfastness in the diaspora. These stories from fieldwork in La Calera and Quillota highlight the production of Palestinian cuisine in diaspora as it is lived daily. For instance, Nadia and Abu Laith hold on to ingredients that they have brought from Palestine and continue to make dishes from the homeland. They intentionally retain memories and a sense of home from Palestine while still engaging in the local context through their restaurant. Other Chilean-Palestinians reconnect with a homeland that they have only heard about in the memories passed down to them. Edu, for example, uses the restaurant as a way to reimagine and reembody the stories he has learned from his family.

Bascunan-Wiley provides a stellar example of how diaspora populations, so important to the Palestinian struggle at home, can embody this struggle through preserving and serving Palestinian food as a form of resistance in the diaspora.

Conclusion: Terroir in a Transforming Territory

As a tool of anthropological methodology, I found my experiment in "planthropology" quite helpful, for beginning to understand the extraordinary labor, shared knowledge, care, and genuine affection that can develop between humans and their plants. In the spring of 2021 I gazed adoringly at my little plants, so pleased when they began to emerge after a long winter. The following week, I was truly horror struck when my next-door neighbors began ambitious home renovations, digging up their front yard and covering half of my plant children in concrete dust! This experience has allowed me to make analogies to the more harrowing experience of many Palestinian farmers, who have had to see their crops or olive trees they have cultivated with such dedication destroyed for the establishment of highways and settlements for illegal settlers in the West Bank. I have learned in a visceral way what it means to put effort into the plants and the land, to take joy in the plant progress. But more importantly, I have learned what it might feel like to have your land encroached upon and your plants destroyed after devoting so much love, worry, and sheer physical labor to them. As the world watches the current yet more horrific Israeli bombardment of Gaza, we have seen far too many children covered in concrete dust and bodies extracted from rubble. Along with far too many of the Gazan people, the plants are long gone, causing some of us to question the Israeli commitments to "greening" the land and preserving "nature" when destroying what remains of cultivable lands in Gaza.[10]

As noted at the beginning of this chapter, the concept of terroir is less than adept at incorporating changes like the radical transformations that settler colonialism produces on the land that is co-opted. The immediate effect is denial of ownership and/or the right to use the land. Part of these transformations have to do with the ways in which the land itself is changed with the remains of the occupation, including the unsightly Apartheid Wall and military waste. I think Demossier's (this volume) use of the concept of "management of uncertainty" in navigating terroir is useful as a concept here, except that the uncertainty in the Palestinian territory is often related to military incursions.

In 2019 I spoke with Emily Jacir, who has transformed her family home in Bethlehem into an artists' residence. They envisioned the garden at Dar Jacir as a revival of urban farming, a place to grow Palestine's beloved edible plants. But before gardening could begin, volunteers had to gather up all the tear gas canisters shot by the Israeli soldiers at the nearby Bethlehem checkpoint. A comparative example is Munira Khayyat's (2022) description of how the people of South Lebanon "wage life" while still suffering from the consequences of military action on their land. Khayyat describes how the region is still occupied by the "rogue infrastructures" of unexploded bombs leftover from the brutal 2006 Israeli assault. Khayyat persuasively revives the concept of "resistance:" in her discussion, resistance is not heroic, glamorous, or the slightest bit romantic. The Lebanese villagers continue to survive thanks to their olive trees and goat herding, as the goats are light enough to graze on lands without detonating the unexploded bombs buried in the ground; heavier creatures like humans will trigger them. Khayyat describes this as a "clever multispecies assemblage" tricking the leftover death implements of war. Rather than the romance of resistance, what is going on here is the more ordinary strategies of "making do" in order to survive, because doing otherwise is unthinkable. As in Lebanon, resistance, including agro-resistance, in Palestine is not romantic. But to not resist, to just give up, give up hope, their land, and their delicious cuisine, is unthinkable. The reciprocal love of the land and its products and the people provides sustenance and much-needed hope.

I do not suggest that we celebrate "terroir without the territory," as if the food itself was enough. I know that a fundamental element of Palestinian steadfastness (*sumud*) is the right of return to their land if they choose to do so. But in the meantime, when many Palestinians cannot return, the capacity to create a taste of Palestine is a means of maintaining connections to their homeland and people. I will close with the words of Palestinian chef, Sami Tamimi, who offered the following thoughts on his Instagram page (19 December 2023), along with his prayers for those suffering in Gaza: "Recipes are more than recipes, they are stories, memories, and a testament to the resilience of those who've handed them down through the generations. So, when we cook these recipes, we not only recreate flavors but also continue the narrative of our ancestors, preserving a rich heritage that transcends time and taste." Creating or recreating their Indigenous food is an essential element of Palestinian *sumud*, continuing the struggle to return to the land to which they belong, despite the horrors visited upon it.

Acknowledgments

I would like to thank my Palestinian interlocutors over the years, including Mirna Bamieh, Baha Hilo, Fadi Kattan, Aisha Mansour, and Vivien Sansour for their insights about the plants of Palestine. I would also like to thank Rana Barakat, Remi Hammami, and Omar Qassis, not only for their unparalleled insights but also for their humor and grace. Some parts of this chapter were presented at the Society of Palestinian Anthropologists, Insaniyyat, 3rd Biennial conference, titled "Pessoptimism: Anthropologies of Palestinian Hope and Uncertainty," in 2021. Nothing gets written in my life without Vaidila Banelis, Bruce Grant, and Paul Manning hearing a great deal about it. I would also like to thank Anna Colquhoun and Katharina Graf for organizing such a terrific brainstorming event in Istria; I was delighted to engage with the co-participants in this volume.

Anne Meneley received her PhD in Anthropology from New York University. She is now Professor of Anthropology at Trent University. She has published in various journals, including *American Anthropologist*, *Annual Review of Anthropology*, *Cultural Anthropology*, *Environment and Planning E: Nature and Space*, *Ethnos*, *Food, Culture & Society*, *Food and Foodways*, *Gastronomica*, *History and Anthropology*, *Jerusalem Quarterly*, *Journal of Palestine Studies*, *PoLar*, and *Religion and Society*. Her current work is on the anthropology of consumerism, anthropology of food, particularly olive oil, walking (quantified and nature walking), mobilities, cities, and human-nonhuman interactions in plant materialities.

Notes

1. See Pappe (2017) for a discussion of the other myths of Zionism.
2. No pseudonyms are used in this chapter. The Palestinian artists, activists, and chefs mentioned here are public figures.
3. States such as Norway and Ireland have recognized Palestine as a state. This is a symbolic move, as the Palestinian Authority has little control over the West Bank and no control over its borders.
4. I am reminded of Stoetzer's (2018) discussion of "ruderal" plants, plants that emerge from the rubble in Berlin.
5. Battir provides a good example of foreign certification being used to help protect Palestinian agriculture: Battir received a UNESCO World Heritage Site certification in 2014, which helped change the route of the Separation Wall. Not only is this wall, often called the Apartheid Wall, a visual blight on the landscape, but it is built on confiscated Palestinian farmland.
6. See Mariam Shahin's wonderful documentary about Sansour, *The Seed Queen of Palestine*: https://www.aljazeera.com/program/witness/2018/12/10/the-seed-queen-of-palestine (retrieved 11 December 2024).
7. Virginia Nazarea's discussion of the tension between scientific vaulting of seeds as a means of preservation versus Indigenous Quechua practices of preservation and nurturing of plant heritages provides a relevant comparison. Thanks to one of the reviewers for this suggestion.
8. Courtney Lewis (2012) notes that ramp foraging was forbidden in North Carolina national parks, but a court case considered whether it ought to apply to Indigenous Cherokee as well as other guests to the park. Thanks to Heather Paxson for this reference.
9. Laila al-Haddad's cookbook *The Gaza Kitchen* has recipes that are originally from the areas of Palestine from which people were displaced after the Nakba; for instance, the cuisine of Jaffa is preserved by those displaced into Gaza.
10. As Isabella Hammad (2024) has recently noted, in the latest Israeli onslaught in Gaza, the "quantity of ammunition dropped on Gaza is equivalent to more than three times that of the atom bomb dropped on Hiroshima."

References

Barakat, Rana. 2023. "Palestine Is about Living in Spite of Everything." Interview with Kelly Hayes, *Truthout*, 7 December. Retrieved 13 December 2023 from https://truthout.org/audio/palestine-is-about-living-in-spite-of-everything/.

Bascunan-Wiley, Nicholas. 2019. "*Sumud* and Food: Remembering Palestine through Cuisine in Chile." *Mashriq & Mahjar* 6(2): 100–129.

Beriss, David. 2019. "Food: Location, Location, Location." *Annual Review of Anthropology* 48: 61–75.

Braverman, Irus. 2009. *Planted Flags: Trees, Land, and Law in Israel/Palestine.* Cambridge: Cambridge University Press.

Habiby, Emile. 2003. *The Secret Life of Saeed, the Pessoptimist.* First published 1974. Translated by Salma K. Jayyusi and Trevor LeGassick. Northampton: Interlink.

Haddad-El, Laila, and Maggie Schmitt. 2012. *The Gaza Kitchen: A Palestinian Culinary Journey*. Charlottesville: Just World Books.

Hammad, Isabella. 2024. "Acts of Language." *New York Review of Books*, 13 June. Retrieved 17 June 2024 from https://www.nybooks.com/online/2024/06/13/acts-of-language-isabella-hammad/.

Hartigan, John H., Jr. 2019. "Plants as Ethnographic Subjects." *Anthropology Today* 35(2): 1–2.

Jensen, Casper Bruun. 2015. "Experimenting with Political Materials: Environmental Infrastructures and Ontological Transformations." *Distinktion: Scandinavian Journal of Social Theory* 16(1): 17–30.

Khayyat, Munira. 2022. "Resistant Ecologies: The Life of War in South Lebanon." *American Ethnologist* 50(2): 1–15.

Khoury, Sari. 2021. "Winemaking and the Search for Palestine's Stubborn Saints." *This Week in Palestine*. Retrieved 13 June 2024 from https://thisweekinpalestine.com/philokalia/.

Lewis, Courtney. 2012. "The Case of the Wild Onions: The Impact of Ramps on Cherokee Rights." *Southern Cultures* 18(2): 104–17.

Manna, Jumana. 2020. "Where Nature Ends and the Settlements Begin." *e-flux* 113 (November). Retrieved 12 December 2023 from https://www.e-flux.com/journal/113/360006/where-nature-ends-and-settlements-begin/.

Meneley, Anne. 2021a. "Hope in the Ruins: Seeds, Plants, and Possibilities of Regeneration." *Environment & Planning E: Nature & Space* 4(1): 158–72.

———. 2021b. "Eating Wild: Hosting the Food Heritage of Palestine." *PoLAR: Political and Legal Anthropology Review* 44(2): 207–22.

Nazarea, Virginia. 2021. "Ontologies of Return: Terms of Endearment and Entanglements." In *Moveable Gardens: Itineraries and Sanctuaries of Memory*, edited by Virginia Nazarea and Terese Gagnon, 253–72. Tucson: University of Arizona Press.

Pappe, Ilan. 2017. *10 Myths about Israel*. London: Verso.

Paxson, Heather. 2013. *The Life of Cheese: Crafting Food and Value in America*. Berkeley: University of California Press.

Stoetzer, Bettina. 2018. "Ruderal Ecologies: Rethinking Nature, Migration, and the Urban Landscape in Berlin." *Cultural Anthropology* 33(2): 295–323.

Wallace, Lewis. 2019. "Human Resilience and Ecological Resistance in the Tear Gas Capital of the World." *Environmental Health News*. Retrieved 16 June 2024 from https://www.ehn.org/human-resilience-and-ecological-resistance-in-the-tear-gas-capital-of-the-world-2637002101.html.

CHAPTER 2

Beating the Bounds of Terroir

A Perambulation of the Micro and Macro Cultures of Cidermaking in Devon, England

Simon Pope and Harry G. West

Introduction

Terroir has recently become an object of interest among anthropologists. As is often the case when anthropologists focus on a term, the definition of terroir has been parsed, subtle variations in meaning have proliferated with examination in various ethnographic contexts, and ultimately the concept has begun to creak and shudder as it has been stretched and, in some cases, tested to breaking point. Some stretching has been literal, for after all, terroir is fundamentally about space/place. Some stretching, however, has been metaphorical—the expansion of the terroir idea in new ways. This chapter tells the story of our work on the outer limits of the terroir idea in the context of apple cidermaking in the county of Devon in South West England. After extending the terroir concept into new scalar dimensions,[1] we ultimately seek to ask whether it might accommodate spatial movements, and transformations through time, of the very products and productive traditions that it has been used to characterize and celebrate.

The Natural and Social Ecology of Devon Cidermaking

Trubek's succinct definition of terroir as "the taste of place" (Trubek 2008) serves as a useful point of departure. Where foodstuffs from anywhere are increasingly available to consumers everywhere, and where the standardization of productive processes has intensified along with the homogenization of tastes, the terroir concept resists the idea that anything can be made anywhere, asserting instead that place matters, and that some things can only be made in specific places. Such assertions, of course, have historically been associated with attempts to secure intellectual property rights over goods fetching a market premium. The "taste of place" definition harmonizes well with the longstanding use of the terroir idea to underpin legal regimes that reserve the use of toponyms in association with selected products to self-governing producers working within bounded geographical domains and adhering to closely specified productive protocols—regimes referred to as, inter alia, *Geographical Indications* (GIs, by the World Trade Organization), *Protected Designations of Origin* (PDOs, by the European Union), or *Appellations d'Origine Contrôlée* (AOCs, by the French state) (Barham 2003; West 2013).

Of course, terroir is not simply about geographical locations of production. More profoundly, the terroir idea asserts the importance of an ecology of production to certain goods. Even the most basic conceptions of terroir emphasize how particular products express the characteristics of the natural environments in which they are made. In viticulture, for example, this has often been articulated with regard to underlying geology (Wilson 1998), but it has also included reference to features such as the slope of the land, its aspect (e.g., "south-facing"), soil composition, weather patterns, and so forth. For other products, different features of the natural environment have been considered fundamental. In cheesemaking, for example, discussions of terroir have referred to the palette of grasses, wildflowers, and other plant species in pastures on which animals graze, or to the temperature and humidity in aging caves or cellars (West 2013).

More recently, others have expanded the terroir concept to include not only the natural ecology in which products are made but also the human dimensions of their contexts of production. They have focused on the people who, it is said, translate the natural environments in which they work into the products in question (Bérard and Marchenay 2008; Trubek, Guy, and Bowen 2010). These interpretations of the terroir idea tend to conceive of makers as part of the natural environment, and to emphasize the continuity of their relationships with the natural world and with their ancestors/predecessors, who also worked within it. Accordingly, makers are generally cast—explicitly or implicitly—as autochthons/indigenes, who draw on traditional knowledge handed down through the generations, and who reproduce such knowledge in situ while practicing their craft, transmitting it to family members or apprentices (an idea with which we critically engage below).

In our work with Devon cidermakers since April 2018, we have come to know a story that can easily be told in this language of terroir. One of us (Pope) is an artist who was commissioned by Arts & Culture at the University of Exeter, and by the Royal Albert Memorial Museum & Art Gallery (RAMM) in Exeter, to lead a project exploring the microbiosocialities of cidermaking through a range of collective artistic works. The other (West) is a professor of anthropology at the University of Exeter who studies artisan food making, the terroir idea, and its use in initiatives to develop food-and-drink-focused cultural economies. We partnered, along with others, in a three-and-a-half-year-long project titled "Here's to Thee: Experiments with the More-than-Human Social Worlds of Devonshire Cidermaking"[2] (Pope 2022).

The project focused on Gray's Devon Cider, a cidery on land that has been farmed by the Gray family—first as tenants and later as owners—for nearly four hundred years. The pound house (where apples are pressed to extract juice) and cellar date to the very early 1800s, meaning that the current inhabitants, Ben and Ruth Gray—along with their young adult sons, David and Theo—carry on a family cidermaking tradition reaching back at least two hundred years. The farmstead is located in Halstow—*stōw* meaning "a place of significance" (often referring to a church or burial ground) in Old English, and *hal* meaning "holy" in Old English, or *heall* meaning "hall" (residence) in Middle English (Gover, Mawer, and Stenton 1931), or *hals* meaning "at the neck of a valley" in Anglian (Higgins 2014)—where it nestles between steep slopes on the north and south sides with views of Dartmoor down the valley to the west. Only 70 of the Grays' 240 acres are suitable for agriculture. On this land, the family and their forebears have grown various crops, including wheat, barley, or oats, as well as turnips or kale for sheep feed (the latter also as a cover crop for pheasants today) and potatoes, or swede, for human consumption; Ben's grandfather grew flax, and Ben has grown hemp (both for fiber). The rest of the land is unsuitable for agriculture due to its heavy clay soils and undulating terrain. Sheep have been grazed on these parcels since Saxon times—preferred over other livestock because they do not damage trees. And this has been crucial in recent centuries because orchards were planted on the steepest, least accessible fields, the oldest dating back to 1795. Today, the farm's mature orchards produce on average seventy-five tons of apples per year, which the Grays transform into approximately twenty thousand liters of cider.

Not only does the lay of the land lend itself to orcharding, but cidermaking is a well-established practice in the county. The first evidence of cidermaking in Devon comes from the neolithic period (Department for Environment 2018). Orchards have been planted in the region at least since Roman times, and they were greatly expanded by the Normans, who were keen apple producers (Derry and Williams 1960: 61; Department for Environment 2018; Crowden 2021: 64). Records dated 1285 show commercial production of cider at Exminster Manor, and a market for cider was well established in Devon by the 1300s (Department for Environment 2018). While the agricultural economy was mixed in late medieval and early modern times—with a somewhat greater focus on beef cattle and sheep for wool in North Devon and on Dartmoor, and a greater emphasis on dairy and arable farming in East Devon and the South Hams—cider was produced in much of the county (Fox 1999; Havinden and Stanes 1999). Along the south coast, cidermaking was for local consumption in the medieval

Figure 2.1. Participants walking to the orchard at the Halstow Wassail. England, 2022. © Robert Darch

period (Fox 1999: 276), but by early modern times came to be oriented toward buyers in Devon's coastal ports, or in London, with some ultimately destined for consumption in Newfoundland (Havinden and Stanes 1999: 288); so valuable was the drink that landlords allowed tenants to plant orchards and accepted cider as a form of payment of rent (Department for Environment 2018). Cider was less prominent in the north and west of the county in the medieval period (Fox 1999: 276), but by the early modern period, it was increasingly produced there for local consumption (Havinden and Stanes 1999: 288); landlords there also used cider as partial payment in kind to attract seasonal labor (Spender 1864).[3]

For these reasons, cider became an essential element of the Devon rural landscape. Samuel Lewis wrote in 1848: "In no part of England are the gardens [meaning orchards] on a more extensive scale than throughout this county [Devon]" (Department for Environment 2018). Knowledge of cidermaking was consequently widespread—a cultural heritage from which makers like the Grays have benefitted for generations. In other words, there is a compelling case to be made for the terroir idea that the environment—natural and human—is an essential contributor to Devon cider.

Terroir at Extreme Ends of a Scalar Spectrum?

Beyond substantiating the importance of ecological and socioeconomic context in the making of Gray's Farm Cider, however, our exploration of cidermaking in Halstow has prompted us to stretch the terroir concept in two scalar directions. First, we have looked for terroir at microscopic dimensions, in the microbial cultures associated with cidermaking. In the preamble to the recently completed arts commission, one of us has written:

> "Here's to thee, Old Apple Tree" we declaim to the apple tree, every year on Old Twelfth Night as part of conventional wassail celebrations [of which more in a moment]. But who or what else takes part in bringing us our cider each year? What of all those things that go unnoticed but whose effects are felt nonetheless? What of the yeasts, living "wild" on the apple skins, that we co-opt into the fermentation process? And what, indeed, of the other microbes that make their home on the cider-press and on the walls of the barn? . . . What of the microbiomes of the people that pick and prune, press and drink the cider each year? How do all these participants relate to each other? What kinds of dependencies do they form? What kind of cooperations or antagonisms? What kinds of collective action, and what kinds of politics do they negotiate among themselves, as a more-than-human community? (Pope 2022)

While it is common knowledge that cidermaking depends upon yeasts, bacilli, and other microorganisms (Beech 1993), and while some research has been done to identify the predominant microorganisms at work in the cidermaking process (Doores and Splittstoesser 1983; Laplace et al. 1998; Cousin et al. 2017; Misery et al. 2020; Al Riachy et al. 2021), little is known about how the array of microorganisms in the process differs from one particular place to another (Bowen and Beech 1964; Abbots 2018: 123–24). In turning attention to this microcultural level, we build on the work of authors who have theoretically framed the more-than-human dimensions of food and eating (Bennett 2007; Sarmiento 2017; Beacham 2018; Elton 2019) and, in particular, on Paxson's concept of "microbiopolitics," which she explored in the context of cheesemaking in the United States (Paxson 2008). We also work in parallel with researchers who have only just begun to explore the microbial dimensions of terroir in the making of other foods and beverages, such as sourdough bread (Landis et al. 2021; McKenney et al. 2021), cheese (Marcellino et al. 2001; Marcellino 2003; Paxson 2008; West 2020), and wine (Liu et al. 2020; Wang et al. 2021).

Second—at the other end of the scalar spectrum—we have looked at terroir's macrocultural dimensions in various cultural practices that not only contribute to the taste "of" cider but also to the cultured taste "for" cider. These practices are shared by communities of people reaching well beyond the orchard, the pound house, and the aging cellar—communities through which cidermaking and drinking is celebrated in particular locales even as the social context of cidermaking craft is reproduced along with the cider itself. Included in this line of enquiry has been not only productive practices but also folkways associated with the wider cultural context of these productive methods, from the terminologies and turns of phrase through which cider is discussed to the calendrical events associated with cider, the stories told about it, and the songs and dances performed alongside its making. We have focused particularly on wassailing.

As one of us describes elsewhere, wassailing is a folk practice through which people wish "good health" to apple trees (Pope 2022). The term is thought to derive from the Old English salutation, *Wæs þu hæl*, meaning "Be of good health," and in its early forms was a "festive occasion with much drinking and pledging of healths" (Cater 2013). Generally held on *Old Twelvey* (17 January in the Julian calendar, in other words, Old Twelfth Night—the end of Christmastide celebrations), the wassail was the "last hurrah" before Plough Monday, which marked the start of the new agricultural year and the return to work in the fields (Parker 2022: 83; Pope 2022). In post-Reformation England the wassail came to be a synthesis of Christian ritual and popular merrymaking (Hutton 1996) that fostered community through collective focus on ensuring a bountiful harvest of apples (Pope 2022). In a typical wassail today, participants gather around a tree—generally believed to be the oldest in an orchard—where an incantation is read, and bread or toast soaked in cider is suspended from its boughs, often by a "wassail queen." Noise is then made, whether by rattling pans or firing shotguns, in order to (depending upon the interpretation) wake the tree, chase away evil spirits, or merely raise the spirits of those attending (Pope 2022). A song is then sung. At the renowned wassail in Whimple, Devon, people sing: "Here's to thee, old apple tree; that buds well, blooms well, bears well; hatfuls, cupfuls, three bushel bagfuls, and all under one tree" (Pope 2022).

By addressing the tree as "thee," such lyrics treat it as another living being, equal to those gathered round it, and upon whom they depend as much as it depends upon them—fellow species bound together in collective mutuality (Pope 2022). What is more, we may see the wassail—along with geographer Edward Wigley, who has studied the contemporary revival of wassailing in England—not only as part of a rich tradition of popular magic endeavoring to transform the nonhuman, material world through the written or spoken word, but also as a practice open to the "interests and attitudes of participating audiences" (Wigley 2021)—a means through which they reproduce the very communities that give cultural context to the production of the cider they celebrate.[4]

Reproducing Living Cultures by Singing to Microbes

Beyond seeing wassailing as an "expression of" cidermaking, "Here's to Thee," conceived of wassailing as a tradition that lends itself to "experimentation with"

Figure 2.2. Ruth Gray of Gray's Devon Cider recites the incantation at the Halstow Wassail. England, 2022. © Robert Darch

the human-nonhuman relationships essential to ecological thought (Gosden 2020). Accordingly, our project constituted a playful interscalar dialogue with, simultaneously, the microcultures and macrocultures of cidermaking, focused on the creation and performance of a new wassail. "Written to be sung not only to the apple trees, but to all who constitute the microbial ecology and more-than-human social world of cider-making at Halstow" (Pope 2022), and sung in various locations on the farm—the orchard, the pound house, the aging cellar—the song takes the form of call and response with microbes, first asking, "Who be I, Who be I, Who be I this night?," and with different answers coming in each verse: "You be the yeast (or lichen, or fungus, or mould, or bacilli) whom we praise with delight!" To the question "Where be I this night?," the answers come as "in the air," "on the (apple) skin," and "in the barrels" for the yeast; "on the branch of the tree, from brown rot and canker pray keep us all free" for the lichen; "underground binding all trees in sight" for the fungus; "on the walls of the pound house" for the mold; and "on the press, where we squeeze the cheese tight" for the bacilli. The song even calls out the flora "in our bellies" (and at the height of the pandemic, the virus [COVID-19] "on the air of our breath"), before celebrating all these entities (except COVID-19) with the blessing "long may they prosper in this holy place."

This new wassail—performed annually since 2020 (with limited participation in 2021 due to the pandemic)—has "inhabit[ed] and transform[ed] the conventions of the apple tree wassail as a way to experiment with more-than-human forms of community, multi-species' relations, and the negotiations that people undertake with microbial life through cidermaking" (Pope 2022). In other words, it has used this historically-grounded macrocultural practice associated with cidermaking to connect with the microcultures—the "Great Good Unseen," as the forces of fermentation were once called in the region (Groom 2014)—also at work in the making of cider.

Mapping Distinctiveness, or Documenting the Transgression of Boundaries?

Our work thus far on the micro- and macrocultures associated with cidermaking in Devon raises questions about how far the terroir idea might be stretched along scalar axes, and whether or not the ecological context to which it refers must always be a strictly delimited place—questions that we hope to explore further in future, as elaborated below. These are particularly timely questions following on a failed application in 2018 by cidermaker James Mcilwraith, on behalf of the Devon Cidermakers Guild, to the UK Department for Environment, Food and Rural Affairs (DEFRA) for a Protected Designation of Origin (PDO) for Devon Cider (Department for Environment 2018). The application argued for the distinctiveness of Devon Cider based on its expression of the environment in which it has historically been produced. In particular, the petition asserted that, because higher rainfall in Devon leads to greater prevalence of canker, Devon cidermakers have historically selected canker-resistant apple varieties. It further asserted that, although Devon cider is made from both native and non-native varieties, apples grown in Devon are "noticeably distinct from the apples grown in other counties" due to the terroir of Devon, namely its climate, soil, and native microflora. Specifically, it claimed that the red soils found in Devon lent a rich color and softer character to Devon Cider.

The application was denied by DEFRA, however, on grounds that it had not "sufficiently established that the quality of characteristics of the product are essentially or exclusively due to the particular geographical environment of Devon." DEFRA rebutted the guild's claims by stating that a number of factors, not unique to Devon, increase susceptibility to canker, and that the varieties of apples used by commercial cidermakers in Devon are not dissimilar to those used in, for example, Herefordshire, challenging the link between the Devon climate and apple varieties. It also pointed to the geological diversity of Devon—

which includes chalk, limestone, red sandstone, granite, and strata defined as the Culm Measures, and Devonian, etc.—with the presence of cider orchards on all these soil types.[5] The Devon Cidermakers Guild responded that Devon's maritime climate is cooler in summer and warmer in winter than Herefordshire and Somerset, with higher rainfall from April to September, and that this altered the phenolic content of Devon apples and affected the character of Devon cider. DEFRA remained unconvinced, responding that research showed "no significant differences between the same apple varieties grown in different regional environments."

Building on "Here's to Thee," we hope to conduct research in future that would further assess the stretching of terroir into the micro and macro ends of the scalar spectrum in the study of Devon Cider. This would entail shifting focus away from questions of soil, climate, and rainfall emphasized in the Devon Cider PDO application and looking instead at the microbes involved in cidermaking in Devon, the folkways through which Devon cider is celebrated, and the relationship of each of these with productive practices. We intend to work with ten cidermakers scattered throughout the county. We plan to sample microbes on trees in orchards and during the first stages of fermentation at pressing to identify prevalent strains and discern patterns of distribution. We also plan to document folkways associated with cidermaking in locales across Devon, and to study how these compare both within the county and beyond, as well as how they contribute to an appreciation of/taste for cider, for the heritage of cidermaking, and for stewardship of the orchards and the broader natural ecologies associated with cider production.

While this data might provide evidence of common micro- and macrocultural factors in the production of Devon Cider, and of differences between these elements in Devon cidermaking and cidermaking elsewhere—something that the Devon Cidermakers PDO petition failed to do with reference to more established measures of the relevant ecology of production—we rather anticipate a more complicated picture emerging from this work. Indeed, we suspect that our findings may further challenge not only the case for a Devon Cider PDO but also terroir orthodoxy more broadly. This is because orthodox conceptions of terroir—including those that see a product being shaped not only by its place of production but also by the people within it—see constituent relationships between people, place, and product as both immutable and immovable. Our examination of cultures—micro and macro—will quite possibly unsettle these assumptions, identifying crucial elements in the ecology of production of cider that move through space and change over time.[6]

With regard to the microbial ecology of cidermaking, our expectations arise from reading research recently undertaken by others on microbial cultures associated with other foods and beverages. Findings are mixed. In a study of six wine-growing areas in southern Australia, Liu et al. found that "microbial diversity responds to the surrounding environment and correlates with wine composition and regional characteristics" (Liu et al. 2020). Similarly, Wang et al. looked at the microbial diversity on grapes in Pennsylvania and concluded that "microbial signatures during fermentation and differential microorganisms and metabolites . . . support impact of regionality on Chambourcin wines" (Wang et al. 2021: 2). However, others have suggested the opposite, asserting that, to some extent, "all microbes are everywhere." Noella Marcellino found similar molds and fungi throughout France in places where cheese was produced and concluded that strains did not group according to region (Marcellino et al. 2001; Marcellino 2003). Wolfe et al. found the community composition of bacteria and fungi on cheese rinds taken from diverse settings correlated with abiotic factors rather than geography (Wolfe et al. 2014). Landis et al. found the myriad microorganisms associated with sourdough to be present everywhere they looked, albeit with variations in the proportions of their prevalence, suggesting that it is specific biotic interactions within sourdough starter culture that account for locally distinct qualities of bread, rather than biogeographic variation in microbial species (Landis et al. 2021; McKenney et al. 2021). As one of us has previously posited, "Some microbes are more mobile than humans, and do not respect the delimitations of space that we live with" (Pope 2022).

Neither do we expect to find forms of expressive culture in Devon cidermaking that are completely unlike those found elsewhere. Wassailing is widespread in England and Wales, even if forms vary (Cater 2013). And Wigley tells us that the contemporary revival of wassailing is characterized by people readily borrowing elements from elsewhere (Wigley 2019: 386–87). What is more, he concludes that the "enchantment" that characterizes contemporary wassailing is "always temporary and changing"—emerging from contingent, local relationships rather than fixed, authoritative "tradition" (Wigley 2021: 887). The same may have been true of wassailing in the past (Hutton 1996). Such movement and mixing of traditions applies to other forms of cultural expression found alongside orcharding and cidermaking. We know that folk songs such as "Widecombe Fair" have traveled widely over time, being sung with revised characters and settings as they have moved from place to place (Gray 2019).

This dynamism is also visible, ironically, when we look at English traditions like "beating the bounds"—a form of communal perambulation with roots in annual, clergy-led crop blessings, or "rogation" ceremonies, held in the fields during early summer since at least the eighth century, and which, following the Reformation and acts of enclosure, took on the more practical function of demarcating parish boundaries (Hutton 1996). Ostensibly about visiting and recognizing boundaries, these ceremonies lead to participants witnessing subtle movements and changes on the landscape, viewing what lies beyond, and pondering the very flows that boundaries strain to hold in check. When accompanying the Grays in the recent renewal of this ritual on their farm, Pope was led to gaze down the

Teign valley to Dartmoor and to remember how cider used to be sold to Dartmoor Prison, in Princetown, where American and French prisoners were held during the Napoleonic Wars and the War of 1812, and how Ben Gray had told him that French soldiers—billeted in Moretonhampstead after their release at the end of the Napoleonic Wars—stole cider from the Grays' farm before returning home. Such stories betray centuries-long dynamics of global dimensions within this place, with cider at the center of the plot.

In fact, beating the bounds can be traced to the Roman occupiers of Britain, with its uptake in England bearing evidence of the movements of cultural practices, along with people, over millennia. Like microbes, cultural forms at the macro end of the scalar spectrum transgress boundaries while their relationships with places change over time, with close examination often revealing traces of movement and transformation.

Conclusion: Is Terroir Any Place for Movement and Change?

What significance might our work on Devon cider at the ends of the scalar spectrum have for the terroir idea? And what implications does it have for geographical indication regimes, which build upon terroir claims? Does the mobility and mutability of these micro and macro elements of a product's ecology of production undermine the terroir idea? Does it subvert the terroir argument—underpinning geographical indications—that some things can only be made in particular places?

Some may argue that there is no place within the terroir framework for such mobile and mutable elements as microbes and folk songs, which move across the landscape and change as they take root in, and adapt to, new places. Some may assert that terroir is fundamentally about place, and that places, by definition, do not move. The trouble with this argument, however, is that the terroir idea flourishes today precisely because places, everywhere, are subjected to dramatic transformation, in significant measure because of flows through them of everything from people and objects to ideas and climatic forces. The embrace of terroir is in significant measure a response to the threats posed by movements and transformations that challenge conceptions of tradition—an idea one of us has expounded upon elsewhere (West 2022). However, like the rituals of beating the bounds, which realize boundedness through repetitive acts of demarcation that render visible the very shifts and movements on the land that such practices seek to forestall, terroir delimits and defines foodways through regimes of governance, such as PDOs, that call attention to the mobilities and mutabilities that the terroir idea seeks to contest.[7] Terroir reasserts the importance of place—not to mention the continuity of particular practices and the products arising from them—because of globalizing processes that cannot be ignored.

We would argue that, in order to preserve the idea—essential to terroir—that ecologies of production matter in the making of food and other things, mobility and mutability must be included in the stories of the places where such ecologies are sustained and reproduced—whether we call this terroir, or not. Our future work with Devon cidermakers will therefore explore how their stories may be conceived of as ones not only of geographical places and the people working within them but also of movement and change of even some of the most elemental and traditional components of cidermaking in these places. It will examine how microbes and folkways, which readily transgress boundaries, are as essential to the distinctiveness of cidermakers' products as the more static components of the places in which they are made—indeed, how the comings and goings of these elements have shaped these places of production along with the people in them and the products that they make. Instead of producing new data points through which cidermakers might assert distinctiveness, in the language of terroir and/or a PDO claim, as historically continuous traditions grounded in fixed places, we will explore whether distinctiveness can more readily be found in complex combinations of elements moving and changing in time, on a landscape in constant—if often subtle—flux. Such stories may not secure Devon cidermakers a PDO, but they may express more sustainable claims to tradition—living traditions—than ones that ignore the dynamic forces at play in ecologies of production in Devon and elsewhere.

Acknowledgments

The project underpinning this chapter was funded by the University of Exeter, Arts & Culture; by the Royal Albert Memorial Museum & Art Gallery in Exeter; by a Partnership Engage Grant from the Social Science and Humanities Research Council, Canada; and by a Project Grant from the Arts Council England. We thank Sarah Campbell at Arts & Culture, Laura Goodband at the RAMM, and Sue Ruddick at the University of Toronto, who facilitated these grants and worked with us in delivery of the project. Jim Causley, Bill Murray, and Mariners Away collaborated in the development and enactment of the project. And above all, we thank Ben, Ruth, David and Theo Gray, who welcomed us into their orchards and pound house, embraced us all, and, to our delight, made "Here's to Thee" their very own.

Simon Pope is an artist specializing in participatory approaches to contemporary art. His recent work takes the form of collective explorations of more-than-human social worlds. This work is often made with artistic collaborators, in partnership with universities and museums, and with researchers from other disciplines. He is Research Associate at the Centre for Rural Policy Research at the University of Exeter, and an Eccles Fellow of the British Library.

Harry G. West is Professor of Anthropology at the University of Exeter (UK), with expertise in agrarian history and political economy, and food and cultural heritage. His research explores artisan cheesemaking and the cultural economy, including how cheesemakers have embraced and transformed the idea of terroir, and how they have adopted innovative methods while reproducing cheesemaking traditions in changing historical contexts. His publications on these themes include numerous journal articles and book chapters. He is Convener of the Master's in Food Studies, Codirector of the Centre for Rural Policy Research, and Lead of Exeter Food: A University Research Network.

Notes

1. See also Grasseni (this volume), who focuses on the politics of scales of production.
2. http://www.heres-to-thee.org.uk (retrieved 11 December 2024).
3. Abbots writes of this phenomenon in Wales, expressed by the adage "no cider, no work" (Abbots 2019).
4. See also Grasseni (this volume).
5. A 1962 geological survey indicates variance even in the geological strata beneath the Grays' farm, while some of these strata share characteristics with places as distant as north Wales (Clayden 1962, 1964, 1971).
6. On the movement of people, foods, and cuisines, see also the chapters by Klein, Sanders, and Garth, in this volume. The chapters by Demossier and Meneley (both this volume) also address material change. And Czerny's chapter (this volume) discusses microbes moving through space or persisting through time.
7. On this dynamic, see also the chapters in this volume by Paxson and Weiss; Grasseni; Colquhoun; Xiao; de St. Maurice; and Jung.

References

Abbots, Emma-Jayne. 2018. "Corporeal Crafting: Tastes, Knowledges and Quality Protocols in British Cider-Making." In *Taste*, edited by Andrea Pavoni, Danilo Mandic, Caterina Nirta, and Andreas Philippopoulos-Mihalopoulos, 111–44. London: University of Westminster Press.

———. 2019. "'Good People Make Good Cider': Crafting Culinary Heritage in Wales and the Welsh Marshes." *Food & History* 17(2): 19–39.

Al Riachy, Reem, Caroline Strub, Noel Durand, Benjamin Guibert, Hugues Guichard, Florentin Constancias, Vincent Chochois, Felicie Lopez-Lauri, Angelique Fontana, and Sabine Schorr-Galindo. 2021. "Microbiome Status of Cider-Apples, from Orchard to Pressing, with a Special Focus on Penicillium expansum Occurance and Patulin Contamination." *Journal of Fungi* 7(4): 244.

Barham, Elizabeth. 2003. "Translating Terroir: The Global Challenge of French AOC Labeling." *Journal of Rural Studies* 19(1): 127–38.

Beacham, Jonathan. 2018. "Organising Food Differently: Towards a More-than-Human Ethics of Care for the Anthropocene." *Organization* 25(4): 533–49.

Beech, F. W. 1993. “Yeasts in Cider-Making.” In *The Yeasts*, edited by Anthony H. Rose, and J. Stuart Harrison, 169–213. San Diego: Academic Press.

Bennett, Jane. 2007. “Edible Matter.” *New Left Review* 45: 133–45.

Bérard, Laurence, and Philippe Marchenay. 2008. *From Localized Products to Geographical Indications: Awareness and Action.* Paris: Centre National de la Recherche Scientifique.

Bowen, J., and F. W. Beech. 1964. “The Distribution of Yeasts in Cider Apples.” *Journal of Applied Bacteriology* 27(2): 333–41.

Cater, Colin. 2013. *Wassailing: Reawakening an Ancient Folk Custom.* Sible Hedingham: Hedingham Fair.

Clayden, B. 1962. *Soils of the Middle Teign Valley District of Devon, Exeter.* Soil Survey of England and Wales.

———. 1964. *The Soils of the Middle Teign Valley District of Devon.* Bulletin of the Soil Survey of Great Britain.

———. 1971. *Soils of the Exeter District.* Memoir of the Soil Survey of Great Britain.

Cousin, Fabien J., Rozenn Le Guellec, Margot Schlusselhuber, Marion Dalmasso, Jean-Marie Laplace, and Marina Cretenet. 2017. “Microorganisms in Fermented Apple Beverages: Current Knowledge and Future Directions.” *Microorganisms* 5(3): 39.

Crowden, J. 2021. *Cider Country: How an Ancient Craft Became a Way of Life.* Castlehead: William Collins.

Department for Environment, Food & Rural Affairs. 2018. *Protected Food Name: Devon Cider: An Application for Devon Cider under the EU Protected Food Name Scheme*, 17 December. Retrieved April 2023 from https://www.gov.uk/government/publications/protected-food-name-devon-cider-pdo.

Derry, Thomas K., and Trevor I. Williams. 1960. *A Short History of Technology from the Earliest Times to A.D. 1900.* New York: Courier Corporation.

Doores, S., and D. Splittstoesser. 1983. “The Microbiology of Apples and Apple Products.” *CRC Critical Reviews in Food Science and Nutrition* 19(2): 133–49.

Elton, Sarah. 2019. “Posthumanism Invited to Dinner.” *Gastronomica* 19(2): 6–15.

Fox, Harold. 1999. “Medieval Farming and Rural Settlement.” In *Historical Atlas of South-West England*, edited by Roger Kain, and William Ravenhill, 273–80. Exeter: University of Exeter Press.

Gosden, Chris. 2020. *The History of Magic: From Alchemy to Witchcraft, from the Ice Age to the Present.* London: Penguin.

Gover, J. E., Allen Mawer, and Frank Merry Stenton. 1931. *The Place-Names of Devon.* Vols. 8–9). Edited by E. P.-N. Society. Cambridge: Cambridge University Press.

Gray, Todd. 2019. *Uncle Tom Cobley and All.* Minneapolis: Mint Press.

Groom, Nick. 2014. *The Seasons: A Celebration of the English Year.* London: Atlantic Books.

Havinden, M., and R. Stanes. 1999. “Agriculture and Rural Settlement 1500–1800.” In *Historical Atlas of South-West England*, edited by Roger Kain, and William Ravenhill, 281–93. Exeter: University of Exeter Press.

Higgins, D. H. 2014. “The Meaning of Old English Stōw and the Origin of the Name of Bristol.” *Transactions of the Bristol and Gloucestershire Archaeological Society* 132: 67–73.

Hutton, R. 1996. *The Stations of the Sun: A History of the Ritual Year in Britain.* Oxford: Oxford University Press.

Landis, Elizabeth A., Angela M. Oliverio, Erin A. McKenney, Lauren M. Nichols, Nicole Kfoury, Megan Biango-Daniels, Leonora K Shell, Anne A. Madden, Lori Shapiro, and

Benjamin Wolfe. 2021. "The Diversity and Function of Sourdough Starter Microbiomes." *eLife* 10: e61644.

Laplace, Jean-Marie, Sophie Apery, Jacques Frëre, and Yanick Ray. 1998. "Incidence of Indigenous Microbial Flora from Utensils and Surrounding Air in Traditional French Cider Making." *Journal of the Institute of Brewing* 104(2): 71–74.

Liu, Di, Qinglin Chen, Pangzhen Zhang, Deli Chen, and Kate S. Howell. 2020. "The Fungal Microbiome Is an Important Component of Vineyard Ecosystems and Correlates with Regional Distinctiveness of Wine." *mSphere* 5(4): e00534-20.

Marcellino, N. 2003. *Biodiversity of Geotrichum candidum Strains Isolated from Traditional French Cheese*. Storrs-Mansfield: University of Connecticut.

Marcellino, N., E. Beuvier, R. Grappin, M. Guéguen, and D. R. Benson. 2001. "Diversity of Geotrichum candidum Strains Isolated from Traditional Cheesemaking Fabrications in France." *Applied and Environmental Microbiology* 67(10): 4752–59.

McKenney, Erin, Rob Dunn, Elizabeth Landis, Benjamin Wolfe, Angela Oliverio, and Matt Shipman. 2021. *Intercontinental Study Sheds Light on the Microbial Life of Sourdough*, 26 January. Retrieved February 2021 from https://news.ncsu.edu/2021/01/the-sourdough-map/.

Misery, Boris, Patrick Legendre, Olivier Rue, Valerie Kientz Bouchart, Hugues Guichard, Jean-Marie Laplace, and Marina Cretenet. 2020. "Diversity and Dynamics of Bacterial and Fungal Communities in Cider for Distillation." *International Journal of Food Microbiology* 339.

Parker, Eleanor. 2022. *Winters in the World: A Journey through the Anglo-Saxon Year.* London: Reaktion Books.

Paxson, Heather. 2008. "Post-Pasteurian Cultures: The Microbiopolitics of Raw-Milk Cheese in the United States." *Cultural Anthropology* 23(1): 15–47.

Pope, Simon. 2022. *Here's to Thee: A Celebration of the Human and Microbial Social Worlds of Devonshire Cidermaking.* Arts & Culture, University of Exeter. Retrieved April 2025 from https://heres-to-thee.org.uk/publication/herestothee_book_online_version.pdf.

Sarmiento, Eric R. 2017. "Synergies in Alternative Food Network Research: Embodiment, Diverse Economies, and More-than-Human Food Geographies." *Agriculture and Human Values* 34: 485–97.

Spender, Edward. 1864. "On the 'Cider-Truck' System in Some Parts of the West of England." *Journal of the Statistical Society of London* 27(4): 526–32.

Trubek, Amy B. 2008. *The Taste of Place: A Cultural Journey into Terroir.* Berkeley: University of California Press.

Trubek, Amy B., Kolleen M. Guy, and Sarah Bowen. 2010. "Terroir: A French Conversation with a Transnational Future." *Contemporary French and Francophone Studies* 14(2): 139–48.

Wang, Hung Li, Helene Hopfer, Darrell W. Cockburn, and Josephine Wee. 2021. "Characterization of Microbial Dynamics and Volatile Metabolome Changes during Fermentation of Chambourcin Hybrid Grapes from Two Pennsylvania Region." *Frontiers in Microbiology* 11 (11 January): 614278.

West, Harry G. 2013. "Appellations and Indications of Origin, Terroir, and the Social Construction and Contestation of Place-Named Foods." In *The Handbook of Food Research*, edited by Anne Murcott, Warren Belasco, and Peter Jackson, 209–28. London: Bloomsbury.

———. 2020. "Crafting Innovation: Continuity and Change in the 'Living Traditions' of Contemporary Artisan Cheesemakers." *Food & Foodways* 28(2): 91–116.

———. 2022. "Terroir Products: A Movable Heritage Feast?" *Review of Agricultural, Food & Environmental Studies* 103(1): 1–27.

Wigley, Edward. 2019. "Wassail! Reinventing 'Tradition' in Contemporary Wassailing Customs in Southern England." *Cultural Geographies* 26(3): 379–93.

———. 2021. "'A Place of Magic': Enchanting Geographies of Contemporary Wassailing Practices." *Social & Cultural Geography* 22(6): 868–89.

Wilson, James E. 1998. *Terroir: The Role of Geology, Climate, and Culture in the Making of French Wines.* Berkeley: University of California Press.

Wolfe, Benjamin, Julie Button, Marcela Santarelli, Rachel J. Dutton. 2014. "Cheese Rind Communities Provide Tractable Systems for In Situ and In Vitro Studies of Microbial Diversity." *Cell* 158(2): 422–33.

CHAPTER 3

Fishnets

Land-Sea Relationalities and Contingencies in Coastal Latvian "Taste of Place"

Guntra A. Aistara

Introduction

The flavorful smoke from a fish hut in the dunes wafted toward me on the sea air as the car wheels crunched over pine cones on a sandy, winding road heading toward the Baltic Sea coast in northwest Latvia. There, in July 2022, I met Jānis, a young man who had taken over his late father's fish-smoking business and campground near the Cape of Kolka, where the waters of the open Baltic Sea and the Gulf of Riga, or the "Greatsea" and "Smallsea" as locals call them, crisscross in alternating waves at a perilous point. The numerous shipwrecks below attest to the potential danger that lurks as skilled local fishers take advantage of fishing in "both seas," depending on the winds.

Jānis was tending a small stand with both hot- and cold-smoked flounder, the fish best adapted to the local sea conditions and most demanded by summer tourists. We walked down the dune to a plateau where Jānis pointed out metal frames sunken into the sandy soil, the removable wooden lids blackened by smoke and shiny from fish oil. He explained:

> These are from my father's day . . . there used to be a—like a tunnel here, and it is where we did our cold smoking. But now, now we do the hot smoking here. That is—you make a little fire underneath here—you dry the fish first, lay them on the rack. Dry them—depending on the weather and other conditions, for about an hour—and then, we primarily do it the *Liv* way, with the pine cones. Here you can see how they've fallen down the sides. We pour the pine cones on the coals, put the fish in there, the lid on—and then they smoke, for about thirty to forty minutes.

The *Livs* invoked by Jānis inhabited twelve fishing villages in northwest Latvia for several thousand years, an area now known as the "Liv coast."[1] Liv culture, however, witnessed a marked decline during the Soviet years when policies aimed to depopulate coastal villages and severed residents from traditional livelihood practices, as well as in the post-socialist era when socioeconomic pressures proved too great to actively revive cultural practices. Today fewer than twenty Liv language speakers remain, and much of their knowledge has been appropriated into Latvian culture as coastal families intermarried and newcomers arrived over generations. Liv cultural heritage is visible mostly in the use of the Liv flag, Liv place names and phrases, and mentions of Liv heritage on tourist sites (Šuvcāne and Ernštreits 2018).

Jānis is one of the few fish smokers on the Liv coast who still uses the pinecone-based hot-smoking pit called a *pepiņbedre.* He learned the technique from his father, who had moved to the region thirty years earlier and had himself learned fishing and smoking practices from his neighbors at the time, many of Liv ancestry. Jānis maintains that pine cones give the fish a distinctive taste, aroma, and color. He said it was the taste imbued by the pine cones that local buyers especially valued because it reminded them of how their grandfather or father had smoked fish: "We started with these methods . . . well, we can't invent some kind of other method and somehow get the same result," Jānis explained. "If you smoked them differently, would they have a different taste?" I asked. "Yes, well . . . then you couldn't use the pine cones . . . then it isn't the same anymore," he replied.

When I met Jānis again in 2024, he again demonstrated the hot-smoking technique with pine cones but did not attribute it as a Liv method. When I asked him about it, he said: "Well, they say it is a Liv method. It's a very, very old method, but we can't prove whether it was Liv per se. I assume they also had many different methods." He seemed uncomfortable having to claim one set culinary heritage narrative.

While Jānis is one of the few fish smokers using the *pepiņbedre,* smoked flounder abounds in every village. Another renowned fish smoker, Valdis, who is of Liv ancestry, reinvented cold fish smoking based on what he remembered from his father's fish smoking, adapting it based on his own observations, the practicalities of having to smoke fish all night on his own, and feedback from elderly neighbor women who remembered previous tastes. In June 2024, he remarked that tourists who come to the Liv coast from other regions simply seek out *kūpināta bute,* or smoked flounder, without much regard for the processes. He compared it to other popular tourist commodities taken to represent a place, such as the carved wooden walking canes sold at a hiking area in Sigulda, in northeastern Latvia. Sometimes Valdis tells tourists he has *kūpināta leste,* and sees their faces fall in disappointment that they will not get what they came for, not realizing that this is the Liv name for the same smoked flounder.

Figure 3.1. Flounder-smoking demonstration at Jānis's place. Latvia, 2024. © A. Valaine

While smoked flounder has become a tourist icon of the Liv coast, what exactly it represents remains somewhat elusive. Each fish smoker has a slightly different technique, resulting in a different texture and taste, yet this variation is glossed over in the imagined *kūpinātā bute* sought by tourists as an authentic commodity representing the place. The taste of the smoked flounder seems to be taken for granted as the "taste of place" without any details attached to it. The tourist imaginary of the smoked flounder is a search for the "authentic" culinary experience, which may obscure complexities of its production process (Pratt 2007). In this chapter, I follow the stories of fishers, fish smokers, and local residents to try to piece together what historic and current processes and practices make up the imagined "taste of place" embodied in the sought-after smoked flounder on the Liv coast.

"Taste of place" is often captured in the literature by the terms *terroir* and its sea-based relative, *merroir.* These concepts describe the specific craft and skill of the producer as well as the particular qualities of the soil or marine environment, respectively, which are seen to impart distinctive tastes on food, wine, or fish (Demossier 2011; Teigen De Master et al. 2019). Yet the desired taste of smoked flounder results from neither just the sea nor only the land, but the intermingling of both. It stems from the fish species, the ecology of the sea, the skills of the fisher and the smoker, and the pine and alder forests that grow in the meager coastal soils and traditionally facilitated access to the sea. Therefore, following "amphibious anthropology" (Gagné and Rassmussen 2016), I argue that rather than one stable conception of "the taste of place" imagined by tourists, the particular qualities of smoked flounder have emerged through more complicated networked relationalities.

Moreover, the taste of the smoked flounder does not stem from an uninterrupted tradition passed down over generations from Liv ancestors. Rather, the coherence of any such narrative is punctured by ruptures and tempered by contingencies of history that make it more difficult to catch, sell, and smoke fish today or to know the real origin of the now-reinvented smoking practices. I analyze this relational network and its contingencies through the metaphor of "fishnets," revealing the inherent instabilities and uncertainties that complicate the simplified "taste of place" of the tourist imaginary.

This chapter is based on interviews with coastal fishers and other residents, as well as ethnographic and archival research along the Kurzeme coast between 2021 and 2024. It is part of a larger project, "Life by the Sea, Revisited,"[2] which traces how the cultural and culinary heritage and ecological perceptions of coastal residents in Western Latvia has changed in the last century. I first discuss the idea of fishnets as a tool for analyzing land-sea relationalities and contingencies. Next, I briefly introduce the distinctive ecology of the Baltic Sea and the western Latvian coastal seascape, then trace historic and contemporary Liv and Latvian interactions with the land and sea in crafting their livelihoods and foodscapes. Finally, I return to the smoked flounder to illustrate how, rather than one straightforward narrative of the "taste of place," it integrates land and sea relationalities and political contingencies in an intricate fishnet.

Weaving Fishnets

I use the metaphor of fishnets here to analyze how the smoked flounder represents both interconnections between the particular ecology of the Baltic Sea and intertwined land- and sea-based livelihoods, and the political and economic restrictions that have governed small-scale coastal fishing and thus limited possibilities in various historic periods.

Coastal Baltic residents have historically woven their livelihoods from connections between the land and the sea. Perhaps even more than farmers who have crafted their farms as landscapes through understanding ecological cycles and their interrelations with other creatures, in what I have called "networked diversities of place" (Aistara 2018), coastal foresters-fishers-farmers are anchored in place by their ability to know, manage, and navigate the ecological interdependencies between these sectors. I show here how these relationalities and contingencies of production and consumption affect the possibilities of producing smoked flounder.

The intermingling of land and sea forms the Baltic seascape, defined by Plaan (2019: 74) as "a relational space of sea and land. It is simultaneously social, material, and subjective: a space where islanders' [or coastal peoples'] views of nature, their identity and their livelihood practices interact with conservation regulations and state power." Amphibious anthropology (Gagné and Rassmussen 2016: 137) is an approach to studying such relational spaces where land and water meet, which aims to show "how the dynamics related to flows of water are constitutive of, and become enfolded into, landscapes. . . . Land relates to landscape and, by extension, to the cultural production of place and to forms of belonging and attachment." Following this approach here allows us to more effectively explore this intersection of land- and sea-based foodscapes in coastal areas rather than perpetuating their division through the separate terms *terroir* and *merroir* in the literature. Like amphibians that spend part of their life on land and part in the water, coastal forester-fisher-farmers have long harvested from both the land and the sea. Over time, their practices have changed the physical seascape as well. The relational seascape is created as much by residents' actions as those of other living beings in the sea, by the constantly flowing waves of the sea as well as the shifting sands of the shore.

The "taste of place" represented by smoked flounder in the tourist imaginary may discount not only the interdependencies of land and sea through which these flavors have developed but also the contingencies that have at times made fish impossible to be caught or eaten. This is similar to the "traditional" food narratives surrounding bread or wine in post-socialist Latvia that obscure Soviet histories as inauthentic (Aistara 2014).

In what follows I show how fishers and smokers have navigated the shifting ecological, socioeconomic, and political conditions that both structure and limit their possibilities, much like fishnets. These in turn represent the relationalities and contingencies that fishers and smokers retell in the more complicated stories that make up coastal Latvian foodscapes.

Brackish Ecologies

The Baltic Sea is the largest brackish, or low-salinity, sea in the world, with only one inlet of salty water from the North Sea near the Kattegat in Denmark (Svedäng 2023). The influx of salt water has become less frequent in the last decades, producing a steep gradient of salt water in the south to near-fresh water in the north (Lehman et al. 2022). This hybrid ecosystem of sweet and salty water makes it, on the one hand, livable for river species that may not be able to exist in salt water, but, on the other, it requires saltwater species that have migrated in from the North Sea and the Atlantic to adapt. Both fish and coastal residents can thus be seen as engaging in a constant adaptation to brackish ecologies.

The most extreme response can be seen in flounder, which has split into two species as an environmental adaptation to these low salinity conditions (Jokinen et al. 2019). European flounder developed new reproductive behaviors to survive: because their eggs' ability to float in deeper water was hindered by low salinity, they began spawning eggs that would sink to the bottom layers in coastal waters (Momigliano et al. 2018). Those flounder with this adaptation, called Baltic flounder (*Platichthys solemdali*), were discovered in 2018 to have become genetically distinct from European flounder (*Platichthys flesus*) and are now considered the only endemic fish species in the Baltic Sea (Momigliano et al. 2018). The Baltic flounder lives more in the north, where there is lower salinity, while the European flounder is more prevalent in the south (Jokinen et al. 2019). It is right around the Cape of Kolka, where the Greatsea and Smallsea intersect, that the two populations meet and where flounder is one of the most important fish. This demonstrates the complexity of brackish Baltic ecosystems, even for their long-term inhabitants.

Furthermore, the sea cannot be ecologically separated from the land that surrounds it. The sandy coastal dunes determine what can grow there, which in turn influence what economic activities are possible. One of the only trees that grows in the sandy soil of the dunes is pine; black alder tends to grow in the wetter areas beyond the dunes, with birch and gray alder forests behind (Kitenberga et al. 2019; Veidemane 2011: 12). It is therefore also exactly the wood from pine, alder, and birch that coastal residents have used to facilitate their access to the sea, and smoke their fish, creating hybrid socioeconomic systems and identities where the land and the sea intersect.

Amphibious Economies and Identities

The Liv way of life grounded in land-sea interdependencies is represented in the three horizontal stripes of the Liv flag: blue for the sea where Livs fished for their livelihoods, white for the sand that greeted them upon return, and green for the pine forests lining the dunes (Šuvcāne and Ērenštreits 2018; Ozoliņa et al. 2022).

The intimately intertwined land and sea have long been the joint foundation for coastal livelihoods. As far back as three thousand years ago, Livs around the Cape of Kolka, whose names for themselves mean "coast dwellers" and "fishermen" (Wierucka 2011), engaged in small-scale fishing, forestry, and farming. Yet rights to fishing have been just as heavily contested as rights to land in various political regimes, making the exercise of fishers' skills contingent upon political power struggles. Fish were included as part of the "tithe" paid by serfs to landlords after the invasion of Teutonic knights in the thirteenth century, a practice extending well into the nineteenth century when Latvia was included in the Russian empire (Cimermanis 1998). In the early twentieth century in independent

Latvia fishing was still mostly used for subsistence purposes and as barter for agricultural products; only in rare cases were fish sold (Cimermanis 1998). The late 1930s saw the formation of the first fishing cooperatives, commercial fishing, and motorboats that were later appropriated into Soviet fishing *kolhozes* (collectives, pl. English; *kolhozs*, sg. Latvian).

Although coastal residents today emphasize that they cannot live from fishing alone, probably this has always been true. Veldre's 1938 (1991) book *Dzīve pie jūras* (Life by the sea) recounts that in the winter, when the sea froze, coastal residents worked in the forests, and on days in the summer when it was too windy to fish, they worked the fields. Forests afforded residents fuel and building materials. Fishing boats in Kurzeme were traditionally built from pine wood, tar to make boats and nets seaworthy came from both pine roots and birch bark, and pine bark was used to make buoys for nets (Šabanovs 2022). Wood was also used to make posts for drying the nets and anchoring boats, as well as to construct breakwaters to collect seaweed. Thus, there could be little fishing or farming without the surrounding forests.

Another key strategy for coastal residents was to integrate fishing and farming. Since at least the 1700s small farmers have been adapting coastal lands to farming by reforesting dunes to prevent erosion and constructing wind-protected fields in the meager, sandy soils (Sture 2012). On the southern Kurzeme coast this formed a distinctive landscape of fields protected by dunes called *aizjomi* (Sture 2012). In the 1930s fishers used to compete for the seaweed even more than for the fish themselves. State support included building breakwaters to help catch four to six times more seaweed (Sture 2012). Every house had its own symbol, which was branded into wooden posts used to mark not only fishnets but also piles of seaweed they had collected. They used horse-pulled wagons and pitchforks to bring the "sea gold" back to enrich their fields with nitrogen and phosphorus:

> The small plots behind the dunes were called "sea gardens" and, thanks to the "sea manure," people could grow "sugar beets as big as stumps." The local coastal villagers believed that the sea was their blessing, that it gave not only fish but also bread and potatoes, which could grow big thanks to the sea manure. . . . It is known that sea manure was also used to feed pigs at that time—dried, washed sea manure was chopped up, a little flour added and fed to the pigs. The sea not only provided the coastal population with fish, but also helped to produce good quality bacon. (Grickus et al. 2021: 12)

Intricate forms of land-sea barter were developed as a type of socioeconomic networking. One fisher-farmer told me that in the old days flounder used to be "traded for meadows," that is, for the permission to mow more fertile inland grasslands to provide a richer hay for coastal livestock. Others recalled loading fish onto a horse cart to bring inland to trade for other food products.

Figure 3.2. Sketch from monument board ethnographic expedition. ZAE 4712/3 Drawing. Smokehouse. Ventspils region. Dundaga municipality, Saunagciems, "Nigliņi" farmstead. Drawn by Aleksandrs Belte, 30 October 1943, with permission from the Latvian National History Museum.

These ecological and socioeconomic exchanges between land and sea have resulted in particular coastal foodscapes. Most fish recipes also include potatoes or dairy products. Yet potatoes could only be grown with additional nutrients provided by the sea, and dairy products were only available if one could afford to feed a cow by gaining access to richer meadows.

Many coastal culinary practices that depend on land-sea intermingling were inherited from the Livs. Attention to Liv cultural preservation began in the 1920s as assimilation into Latvian culture was already marked, and Liv language speakers remained active on the coast well into the Soviet period. A 1943 ethnographic expedition documented how Livs sometimes used old boats that were no longer seaworthy, sawed in half and placed upright to form the walls of the smoke shed, as seen in figure 3.2. The tarred and seawater-impregnated walls of the boat would likely have also added to the aromas and flavors of the smoking process.

The ethnographic materials document hot-smoked flounder called *pepiņi* and smoked in a specially dug pit in the ground covered by a wooden door, much like the practice Jānis demonstrated. Cold-smoked flounder was smoked in either the repurposed old boat or in a specially built wooden smoke shed. In both cases the initial fire was made with alder and the smoke maintained with the addition of pine cones to guarantee a golden color.

Land-sea exchanges thus also determined the taste of the smoked fish, as a kind of forest terroir. Food studies scholars have explored how the flavors of different woods change the tastes of smoked meats and fish. While the use of alder wood is well known in fish-smoking recipes due to its neutral properties, such as cold-smoked salmon with alder wood in Alaska (Jacobsen 2010), I have found the use of pine cones mentioned only in the Baltic. All of the smokers with whom I spoke mentioned that pine wood itself is not good for smoking, but those few that use pine cones mention that it helps brown the skin without imparting strong flavors.

Integrated land-sea livelihood strategies also become ingrained elements of both Liv and Latvian coastal identities. Most Latvian coastal residents have told me they could not live without the harsh winds and sea air: "If you have been by the sea since your childhood, what else would you do? . . . I love this place and the sea. When you haven't been in the sea for a while, it pulls you, like a magnet. I have to say, I can't imagine [living] without it." Yet one of the consequences of both Soviet and current developments has been the separation of these intertwined livelihoods and identities.

Forced Separations, Toxic Legacies

During Latvia's occupation by the Soviet Union, the entire Kurzeme coast was also the westernmost border of the Soviet Union. The coast was a closed military zone; the sea was behind a barbed wire fence, accessible only in certain places and at certain times of day. Guards tediously raked the sand every evening to be able to discern unauthorized movements on the beach; relatives from other areas needed special permits to visit. One author who spent every childhood summer living with her Liv grandparents on the Kolka coast said she first saw the cape itself only after independence in 1991.

The barbed wire fence that separated the sea from the land also represents both Soviet and current attempts to segregate fishing from agriculture, the effects of which still reverberate through coastal seascapes and foodscapes. After 1948 all independent farmers were forced to join collective farms called *kolhozes*. Soviet policies aimed to depopulate coastal villages by relocating people to urban centers or fishing towns. Residents from smaller coastal villages were forced to either burn their boats and work on the agriculture *kolhozs* or move to the nearest port to join a fishing *kolhozs*. Most fishers from the smaller Liv fishing villages had to relocate to the town of Kolka, which had a fishing *kolhozs* and cannery.

This forced separation between intertwined identities, becoming either fishers or farmers, also severed ties to place and community. As one fisher whose father relocated to join a fishing *kolhozs* told me, families who moved were called traitors in their old village for abandoning home. At the same time, archival records show that they were regarded as potentially disloyal to their new collective, repeatedly reprimanded in *kolhozs* administrative meetings, and many eventually kicked out.

As access to fish was officially controlled by the *kolhozs*, and all catch had to be centrally deposited for either processing in local factories or fresh export to Moscow, fresh local fish took on new value as a limited commodity. It was used for everything from greasing deals (e.g., to build a new *kolhozs* building) to giving informal "favors" (e.g., to graduate), and presenting as a treasured gift to inland friends and relatives. Guards checked fishermen for hidden stashes (though these often passed "unseen" through holes in the fences), but "fishwives" routinely smuggled fish to smoke and deliver to ministry workers in Riga. Fish, then, were an important element of the informal economy.

The segregation of land from sea through the industrialization of both fishing and agriculture has had severe consequences. After World War II, larger fishing vessels and trawlers both in the Soviet Union and in other Baltic Sea states precipitated overfishing. This coincided with the industrialization of agriculture. As synthetic fertilizers replaced more circular systems based on seaweed and manure, the Baltic Sea became heavily polluted from decades of intensive agricultural runoff. Excess nutrients deplete oxygen levels, resulting in eutrophication, toxic blooms, and fish kills. The most recent Helsinki Commission State of the Baltic Sea report (2023) indicates limited improvements despite decades of reporting on the problems and working internationally to solve them.

The mental separation of the land from the sea also rendered the sea as a toxic dumping ground for chemical weapons after the war (Polak-Juszczak and Richert 2021). Baltic Sea fish have been found to have high levels of arsenic, dioxins, and other chemicals. Environmental organizations have reported that Baltic fish may be too toxic to eat. Large trawlers continue to fish large amounts of herring and sprats, which are processed into fishmeal, leaving fewer livelihood options for small-scale coastal fishers. This toxic legacy continues to affect coastal residents.

Contemporary Contingencies

Since renewed independence after 1991, various actors have tried to recreate land-sea connections, only to be entangled in new obstacles and contingencies. In the 1990s *kolhozes* were disbanded, and the boats, fishing gear, and inventory could be privatized by individuals. It was a chaotic and difficult time, but one brimming with possibilities. One fisher, Žanis, from Kolka, remembered the moment when private individuals could first freely visit the seaside and fishers were overwhelmed with new demand: "Well, actually, maybe we are a little at fault for that [overfishing]. At that moment—when the first independence years were exploding—then the flounder was very weak. But, well . . . if there is someone to buy it, bring it ashore! . . . And they bought it—all those skinny flounder! Business boomed—cars lined up. Now sometimes you have to beg—you don't know where to put the fish."

When I asked who came in the 1990s to wait in line for fish, he replied: "Everyone! Everyone drove out here. You wouldn't believe it!" Like bananas, another good that exploded in the post-Soviet years because it had not been easily accessible in the Soviet Union, smoked flounder sales boomed. Some customers would purchase several buckets of fish and drive inland, selling fish door-to-door at farms along the way. This boom eventually went bust, however. Žanis noted: "At that time there were fish, but they didn't have a price—now it's the reverse."

Thirty years after independence, fishers are struggling once again with the interdependencies of brackish ecologies, amphibious economies, and forced separations. Flounder is still an important fish that thrives on the Liv coast. As Žanis told me: "For us here in Kolka, . . . our one constant fish is the flounder. The other fish we catch are just passing by." Yet catching and smoking them involves navigating multiple contingencies.

Ecologically, the overfishing, pollution, and eutrophication has changed the sea dramatically. Farmers who returned to fishing encountered entirely new fish, such as the invasive round goby. One fisher said: "When we first went back to the sea, and it showed up in our nets, we didn't know what to do with it . . . what kind of beast it was." Round goby arrived in the Baltic Sea from the Black Sea in the late 1990s and made it to the Latvian coast within the last ten years. They have also now adapted to the brackish waters, growing larger than in their place of origin, and even becoming fishers' mainstay in some areas. Flounder have become harder to catch both because they must now compete for food with the round goby and because the flounder go farther from shore in search of cooler waters as the climate warms. Meanwhile, the one conservation success in the last decades is the resurgence of gray seals, but for fishers they are furry enemies who destroy their expensive nets and compete for prized salmon and cod.

And while land-sea interdependencies are still important economically, a number of new barriers force separations between livelihoods and foodways. Ironically, fishers had to destroy boats again when joining the European Union, echoing their burning of boats when they joined the Soviet Union. Due to overfishing, new member states were required to reduce their fleets, and some fishers accepted compensation in exchange for cutting up their boats. Fishing quotas also limit catch of specific fish at certain times to allow them to spawn or recover, but these are seen as unfair by small-scale coastal fishers who do not feel they contribute to overfishing.

Fishing is still combined with forestry work and odd jobs. As Zigis noted: "You can't live from fishing alone. You still go cut trees in the forests in the winter and do everything you can." He went on to explain, however, that combining fishing with agriculture is now difficult. While many fishers own coastal land, these activities are now difficult to integrate because of the larger scales required to make them work economically: "You really can't combine these two things: fishing and farming. So, for example, if you have to spray your field when it is the round goby [season] in the spring, or you have to harvest the grains in the fall when you have to fish the salmon, how will you combine them?"

Zigis still relies heavily on land-sea barter as a means to compensate for this inability to combine fishing and farming. He explained:

> I don't buy potatoes. Neither potatoes nor carrots nor beets—I neither plant them nor buy them. For that I have a friend who grows them. I just go visit him—if I have some fish, I give them to him. Let's say, in the spring I have more flounder. I go and bring him the flounder. It doesn't matter how much, let's say two to three boxes—I don't mind. He puts them in the freezer and has them. He lives beyond Kuldīga, where they don't have fish, so he is overjoyed. And I, whenever I am going out that way, I stop by. I can always go there and pick up some potatoes, beets, onions, eggs, whatever I need. We don't even calculate it, really.

As fishing and farming have declined, tourism has taken their place as a coastal activity, but this poses new challenges. Fishers complain that safety laws make it difficult to take tourists out on their boats to demonstrate fishing. Sometimes fishers are frustrated that their access to the coast is also inhibited by protections put in place for other endangered species.

Both Jānis and Žanis, from whom he buys the fish he smokes, tell me that it is nearly impossible to both catch and smoke fish. Žanis experimented with smoking fish to sell to a friend who opened a tavern in an inland town until his neighbors complained about too much smoke. Jānis took over only his father's smoking business, considering the bureaucracy governing fishing too complicated.

Cold smoking is becoming rarer both because long storage is no longer necessary thanks to refrigeration and because it is more time-consuming. The drier and harder cold-smoked fish is still appreciated by locals for its distinctive texture and taste, but most fish smokers have now adapted their processes. Jānis makes cold-smoked fish in a wooden hut that takes twenty hours rather than several days. Valdis mentions that he does not have the time or the helpers to collect the pine cones. His more modern version of the smoke shed has a brick and concrete foundation that extends twenty centimeters up the sides to help minimize the fire risk, and he uses sawdust rather than pine cones, which is faster and easier to come by. Fish smokers also face new challenges, such as EU regulations on benzopyrenes. All of these barriers and contingencies act as traps, or as current realities complicating amphibious relationalities.

Fishnets: Navigating Relationalities and Contingencies Beyond Terroir and Merroir

The "taste of place" of the smoked flounder on the Liv coast is determined by brackish ecologies, amphibious economies, and toxic legacies. When Jānis sells a tourist a flounder, caught by Žanis off the coast near Kolka, smoked using an old (possibly Liv) smoking technique he learned from his father, it embodies the place where the Greatsea meets the Smallsea on the edge of the pine forest that has long facilitated access to the sea. Its taste, however, is not based just on *merroir*, or the interaction of the brackish sea with the flounder that speciated to adapt to the low salinity of the water. Nor is it merely the forest *terroir* of the alder wood and pine cones, which grow on the meager soils of the Baltic coast, used to smoke the fish. It represents a much more ambiguous set of amphibious relationalities that have determined both historic and contemporary land-sea networks and contingencies that limit the ability of Žanis to catch the fish and Jānis to smoke it.

Žanis possesses artisanal fishing skills, but the sea may be too windy or too warm; the flounder may have gone too deep and far due to climate change; there are bureaucratic hurdles for catching the fish, which are fewer and thinner. Meanwhile fishers must compete with both invasive fish like the round goby and with hungry gray seals for fish, both of which are also adapting to climatic change. Thus, the taste of the flounder is not only determined by the fact that Jānis is following his father's recipe, allegedly passed down from the nearly extinct Livs, whose legacy lives on in culinary heritage artifacts. When Jānis smokes the product, the level of benzopyrenes may be too high, or the fish may have too much dioxin for high-risk groups to eat, or there may be too few tourists traveling to Kolka anymore amid economic crises and emptying villages to make fishing a viable practice. The taste of place is steeped in these amphibious histories and the ability to navigate contemporary contingencies.

Neither the terms *terroir* nor *merroir* accurately capture the coastal foodscapes that have developed based on land-sea interconnections in Latvia. The use of these as separate terms may also recreate some of the land-sea segregations that have divided coastal residents historically. Finally, the stability implied by such terms does not account for the contingencies that lead to some of the food choices people have available today. This calls for embracing the uneven cultural heritage and intertwined livelihoods of land and sea that construct the "taste of place," and highlighting, rather than obscuring, these histories, relationalities, and contingencies.

Acknowledgments

I would like to thank all of the people who agreed to be interviewed, who participated in the ethnographic expeditions, and who have assisted with transcription. I would like to thank the editors and other contributing authors, as well as Ginta Elksne, Miķelis Grīviņš, Karen Hèbert, Diana Mincyte, Signe Pucena, Ieva Puzo, Ieva Vītola, and Sanita Zvidra for thoughtful comments on earlier drafts, lectures, and discussions on the topic. All errors remain my own.

Guntra Aistara is an environmental anthropologist whose research lies at the intersection of political ecology, food sovereignty, and environmental justice. Her research interests include organic agriculture movements, agrobiodiversity and seed sovereignty, agroecology, permaculture, culinary heritage revivals, and multispecies ethnography. Since 2021 she has been working on a project "Life by the Sea, Revisited" that seeks to investigate how coastal residents' knowledge, fishing and food-production practices, social and ecological relations, and sense of place have been transformed over the last century in the context of profound changes in political regimes, fisheries management structures, and climatic and ecological change.

Notes

1. The Livs are Finno-Ugric people who split into several cultural groups fifteen hundred years ago (Wierucka 2011). The height of Livonian culture was around the tenth and thirteenth centuries. After six hundred years of German rule in the current territory of Latvia, the Livs slowly intermingled with the ancient Baltic tribes of Latvia. See: http://www.livones.net/en/vesture/the-livonians-in-ancient-times (retrieved 11 December 2024).
2. The project includes ethnographic expeditions together with researchers from the Social Science Research Center of Riga Stradiņš University, the Latvian Oral History project, the Latvian National History Museum, and the interdisciplinary art center Serde. We are grateful for financing from the Latvian Foundation, the Kurzeme Regional Culture Fund and Central European University. All names are pseudonyms and all translations are my own.

References

Aistara, Guntra A. 2014. "Authentic Anachronisms." *Gastronomica: The Journal of Food and Culture* 14(4): 7–16.

———. 2018. *Organic Sovereignties: Struggles over Farming in an Age of Free Trade.* Seattle: University of Washington Press.

Cimermanis, Saulevedis. 1998. *Zveja un zvejnieki Latvijā 19. gadsimtā* [Fishing and fishermen in Latvia in the nineteenth century]. Riga: Latvian Academy of Sciences.

Demossier, Marion. 2011. "Beyond Terroir: Territorial Construction, Hegemonic Discourses, and French Wine Culture." *Journal of the Royal Anthropological Institute* 17(4): 685–705.

Gagné, Karine, and Matthias Borg Rasmussen. 2016. "Introduction–An Amphibious Anthropology: The Production of Place at the Confluence of Land and Water." *Anthropologica* 58(2): 135–49.

Grickus, Armands, Ligita Kokaine, and Zaiga Ozoliņa. 2021. *Apskats par makroaļģu audzēšanas, vākšanas un uzglabāšanas regulējumu Latvijā* [An overview of regulations on growing, harvesting, and storing macroalgae in Latvia]. Rīga: INTERREG. Retrieved November 2023 from https://www.kurzemesregions.lv/wp-content/uploads/2021/09/Makroaļģes_normatīvais-regulējums_apskats.pdf.

Jacobsen, Rowan. 2010. *American Terroir: Savoring the Flavors of Our Woods, Waters, and Fields.* London: Bloomsbury.

Jefremova, Lidija. 1963. "Kultūra un sadzīve Videmes zvejnieku kolhozos [Culture and social life in Vidzeme fishing kolkhozes]." *Arheoloģija un etnogrāfija.* 5th ed. Rīga: Zinātne.

Jokinen, Henri, Paolo Momigliano, and Juha Merilä. 2019. "From Ecology to Genetics and Back: The Tale of Two Flounder Species in the Baltic Sea." *ICES Journal of Marine Science* 76: 2267–75.

Kitenberga, Mara, Igor Drobyshev, Didzis Elferts, Roberts Matisons, Andis Adamovics, Juris Katrevics, Mats Niklasson, and Aris Jansons. 2019. "A Mixture of Human and Climatic Effects Shapes the 250-Year Long Fire History of a Semi-natural Pine Dominated Landscape of Northern Latvia." *Forest Ecology and Management* 441: 192–201.

Lehmann, Andreas, Kai Myrberg, Piia Post, Irina Chubarenko, Inga Dailidiene, Hans-Harald Hinrichsen, Karin Hüssy, Taavi Liblik, H. E. Markus Meier, Urmas Lips, and Tatiana Bukanova. 2022. "Salinity Dynamics of the Baltic Sea." *Earth System Dynamics* 13: 373–92.

Momigliano, Paolo, Gaël PJ Denys, Henri Jokinen, and Juha Merilä. 2018. "Platichthys solemdali sp. nov. (Actinopterygii, Pleuronectiformes): A New Flounder Species from the Baltic Sea." *Frontiers in Marine Science* 5: 225. Retrieved November 2023 from doi: 10.3389/fmars.2018.00225.

Ozoliņa, Lolita, Valts Ernštreits, Kadri Koreinik, and Ieva Vītola. 2022. "The Manifestations of Livonian Intangible Cultural Heritage across the Latvian and Estonian Border: Framing Early Field Notes from Research Sites." *Eesti ja soome-ugri keeleteaduse ajakiri. Journal of Estonian and Finno-Ugric Linguistics* 13(1): 233–56.

Plaan, Joonas. 2019. "Knowing and Perceiving the Seascape: Local Knowledge, Human-Environment Interactions and Materiality on Kihnu Island, Estonia." In *Dwelling in Political Landscapes*, ed. Ana Lounela, Eeva Berglund, and Timo Kallinen, 74–89. Helsinki: Studia Fennica.

Polak-Juszczak, Lucyna, and Joanna S. Richert, 2021. "Arsenic Speciation in Fish from Baltic Sea Close to Chemical Munitions Dumpsites." *Chemosphere* 284: 131326. Retrieved November 2023 from https://doi.org/10.1016/j.chemosphere.2021.131326.

Pratt, Jeff. 2007. "Food Values: The Local and the Authentic." *Critique of Anthropology* 27(3): 285–300.

Sture, Inese, 2012. "The Rise and Fall of the *Aizjomi* Landscape." *Geographical Review* 102(4): 427–45.

Šabanovs, Jānis. 2022. "*No kā būvēta 19. gadsimta zvejnieka laiva*?" [From what was the 19th century fishing boat built?] and "*Priedes izmantošana 19. gadsimta zemnieku dzīvē*" [Uses of pine in 19th century farmers' life]. Rīga: Latvijas nacionālais vēstures muzejs. Retrieved 19 November 2023 from https://emuzejs.lnvm.lv/resursi/galerijas-un-virtualas-izstades/galerijas/airis-mozus-un-radio-koks-latvijas-vesture/laivas and https://emuzejs.lnvm.lv/

resursi/galerijas-un-virtualas-izstades/galerijas/airis-mozus-un-radio-koks-latvijas-vesture/priedes-izmantosana.

Šuvcāne, Baiba, and Valts Ernštreits. 2018. "Chasing Livonian Heritage on the Livonian Coast." *Eesti ja soome-ugri keeleteaduse ajakiri. Journal of Estonian and Finno-Ugric Linguistics* 9(2): 109–28.

Svedäng, Henrik. 2023. "The Development of Fish Stocks and Fisheries in the Baltic Sea Since the Last Glaciation." In *Oxford Research Encyclopedia of Climate Science*, ed. Matthew C. Nisbet, Shirley S. Ho, Ezra Markowitz, Saffron O'Neill, Mike S. Schäfer, and Jagadish Thaker, online. Oxford: Oxford University Press. Retrieved 1 June 2023 from https://doi.org/10.1093/acrefore/9780190228620.013.902.

Teigen De Master, Kathryn, James LaChance, Sarah Bowen, and Lillian MacNell. 2019. "Terroir in Transition: Environmental Change in the Wisconsin Artisanal Cheese and New England Oyster Sectors." *Sustainability* 11(10): 2969. Retrieved November 2023 from doi:10.3390/su11102969.

Veldre, Vilis. 1991 [1938]. *Dzīve pie jūras: vērojumi Latvijas jūrmalas zvejniekciemos no Kolkas līdz Ainažiem* [Life by the sea: Observations in Latvian fishing villages from Kolka to Ainaži]. Rīga: Latvijas kultūras fonds.

Veidemane, Kristine. 2011. "The Impact of Driving Forces and Protection Policies on Future Coastal Landscapes: A Case Study of Latvia." In *Global Change and Baltic Coastal Zones*, edited by Gerald Schernewski, Jacobus Hofstede, and Thomas Neumann, 193–210. Dordrecht: Springer.

Wierucka, Aleksandra. 2011. "People from Under the Lone Oak: Using Culture for Constructing Identity in Local Livs' Community." *Current Issues in European Cultural Studies, Linköping Electronic Conference Proceedings* 62(17): 159–68.

Zirnīte, Māra, Vaira Strautniece, Uldis Krasts, Ernests Mūrnieks, Katrīna Vasiļevska, Gundega Blumberga, and Amanda Jātniece. 2021. *Lūžkilā* [In Lužkila]. Rīga: Latvijas mutvārdu vēstures pētnieku asociācija "Dzīvesstāsts" un LU Filozofijas un socioloģijas institūts.

CHAPTER 4

On Being Placeless?

The Case of Vegan Cheeses

Sarah Czerny

Introduction

I was sitting in a café in a small hilltop village in Sardinia on an unseasonably warm day in November. The views from this village were of the pastures below that were filled with sheep grazing in them. In the café there were some local farmers who were talking about their work, and how they kept sheep to make cheese out of their milk. According to the conversation that was unfolding, these sheep were an important part of Sardinian life because of the cheeses, where cheesemaking was an important way of life in these parts.

I had not gone to this village to research "Sardinian cheesemaking," or even dairy-based cheesemaking. Rather, I had come on a short visit to speak to vegan cheesemakers in the area about their work. But during this visit, the relation between animal-based cheesemaking and plant-based cheesemaking had caught my interest because of what seemed to be an irreconcilable difference between these "different" forms of cheesemaking. It was something I had already observed in other parts of Europe (France, Croatia) while doing research on plant-based cheesemaking: that these forms of cheesemaking were often operating in quite separate constellations of relations, where they were often conceptually held in opposition to one another. It was what caused an apparent "friction" between them. Even on this short visit, I had noticed that the same thing appeared to be happening: while all the cheesemakers were living together in the same place, they were working in quite different ways and separately.

On this day in the café, I was with a colleague who was doing long-term research in the area, and while speaking to the farmers we had asked them whether they had ever tried vegan cheeses. Other people we had spoken with in the village had tried them, or had wanted to try them, saying that they found them interesting because of various health reasons, such as lactose intolerance. They

Figure 4.1. View from the village. Sardinia, 2023. © Sarah Czerny

said that they could not eat dairy-based cheeses, which they missed, and these plant-based cheeses offered a potential alternative. Yet the response of the farmers in the café was a resolute "no" when we asked if they had tried them or had any interest in trying them. One farmer explained that vegan cheeses were not for people who lived in these areas, and since they were made out of nuts, they were really nothing more than "nutcakes." According to what he said, these cheeses were not cheese at all. As the conversation progressed, during which it seemed he was quite opposed to vegan cheeses, I asked him if this form of cheesemaking bothered him.

When speaking to people in other locations, beyond Sardinia, about vegan cheesemaking, some people had told me that they considered the labeling of plant-based cheeses as "cheese" to be a form of "false advertising," in the sense that they were plant-based cheeses "masquerading" as "real" cheeses. But this farmer said that he did not see this as a problem, explaining that he supported the people who were making plant-based cheeses because they were good for the "economy." He said it was important that young people (as he saw the plant-based cheesemakers) move into rural areas, because they stimulated business and employment for the people living there. Thus, he thought that the people who were making these cheeses were doing a good job and should be supported.

Initially, his response confused me because it seemed to be in almost direct opposition to what he had said earlier, that these plant-based cheeses were not cheeses at all and he did not ever want to try them. But he added that while it did not bother him if people from elsewhere ate such cheeses, people from his area would not understand them. His explanation was that people from his area could only appreciate Sardinian cheeses, because they were part of the land that these cheeses were made in. It was because they were Sardinian that they could really understand these cheeses. In contrast, he said that vegan cheeses were not a part of traditional Sardinian cheesemaking, which was why they were not for people "from these parts."

It is his suggestion that only certain people can appreciate a particular cheese because they are "from" the place where it is made that I want to consider in this chapter. In my mind, this sense of appreciation is closely related to how we know things—in this case, cheeses. It seems to closely resonate with the concept of terroir, and its relation to a particular place. In their afterword to this volume, Paxson and Weiss write that terroir is "frequently used as a descriptor of the ways that food is an expression of place." In these terms, terroir serves to make food "knowable" through the way that people connect it to a particular place, where Harry West (2022) has suggested that terroir is often conceptually formed on a triad of "people-place-product." As such, through the way that people conceptually root foods to a particular geolocation, they become identifiable by others through a specific relation to a locality. This can be seen in Elizabeth Barham's description of terroir, which she describes as being "an area or terrain, usually rather small, whose soil and microclimate impart distinctive qualities to food products" (2003: 131). It is also visible in Daniel Gade's point that terroir "claims that the special quality of an agricultural product is determined by the character of the place from which it comes" (2004: 849).

But a point that Paxson and Weiss (this volume) also make is that we should not always think of this relation between food and place as only going in one direction. They argue that it might be useful to consider this relation the other way around, where we study how places become knowable through food so that "we can further an understanding of the many ways that places come into being and become *knowable*" (Paxson and Weiss, this volume, emphasis added). In terms of how foods become knowable, this means that knowability is elicited in both directions: as much as foods become knowable through their connection to a specific place, places also become knowable through the way they are connected to a specific food. This is critical when one thinks about Paxson and Weiss's point about knowability in terms of West's (2022) triad of "people-place-product." It would seem that each figure (people, place, or product) has the potential to become knowable through its relation to the other two figures or positions in the triad. In this sense, people also become knowable through their relation to a place and product, as do products through their relation to place and people. In this sense, each figure in the triad is made known through the other two positions, and this works in all directions.

On Being Placeless?

This question of knowability is important with regards to plant-based cheeses because initially they seem quite "placeless"; it does not seem possible to connect them to one known and identifiable place. This creates the effect of having no terroir, which raises the question: Does this apparent lack of place also mean that the people making and eating plant-based cheeses become unknowable? When thinking about them in the European social context, as I do here, plant-based cheeses appear to challenge what might be thought of as the usual "intellectual coordinates" (Strathern 1991: xv) of how cheeses are most often thought of. This supports a point that Tobias Linné and Ally McCrow-Young have said in their writing about plant-based milks in general, where they write that at "an ontological level, the development of plant milk raises many questions" (2017: 211).

Correspondingly, plant-based cheeses trouble the usual reference points that are employed to determine a cheese as being a "cheese," which becomes especially evident when one holds them in a comparative position with dairy-based cheeses. Perhaps the most obvious is that they are not made using animal milks, where it is precisely the absence of animal milk that raises the question of whether these products can actually be thought of as cheeses. In European Union legislation, only products that have been made from animal milk, where milk that is defined as a "normal mammary secretion obtained from one or more milkings without either addition thereto or extraction therefrom," are cheese. As a result, anything that does not come from a "normal mammary secretion" cannot be legally sold as cheese, where a judgment by the Court of Justice of the European Union states that "purely plant-based products cannot, in principle, be marketed with designations such as 'milk,' 'cream,' 'butter,' 'cheese' or 'yoghurt,' which are reserved by EU law for animal products." Consequently, according to these legislative measurements, cheeses made from plant-based milks are not cheese.

However, this narrative that plant-based cheeses are not cheese is not settled. People who make and eat plant-based cheeses dispute this, where they counter-argue that their "products" can be thought of as cheeses because of the methods that have been used to make them. In my conversations with plant-based cheesemakers, they said that because they ferment and age their cheeses, and do so using very similar methods to the way that cheeses are made from dairy milks, they are cheeses. They explained that many of the recipes they use are based on "well-known" dairy-based cheese recipes, which is evident in the labels they use to describe these cheeses. For instance, Cashewbert is a cheese that is made using the same microbes that are used for camembert, and due to the resulting white mold on the rind of the cheese, it looks very similar to a camembert. The same can be said about another cheese, the Bluebert, where *Penicillium roqueforti* is used in the fermentation process, which results in a cheese that looks similar to a Roquefort cheese.

As a result, and in terms of knowability, these differing perspectives on what makes a cheese a cheese raises a wider question of whether foods are made knowable based on the way they are made or based on the ingredients that are used to make them. Nevertheless, it is not only the point that these cheeses are not being made from animal milks that makes them a challenge in terms of how, or even whether, they are "known" as cheeses. When one does focus on their relation to a particular geolocation, these cheeses do not appear to be "from" anywhere. This can be seen in the ingredients that are used to make them. For example, in the European social context, these cheeses are most often made using cashew nuts, which are imported from outside of Europe, for instance from Vietnam. Other ingredients, such as transglutaminase, an enzyme that is used to bind the cheesemaking ingredients together, are produced in "the laboratory." This, again, elicits a sense of placelessness. When people who questioned whether these were "real cheeses" spoke about such laboratory-produced ingredients, they sometimes referred to them in terms of being "artificial" or "not natural" precisely because they came from a laboratory. This is also the case with the microbes that are used in fermented plant-based cheeses, since they are imported from larger companies who specialize in producing cheesemaking microbes. Thus, in narratives about plant-based cheeses, even the microbes in the cheeses are not thought of as connecting them to a particular location. As a result, and similar to what Linné and McCrow-Young have written about almond milk, they appear as "a decidedly global food product" (2017: 210), where they seem to come from everywhere and nowhere at the same time.

In addition, when we think about plant-based cheeses in terms of the triad of people-product-place, the people who are making these cheeses also do not appear to "come" from one place either. For instance, the recipes and knowledge that are used to make the cheeses are ones that have not been passed down through the generations, in the form of a "family tradition" where the family is thought of as belonging to a particular place. Most often they come from social media groups, where interested cheesemakers share tips and offer advice on how to make them. Subsequently, these cheeses are not thought of as being locatable through the people who are making them, in that they acquire the characteristics of a particular place from those who produce them. And as is visible in some of the chapters in this volume, this appears to stand in slight contrast to how others are negotiating this relation between food and place. In these accounts, authors describe how it is through the preparation, and also the eating, of particular foods that a particular place can be summoned.

For example, Colquhoun (this volume) describes how some producers of Istrian *pršut* import the pork from other places. Thus, in what seems to follow a similar form in terms of the "origins" of the ingredients that are used to make plant-based cheeses, the critical ingredients that are used to make these hams are also brought in from elsewhere. But as Colquhoun draws out, it is through the work of the people in Istria, the Istriani (Istrians), that they fashion these hams into Istrian *pršut*. As such, hams that are thought of as being *domaće* become Istrianized through the Istrianness of those who are making them. Thus, these foods are localized through the work of the people who make them. In this sense, these foods acquire their place from the perceived qualities of the people who make them and, in turn, come to elicit the place that these people are associated with.

Yet with regard to plant-based cheesemaking, drawing a similar conclusion poses a challenge. Since the recipes and the people who make them are not thought of as coming from one singular, identifiable place, they are not considered to possess the qualities of any particular place. As such, in their work, "the people" who make plant-based cheeses are not seen to infuse the cheeses they are making with the qualities of a particular location. Indeed, when one thinks of how one might locate plant-based cheeses, the most apparent location is that of the *virtual* sphere. The ingredients used to make these cheeses are purchased online, they are very often sold online, and the recipes that are used to make them are developed and exchanged online.

I would argue that one consequence of these cheeses appearing to sit the closest with a "virtual" location is the effect this has on how they are known. It starts to raise questions about their "realness" or "authenticity." The multisited origin of their ingredients, the sense that the people who make them do not come from one particular place, as well as the point that the recipes are shared in the virtual space all serve to elicit this sense of them not being quite real. And further, this sense of them not being quite real is augmented by the legislative framework that determines that they are not cheeses because of not being made using animal milk.

Here it is useful to think about what is happening through the concept of ferality, and not fitting in. In Catie Gressier's writing about feral meat eating in Australia, she describes how feral meats engender a sense of being out of place (2016: 52), which in my mind shares a number of parallels with the way that plant-based cheeses are thought of. Their "out of placeness" comes not from a quality that they essentially possess, but as Mary Douglas (2001) has said some time ago, from how they do not appear to fit what might be thought of as the dominant ways that food is most often analytically located. What feral meats and plant-based cheeses both share is that their "out of placeness" is elicited because of the way they are held in a comparative relation with a more dominant analytical counterpart: livestock-based meats or dairy-based cheeses. In terms of feral meats, Gressier writes that feral meats do not seem to fit because they "are not normalised in local culture and do not have a long tradition in much of the community" (2016: 62). Thus, their lack of fitting, or "out of placeness," comes from how they are set in a comparative relation to the consumption and production of livestock-based meats, which can be thought of as the dominant form of meat eating. The effect of this comparison is that they do not seem to quite belong, and in turn are thought of as being feral.

An additional point that Gressier has made about feral meat, which also sits closely with the way that plant-based cheeses are spoken about, concerns the "ideological commitment" of those who are eating it. She writes that "the majority of feral meat eaters do not do so lightly, but out of a *strong ideological commitment* to various principles" (2016: 62, emphasis added). This suggests that not only can the production of food help to evoke a particular place, but its consumption can also evoke a particular type of person. By relating the eating of feral meat to a particular ideological position, the person eating this meat takes on a particular form themselves, which in turn makes them knowable as a particular kind of person.

I suggest that one can see something similar in how people approach plant-based cheesemaking and the eating of plant-based cheeses. As I have already mentioned, a very audible interest, if not the most audible interest, that people have in making plant-based cheeses, as well as eating them, is that they are *not made* from animal products. They are not made using animal milks, nor are they made with any other ingredients of animal origin, such as rennet or the medium in which the microbes are grown that are used to make them. Nevertheless, while this is perhaps the most audible interest in making and eating plant-based cheeses, it is not the only one. When discussing why they eat plant-based cheeses, some made the point that they did so *not* because they were vegan but because they were lactose intolerant. Thus, and as I touched upon earlier, they emphasized a health condition, such as lactose intolerance, meaning they could not eat or consume dairy-based products. In our conversations it was very apparent that they wanted to distance themselves from veganism.

This, I suggest, draws out another facet concerning how people work to make themselves knowable through the making and eating of cheeses. Since different people do this differently, a form of tension is elicited. Through the way they negotiate themselves, and each other, in relation to these cheeses, they are fashioning themselves, and are fashioned by others, as *being particular kinds of persons*. This was also evident in the discussion that opened up with the farmer after he had made the point that people from his area did not eat such cheeses. This concerned the gender roles of the animals whose milk made dairy-based cheeses from the local area; he made the point that rather than these cheeses "taking life," they "gave life." In his mind, the ewes who produced the milk were able to fulfill themselves as mothers. This suggested that his refusal to eat vegan cheeses, or even to try them, was closely related to the *gender roles* of those both producing and consuming these cheeses, which resonates with literature that considers the relation between meat eating and masculinity (e.g., Adams 2000). As a result, when one thinks about the eating of plant-based or vegan cheeses in terms of "ideological commitment" and how a person's veganness can be elicited through making and eating these cheeses, different people approached this in different ways, depending on how they negotiated their own relation to veganism. Some of those producing and eating them wanted to emphasize their commitment to veganism, whereas others were keen to distance themselves from it.

But what I want to suggest here is that while these different "consumers" approach these cheeses in quite different ways, and offer quite different, even opposing, narratives about their relation to these cheeses, the underlying analytical framework that they use is the same.[1] While the person who is "produced"—or perhaps, better put, made visible—in this relation appears different according to the products and places they have related themselves to, the analytical frame they use is the same. Where there is a difference, however, is that vegan cheesemakers work with a different form of place: "the environment." As such, while they root their cheeses "in place," or perhaps better put "emplace them" to make them knowable, the process involves a form of place that is broader than those narratives of terroir that emplace foods into a particular known locality. And the question I want to ask here is, how different is "the environment" to "place" in these constructions, and indeed what are the differences when one looks at how plant-based/vegan cheesemakers are using it?

Environmental Interests

To think about this further, I want to continue discussing it in terms of ideological commitments and the relation between place and geolocation. When talking with plant-based cheesemakers, they did sometimes talk about an interest they had in trying to incorporate local ingredients into their cheeses. These were ingredients, such as local herbs or local drinks, that they either added before the fermentation process started or used to wash the rinds with. For instance, when making cashew paste, they would add these herbs to it, or while the cheeses were fermenting, they would wash the rind every few days with a local beer or spirit to try to develop a particular taste and color. Returning to the concept of terroir with this in mind, this interest initially seems to challenge the suggestion I made earlier that these cheeses are placeless. Through this interest in using local ingredients, the cheeses are localized, which is further confirmed by the way that the cheeses are given names that associate them with these local ingredients. Furthermore, cheesemakers spoke about their interests in the "old recipes" of their localities, recipes that they were trying to incorporate into their cheesemaking, thereby foregrounding the concept of locality. Often when talking about this they would mention a recipe from the nineteenth century that used a mixture of potatoes and dairy milk. Other cheesemakers said that they had researched local archives or spoken to people from the older generations of their locality to see if there were any plant-based cheese recipes. Again, their interest was to see how they could connect their cheeses to the locality where they were based.

But what was also apparent was that they did not express this in terms of wanting to give their cheeses a "local identity" in the sense that they wanted to make their cheeses knowable by attaching them to a particular place. It was not that they wanted to elicit a sense of "tradition." Rather, a point that some made, especially when they were talking about how they imported ingredients from elsewhere, was that the reason they were interested in localizing their cheeses was to reduce the "environmental impact" or "carbon footprint." One narrative that is often heard about plant-based cheeses, which once again relates to plant-based milks (Linné and McCrow-Young 2017), concerns the environmental impact of these foods and how they are made. In turn, this is connected to broader claims about vegan/plant-based diets in general, where vegan/plant-based diets are often presented as being more environmentally friendly than diets that involve the consumption of animal products, such as dairy or meat. They are often presented as being part of a "greener," more environmentally sustainable diet than a meat-eating diet. Again, these assertions are shaped according to the same analytical aesthetic that turns on holding them in contrast with dairy-based cheeses. For instance, when talking about the "carbon footprint" of cheesemaking, people set plant-based cheesemaking in opposition to large-scale industrial dairy farming that produces high levels of methane. When talking about the "greenness" of plant-based milk and cheeses, people often offer the statistic that the livestock sector is responsible for 14.5 percent of anthropogenic greenhouse gas emissions (Grossi et al. 2019: 69) at the global level and give examples of how dairy farmers are being subsidized to shift away from dairy farming to farming plant-based crops in order to remedy this.

The interest in making "environmentally friendly" cheeses made these cheesemakers look to locally grown "bases" for their cheeses in developing local recipes. For example, they sometimes spoke about potatoes as a potential cheesemaking base since they could be grown locally and not require the import of ingredients, such as cashew nuts, from elsewhere. They were more than aware of the point that importing ingredients, often by air transport, from the "other side of the world," challenged narratives that foregrounded the environmental sustainability of their cheeses. Thus, similar to Gressier's (2016) point about the "strong ideological commitment" of those who consumed feral meats, this interest in the local was closely connected to the ideological commitment of those making and eating these cheeses to shape them into "environmentally friendly" products. Instead of localizing these cheeses to connect them to a *specific* locality and thus infuse them with the qualities found in that location, cheesemakers used this interest in localizing them to turn on an interest in foregrounding their "ideological commitment" of being "environmentally aware."

Notably, therefore, they emplaced their cheeses into a specific locality not to imbue them with qualities that they considered to come from a particular terroir but to find a way to make them knowable so they fit their commitment to a broader ideology: environmental sustainability. It is an interest that turns on distance, where they approached "place" on slightly different terms. The geolocation of where they made their cheeses was important to them in terms of how the distance/proximity of the ingredients they used could make their cheeses knowable as "green" products.[2]

But this is not the only way that plant-based cheesemakers refer to the "environment" in their cheesemaking. An issue that is faced by both vegan and dairy cheesemakers alike is "environmental contamination." Due to the cheeses' contact with the environment where they are being aged, microbes that are already living in that environment can become a part of the culture living in the cheeses. One vegan cheesemaker said that environmental contamination was one of the biggest problems he had in his work. At a certain point during the aging process, a yellow mold would start to grow on his cheeses, and he would have to throw them away. While the mold was not dangerous for human health, it caused large yellow spots to form on the cheese, and he told me that he knew customers would complain about this, so they could not be sold. In order to try to resolve the problem, he carried out a lot of experiments to see where the source of this contamination was. These experiments included changing the producers of the raw cashew nuts that the milk was made from, aging the cheeses in other locations, and seeking advice from the microbiology department at the local university. The results of these experiments proved to him that the mold was coming from the location where the cheeses were being made.

This was also confirmed by the microbiologist from the university, who said that it was not just one type of microbe that was affecting the cheeses but a "whole football team" of them. The microbiologist's hypothesis was that these microbes had been living in the cheesemaking premises for a long time and were probably a legacy from when the premises used to be the village shop. Even though the shop had long since closed, the cultures lived in the brick walls and were now contaminating the cheeses. This was a huge problem, the cheesemaker said, because not only did the cultures produce unsightly molds on the cheeses, the question was also raised about whether his cheeses were still vegan. There was a possibility that some of these molds had come from animal products that were previously sold in the shop, such as sausages or dairy cheeses. As he explained, for some vegans this would be an issue, and he could not sell them in good faith as vegan cheeses. The only way he had found to control them was to use aqueous ozone cleaners on his premises before each fermentation cycle. This process was expensive and time-consuming, and if he could not find a better way for him, the cheeses, and the microbes from the food shop to live harmoniously together, he would have to move away and find somewhere else to work.

Thus, when one thinks about this in terms of place, the location the cheeses were being made in clearly affects the fermentation process. Due to the yellow mold, they were considered by the cheesemakers to be unsellable, and instead of being an edible product became waste. As such, their relation to the locality where they were made involved a constant negotiation between the cheesemaker and the microbes that lived there. Thus, while this cheesemaker also used recipes found online, sold almost exclusively to customers online, and imported ingredients from elsewhere, the microbes situated his cheeses in a particular locality. As Paxson (2010) has described, cheesemakers consider the presence of environmental microbes as one of the ways cheeses acquire their terroir, in that they become a part of the microbial cultures in the cheeses. Through these microbial exchanges, the cheeses become a part of, and are shaped by, the locality in which they are aging. What is notable, though, is that for cheesemakers, the interaction of the cheeses with the locality in which they are made is not something the cheesemakers want—it is often spoken of as an intrusion.

When we turn to think about this in terms of terroir, in terms of the people-product-place triad that West (2022) described, the environment does not take the form of an abstract concept. My interlocutors also spoke about the environment having a direct material effect on their cheeses, which they had to deal with in their work; in this form, as one of contamination, the environment was something they wanted to avoid. What is critical to note here is that there is a conceptual shift at work in terms of how place is being used. Rather than the environment being thought of on global terms, in this specific case it was localized due to concerns about contamination. I would therefore argue that there are different renditions of place at work here in this conceptualization of environment, where these are only two renditions, and there are potentially many more. In the first, which foregrounds "environmental sustainability," the environment took the form of an ideological commitment that helped to shape those who were making and eating these cheeses as being environmentally aware. One cannot say that in this form the interest in the environment was completely abstract since this interest did influence the material form of the cheeses. Nonetheless, this interest in making their cheeses environmentally sustainable was something that the cheesemakers themselves were animating, where the environment was something that they were working on or with. In the other rendition, the form that was audible in narratives about "environmental contamination," the environment was treated as problem and something that needed to be resolved. Thus, at some points, cheesemakers themselves intentionally elicited the environment, such as in terms of presenting their cheeses as being environmentally friendly, and at other points they tried to submerge it, when it seemingly intruded, such as in the form of environmental contamination.

Conclusion

When one thinks about plant-based cheeses and their relation to place, it is clearly not the case that place is never present. Nor, I think, is it possible to suggest that vegan cheesemakers are conceptualizing place by using a different analytical aesthetic than dairy-based cheesemakers. In this sense, the form being given to place in the "environment" is submerged or foregrounded according to the interests of those offering these accounts. Each rendition of the environment, where different aspects are either foregrounded or submerged, also has the capacity to alter how these cheeses are made knowable. When the environment is spoken about in relation to these cheeses, in terms of environmental sustainability or environmental friendliness, the cheeses in turn take on these qualities. But when the environment is spoken about in terms of environmental contamination, they take on a different guise. In this sense, the place they are working with shifts according to their interests and the meanings they give to it.

What is important here is the effect this has on the people who are part of the "people-place-product" (West 2022) triad. Each rendition of place has a different effect on the form the person takes. As Strathern has written, while the way villagers in the UK talk about their villages appears the same, the effect can be different because of the different relations they are in (1991: 25). In this case, both approaches to cheesemaking say something about those who are making or eating the cheeses; for instance, one person's veganness can be either confirmed or challenged depending on how the environment is being spoken about. In contrast, and as I heard when listening to those who rejected eating vegan cheeses, a person's masculinity can be confirmed or challenged through their consumption of these cheeses. As such, and depending on which figure (person, product, or place/environment) they foreground in their narratives, different effects are elicited, where all involved can take on different forms according to the analytical perspective that is taken. Sometimes people are made knowable through the product and the way they relate it to a place, whereas other times place is made knowable through the people and the way they relate it to a product; at yet other times, the product is made knowable through the way that people and place are related to each other. Thus, when we think about plant-based cheeses on these terms, it becomes much harder to say that they are placeless, or that place is not important in their making. Place is constantly present, where it is being negotiated in different ways by different people according to their own interests.

Acknowledgments

I would very much like to thank Anna Colquhoun and Katharina Graf for their comments and suggestions, and all those who attended the writing retreat in Istria.

Sarah Czerny is a social anthropologist who works as Associate Professor at the University of Rijeka. She has done research on interspecies milks and has written the book *Absent Interests: On the Abstraction of Human and Animal Milks* (Leiden: Brill). She teaches courses on anthropology and urban ecology.

Notes

1. In Tony Crook's (2007) writing on the "textual person", he discusses how anthropological texts have a shared aesthetic to them in the sense of the structure that is used to write them in (Crook 2007: 299–330). This is what I am referring to here.
2. In his account on the shared aesthetic in anthropological writing, Crook (2007) stresses the importance of the distancing trope and how it is used to make "textual persons" visible (Crook 2007: 299). I see the same mechanism to be at work here.

References

Adams, Carol. 2000. *The Sexual Politics of Meat: A Feminist-Vegetarian Critical Theory*. 10th anniversary ed. New York: Continuum.

Barham, Elizabeth. 2003. "Translating Terroir: The Global Challenge of French AOC Labeling." *Journal of Rural Studies* 19(1): 127–38.

Crook, T. 2007. *Anthropological Knowledge, Secrecy and Bolivip, Papua New Guinea: Exchanging Skin*. Oxford: Oxford University Press.

Douglas, Mary. 2001. *Purity and Danger. An Analysis of Concepts of Pollution and Taboo*. First published 1966. London: Routledge.

Gade, Daniel W. 2004. "Tradition, Territory, and Terroir in French Viniculture: Cassis, France, and Appellation Controlee." *Annals of the Association of American Geographers* 94: 848–67.

Giampiero, Grossi, Pietro Goglio, Andrea Vitali, and Adrian G Williams. 2019. "Livestock and Climate Change: Impact of Livestock on Climate and Mitigation Strategies." *Animal Frontiers* 9(1): 69–76.

Gressier, Catie. 2016. "Going Feral: Wild Meat Consumption and the Uncanny in Melbourne, Australia." *Australian Journal of Anthropology* 27: 49–65.

Linné, Tobias, and Ally McCrow-Young. 2017. "Plant Milk: From Obscurity to Visions of a Post-dairy Society." In *Making Milk: The Past, Present and Future of Our Primary Food*, edited by Mathilde Cohen and Yoriko Otomo. London: Bloomsbury.

Paxson, Heather. 2010. "Locating Value in Artisan Cheese: Reverse Engineering *Terroir* for New-World Landscapes." *American Anthropologist* 112(3): 444–57.

Strathern, Marilyn. 1991. *Partial Connections*. Lanham: Rowman & Littlefield.

West, Harry G. 2022. "Terroir Products: A Movable Heritage Feast?" *Review of Agricultural, Food & Environmental Studies* 103(1): 1–27.

CHAPTER 5

What's Mine Is Mine and What's Yours Is Mine

The Terroirism of *Nash* in Russian Culinary Colonialism

Melissa L. Caldwell

Introduction

During my ethnographic fieldwork in Moscow in the late 1990s, a university student said something that has stayed with me. In response to my invitation to reflect on the growing popularity and availability of foreign foods in Russia at that time, she responded directly and simply with the statement, "Russian [bodies] prefer Russian foods."[1]

The young woman's comment came at a moment of profound cultural and culinary transformation in Russia. Like many formerly Soviet countries in the first years following the dissolution of the Soviet Union, Russia was experiencing a rapid expansion and diversification of its economy. Foreign companies and global brands recognized the opportunities posed by what was described as the "wild west" of the post-Soviet world to introduce their products, services, and values to consumers they believed desired foreign, and most notably, Western products (Caldwell 2002, 2004). In many respects, Moscow was the epicenter of a global "culinary colonialism" marked by the proliferation of foreign and transnational food products, restaurants, grocery stores, and preparation and consumption practices that were transforming Russian food cultures and preferences.

McDonald's was one of the most visible foreign companies to set up shop in Moscow, with the first three restaurants located prominently in the city center near the Kremlin and other historically and politically important Russian sites. Pizza Hut, Kentucky Fried Chicken, Baskin Robbins, Dunkin Donuts, and Subway were just some of the many other global food companies that opened restaurants and cafés in Moscow and beyond. Reflecting the power of capitalist

Figure 5.1. An inflatable version of Ronald McDonald, McDonald's iconic representative, sits on the grounds of a restored royal estate for the American Chamber of Commerce July Fourth festivities. Moscow, 2007. © Melissa L. Caldwell

advertising strategies, billboards along city streets and highways, advertisements on television and radio, lifestyle magazines, and "product hostesses" in public venues introduced and promoted a wide array of foreign food products and consumer practices. Even the physical spaces of Moscow and other Russian cities and towns were occupied and rearranged by the many foreign grocery stores that redesigned storefronts, suburban lots, and shopping centers.

Foreign culinary colonialism was thus an ever-present reality of daily life, even as it was accompanied by the redevelopment and expansion of Russia's domestic food industry, a sector that increasingly encouraged Russian consumers to "buy (and eat) local" by invoking themes of patriotism and heritage. Consequently, Russian consumers found themselves pulled between two radically different markets: one marked by Western food companies, brands, and experiences, and one marked by an emergent and explicitly nationalist Russian food industry that associated taste with the nation (Caldwell 2002). To navigate and make sense of these different possibilities, and to position themselves within the competing political values assigned to these different consumer systems, Muscovites and other Russians invoked linguistic markers to distinguish between what was Russian (*nash*, or "ours"), and what was not Russian (*ne nash* ["not ours"] or even *chuzhoi* ["foreign"]).[2]

Several years later, as foreign foods were becoming more fully integrated—and invisibilized—into local Russian food cultures such that many had become perceived as Russian, *nash* had become a fluid marker of preference and incorporation. McDonald's was perhaps the most notable case of being accepted and perceived as *nash*, especially as french fries and milkshakes became ubiquitous staples in Russian cuisine (Caldwell 2004), but other examples included the dairy product line owned by Pepsi and a chain of Japanese restaurants that was started by a Russian entrepreneur and then expanded into other countries as an authentically Russian enterprise. What did it mean that Russian bodies preferred Russian foods when those foods had originally come from elsewhere?

By the mid-2010s, the idea of an association between authentically Russian bodies and Russian foods took on yet another layer of complexity in an advertising campaign for a Russian brand of kvass. Kvass is a fermented, nonalcoholic beverage whose flavor and texture can best be described as a cross between dark beer and cola. One of the few beverages consumed cold in Russia, kvass is a refreshing choice after activities that heat and tire the body, such as sports, sessions in the *banya*, or hard work during hot summer days. One advertisement featured several athletic-looking men wearing sports gear for their favorite team and discussing what to drink. The tag line for the ad stated: "*Net kolanizatsii. Kvas—zdorov'e natsii!*" ([Say] No [to] cola-nization. Kvass is the health of the nation!) With this pun on the word *colonization,* Russia's version of the "cola wars" presented a provocative take on national discomfort with the effects of foreign food products on Russian bodies. Very emphatically, the ad campaign suggested, the very health of the nation's bodies was at stake—and in danger of colonization by foreign foods.

In 2022, roughly twenty-five years after I first collected the young woman's statement about Russian foods and bodies, Russian consumers experienced another series of profound political, cultural, and culinary transformations, when Russia invaded Ukraine and launched a brutal war of occupation and dispossession. As part of a global boycott campaign to pressure the Russian government to end the war and withdraw from Ukraine, many foreign and transnational companies closed their Russian operations and withdrew their products from Russian stores. In retaliation, the Russian government enacted harsh restrictions against foreign citizens, enterprises, and governments, causing most foreigners from "Western" countries and their allies to leave Russia. Although such measures have occurred at various moments of extreme geopolitical turmoil in Russia over the past twenty-five years, they have typically been relatively brief in duration.

By contrast, the events following the invasion of Ukraine have been the most extreme and consequential. Perhaps the most prominent and surprising development was that McDonald's closed its operations, sold its stock to a Russian businessman, and exited the country (Kim 2022; Rainey 2023). Within just a few weeks in spring 2022, by pushing out, seizing, and redefining what was formerly "foreign," Russia pushed back against its "culinary colonizers" by reinforcing an explicitly Russian—*nash*—supremacy over its food system. Not coincidentally, at the same time, Russia's invasion and occupation of Ukraine was playing out through the seizure of prime agricultural land, expropriation of Ukrainian agricultural products, and blockades of Ukrainian grain that prevented shipments from reaching consumers throughout the world. Russia had become the colonizer of the Other and was claiming Ukraine's food as its own.

When viewed through the lens of these particular historical moments that bookend Russian consumers' efforts to make sense of the presumed national origins of the foods they consume, the young woman's comment that "Russian [bodies] prefer Russian foods" can be understood to have multiple meanings that, in turn, highlight both the ambiguity and perceived certainty of Russianness. By positioning herself—and her body—within an explicitly Russian foodscape that, in turn, is presumed to nourish uniquely Russian bodies with Russian taste preferences, the young woman highlighted the fact that food preferences are deeply infused with national and even international politics. At different moments, Russian foods, sensory experiences, and bodies have been made by ingesting local, domestic products, by transforming foreign foods into local foods, and even by seizing and claiming foreign foods as rightful national patrimony. Above all, what these events show is that Russianness—*nash*—is not merely a patriotic invocation of heritage and identity but an oppressive political project of colonialist national expansion and assertion of national exceptionalism and supremacy.

This chapter examines how Russian foods and taste preferences have come to be perceived and formalized as *nash*, or Russian. I argue that these processes of making things Russian—what I am calling "nashification"—are embedded within Russian colonizing projects of national expansion and consolidation that are explicitly focused on the land in which foods are grown and consumed. Consequently, *nash* is a Russian philosophy of terroir that valorizes national soil as the indisputable progenitor of uniquely and exclusively Russian foods, tastes, bodily dispositions, and people. Yet as this discussion shows, the placemaking strategies of nashification are not neutral but are embedded within explicit political projects of seizure, occupation, appropriation, and reinvention, such that soil is transformed into territory, and the foreign becomes indigenous. Attending to the political processes through which nashification happens sheds light on how philosophies of terroir can be contested, oppressive, and violent. As such, this chapter contributes to rethinking the positive aesthetics of terroir and instead considers how terroir can be wielded as an instrument of violence.

In the discussion that follows, I first discuss the importance of place and soil in Russian projects of nashification, with particular attention to territorial expansion and its role in mythologies of an idealized Russian nation and Russian person. I then present examples of foreign foods that have been incorporated into Russian cuisine before addressing how these processes of incorporation have taken place over the past several centuries. As this discussion shows, the production of *nash*, the Russian philosophy of terroir, has a more malevolent side that comes through with Russian assertions of superiority, occupation, and dispossession. Ultimately, I show how *nash*, and terroir more generally, is something that is generated and officialized through political struggle.

Soil and the Territorialization Project of Nashification

Within the Russian culinary lexicon, place matters greatly as both a "locational philosophy of taste" (Trubek 2008: 8) and a signal of authentically local or national production and legitimacy (Caldwell 2011). In the 1990s and 2000s my Muscovite informants regularly queried market vendors about the origins of the foods they were selling. Vendors and consumers alike claimed to be knowledgeable about which regions were known for producing the best fruits, vegetables, and dairy products. The names of certain breads and cheeses were identified by the regions or distinctive regional styles of origin. Customers, vendors, and marketers deployed the linguistic marker *nash* alongside regional place-names to denote foods and food styles that were produced domestically and, more importantly, understood to be authentically Russian.

More than indicating places of origin for foods, however, *nash* expresses the idea of a uniquely Russian nation that emerges from the land—from the very soil—from which that nation emerged. Land, and most specifically soil, is critically important to Russian conceptions of the nation and the space that constitutes the nation.[3] As Erley has described in her account of soil as the material basis of Russian life and culture, "soil is the material foundation of civilizations, economies, and lifeways. . . . Soil is the material index of 'place' and 'home'" (2021: 1). Soil is also the progenitor of living Russian things, both human and nonhuman.[4] Russian geographer Lev Gumilev theorized that a central component of the Russian nation is *ethnos*, a concept of collective being that grounds a specific group of people (in this case, the Russian collective)—and their bodily experiences—in a specific geographic region and geologic time (see Caldwell 2011: 125). Yet *ethnos* is more than a biogeographic concept, however, as it also invokes "'bio-psycho-social' collectivities" that are passed from one generation to another (Oushakine 2009: 83). Similarly, Ries has observed that the Russian concept of motherland, *rodina,* "is habitat, nature, soil . . . it's a very fermenting thing. Upon or within it, history takes place" (1997: 29). Paxson has added that the concept *rodnoi,* which denotes relatedness especially in the sense of connection to the *rodina* (motherland) and the *narod* (nation, collective), "is a term with earth and soil in it, as well as ancestral rootedness" (2005: 53; see also Ely 2000).[5] Consequently, at the core of Russian ideologies of the nation is a narrative of birth, emergence, and regeneration from and through engagement with the soil of the nation. Most notably, it is a national theory of exclusivity and exceptionalism (see Bassin 1991: 4).

The *ethnos* ideal, with its connotations of primordial soils and a "pervasive discourse of the organic, rooted nation" (Erley 2021: 11), appears vividly in Russian food traditions that emphasize that the soils in which Russian foods are grown imbue them with particular qualities and sensory experiences that, in turn, produce particular bodies that can appreciate and respond to those qualities and experiences (Caldwell 2007). In this logic, *nash* is a classificatory system that Russians use both to identify themselves, the nation, and things that come from that nation and to define the sensory qualities of the things that belong to the nation. As such, *nash* is a system of terroir that associates taste, identities, and values with particular places, and it exemplifies what Trubek has suggested is a defining feature of terroir—"dirt in a certain place" (2008: 54).

Yet *nash* does not denote just any land or soil, no matter where it is located. Rather, *nash* denotes soil that has been converted into territory, that is, specific lands that have been recognized, claimed, and demarcated by specific political boundaries and histories. In other words, it is soil with politics. Beyond delineating particular places and associating them with particular qualities and sensory experiences, nashification is a process of knowing, appropriating, and owning those places, the foods grown in those places, the qualities they possess, and the bodies that emerge from and can experience those qualities.

Moreover, Russian soils, and by extension Russian territories, have long been unstable. Over the past several centuries, not only have geographic boundaries moved, but so has the very soil that is mythologized for producing the Russian nation, its people, and its products (Erley 2021; Anonymous 2023). In very material ways in the eighteenth and nineteenth centuries, Russia's imperial leaders moved the country westward, both geographically and symbolically, with the efforts by Peter I (Peter the Great) to position Russia within Europe by creating what is now the city of St. Petersburg out of virtually nothing but swampland and water. This movement and depositing of soils to create and extend Russian territory has been repeated over the centuries, most notably during Russia's seizure of Crimea and its present war in Ukraine.

Consequently, nashification is a project of colonization through which Russia has enlarged the nation through the appropriation of territory, the extraction of the national and cultural resources found in those territories, and the reinvention of those resources as only and always autochthonously Russian (see Sunderland 2000).[6] As these resources are redefined as Russian, they are also remade into things that are understood to be the legitimate entitlement for Russian consumers. In other words, members of the authentic Russian nation have the right to consume the products that originate from the territory of the Russian nation, wherever and however that Russian nation is defined. And by extension, sensory perceptions of those products are claimed as authentically and exclusively the purview and possession of the Russian nation. The next section explores some of the foreign tastes that have been made Russian and instantiated into the Russian culinary palate.

Rooting National Tastes in National Places

In their history of Russian and Central Asian food cultures, Glenn Mack and Asele Surina write that "Russian food (*pishcha*) . . . is any food immediately and inherently familiar to and embraced by Russians as *nasha*, the Russian word for 'our,' be it spicy Korean carrot salad or Crimean Tatar meat pies (*chebureki*)" (2005: 4), a sentiment expressed repeatedly by my own informants, who defined Russian food as whatever appealed to their taste buds.

At first glance, this perspective suggests an inclusive approach to diversity within a multiethnic country like Russia. In some cases, Russian foods have retained a sense of "foreignness" even as the "foreignness" has been fully integrated into Russian culinary practices, as has happened with French cookery styles. For several centuries the Francophilia of the royal family ensured that courtly life drew heavily on French cultural traditions, from language and architecture to clothing fashions and cuisine. Over time, even as the formal presentation style associated with different national culinary trends persisted in Russia with distinctions of *à la russe* versus *à la française*, individual dishes and ingredients gradually became incorporated into Russian cuisine, so that French-style sauces or jellies, for instance, were presented simply as part of daily Russian cuisine. Such incorporations are apparent in quintessentially Russian cookbooks like Elena Molokhovets's *A Gift to Young Housewives*. Originally published in 1861, Molokhovets's cookbook was for many decades "the" classic cookbook and household manual that instructed young Russian women in the art of keeping a Russian home. In the way that cookbooks reify and institutionalize particular culinary styles as anthropologist Arjun Appadurai and others have described (e.g., Appadurai 1988), Molokhovets's manual effectively codified Russian cuisine for generations.

By the 2000s, the appropriation and integration of French cookery styles into Russian cuisine was readily apparent both in ordinary Russian confection styles and in the trend of French-style bakeries that had emerged in Moscow at the time. French styles were even included in Russian "heritage restaurants" that were meant to capture "traditional" Russian culinary and cultural styles from Russia's past. Moscow's Pushkin restaurant was a notable example: the restaurant occupied a renovated estate in the center of Moscow and was designed to look like a noble estate from the time of the beloved Russian poet and novelist Alexander

Pushkin at the beginning of the nineteenth century. The interior decorations of lighting fixtures, wallpapers, and tables recreated French interior decor, while the servers and security guards were dressed in French-themed costumes and powdered wigs. The café's menu featured almost exclusively French-style cakes and pastries.

Less marked, but no less significant, than these European culinary trends are influences from other parts of Russia's heritage, namely its Asian heritage drawn from its southern and eastern regions and neighbors. As Joyce Toomre, the scholar of Russian cuisine who translated and annotated Molokhovets's cookbook for a new generation of Russian culinary enthusiasts, points out, Asian influences are everywhere in Russian dishes, if one only knows where to look. Tea, spices such as saffron and cinnamon, and fermentation practices that are today intrinsic to Russian cuisine have their roots in the Caucasus, Central Asia, Siberia, India, and China (Toomre 1992: 15-20). Already by the seventh century A.D., there are records of Chinese tea and Turkic foods such as yogurt, kebabs, dumplings, and halvah in what is now Russia, and by the tenth century A.D. nuts, fruits, and spices had appeared via the trade networks of Scandinavians and Byzantine Greeks (Mack and Surina 2005: 26–57). The sixteenth-century household manual the *Domostroi* contains references to spices such as "saffron, garlic, hops, cloves, nutmeg, ginger, hemp seed, lemons, horseradish, mace" (Mack and Surina 2005: 27). A quick glance at the recipes in Molokhovets's cookbook reveals further borrowings, such as rice pilaf, which has since morphed into the ubiquitous Russian rice dish *plov'*.[7]

Yet even as Russian cultural ideologies of *nash* have created an internally diverse cuisine made possible by global trade movements, looking beyond the seemingly broad embrace of *nash* reveals less benign dynamics and motives. Assertions by Russian consumers that their bodies can recognize and prefer authentically Russian tastes belies the reality that when the foreign is claimed and remade as Russian, this is a project of colonial nation-building that has been enacted through the forcible appropriation and dispossession of the Other.

Making the Self through Seizing the Other

Seizure has long been an intentional tactic of the Russian nation-state to define itself, to accommodate its own internal diversity, and most importantly to locate itself through political, legal, and cultural frameworks of settler colonialism. In many respects, Russian imperial leaders presented their colonial activities not as conquest but as forms of benevolent integration, a dynamic that Daniel Brower has termed "triumphant nationalism" (1994: 371). During Russia's imperial era of exploration and consolidation, imperial agents—cartographers, Orthodox priests, health officers, tax collectors, and other officials—traveled both within the known boundaries of the Russian Empire and to more rural and distant areas far beyond the metropole. Because of the contiguity of the lands through which Russian imperial agents moved, it was presumed that the regions into which they intruded were already part of the Tsarist Empire. They simply had *not yet been* discovered and mapped, a point that Valerie Kivelson makes in her study of how Russian cartographers identified and claimed the Russian Empire through mapping (Kivelson 2006). Wherever the imperial power or its designees ventured and then located representationally on maps, that was where the nation existed. This was a form of knowing and laying claim to the nation by discovering its parameters and extending its formal boundaries, a process that Mark Bassin has described not as colonizing but as extending "an *ecumene* of Russian settlement" (1991: 11). Thus "Russia" as a national territory existed by virtue of claims of preexisting ownership (see also Bassin 1991; Erley 2021).

As part of this imperial project of extending and reifying the boundaries of the Russian Empire, colonial agents seized not only geographic spaces but also local cultural products and practices, which they then repatriated back to the empire's center for incorporation, materially and legally, into the national cultural heritage. Ethnographic museums, such as the ones created by Peter I in the early eighteenth century, are filled with cultural artifacts collected from Russia's colonial encounters, including dishes, cooking implements, and even foods. These "collecting practices" included the gathering of culinary influences from the West and the East, as members of Russia's royal family traveled abroad and brought back foods and recipes with them. Tsar Alexander I offered French chef Marie-Antoine Carême employment in the royal court (Goldstein 1995: 691)—an offer that would have continued the Russian ethnographic tactic of "collecting" people and turning them into Russian heritage objects, had Carême accepted.[8] In other cases, the Russian imperial court drew on Russia's trade networks in and through Asia to collect unfamiliar foods, which they then transformed into Russian cultural objects that were offered as diplomatic gifts, including official meals, to foreign visitors (Mack and Surina 2005: 27; Soroka 2022).

By the nineteenth century, these colonial orientations of seizure and unquestioned ownership were evident in philosophies of Slavophilism that promoted both Russian distinctiveness and assertions that the Russian nation legitimately "owned" whatever it seized, occupied, and controlled. Notably, some of these Slavophilic philosophies emphasized the biological and ecological roots of colonialism, whereby proponents advocated colonization of other regions through the takeover of land and the physical transplantation (and grafting) of people, plants, and even soils (Erley 2021: 24–28).

Historically, then, agriculture became a critical site for Russia's projects of colonization through seizure and transplantation, and Russian nationalists looked to regions such as the Crimea and what is now Ukraine not only to grow food for the Russian nation but also to export grain that it labeled "Russian" to Europe.

These projects continued into the Soviet period, as Russia (as the center of the federation) moved into Central Asia and appropriated agricultural production there (Erley 2021: 46–47, 88–91). Most recently, Russia's invasion of Ukraine has entailed attempts to expropriate Ukraine's agricultural land, with geographer Vera Smirnova (2023) noting that Russia had, as of 2023, seized more than 20 percent of Ukraine's farmland.

Russian practices of claiming farmland for its own nation have also included installing its own people in those regions as the legitimate occupiers and food producers. Sunderland has argued that in the imperial period there were two different words for colonization in Russian: *kolonizatsiia*, which refers to the physical settlement of land and the incorporation of land into imperial rule, and *pereselenie* (resettlement), which referred to the "agricultural migration" by peasants to different territories (Sunderland 2000: 212). As Sunderland points out, the movement of peasants (and other migrants) into new territories was presented as a form of "correct colonization" because it relied on a notion that uncolonized spaces were empty and this process of moving people and culture into these empty spaces was a way to fill them with productive life (Sunderland 2000: 217). Erley has described similar practices of claiming and seizing that continued into the Soviet period and reflected civilizational beliefs that the original inhabitants of the regions were incapable of caring for the land and farming and needed to be replaced by Russians (Erley 2021).

Seizure, occupation, and control were critical first steps in Russia's practices of culinary colonialism, but the next steps of nashification to turn the foreign into Russian were made possible by state-level forms of bureaucratic management such as regulation, standardization, and codification. As the following section shows, the colonial Russian state deployed bureaucratic techniques to manage foreign foods and food practices, incorporate them into the official Russian culinary lexicon, and ultimately consolidate a recognizably "Russian" flavor profile and sensory preference.

Nashification as Singularization and Consolidation

By the nineteenth century, Russian state-making efforts increasingly emphasized the value of routinization, science, and technology, themes that were important for how foods, taste preferences, and their grounding in Russian soil came to be made Russian. Health and media were two key areas in which this played out. As part of its efforts to codify and singularize Russian food practices, the state created bureaucratic departments to monitor and legislate information about agriculture, food, and health and opened public exhibitions as forums for practical and moral education (Smith 2008: 134–41). At the same time, the state's emphasis on science and technology merged with the emerging field of food science and industrial food production and the legislation of food safety and hygiene. Food safety regulations had distinctive national interests, as state public health measures to ensure food safety and quality focused on determining and evaluating the domestic or foreign origins and flavors of foods (Smith 2008: 179).

In this same period, the growth of both the publishing industry and state bureaucracies intersected to further define and naturalize food cultures that were intended to be appropriate for the Russian nation. Cookbook authors, who were at different moments chefs, reformers, and housewives, effectively contributed to the codification of a distinctive and singularizing Russian cuisine through the recipes they included. Such publications were meant to be conduits of change by spreading information about new methods of agriculture, food production, taste, and health (Smith 2008). Perhaps more important were the annotations these documents provided to explain and justify particular dishes, ingredients, and styles. As Alison Smith documents, nineteenth-century cookbooks, household manuals, and annotated translations of foreign cookbooks and housekeeping manuals were instructive not as repositories of information but as cultural interpretations about the value of that information (Smith 2008). Specifically, both cooking commentators and health reformers focused on domestic/foreign interactions and offered suggestions for the types of foods best suited to Russian diners. In some cases this meant advising Russians against consuming "foreign" foods—such as a recommendation to avoid highly refined French foods because they would aggravate Russian digestive tracts—and in other cases it offered possibilities for incorporating "foreign" foods into the Russian diet (see Smith 2008). Ultimately, through these proscriptions, Russian authorities and their proxies created a bureaucratic process through which Russian food practices became officially recognized and standardized as belonging to a defined Russian culinary system.

Soviet-era socialist planners employed similar measures to create a pan-Soviet culinary heritage. Foods and food practices from across the USSR were codified, regulated, and transformed into state property through a centralized food sciences bureaucracy. Cookbooks, recipes, and menus from across the Soviet Union were standardized at the center, resulting in a singular national—or even civic—cuisine that was managed by the state and then redistributed throughout the entire USSR (see also Mack and Surina 2005). Not coincidentally, even though the USSR was established in theory as a federation of republics with equal standing, in practice Russia occupied the central and dominant position. After the dissolution of the Soviet Union in 1991, although the formerly Soviet republics became independent, autonomous countries and reclaimed their respective histories and heritages, Russia retained ownership and control over the things, traditions, and histories that had been brought to the center.

In the post-Soviet period, Russia's cuisine continued to expand and standardize by incorporating ingredients and dishes from its Asian regions and neighbors.

Korean salads, complete with bean sprouts, tofu, and kimchi, are ubiquitous in outdoor markets, fresh salad bars in state-of-the-art supermarkets, and even specialty "Russian foods" shops that cater to expatriate Russians elsewhere in the world (see Caldwell 2015).[9] One of the most notable examples of the remaking of Asian food as Russian is evident in the widespread popularity of sushi beyond cosmopolitan cities such as Moscow and St. Petersburg into provincial towns far from open harbors and major airports. From fancy Japanese restaurants to small sushi bars located in grocery stores, hamburger stands, pizza joints, Chinese take-away counters, and restaurants specializing in traditional Russian buffets, sushi has become an ever-present side dish—and even accompanying condiment—in Russians' everyday diets.

Sushi's power to represent the Asian "exotic" in Russian culinary culture was obvious, as represented by stylized performances of Japanese culture by young Russian women who dressed as geishas and maikos and by the young men who dressed as samurai and provided "security" and "face control" at the front door. Some Japanese restaurants even offered stylized performances of sumo wrestling for customer-tourists. The deliberate display of the exoticness and uniqueness of Japanese cuisine ends at these cultural performances. The actual dishes served in these settings themselves bear only superficial visual resemblance to Japanese cuisine.

Through processes of appropriation and translation into Russian culinary practices, sushi and other Japanese foods have been homogenized and standardized such that the flavor and textures associated with Japanese cuisine have largely disappeared. Russian acquaintances who had prior experience with Japanese dishes from personal travels in Japan or through friendships with Japanese citizens lamented what they described as the blandness of Russian versions of these foods: wasabi that lacked bite, noodles that were served lukewarm and rarely fully hot or cold, miso soups that were largely flavorless, and sashimi that was rarely served raw. One of the most common ingredients in Russian sushi was American-style cream cheese, which meant that different types of sushi tasted the same. This uniform and generic flavor palate and aesthetic style was relatively constant across Russian restaurants, sushi stands, and grocery store packages. As a result, only the external cues of Japanese culture changed slightly from restaurant to restaurant, while the dishes did not. The nashification of Japanese food did not end with its homogenization, however, but continued with its conversion into a distinctively Russian export cuisine. Originating in Russia and domestically owned, Russia's primary Japanese restaurant chains eventually expanded into Eastern Europe, effectively transferring Russian culinary ideals and flavor palates to foreign lands.

Russian consumers have continued to use nashification tactics to claim Georgian dumplings, Uzbek pilafs, and more general Slavic dishes such as borshch not just as uniquely and autochthonously Russian but as the source for the unique sensory qualities that produce Russian bodies and the Russian nation. In the mid-2010s, when Russia was engaged in a dispute with the European Union and had officially banned imports of EU products, Russa quietly continued to import those same foods after they had been diverted through Belarus where they were repackaged and relabeled as Belarussian and Russian.

Most recently, these processes of nashification have been on full display in Russia's conflicts with other formerly Soviet republics, most notably Georgia and Ukraine. In Georgia, one of the most significant wine-producing regions for the Soviet and now post-Soviet world, Russian investors and consumers have sought not only to claim Georgian territory but also to influence Georgian winemaking styles and distribution chains to favor Russian markets (Brown n.d.). As Rikki Brown has documented, Georgian winemakers have recognized Russian colonial and occupationist efforts and have reinvigorated authentically Georgian wine production and taste preferences as forms of resistance (Brown n.d.).

The situation with Russia's war in Ukraine is even more explicitly about seizing territory and claiming that it is rightfully and authentically Russian. In the wake of Russia's invasion of Ukraine in February 2022, many foreign companies withdrew from Russia, often exerting pressure on one another to do so. Russia's food world changed quickly and dramatically as foreign foods disappeared and restaurants closed down. Most remarkably, McDonald's first closed operations temporarily and then made the decision to terminate its Russian franchise by selling off its stock to a Russian investor. The restaurant was quickly rebranded as Vkusno i tochka (Simply Delicious). Ironically, even as the restaurants were rebranded as authentically Russian, and even though McDonald's did not sell its recipes or license to use McDonald's-branded products or foods, the new outlets continued to use McDonald's packaging but with the name blacked out and prepared foods that resembled McDonald's products. In effect, the nashification of McDonald's became complete.

More dire and catastrophic are the consequences of Russia's violent efforts to seize Ukraine and incorporate it into Russia. In late December 2023, a poster on X (formerly Twitter) wrote that a restaurant in one of the St. Petersburg airports had renamed their "traditional Ukrainian borscht" as "Little Russian borscht." The image included in the tweet showed the menu, with the new name in Russian ("*Malorossiiskii borshch*") and the previous name identifying the dish as "Ukrainian borsch" in English.[10]

Central to Russian efforts to incorporate Ukraine is control over Ukraine's agricultural production. Before and during the Soviet period, Ukraine was recognized as the "breadbasket" for the rest of the Russian and Soviet empire because of its production of grain and other agricultural products. Into the 2000s, although Ukraine has emerged as a key supplier of grain and other foodstuffs to many countries around the world, Russia remained a prime importer. Not only have Russian forces been attempting to seize Ukrainian farmland, they have also been actively destroying Ukraine's grain supplies and preventing other supplies

Figure 5.2. Foreshadowing the events of 2022, when McDonald's was replaced by a Russian imitator, this former location of a Pizza Hut restaurant was occupied in the early 2000s by a Russian chain called "Nasha Pizza." Moscow, 2005. © Melissa L. Caldwell

from reaching their intended markets. These cruel, catastrophic moves make sense within a logic in which those properties are understood to belong to Russia and not to anyone else, including Ukrainians. At the same time, Russian troops have been sent to Ukraine without adequate food supplies, forcing them to occupy and seize food stores from ordinary people.

Even stranger are the reported thefts of chernozem, the black Ukrainian soil celebrated for its rich nutrients, and the transfer of this soil to Russia for sale (Anonymous 2023). Thefts of Ukrainian soil, and by extension thefts of the soil's capability to generate the food of the nation, show how long-standing Russian traditions of connecting soil, food, bodies, and the nation persist.

The Terroirism of Culinary Colonialism

Although philosophies of terroir often privilege, even idealize, connections between taste and place, the Russian case of culinary colonialism reveals that the actual dynamics that make terroir possible are often far less savory. Claims about the sensory aesthetics of terroir obscure the political machinations by which those claims came to be and to be believed. More troubling, as the Russian case shows, terroir can be the product of violent oppression and dispossession. The Russian case also illuminates how philosophies and processes of terroir can be mobilized in the pursuit of national expansion. Nashification is, ultimately, a colonial tactic of turning soil into territory in order to stake out the boundaries of the nation, even as those same tactics move the boundaries of the nation, especially when foods and agricultural soils are the things that are moving.

More broadly, the processes of nashification offer a productive lens for rethinking terroir's premise about the significance of place for infusing particular qualities into foods and food experiences. When colonial powers like Russia embrace terroir as a tool of expansion, the presumed placeness of food experiences becomes unstable and even elusive. When soils, places, and nations move, what happens to ideals about the sensory qualities and experiences that are presumed to be attached to those places? Who is authorized to make those connections and for what purposes? As Erley astutely noted, "Soil does not always behave as it is meant to" (2021: 3). Neither, apparently, does the taste of place.

Ultimately, Russian nashification shows that the concept of terroir is something that deserves caution, because it is not necessarily as pleasurable and desirable as it might otherwise appear. When Russian bodies prefer foods that are Russian because they are seized by Russians in order to fortify Russian bodies and the Russian nation, terroir enables practices of exclusion and exceptionalism. More importantly, when terroir is wielded as a tool of nation-making processes that connect control of the soil with the nourishment of an ethnically monolithic nation, it becomes a conduit for assertions of political dominance, aggression, and even violent ethnic cleansing.

Acknowledgments

Much earlier versions of the ideas in this chapter were presented in my Distinguished Lecture for the SOAS Food Studies Centre and in a lecture presented to the food studies and Russian studies programs at New York University. I am grateful to my colleagues at those presentations for their feedback, with special thanks to Krishnendu Ray, Marion Nestle, Jakob Klein, Harry West, and Anne Murcott. I was delighted to have been invited to participate in the "Beyond Terroir: Situating Food, Taste, and Place in Cross-Cultural Comparison" workshop, organized by Dr. Anna Colquhoun and Dr. Katharina Graf and hosted by SOAS, so that I could develop these ideas more fully and to make sense of how they connected with Russia's war on Ukraine. I am grateful to my fellow participants in that workshop for their suggestions, and I owe special thanks and appreciation to Anna and Katharina for their thoughtful guidance and encouragement.

Melissa L. Caldwell is Professor of Anthropology at the University of California, Santa Cruz. She has been conducting research in Russia since the early 1990s. She has written on such topics as food nationalism, culinary tourism, gardening and natural foods, summer cottages, and the social experience of hunger and food assistance. Her publications include *Living Faithfully in an Unjust World: Compassionate Care in Russia*, *Dacha Idylls: Living Organically in Russia's Countryside*, and the edited volumes *Ethical Eating in the Postsocialist and Socialist World* (coedited with Yuson Jung and Jakob K. Klein), and *Why Food Matters: Critical Debates in Food Studies*.

Notes

1. Writing about Imperial Russian taste preferences, Alison Smith similarly argued (2008: 70) that "the Russian diet, whatever it truly was, suited the Russian body."
2. Because there are multiple transliteration systems for Russian, there are occasionally differences in English spellings of Russian words. When transliterating Russian words, I have followed the U.S. Library of Congress system of transliteration. When I am quoting transliterations from other people, I have retained their spelling.
3. Trubek (2008) has made a similar observation for the case of France, which has had a very different political, cultural, and agricultural history than Russia.
4. Soil is also the repository for dead Russian things (e.g., Erley 2021).
5. For longer discussions of these connections, especially the etymological connections between these concepts, see Caldwell (2011) and Ely (2000).
6. See also Sunderland's distinction (2000) between colonialism as a national project grounded in an intrinsic and exclusionary/nationality-based identity (*Russkaia*) and colonialism as a dynastic project (*Rossisskaia*) grounded in an inclusionary civic identity tied to citizenship.
7. See also Smith (2008: 151) for details on what she calls Russia's "Asiatic Table."
8. Although Carême apparently traveled to Russia, he never, in fact, cooked for Tsar Alexander (Goldstein 1995: 691).
9. See Caldwell 2015 for a longer discussion about the extent of Korean cuisine in Russia and the history of Korean migration to Russia.
10. See Kivelson (2008) for a longer discussion of sixteenth and seventeenth centuries Russian imperial expansion into "Little Russia," as Ukrainian lands were known at that time.

References

Anonymous. 2023. "Stolen Ukrainian Black Soil on Sale in Russian Stores." *Ukrainian World Congress*, March 30, 2023. Retrieved 20 December 2023 from https://www.ukrainianworldcongress.org/stolen-ukrainian-black-soil-on-sale-in-russian-stores/.

Appadurai, Arjun. 1988. "How to Make a National Cuisine: Cookbooks in Contemporary India." *Comparative Studies in Society and History* 30(1): 3–24.

Bassin, Mark. 1991. "Russia between Europe and Asia: The Ideological Construction of Geographic Space." *Slavic Review* 50(1): 1–17.

Brower, Daniel. 1994. "Imperial Russia and Its Orient: The Renown of Nikolai Przhevalsky." *Russian Review* 53(3): 367–81.
Brown, Rikki. N.d. "Layered Occupation: Terroir and Sovereignty in the Republic of Georgia's Wine Economy." PhD diss., in progress. Santa Cruz: University of California.
Caldwell, Melissa L. 2002. "The Taste of Nationalism: Food Politics in Postsocialist Moscow," *Ethnos* 67(3): 295–319.
———. 2004. "Domesticating the French Fry: McDonald's and Consumerism in Moscow." *Journal of Consumer Culture* 4(1): 5–26.
———. 2007. "Feeding the Body and Nourishing the Soul: Natural Foods in Postsocialist Russia." *Food, Culture & Society* 10(1): 44–71.
———. 2011. *Dacha Idylls: Living Organically in Russia's Countryside*. Berkeley: University of California Press.
———. 2015. "The Visible and the Invisible: Intimate Engagements with Russia's Culinary East." In *Tasteful Trends: Identity, Power, and the Mobility of East Asian Foods*, edited by Kwang-Ok Kim, 129–49. New York: Berghahn.
Ely, Christopher. 2000. "Critics in the Native Soil: Landscape and Conflicting Ideals of Nationality in Imperial Russia." *Ecumene* 7(3): 253–70.
Erley, Mieka. 2021. *On Russian Soil: Myth and Materiality*. Ithaca: Cornell University Press.
Goldstein, Darra. 1995. "Russia, Carême, and the Culinary Arts." *Slavonic and East European Review* 73(4): 691–715.
Kim, Lisa. 2022. "McDonald's Shuts 800 Restaurants in Russia over Ukraine Invasion." *Forbes*, 8 March 2022. Retrieved on 21 December 2023 from https://www.forbes.com/sites/lisakim/2022/03/08/mcdonalds-shuts-800-restaurants-in-russia-over-ukraine-invasion/?sh=29f3355c4dd1.
Kivelson, Valerie. 2006. *Cartographies of Tsardom: The Land and Its Meanings in Seventeenth-Century Russia*. Ithaca: Cornell University Press.
———. 2008. "'Between All Parts of the Universe': Russian Cosmographies and Imperial Strategies in Early Modern Siberia and Ukraine." *Imago Mundi* 60(2): 166-81.
Mack, Glenn R., and Asele Surina. 2005. *Food Culture in Russia and Central Asia*. Westport, CT: Greenwood Press.
Oushakine, Serguei Alex. 2009. *The Patriotism of Despair: Nation, War, and Loss in Russia*. Ithaca: Cornell University Press.
Paxson, Margaret. 2005. *Solovyovo: The Story of Memory in a Russian Village*. Bloomington: Indiana University Press and the Woodrow Wilson Center Press.
Rainey, Clint. 2023. "How McDonald's Won Russia—And then Lost It All." *Bloomberg*, January 3, 2023. Retrieved on 21 December 2023 from https://www.bloomberg.com/news/features/2023-01-04/mcdonald-s-won-big-in-russia-until-the-ukraine-invasion.
Ries, Nancy. 1997. *Russian Talk: Culture and Conversation during Perestroika*. Ithaca: Cornell University Press.
Smith, Alison K. 2008. *Recipes for Russia: Food and Nationhood under the Tsars*. DeKalb: Northern Illinois University Press.
Smirnova, Vera. 2023. "Land Theft and Land Abandonment: Property Question and the War in Ukraine." Paper presented at the Association for Slavic, East European, and Eurasian Studies meetings, 30 November 2023, Philadelphia.
Soroka, Marina. 2022. "Diplomats' Wives and the Foreign Ministry in Late Imperial Russia, Four Portraits." *Aspasia* 16: 149–70.

Sunderland, Willard. 2000. "The 'Colonization Question': Visions of Colonization in Late Imperial Russia." *Jahrbücher für Geschichte Osteuropas* (Neue Folge) 48(2): 210–32.
Toomre, Joyce. 1992. "Introduction." *Classic Russian Cooking: Elena Molokhovets'* A Gift to Young Housewives. Translated by Joyce Toomre, 1–89. Bloomington: Indiana University Press.
Trubek, Amy B. 2008. *The Taste of Place: A Cultural Journey into Terroir*. Berkeley: University of California Press.

Part II

Laws

CHAPTER 6

The *Domaće* Relations of Cured Pork

"Homemade" Resistance to Terroir Products in Croatian Istria

Anna Colquhoun

Introduction

> Istrian ham? Motherf****r! This is not genuine Istrian ham because it's made on a large scale by factories who import the pigs' legs, not even the whole pigs, from Slavonia, Hungary, the Netherlands, and who knows where. Real Istrian ham is *domaće* ham—made on a small scale at home using pigs reared here. They must be reared here. The price may be the same, but the taste is totally different. Istrian ham is bullshit, just a marketing story to make money. You can't get *domaće* ham in the shops, you need to know someone. My friend makes the best. Next time you want to buy some call me and I'll arrange it for you. (Darko,[1] family farmer and pork producer)

Air-dried ham (*pršut*, pronounced /prˈʃut/) is widely considered one of the local specialties of Istria, a peninsula in the north Adriatic comprising the northwest region of Croatia and small parts of Slovenia and Italy. In 2015 a European Union PDO (Protected Designation of Origin) geographical indication (GI) for "Istrian ham" ("*Istarski pršut/Istrski pršut*")[2] was introduced, the subject of my question to Darko that triggered his vehement response. The PDO was hailed by regional politicians as a huge success, and as essential for the protection of the food as an "autochthonous" product.

By their supporters, PDOs are considered a defense against the globalization and industrialization of food systems: conserving territories' distinctive and traditional food cultures, awarding collective intellectual property rights to producers, thereby protection from imposters, and ultimately aiding rural development. They are based on the French concept of terroir: products must demonstrate that "the quality and characteristics of the product are due exclusively or essentially to the geographical environment, including natural and human factors" (Barham and Sylvander 2011: xiv). That particular foods and their qualities are associated with geographical territories is also widespread in European tourism discourses, reflected in terms such as "regional cuisine" and "local specialties."

PDO *istarski pršut* comes with solid "local" credentials: it must be made in Istria, Istrian style, and use meat from within Croatia, all verified through a certification system. Nevertheless, the topic touched a nerve. Many, like Darko, consider *istarski pršut* inauthentic and poor quality. This chapter considers why by paying attention to what he contrasted it to: *domaće* ham. Rather than "terroir," "local," or "*istarski*," the word most often used to denote good cured pork is *domaće* (pronounced /ˈdomat͡ɕe/), usually translated from Croatian as "homemade." *Domaće* and terroir are both concepts concerned with food, place, and taste, and actors use both to authenticate cured pork in Istria. Here I explore how they operate differently, in dialectical tension with each other, and with what consequences.

The chapter is based on fieldwork in Croatian Istria from 2017 to 2019 and ongoing lived experience in the region. It centers on the work of three *agroturizam* (farm tourism) families to make *domaće* pork products for their *konobe* (taverns).[3] While *domaće* cured pork also plays important roles within consumption practices, here I focus on relations of production and exchange.

The ethnography demonstrates that *domaće*, unlike the terroir logic of EU GIs, does not refer to a territorial understanding of place, style of production, or taste. Instead, I argue pork is made *domaće*, and thereby good, through morally imbued social relations of production, which mediate territorial understandings of taste and place. These are the "*domaće* relations" of cured pork, which are themselves reproduced through its making. Being a property of relations, not things, means *domaće* is flexible, allowing producers to autonomously and successfully make cured pork *domaće* in different ways. I argue the *domaće* versus *istarski pršut* debate was not a case of restorative nostalgia for a bygone era when more families kept and processed pigs at home, but rather a practical line of defense against, and moral critique of, the political economy surrounding PDO *istarski pršut*.[4]

Istria

The Istrian peninsula is a borderland region, for centuries divided between the Venetian Republic and Austrian Empire, acquired by Italy between the world wars, then by the socialist republic of Yugoslavia until 1991, and entirely within the European Union (EU) since 2013 when Croatia joined. This chapter concerns the interior of the Croatian part, sometimes called the "hinterland" of the more populated, urban, demographically diverse, and tourism-centered coast.

Here, until the 1990s, it was common to combine factory work with smallholding. Homegrown/made food and drink were for household use, informal trade, gifting, and sharing, and were important for reproducing social relations, particularly homemade cured pork and wine, which still hold high cultural and social significance. People remember the annual pig slaughter as an important event, when extended family and neighbors gathered to transform the animal into a series of parts: blood and offal to use immediately in the post-work feast; prize cuts like the legs and loin salted for high-value cured meat, appropriate only for special occasions, important visitors, or sale; diverse scraps combined to make much-loved sausages; and everything else from snout to tail preserved to use as flavoring for family meals. The pig and its pork were embedded in social, economic, and ecological relations, with feeding and curing practices partly dependent on terrain and climate. During the 1970s and 1980s *pršut* was also made by a couple of state-owned/controlled companies to supply the coastal tourism industry (Šišović 2021: 34).

After the wars and breakup of Yugoslavia, the economy rapidly transformed, starting with the closure of many factories and opening of private businesses. The tourism industry made a quality turn and now includes increasing rural, cultural, and gastronomic tourism. In the 1990s tourism demand for "typical" products like *pršut* was high, and, in the absence of any large, registered producers, tourism companies used agents to source thousands of hams from unregistered smallholders (Kocković Zaborski 2018: 198). Meanwhile, with opened markets and the arrival of supermarkets, small-scale farming was becoming less viable, and tourism-related jobs did not leave time for agriculture. Consequently, many village households gave up livestock, including pigs.

Those who continued pork production faced increasing barriers as pressure grew to comply with onerous new veterinary and food safety regulations. As in other post-socialist EU accession countries, these processes of "Europeanization" have proved highly problematic for small producers, who lack the economic means to "modernize" facilities and meet EU standards (Dunn 2003; Aistara 2015; Czerny 2018). The Croatian state tries to reduce the "gray" economy by encouraging producers to register and consumers to demand receipts. However, it still flourishes in Istria, where many view "Zagreb" with contempt, seek to bypass onerous regulation and taxes, and instead cultivate social and economic autonomy (cf. Smith and Grasseni 2020). Acquiring goods, services, or favors through a social connection (*veza*) is thus commonplace, as in the wider region (Cann 2007; Brković 2017).

Since Croatian independence, a regionalist party has dominated local politics, promoting Istrian autonomy and distinctive cultural identity (Ashbrook 2008; Ballinger 2003). Most of my interlocutors self-identified as "Istrian" above "Croatian." Within the everyday, "Istrianity" is particularly noticeable in dialect, music, and food. Regional assembly (Istria County) policy includes seeking multiple EU-funded cultural and economic development projects and obtaining EU GIs. These help flag Istria's independence from Zagreb, boost export, and brand Istria as a high-quality gastronomic destination (cf. de St. Maurice, this volume).

Cured Pork Geographical Indications

In the late 1990s, as concern grew over the quantity of "illegal" ham production in Istria, the regional assembly launched a project to define, standardize, and ultimately protect "Istrian ham." This involved scientific research into the "best" way to cure ham and the definition of all production stages. The Association of Istrian Ham Producers was founded in 1998, "Istrian ham" was registered with the Croatian State Institute for Intellectual Property in 2002, and, with regional assembly support, the association successfully acquired the EU PDO in 2015 (Kocković Zaborski 2018; Šišović 2021).

The designation ascribes the unique qualities of *istarski pršut* to both the natural and cultural terroir of Istria, in particular the *bura* wind that dries the ham and the tradition of preparing hams in an "almost unique" way, including the use of Mediterranean herbs and a particular butchering technique.[5] As Harry West elaborates, this terroir-based logic assumes static and durable links between product, people, and place (2022). It imagines a unified group ("Istrian farmers"), with a shared distinctive culture ("tradition"), which both map to a defined territory with a particular (presumably unchanging) climate, and have done so for an unspecified long time ("many generations"), resulting in one recipe for *pršut*. The special taste of Istrian ham is thereby rooted in a territorial conception of place.

To label your ham "*istarski pršut*," one must comply with specifications concerning raw ingredients, production methods, packaging, labeling, and the organoleptic qualities of the finished product. The PDO allows meat to come from almost anywhere in Croatia. This is unusual for PDOs, which usually require key ingredients to be sourced within the named geographical region, but was allowed due to Croatia being new to the EU. The PDO permits a range of pig feeds and requires pigs to be at least nine months old and 160 kilograms at slaughter (EUR-Lex 2015). As a legal protection and marketing device within the formal economy, certified producers must also have registered HACCP-compliant production facilities.[6] This combination of standardization and distinctiveness is what the PDO needs to operate on the EU market, offering distant consumers a differentiated "taste of place" (Trubek 2008). It is sufficiently embedded—in the territory of Istria—while sufficiently disembedded—from "traditional" practices—to allow increased production and wider trade.

More recently the association expanded to include producers of "other traditional cured pork products" with an eye to further GI applications. First will be

"Istrian sausage" (*istarska kobasica*), for which a PGI (Protected Geographical Origin) application was in preparation during my research. PGIs are less restrictive than PDOs, and it was expected that this one would allow meat sourced from across the EU. The regional rural development agency, which helps producers' associations apply for GIs, explained this was necessary since pig rearing in Istria is too small-scale.

Along with the municipal mayors of Tinjan and Sveti Petar u Šumi and certain food writers, these actors have been instrumental in preparing for the GIs and shaping ideas and practices concerning *pršut* and *kobasica* within Istria. Initiatives have included new annual ham and sausage festivals,[7] culinary training events, publications, and ham and sausage "museums." At the 2019 "International Ham Fair" in Tinjan, producers of PDO Istrian ham and invited ham producers from Spain, Italy, Slovenia, and elsewhere filled a large marquee, offering direct sales, and were judged in competitions for best Istrian ham and best internationally, thus elevating *istarski pršut* to a global stage. An "association for sensory analysis" called Gustus, headed by the person leading the regional assembly's GI strategy, offered guided ham tastings, advertised as the opportunity to learn "what distinguishes Istrian ham from other Croatian and European hams" (Galić 2019). *Istarski pršut* is also available at some shops and restaurants, particularly those catering to tourists, and online or on-site from the handful of—generally larger—certified, cured pork producers.

The "With a Sausage into the EU" festival in Sveti Petar u Šumi that same year included competitions for best "Istrian sausage" and best "Istrian sausage in the old way." While the former was for registered producers, the latter was for "small producers of homemade (*domaće*) sausages," meaning in this case unregistered producers, the aim being, according to prior promotions "to contribute to the preservation of the traditional production of Istrian sausage as intangible cultural heritage of our region, as well as to contribute to the education of home-based sausage producers" ("Tri Dana Istarske Klobasice" 2019). Gustus organized "expert" judging panels, with scores for qualities such as "correctness of shape," "intensity of red color," and "presence of positive scents characteristic of the product" analyzed by statistics software provided by a company specializing in food certification compliance. Certificates were awarded in the main hall, which was packed with cured pork producers from Istria and beyond selling their wares, including the region's and Croatia's biggest brands. The festival thus does what its name suggests: through annual competitions producers are encouraged to formalize and standardize their production and see the value in doing so for an expanded market. Festival organizers were explicit about their aim to "improve" and increase overall registered production since this was necessary for the PGI application.

The PDO and PGI-in-progress are thus embedded in regulatory regimes for food specificity, safety, and trade in order to circulate on the EU market as "European products" (Welz 2015).[8] This advantages larger producers able to modernize production and wishing to export (West 2013), and suits regional politicians and affiliates working to promote Istria as a destination, while excluding producers who wish to make their cured pork good in other ways, for a different market.

Domaće Cured Pork

In popular discourse, distrust of food from unknown and faraway places is common, reflecting unease over entry into capitalist and globalized food systems. In this context, *domaće* circulates symbolically and materially as the alternative: food that is from "here," "ours," "natural," and "good."[9] *Domaće* is a dense and slippery concept. So, for example, "*domaće* eggs" means eggs produced by a smallholder, not by large-scale agriculture; "*domaće* bread" means homemade bread rather than bought bread; and "*domaće* specialties" means local/our traditional dishes, not those representative of elsewhere/others. The meaning can be ambiguous—so, for example, "*domaće* food" might mean homemade or local style, and "*domaće* meat" might mean meat from a smallholder or from Croatia. *Domaće* is deictic, relying on an understanding of the implied "we" and "here." It thus denotes boundaries between foods, people, and places, although it can do so flexibly or ambiguously. It almost always denotes good food and is associated with, although not limited to, that produced and exchanged outside the formal economy (Colquhoun 2019, 2024).

Despite the promotional and educational efforts surrounding GI ham and sausage, the vast majority of my interlocutors, even some of those involved in the GI strategies described above, told me *domaće* cured pork was superior. At least one PDO ham producer also offers their own noncertified *domaće* version for discerning regulars. A museum curator, Lara, complained: "Real ham is *domaće* ham. Some people still grow pigs and make ham in the same style as fifty years ago, but very few. Now this ham has a very high value, and yet it's illegal, like drugs. Ham is the example I am giving now because this is closest to my heart, and it hurts me the most."

What, exactly, "*domaći pršut*" refers to is not a settled matter, as I explore below, but in such statements, it usually means that it is made by a smallholder from a heavy pig that he (for it is usually he) reared or at least fattened himself on homegrown crops. As more households give up pigs, *domaće* cured pork is therefore harder to find. As family, friend, or neighbor of a producer, you may be lucky enough to be gifted some. To buy it is harder. Supply is small, production often unregistered, and sales—especially if "on the black" (*na crno*)—go to or through known contacts. Hence Darko's offer to broker my access to his friend's *pršut*.

Domaće cured pork is also offered in *konobe* at *agroturizmi*. By law, and guest expectation, the food at *agroturizmi* is homemade from at least partly home-pro-

Figure 6.1. Cured pork and cheese are typically served as a cold starter at *agroturizmi* and other *konobe*. This platter includes *pršut* and *kobasica*. Istria, 2014. © Anna Colquhoun.

duced ingredients. Here, *domaće* food is in especially high demand from guests from urban areas of Istria and neighboring regions, who consider it natural, traditional, and quintessentially Istrian. They seek out, and discern, *domaće* cured pork, while guests from farther afield expect only to find Istria's iconic ham and may not discern the *domaće* difference (Colquhoun 2024).

Making Pork *Domaće*

I participated in pig-processing days with three families who produce cured pork to supply their *agroturizam konobe*, partially, if not fully, in compliance with the relevant regulations. They shared many ideas and practices; nevertheless, each made their pork *domaće*, and thus good, differently.

Darko and his family run a successful *agroturizam konoba* open only on weekends to allow time for agriculture and food preparation during the week. Darko rears his own pigs, feeding them corn, barley, pumpkins, turnips, and greens, and growing them slowly, to slaughter only once they are two years old and around two hundred kilograms. He processes twenty to forty each winter to provide the *konoba* with a mixed charcuterie platter and other cuts. It is impossible to order a plate of just *pršut*, which indicates to discerning guests the fact Darko processes whole pigs. Having whole pigs also, he explained, allows him to make good sausages, since they use meat from across the carcass. For Darko the biggest problem with *istarski pršut* was the importing of pork legs rather than the use of "autochthonous"[10] Istrian-grown pigs, of which he thought there should be many more.

Darko's *pršutana* (ham/pork processing room) was pristine, kitted out with expensive machinery, stainless steel workbenches, and an electric fly killer. To better control temperature and humidity, the windows and fireplace had been retired in favor of air-conditioning. Given the risk of losing too much if anything went wrong, Darko insisted there was no other way. He was proud of his "industrial" production, as he called it, and the speed with which he could single-handedly transform a whole pig, compared to the multiday event it had been for his father and his friends. He explained their *agroturizam* is a new kind, with "modern production."

The cuts of meat here have different names to just a few villages away, something many producers stressed to evidence the linguistic and cultural variety across the peninsula. Darko also emphasized that each family has its "own recipes," its "own tradition," such as his sausages. This recipe—using white wine, garlic, and rosemary—he told me, goes back forty years, and since Darko took over from his father, he has made some changes: more pepper, less salt, and the addition of nutmeg.

I told Darko I was making *panceta* (bacon) and sausages at home, and he queried my meat. My local butcher had described it to me as *domaće*, but Darko was suspicious; he did not trust this unknown butcher, nor the labeling in shops. For Darko anything labeled "*domaće*," as meat is in supermarkets to indicate Croatian origin, or branded "*istarski pršut*" for that matter, was all "just politics" and "bullshit"—"a marketing story to make money."

Despite Darko's strength of opinion regarding the superiority of his *domaće* pork, I learned the family themselves rarely ate these products. Their *domaće* pork was mostly for their *konoba*, where it generates considerable cultural, social, and economic value as products that many of their guests seek out.

***

Nada runs an *agroturizam* with a handful of pigs and chickens and a *konoba* only open for group bookings. I participated the day she, her husband Valter, and his friend processed a whopping 280-kilogram two-year-old sow. Nada was most keen to stress the Istrian nature of their products: the meat was Istrian because the pig was raised here eating the traditional pig feed of squashes, greens, and other vegetables, not concentrate. It was therefore slowly grown into a large pig, which made the meat dark, natural, good quality, and *domaće*. The garlic and wine in the sausages also had to be *domaće*: garlic from her garden and wine from an acquaintance rather than a shop. Secondly, the recipes were Istrian style, employing Mediterranean ingredients like bay and rosemary. And thirdly, in Istria the *bura* wind meant little or no smoke was needed during curing, unlike elsewhere in Croatia. Nada also wanted me to know they only serve their own pork products; she "won't buy them from the shop."

The work was carried out across two rooms—Nada's spotless *konoba* kitchen and Valter's more ramshackle *lišjera,* an outhouse for processing and drying meat. In the latter Valter and his friend cut, salted, and hung the meat, using the open window and a tiny fire in the large traditional-style fireplace to dry it. I learned that despite the *bura* that day, a little fire was still needed, more so on rainy days. Indeed, I have heard producers complain that with climate change winters are getting wetter, making it harder to cure pork without smoke. In the kitchen Nada employed an electric saw, vacuum-bagging machine, freezer, and other kit to ease the workload and preserve semi-dried sausages and other parts for the months ahead. Getting the impression the *lišjera* was a male space, I spent most time in the kitchen.

As I had seen elsewhere, the pelvic bones were removed from the hams, contrary to the PDO definition. The sausage recipe was similar to Darko's, with differing quantities, and additionally used bay. Like Darko, Nada used nutmeg, calling it her "secret ingredient" and adding, "I know it's not from here, not traditional, and has only been available in Istria for about fifty years, but my father used it in his recipe, and so I do too." But, she assured me, the sausages were still Istrian because they used *domaće* meat.

Ending this pig's life had been hard for Valter, who had named her and cared for her. He was emotional, admitting he had had to leave when the slaughterman came. He does not often eat meat, neither Nada for health reasons, and were it not for the *konoba* they would not keep animals. But for Nada, serving traditional Istrian and *domaće* food was important for her sense of Istrian identity and pride, and her *konoba*'s *domaće* reputation.

The small number of pigs meant their meat might not last the year. In a modification to Nada's answer, Valter told me that when it runs out, they "only buy from someone we know, or a friend of a friend." Would he need to see for himself how the animal was raised? "No, it just needs to be a friend, so then you know it's not just a story, you know what they say is true." Like Darko, he completely trusts knowable social networks but not branded shop-bought meat, including certified *istarski pršut,* diplomatically referring to the latter as "edible, but not for me."

***

In the twenty-plus years the Benčić family have run their *agroturizam* they have progressively specialized in wine and olive oil and reduced animals, spending time instead on the *konoba*, open seven days a week. Chef-proprietor Alen does

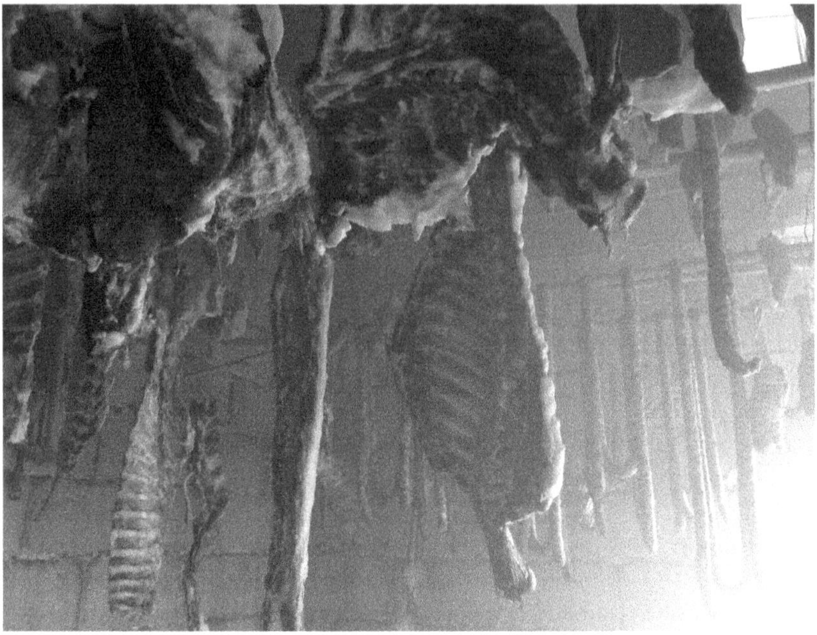

Figure 6.2. Cuts of pork, including ribs and sausages, hanging to dry in a *lišjera*. Istria, 2016. © Anna Colquhoun.

not have time to raise the number of pigs his *konoba* needs, nor do they have the scale of land needed to grow feed. So, during the winter I helped, he bought several whole pigs plus additional legs to meet the additional demand for Istria's famous *pršut*.

The pigs were sourced from the Croatian interior—that is, outside Istria—a fairly common practice since other regions are far bigger pork producers. These were from the neighbor of Alen's mother's brother and collected by Alen's father Milan in their van. Alen assured me they were *domaće* pigs, which had eaten "natural" *domaće* food, and were not from a "farm." By "farm" (*farma*) my interlocutors meant a large "industrial" livestock enterprise. Alen also explained it was cheaper to buy the whole animal from "a place like this," especially without a middleman, and that "this way I know what's in it, I can tell people it's *domaće,* and people say wow I want to buy some!"

Knowing this family well, I was able to join the men—Alen, Milan, Milan's friend, and Alen's father-in-law—in the drafty breezeblock *lišjera* to help process the pigs, increasingly accompanied by wine, banter, and morsels cooked over the smoldering fire. As one explained, "A *lišjera* is a place where men make cured meat and do other winter jobs, and drink by the fire." Here we processed one and a half pigs on a large, well-worn wooden table. Aside from a calculator to determine the weights of salt and pepper for the sausages, no electrical equipment was used. The rest was done by hand and eye, with Milan and his friend advising.

For Alen, most important for making good cured meat was style of production, which must be "traditional." He was proud of his "real" *lišjera* and *podrum* (cellar for aging), and adamant that even a properly home-grown pig could not make *domaći pršut* if the production facilities were modern style, as they are inside a PDO producer's *pršutana*: "This is not *domaći pršut*! For *domaći pršut* you need the *bura* and the earth floor. With an earth floor the *pršut* takes the humidity it needs, not what it's given by the air conditioning." When income from the *konoba* has allowed Alen to finally pay off the loan taken out to build it, he may build a small fully compliant processing room, but this would only be "to show the inspectors" while the majority of production would continue in the *lišjera*.

Here the sausages were made with garlic, bay, and rosemary, but this time no nutmeg or wine. As elsewhere, Alen stressed the importance of following patrilineal family tradition, and also as elsewhere I learned of tweaks made along the way. Alen concluded, "You know for yourself the best recipe." Importantly, these sausages were recognizably theirs: when his sister popped in to try some cooked in the fireplace, she confirmed: "It tastes like *our* sausages, how they always taste. So I like it!"

I recounted making my own, with meat from a trusted butcher, using only rudimentary kit and the *bura* for drying, but learned these were not *domaće* since I had added paprika, which is what people do in Slavonia (eastern Croatia).

The *Domaće* Relations of Cured Pork

Darko, Nada, and Alen variously articulated, and utilized, important connections to place to create their *domaće* pork: pigs and pig feed grown on Istrian territory, the *bura* wind, and "Istrian" recipes. However, in themselves, these connections to Istrian territory, climate, and culture were not sufficient to make good pork, nor all necessary. Other things were important, indicating how *domaće* pork brings people, place, and taste into relation rather differently to the terroir logic of the PDO. Here I use *domaće*'s etymological Serbo-Croat root—*doma*, meaning *home*—to elucidate this, and argue that *domaće* is a property of flexible social relations rather than of fixed things. These are the "*domaće* relations" of cured pork.

More than a physical space, "home" is a set of social relations that are at once economic and moral.[11] Likewise, the salient places of production for my interlocutors were not the geographical territory of Istria, but morally imbued configurations of economic and social relations. And like "home" can scale from the individual household to a town, region, country, or even mobile sense of belonging, so for my interlocutors the scale of relevant socioeconomic configuration varied. For Darko, autonomous production of pigs on the family's land was most important, and he supported the same at regional scale. For Nada and Valter, the unit of production had to be family based and could incorporate wider networks only if socially embedded and thus trustable. And for Alen, these knowable networks could extend beyond Istria, utilizing matrilineal kinship ties. For all, *pršut* making was indivisible from the social and economic relations of pig production and exchange. For Alen, the *lišjera* and *podrum* were also essential places, where men knew how to work with the *bura*, fireplace, soil, and one another to cure meat. As in the other cases, his cured pork's value lay in the household's ability to autonomously produce it, and in its contribution to the economic and social reproduction of the household. This forms the morality of *domaće* cured pork production and distinguishes it from "marketing stories just to make money." Making *domaće* cured pork therefore relies on morally imbued socioeconomic relations and helps reproduce them.

Like "home" only has sense in relation to a subject—"my home"—rather than being simply a place on a map, *domaće* is also known subjectively and relationally. The "we" of *domaće* is crucial to its sense, and the salient taste of place is more "ours" than "Istrian." Darko, Nada, and Alen were all concerned about creating cured pork that continued their own "family tradition" while also being recognizably "Istrian." The recipes used and tastes achieved had to satisfy both. As Alen's sister commented: "It tastes like *our* sausages. So I like it!" This allowed considerable variation between producers and over time, with all families evolving their recipes over generations. Indeed, variation itself was seen as typically Istrian, hence the stress on microregional diversity of pork vocabulary. Paprika was, however, a step too far, since it referenced Slavonia, so it would "only be *domaće* for them," as Alen explained. The production of *domaće* cured pork therefore symbolically, and materially through practice and taste, reproduces individual families and the sociocultural category of Istrian, and connects them. This echoes Melissa Caldwell's description of *nash* (our) food as a "socialized system of consumption" reproducing Russians and Russianness (2002; see also this volume). However, for my interlocutors, *domaće* was more a system of production, which held as much or more relevance for reproducing individual family identity as Istrian. *Domaće* cured pork is therefore similar to *domashno vino* (homemade wine) in Bulgaria, which Yuson Jung describes in this volume as evoking a social imaginary connecting families to their heritage and land through the winemaking practice. In Istria there is a notable gender dimension to this: most pig processing is done by men, and recipes are largely passed from father to son. Cured pork making thus helps reproduce the family as patrilineal and patrilocal.

While "home" often conjures the past, sometimes nostalgically—where we "are from"—it can also reference the future—"homemaking." Likewise, *domaće* may reference the past—Alen's invocations of "traditional" methods—or the future—Darko's "modern production" and aspiration for a more agriculturally autonomous region. And in all cases *domaće* accommodated change, with recipes and/or production methods evolving over generations rather than being embedded in a temporal period (cf. Klein, and Sanders, both this volume).

Finally, as appreciating the materialities of "home" concerns recognizing the configurations of social, economic, and moral relations and histories embedded in things, so, too, discerning *domaće* is more about recognizing the relations discussed above than particular organoleptic qualities. For my interlocutors, the taste of *domaće* pork is a conflation of values: it is considered good by virtue of being morally, socially, and organoleptically good. When eating *domaće* food, people will often comment on it being "good" (*dobro*), and "domaće," but are unlikely to discuss organoleptic qualities. To do so seems impolite, not the point. "Too much philosophizing" about food, as people call it, is considered inappropriate. Instead, it is just *dobro*, but in multiple senses.

This indicates an important dimension to *domaće* taste: it is unabstractable from its relations of production and exchange. This is quite different to conventional terroir products such as those protected by GIs, which are apparently objectively knowable by anyone anywhere due to their organoleptic qualities. A Chablis wine has detectable terroir for drinkers anywhere and can be externally validated as doing so (see Jung, this volume). My interlocutors were generally suspicious of labels and marketing "stories." Instead, *domaće* food is validated through knowable social relations, such as the pigs Alen bought via his kin network, and the *pršut* Darko recommended to me from his friend. So, while terroir-legitimated products like PDO *istarski pršut* are certifiable by third parties, *domaće* products are "relationally" authenticated (see also Jung 2014; Graf 2015; Czerny 2018).

Since *domaće* is a property of relations, not things, it is flexible. The ethnography shows it is possible to make *domaće* cured pork very differently: Darko emphasized the provenance of the pigs—as both his own land and Istria—and use of spotless "modern" and "industrial" equipment; Nada stressed the Istrianness of both the pig-feeding practice and her cured pork recipes, and her small-scale home operation; and Alen was happy to buy a pig from outside Istria as long as it was *domaće*, and insisted on "traditional" methods and spaces. Despite the differences in practice and belief, all were able to successfully claim their cured pork was *domaće* due to their use of *domaće* relations to produce it. *Domaće* cured pork production is thus flexibly embedded in territories, production logics, and temporal registers. This works well for my interlocutors as they negotiate the pressures and opportunities around them: high demand for *domaće* food yet limited land and labor to produce it; politicized Istrian identity yet also pride in individual family and microregional distinctions, and transregional kin affiliations; a flourishing informal economy yet increasing pressures to be legible and governed by the state. Unlike the terroir logic of PDOs—which asserts a fixed taste from a fixed place, connected through a fixed recipe—*domaće* is flexible, reflecting, and accommodating changing social, economic, and political contexts, be it those of the household, region, or wider state. It also accommodates a changing climate, allowing use of smoke when needed.

Domaće Cured Pork as Resistance and Critique

The flexibility of *domaće* allows producers to stress different credentials when making *domaće* claims, as they did to me. In each case they highlighted a difference between their production and that associated with the PDO—be it home-grown or slowly grown heavy pigs, small-scale operation or traditional methods—helping to create the contrasting superior *domaće* value of their pork. As Alen said, "People say wow I want to buy some." He used the values of *domaće* to justify avoiding regulations and continue using his informal social networks and "traditional" *lišjera* for as long as possible. Darko, Nada, and Alen may not legally be able to call their *pršut* "Istrian," but they can call it *domaće*, which creates significant economic, social, and cultural value. Being able to make their own *domaće* cured pork asserted their families' long-standing connection to the land and "autochthonous" Istrian identity, and significantly aided their *agroturizam* reputations. This explains why—as in the past—these families generally only ate the less valuable parts of the pig, saving the rest for sale. In the context of PDO *istarski pršut* making exclusionary claims to authenticity, plus increasing pressures to comply with HACCP and be fully legible by the state, I see these practices and articulations of *domaće* cured pork as a practical line of defense, and social and economic resilience strategy, similar to those Diana Mincyte found within informal raw milk relations in Lithuania (2009).

My interlocutors thus challenged the PDO's monopoly on authentic, high-quality Istrian ham. Through comparison to *domaće* ham this challenge is implicitly moral and political. When Darko complained that "the price may be the same but the taste is totally different," he was highlighting the quality—and moral—discrepancy he saw between his own and PDO ham: both fetched the same price yet while his was the result of hard, and moral, work—pigs slowly reared by himself in Istria, for the sake of household reproduction—the latter was based on cheaper, lower-quality inputs with value added by name only—that is, the "Istrian" labeling. As he continued, "'Istrian ham' is . . . just a marketing story to make money." His assertion that certification was "just politics," a common phrase meaning high-level political declarations deemed meaningless to everyday people, indicated he saw Istria-EU projects such as the PDO as more about scoring political points and benefiting the few than conserving Istrian culture or supporting pig and ham production in Istria (cf. Bardone and Spalvēna 2019). But he would unlikely be so explicit since "being political" is generally avoided and criticizing regional bodies can reportedly court problems. As the ethnography suggests, vocalized critique of *istarski pršut* focuses on pig rearing and ham making. *Domaće* is thus a way of being political without being political (cf. Avieli 2012, 2018).

So *domaće* can function as moral discourse, a way of judging foods and their producers. Producers may use it to critique others, but it can also be turned on them. As Heather Paxson noted regarding cheesemakers in the United States using terroir to describe their cheeses and practices, combining a value-laden critique with a value-adding label is tricky (2010). There is the concern that others may doubt your *domaće* credentials, as Darko doubted my butcher's meat. This was Nada's greatest concern and explains her emphatic denial of using shop-bought meat. Such was the pressure she and Valter felt to produce *domaće* cured pork for the *agroturizam* that they did it despite the slaughter of cared-for animals being traumatic. So, while *domaći pršut* may not have a formal EU governance regime, it is subject to an informal, diffuse governance that pressures producers and also limits who can produce *domaće* cured pork, linked as it is to Istrian identity and social networks.

Conclusion

In Istria cured pork is socially, culturally, and—for some still—economically very important. But the position of cured pork is in flux, with small-scale pig rearing and processing in decline, and new companies entering the field using pork from elsewhere. This raises the stakes; cured pork matters and is highly emotive. As Lana said, *pršut* "is closest to my heart, and it hurts me the most." In this context the meaning and value of both PDO certification and *domaće* is intensified. At the risk of oversimplification, I have presented the debate as it was presented to me by the producers I worked with: *istarski* versus *domaće*.

Actors working with both are concerned with relations between food production, place, and taste, but they conceptualize and practice them very differently. PDO actors use terroir to reify geographical place—a homogenized conception of Istria, with distinctive and timeless nature and culture—and reify taste—as organoleptic, and reflective of this geographical place. This has consequences: it requires standardization, allows third-party certification, and functions to market ham as "the taste of place" in an expanded EU market, an advantage for larger producers. Meanwhile, for producers of *domaće* cured pork, these geographical notions of place and taste are mediated by morally imbued social relations of pig and pork production. These *domaće relations* are important for both making and tasting good cured pork. This has consequences, too: it allows variation and flexibility, reproduces (patrilineal and patrilocal) households and their informal social networks, and situates taste in knowable social relations. *Domaće* cured pork is *relationally authenticated*, which facilitates direct and informal sales, and resists third-party interference. The comparison demonstrates how place and taste are co-constitutive in each case, but with very different consequences due to the differing ways they are constructed. In other words, place and taste are not givens but worked on by actors for certain reasons. *Domaće* and terroir are therefore dynamic social constructs with efficacy.

Istaski pršut and *domaći pršut* exist in dialectical relationship. *Istarski pršut* was born out of concern over unregulated, unregistered pork production, and is presented as the certified authentic, safe, and quality option. This animated *domaći pršut* as practical resistance and moral critique, presented with opposing values of autonomy, trust, family and Istrian pride, and living traditions. The existing PDO and the PGI-in-preparation encourage producers and consumers to opt for standardized and certified products and formalized economic relations. But as *domaće* cured pork is threatened, it takes on intensity, as people use it to resist not only the PDO but also the wider processes of market integration and European food governance of which it is part.

We can see, then, that the problem with PDO *pršut* was not a case of restorative nostalgia for a bygone era, when food was literally "homemade," but has a lot more at stake, which paying attention to the wider "home" meanings and practices of *domaće* has helped reveal. Taste-place concepts like terroir and *domaće* can wield considerable power and need to be analyzed as such. With the introduction of further cured pork GIs in Istria, time will tell what impact they have on producers' and consumers' understandings of pork quality, its place, and taste, and on *domaće relations* of production.

Acknowledgments

I thank this volume's contributors for their helpful comments on drafts of this chapter, particularly Jakob Klein, Katharina Graf, Sarah Czerny, Harry West, James Staples, and Yuson Jung. Above all, I thank my interlocutors in Istria, in particular the families who welcomed me into their pork production spaces and shared their knowledge, practices, and perspectives.

Anna Colquhoun is a social anthropologist and Research Associate at the SOAS Food Studies Centre. Her PhD thesis, *Making Local Specialities: Food, Place and Value in Istria*, examined the intersections of making food, place, and value in this rapidly changing borderland region. Her research interests include culinary tourism and the cultural economy, hospitality and cooking, and localized and post-socialist food systems. Anna has a degree in Anthropology and Archaeology from the University of Cambridge and an MA in the Anthropology of Food from SOAS. She has worked in international development, culinary education, food writing, consultancy, and hospitality.

Notes

1. I use pseudonyms to protect my interlocutors' identities.
2. The final designation included the name in both Croatian and Slovenian languages, with the production area including both Croatian and Slovenian Istria. As my research concerned Croatian Istria I use *istarski pršut* hereon to refer to the PDO-protected ham.
3. *agroturizam*, pl. = *agroturizmi*; *konoba*, pl. = *konobe.*
4. For comparison, see Jillian Cavanaugh's work (2007) on salami in Bergamo and Alison Leitch's work (2000) on *lardo* (cured pork fat) in Colonnata, both in northern Italy. In both cases, as in Istria, the production of locally meaningful cured pork products became enmeshed in vibrant debates over authenticity, EU food governance regimes, and the commoditization and privatisation of cultural products.
5. For example, removing the foot, skin and subcutaneous fat, but not the pelvic bones.
6. Hazard Analysis and Critical Control Point (HACCP) is a system that identifies, evaluates, and controls hazards to food safety, and is mandatory for registered food businesses across the EU.
7. The Internacionalni sajam pršuta (The International Ham Fair) has been held in the town of Tinjan each autumn since 2007, and the springtime S klobasicom u EU (With a Sausage into the EU) festival in the nearby small town of Sveti Petar u Šumi since 2013. Both have since spawned summertime sister events, more targeted at tourists.
8. Gisela Welz has identified such regimes as tools for creating "things that either would not exist without the European Union, or have been infused with EU-generated qualities to such a degree that something new has come into being" (Welz 2015: 150; see also Gille 2016).
9. With parallels to other post-socialist contexts (see for example Caldwell 2002, 2007; Gabriel 2005; Matijevic and Boni 2019; Mroczkowska 2019).
10. By this he was not referring to specific breeds but rather to rearing on the land in Istria. Breed was not important to any of my interlocutors.
11. For a summary of the anthropology of home (and house) see Samanani and Lenhard (2023 [2019]).

References

Aistara, Guntra A. 2015. "Good, Clean, Fair . . . and Illegal: Paradoxes of Food Ethics in Post-Socialist Latvia." *Journal of Baltic Studies* 46(3): 283–98.

Ashbrook, John. 2008. *Buying and Selling the Istrian Goat*. Lausanne: Peter Lang.

Avieli, Nir. 2012. *Rice Talks: Food and Community in a Vietnamese Town*. Bloomington: Indiana University Press.

———. 2018. *Food and Power: A Culinary Ethnography of Israel*. Berkeley: University of California Press.

Ballinger, Pamela. 2003. *History in Exile: Memory and Identity at the Borders of the Balkans*. Princeton: Princeton University Press.

Bardone, Ester, and Astra Spalvēna. 2019. "European Union Food Quality Schemes and the Transformation of Traditional Foods into European Products in Latvia and Estonia." *Appetite* 135 (April): 43–53.

Barham, Elizabeth, and Bertil Sylvander, eds. 2011. *Labels of Origin for Food: Local Development, Global Recognition*. Wallingford: CABI Books.

Brković, Čarna. 2017. *Managing Ambiguity: How Clientelism, Citizenship, and Power Shape Personhood in Bosnia and Herzegovina*. New York: Berghahn.

Caldwell, Melissa L. 2002. "The Taste of Nationalism: Food Politics in Postsocialist Moscow." *Ethnos* 67(3): 295–319.

———. 2007. "Feeding the Body and Nourishing the Soul: Natural Foods in Postsocialist Russia." *Food, Culture & Society* 10(1): 43–71.

Cann, Sarah C. 2007. "The Politics of Ethnic Identity in Everyday Life at the Local Level in Croatia." PhD diss., University of Edinburgh. Retrieved July 2024 from https://era.ed.ac.uk/handle/1842/29051.

Cavanaugh, Jillian R. 2007. "Making Salami, Producing Bergamo: The Transformation of Value." *Ethnos* 72(2): 149–72.

Colquhoun, Anna. 2019. "Making Good Meat: From Draft Animal to Local Speciality." *Gastronomica* 19(1): 94–95.

———. 2024. "Making Local Specialities: Food, Place and Value in Istria." PhD diss., SOAS University of London.

Czerny, Sarah. 2018 "A-Pasteurianism in Croatian Dairy Work: Another Form to Human-Microbial Relations." *Canadian Slavonic Papers* 60(3–4): 354–74.

Dunn, Elizabeth C. 2003. "Trojan Pig: Paradoxes of Food Safety Regulation." *Environment and Planning A: Economy and Space* 35(8): 1493–511.

Gabriel, Cynthia. 2005. "Healthy Russian Food Is Not-for-Profit." *Michigan Discussions in Anthropology* 15(1): 183–222.

Galić, Cristian Bruno. 2019. "Obilje okusa, mirisa i doživljaja: Od 18. do 20. listopada U TINJAN STIŽU PRŠUTI IZ DESET EUROPSKIH ZEMALJA." *Glas Istre*. Retrieved July 2024 from https://www.glasistre.hr/istra/obilje-okusa-mirisa-i-dozivljaja-od-18-do-20-listopada-u-tinjan-stizu-prsuti-iz-deset-europskih-zemalja-599333.

Gille, Zsuzsa. 2016. *Paprika, Foie Gras, and Red Mud: The Politics of Materiality in the European Union*. Bloomington: Indiana University Press.

Graf, Katharina. 2015. "Beldi Matters: Negotiating Proper Food in Urban Moroccan Food Consumption and Preparation." In *Halal Matters: Islam, Politics and Markets in Global Perspective*, edited by Florence Bergeaud-Blackler, Johan Fischer, and John Lever, 72–90. London: Routledge.

Jung, Yuson. 2014. "Ambivalent Consumers and the Limits of Certification: Organic Foods in Postsocialist Bulgaria." In *Ethical Eating in the Postsocialist and Socialist World*, edited by Yuson Jung, Jakob A. Klein, and Melissa L. Caldwell, 93–115. Berkeley: University of California Press.

Kocković Zaborski, Tanja. 2018. "Transformacija istarske prehrambene tradicije u turističkim seoskim gospodarstvima (Transformation of Istrian food tradition in rural touristic farms)". PhD diss., University of Zadar, Croatia. Retrieved July 2024 from https://urn.nsk.hr/urn:nbn:hr:162:134430.

Leitch, Alison. 2000. "The Social Life of Lardo: Slow Food in Fast Times." *Asia Pacific Journal of Anthropology* 1(1): 103–18.

Matijevic, Petra, and Zofia Boni. 2019. "Introduction: Losing Appetite for the EU? Tensions around Food in Central and Eastern Europe." *Appetite* 140 (September): 305–8.

Mincyte, Diana. 2009. "Self-Made Women: Informal Dairy Markets in Europeanizing Lithuania." In *Food & Everyday Life in the Postsocialist World*, edited by Melissa L. Caldwell, 78–100. Bloomington: Indiana University Press.

Mroczkowska, Joanna. 2019. "Pork Politics: The Scales of Home-Made Food in Eastern Poland." *Appetite* 140 (September): 223–30.

Paxson, Heather. 2010. "Locating Value in Artisan Cheese: Reverse Engineering Terroir for New-World Landscapes." *American Anthropologist* 112(3): 444–57.

Samanani, Farhan, and Johannes Lenhard. 2023 [2019]. "House and Home." In *The Open Encyclopedia of Anthropology*, edited by Felix Stein. Facsimile of the first edition in *The Cambridge Encyclopedia of Anthropology*. Retrieved July 2024 from https://www.anthroencyclopedia.com/entry/house-and-home.

Šišović, Davor. 2021. *Istarski Pršut*. Tinjan: Udruga Proizvođača Istarskog Pršuta. Retrieved July 2024 from https://www.istarski-prsut.eu/.

Smith, Robin, and Cristina Grasseni. 2020. "Ambivalent Solidarities: Food Reconfigurations in Croatia and Italy." *Anthropology Today* 36(1): 12–16.

"Tri Dana Istarske Klobasice Po Starinksi; Prvi put se ocjenjuju i tradicionalne istrijanske kobasice iz kućne radinosti." 2019. Glas Istre, 26 January. Retrieved July 2024 from https://www.glasistre.hr/pula/tri-dana-istarske-klobasice-po-starinskipo-prvi-puta-se-ocjenjuju-i-tradicionalne-istrijanske-kobasice-iz-kucne-radinosti-579799.

Trubek, Amy B. 2008. *The Taste of Place: A Cultural Journey into Terroir*. Berkeley: University of California Press.

Welz, Gisela. 2015. *European Products: Making and Unmaking Heritage in Cyprus*. New York: Berghahn.

West, Harry G. 2013. "Appellations and Indications of Origin, Terroir, and the Social Construction and Contestation of Place-Named Foods." In *The Handbook of Food Research*, edited by Anne Murcott, Warren Belasco, and Peter Jackson, 209–28. London: Bloomsbury.

———. 2022. "Terroir Products: A Movable Heritage Feast?" *Review of Agricultural, Food & Environmental Studies* 103(1): 1–27.

EUR-Lex. 2015. "Publication of an Application Pursuant to Article 50(2)(a) of Regulation (EU) No 1151/2012 of the European Parliament and of the Council on Quality Schemes for Agricultural Products and Foodstuffs." *Official Journal of the European Union*, C 186/9. Retrieved 8 April 2025 from https://eur-lex.europa.eu/legal-content/GA/TXT/?uri=CELEX:52015XC0605(01).

CHAPTER 7

From Terroir to Viticultural Bricolages

Facing Environmental Challenges in Burgundy

Marion Demossier

Introduction

On 22 September 2021, during a visit to one of the Burgundian domains[1] that I first studied more than thirty years ago, I witnessed a heated discussion between a father, Vincent,[2] in his sixties, and his youngest son, Clément, in his thirties. Several opinions were expressed, with a clear generational divide, around the need to adapt, or not, to possible climate change scenarios, and on the reality of climate change. This conversation was not, in itself, so remarkable considering that the wine profession is well known for having climate change sceptics among its members. Later in that year I had the opportunity to discuss with Clément the nature of the altercation I had witnessed, which had by then been fully resolved. As Clément commented: "We talked about the transmission of the domain, so a few things needed to be agreed on, especially in terms of giving me leeway for rethinking wine production. I have lots of questions about what we have been doing."

This vignette alerted me to the peculiarity of terroir viticulture and how the production of labor is largely conditioned by a wide range of factors contributing to what Anna Krzywoszynska (2015) refers to as the management of uncertainty. In the context of a changing climate, these uncertainties have become more challenging due to the greater frequency of extreme meteorological events and the extent of knowledge now required to maintain existing levels of quality wine production. Moreover, a generational divide often opposes two very different views of the world of wine. On the one hand, that of the conventional viticulture associated with the AOC (*Appellation d'Origine Contrôlée*),[3] and, on the other, that of the new regime of viticultural adaptation where risks, uncertainties, and innovation are common alongside environmental consciousness, calling into question terroir as the relationship between place and taste.

By terroir ideology I refer to the national construction of a particular relationship established between place, taste, and people (Bohling 2018; West 2022), which became the cornerstone of French viticultural modernization during the 1930s and served consequently as a model for quality food standards. In Burgundy where I conducted my long-term fieldwork (Demossier 2018), this ideology established through highly controlled wines supposed to taste a particular way each year and reflecting the taste of place rely on the use of fertilizers and pesticides that were part of the modernization that French vineyards had to embrace following the spread of viticultural diseases and pests at the end of the nineteenth century. The AOC system based upon the connection between place, taste, and quality has been locally defined through a list of specifications and reference to *usages locaux, loyaux, et constants* (local, fair, and constant practices) often inherited from nineteenth-century scientific knowledge (e.g., the Guyot method of pruning or yields). It provided the foundation for a monocultural and viticultural model of excellence incarnated by scientific rationality and progress through typicity (taste and place controlled each year through the AOC syndicates), which inspired a model of terroir viticulture. The environmental shift of the 1970s has come to increasingly question this true expression of place through a more environmentally caring focus on place and the plant.

Most of the current literature on wine and climate change conflates the environmental shift of the 1970s with climate change adaptation, even though they need to be analytically separated. The organic movement developed in opposition to the rise of agroindustry in the immediate postwar period and later developed in viticulture to include a range of organically oriented groups from biodynamic wines to *vins nature* (Bivar 2018; Pineau 2019).[4] Climate change adaptation, on the other hand, took its impetus from the 2015 Paris agreement as a top-down agenda promoted by climatologists, activists, and viticultural experts. It is only recently, with the definition of climate change adaptation in viticulture, that the notion of risk has taken on another meaning, implying the constant necessity for wine producers to question their existing cultural practices in the face of more frequent and economically challenging climatic accidents.

Environmental shift and climate change adaptation had a specific resonance[5] in the case of the wines from Burgundy where the terroir model serves as a global reference (Demossier 2011, 2018). Terroir came to be closely associated with wine production at a time when the AOC model started to emerge in France as a result of economic, political, social, and cultural upheavals in the context of the 1930s economic depression. It is worth noting that the AOC is the historical product of the negotiations led by collectives of local producers grouped into AOC syndicates that claimed a product's typicity and its relationship to the natural and human factors of place (Barham 2003; Jacquet 2009; Fourcade 2012) as a way of fighting frauds. Wine producers within the AOC have to conform strictly to the specifications (known as *cahier des charges*) they have agreed upon if they want to be able to claim the label. For those unhappy with the AOC system, changing the rules has proven to be difficult, even impossible,[6] to achieve, obliging them to join the Vin de France category.[7]

Terroir will be the starting point of our investigation through its legal definition, but also in its unbounded, dynamic, and transnational nature (see Pope and West as well as Staples in this volume). This chapter seeks to question the ontologies of terroir (from work to care) by examining how different historical socioeconomic contexts produce diverse conditions for individual kinds of environmental engagement and how they shape care ontologies. My argument is that different care ontologies are ethnographically observable and that they contribute to both the collective shift toward the care for the plant and how producers craft their individual understanding of place and taste. For the conventional wine producers, working the land (*travailleurs de la vigne*) is the core value of their professional identity. The emphasis is placed on direct contact with vines, hard labor, and the micro-knowledge they have acquired of their plots. Work in this context refers to both the legacy of their social emancipation through productive ownership of vineyards and the terroir model of conventional viticulture. This model (see also Jung's chapter, this volume, for the importance of social imaginary of place in relation to taste and the Bulgarian discussion over quality) is now facing scrutiny from younger wine producers eager to embrace the environmental turn while adapting to climate change. For the more environmentally engaged older wine producers and the younger generations that have been able to acquire more formal education,[8] caring has become the leitmotif of their viticultural approach and practices. The concept of care is defined by scholars working on the study of wine production as a careful observation of the plant as well as a sense of responsibility for its well-being or health (Krzywoszynska 2015; Boke 2020; Foyer, Hermesse, and Hecquet 2020). These areas of tensions are what I seek to explore in order to better comprehend the nature of environmental engagement and its impact on the place of taste.

From Work to Care: Shifting Environmental Narratives and Practices to a Postindustrial Context of Climate Change Adaptation

I refer to the term *bricolage* in the title of this chapter, partly inspired by Claude Lévi-Strauss's definition of *bricolage* (1962) as the skill of using whatever is at hand and recombining them to create something new. The term has been employed in relation to natural wine production (Blanc, Chartier, and Cohen 2022) but needs to be applied more broadly. It seeks to capture the wider range of viticultural alternatives that producers engage with, in the context of climate change adaptation, and how knowledge is socially constructed. I seek to adopt a long-term historical approach that draws upon an ethnographic close-up focusing on three generations of wine producers and how they understand, feel, and engage with wine production, science, and the environment to produce the taste of place.

Two different case studies—Lucien, a retired conventional male winegrower, and Jeanine, a female well-established leader—will be explored in more depth in this section to engage with the shift in narrative and practices from work (Lucien) to care (Jeanine). Despite their respective domains being only a few miles apart, Lucien and Jeanine share very little in terms of their everyday life, even though they are located in the same area of production. They produce different AOCs, belong to distinct AOC syndicates, and are far apart in terms of their viticultural education and training. They might possibly have met each other at regional wine events, but they are divided on the definition of terroir. If their identities as wine producers refer to different generations and agricultural approaches (one conventional and the other nonconventional),[9] they remain both extremely vocal on viticultural matters. Moreover, they incarnate the historical shift between work and care.

For older Burgundian winegrowers, working the land has been key to their experiential knowledge and the construction of a distinct professional identity facilitated by their increasing recognition as wine artisans, a process encapsulated in their slow socioeconomic emancipation from a wine market dominated by the local *négociants* (wine merchants) (Demossier 2011, 2018; Arceño 2022). Incarnated by the symbolic visible materiality of the *tracteur enjambeur* (grapple tractor), these older producers embraced modernity expressed through mechanization. Working both outside and in the cellar, their professional identity was synonymous with the everyday working life of the *vigneron* (here I emphasize the term *winegrower* as incarnating the key figure of French terroir viticulture). Mechanization and agricultural modernization facilitated the establishment of this conventional form of monoculture, which is rooted in terroir ideology and obsessed with economic rationality and the control of pests and diseases. This is visually incarnated through the aesthetic landscape of *belles vignes* ("beautiful vines," an expression often used by older wine producers), presenting carefully ordered rows of well-manicured and neat vineyards. From the 1970s onward, the rise of tourism and greater technical developments such as bottling *à la propriété* (on site) opened up new opportunities for winegrowers, defined around specific ethical values attached to physically working the land (Demossier 2011, 2018; Compagnonne 2014). Most of their vineyards were relatively small in size and required labor-intensive horticultural skills.

As Lucien, a well-reputed and now retired *vigneron* in his eighties, explained to me: "To my knowledge I am the fifth generation of winegrowers thanks to family inheritance, and viticulture has been my main preoccupation and passion throughout my working life." This enduring relationship to viticulture through its constant and demanding work is manifold. It covers the whole calendar year and involves soil preparation, repairs and replanting, pruning, lifting of the branches, trimming the vine, and protecting the vine from diseases. Each climatic year might pose different challenges. Attention to weather conditions is crucial to the planning of viticultural activities. The high value that is attached to work and viticultural experience is best encapsulated by a letter I received in 2019 from a retired local producer who wanted me to document his long life as a *vigneron*. His letter started with a flamboyant and illuminating narrative constructed around his care for the plant and his enduring struggle to communicate with science. It is a story I often come across when interviewing producers of his generation, characterized by personal and close contact to the vineyard and the often hard labor punctuating their life since childhood.

Like Lucien and others who witnessed the move to modern viticulture, the environment equated with hard labor, seasonal and climatic variations, and the memory of difficult vintages requiring constant adaptation to seasons and meteorological variation. The environment was described by wine producers like Lucien as something to control and manage both through hard labor and the recourse to advice given by sellers of pesticides and fertilizers, who were always on call when disaster struck. Strong sentiments against other wine producers keen to experiment with organic viticulture were encapsulated in comments from Lucien about the laziness of these producers when they allowed the grass to grow between the vine rows. As most of the producers did not have access to viticultural training schools, they had to rely on their parents' and then their own experience to produce their wines with the support of the oenologist. Pleasure and pain epitomized their visceral relationship to the vineyard and wine production (see also Meneley's chapter, this volume, on plant anthropology and how plants are left out of the "species turn"), and these sentiments are captured by Lucien's narrative: "I wanted to voice my feelings about the vineyard after having devoted my life to her, to watch her, to listen to her live and breathe like if she was part of my body, when she suffers, I suffer and when she rewards me, I thank her." This gendered, romanticized, and poetic emotional connection to his vineyards contributes to the narrative associated with the control of the environment and how the feminine humanization of the vineyard transcends labor.

Lucien's attention to detail during his professional life led to quarrels with scientific experts and professional organizations, especially in regard to specific diseases observed in his own vineyards. He loved writing to scientists and provoking debates in local professional circles, and his views were always in tune with the terroir ideology, often unapologetic about the use of fertilizers and other pesticides seen as necessary to fight diseases. For him, respecting the environment is described as engaging with progress so as to preserve the economic viability of the family domain. Furthermore, his lack of formal education was certainly an explanation for his sense of not being heard in the profession when talking about viticultural diseases: "My father did not send me to the local viticultural school. He wanted to teach me the work of the winegrower, he loved to show me examples of poor viticultural practices from students coming out of the viticultural school." On several levels, Lucien embodies the commonsense attitudes of a terroir wine producer, with a solid empirical knowledge of the vineyard and a good understanding of practical winemaking, but no great interest in taste. For him, terroir is a concept wrapped up with a conventional agriculture, and it offers a way to manage uncertainties and risks in a more stable climatic environment. Today he remains extremely skeptical of the younger generations and sees some of them as only interested in profit and personal reputation. He is also wary of the organic wine producers' movement, which he sees as unreliable and not scientifically grounded.

At the other extreme of the viticultural spectrum we have the example of Jeanine, whom I first met in the 1990s. She is an organically committed producer involved in the local professional landscape and eager to engage with the family domain, located at the edge of the emblematic Côte d'Or vineyards. Jeanine, who obtained degrees in Agronomy and Oenology, is well known and respected outside of Burgundy, and she is one of those rare female leaders who have played an important role in bridging viticulture with science and critically engaging with terroir specifications. She can be described as a radical and caring wine producer in the sense that she is proposing "other arrangements of the possible" (Arora and Van Dyck 2021: 255), and she also emphasizes constant care as the way forward as far as viticultural matters are concerned. Her narrative is one of embodied experiences, ongoing experimentation, and a call for alternative viticulture. For Jeanine, environmental care is seen as the care for the plant, and its productive outcome the wine, and this is paramount to her professional identity as a female wine producer. Over the years, I have met with her and, more recently, her equally engaging and well-educated husband to discuss matters related to terroir. I have also been able to follow her on Facebook, where she posts about her viticulture experiments that are central to her radical care of the vineyard. For Jeanine, terroir and the AOC have always been constraining, and she has been part of a group of French wine producers eager to engage with the INAO (Institut National des Appellations d'Origine) and reform the understanding of typicity (Demossier 2011).

Lucien and Jeanine exemplify some of the dominant positions encountered in the field, especially as far as conventional and nonconventional viticulture are concerned. If Lucien believes that his generation did know it all in terms of weather and climate change, Jeanine is more nuanced and careful when reflecting on her own approach and practices, and she refutes any labels given to her. I would argue that Jeanine has over the years cultivated a skilled vision (Grasseni 2018: 269) defined as "the result of a complex relationship between attention, habit, representation and a broad understanding of history and context." The relatively recent and rapid economic success of the terroir story in Burgundy has shifted the meanings and values attached to working the land to a more refined and piecemeal engagement with the environment and the site of production defined through care. Younger generations have different sets of values with an emphasis on the management of the winery and making wines, occupations that are less personally labor intensive than going to the vineyard. For some of the younger producers, the vineyard remains the place for producing quality in wines, with a greater focus on caring for the plant; their engagement is, in practice, more limited as they increasingly use an external workforce for some of the key activities. In this context, different types of skills are mobilized, and producing quality wine is often attached to the overall decision-making process defined as more strategic than before, as well as educating the specialist workforce they need rather than facing the harsh reality and nitty-gritty of working the land. This evolution has led to a greater labor division between viticulture, on one hand, and the work of winemaking in the cellar, on the other. It is now comparatively rare that winegrowers combine both of these occupations on an equal footing.

If Jeanine does represent a sort of exception (she is often described as not fitting any box by other producers) in this changing landscape where environmental engagement has been slower compared to other regions, such as the Loire valley or the Beaujolais, she nevertheless illustrates the broader environmental turn. As Clément, the son of Vincent, commented, "I do not agree with everything she says, but it is interesting." Following Jeanine's daily online observations and comments on what matters to the vineyards, one finds it obvious that a new form of political ecology is emphasized and the terroir framework is no longer adequate when facing climate change. For Jeanine, other possible futures are the key to adaptation, "I am studying sustainable solutions (tarps are used to suppress weeds between vines without having to use herbicides), even if it means doing without the AOC if it continues to ban them." Her Facebook page illustrates the ways in which innovation and experimentation have become integrated as part of the search for more sustainable practices, with even the taboo topic of pesticides and their effects on workers' well-being discussed while other matters such as the use of plastic is not part of the conversation. A snapshot presents the site accompanied by Jeanine's comments: "Near the home the test without sulfur[10] or copper continues[11]. Still no oidium-fungi causing disease in plants this morning. . . . What a pleasure to work in a vine that does not burn our skin or nose." While another post describes biodiversity as "some nice encounters: a shell of a snail and of course ladybugs." Of course, her care transforms into a form of activism but has not yet generated a collective response, and she knows how difficult it is to shift the terroir ideology: "Stopping the use of synthetic molecules in viticulture in the short or even medium term: such is the challenge. Or at least the need. . . . Sad to see that big domains and négociants are not very present, in Burgundy as elsewhere."

I have explored how narratives and practices of work and care that have been central to the discursive realms of winegrowers' self-identification have been deployed in different historical contexts and across the generational divide, signifying the emergence of a new political ecology of wine production. At the center of this shift, terroir and its ideology have come to be intensively debated with a clear shift toward care, defined as a more fragmented and reflexive engagement that is not directly associated with human labor. If these terms are still commonplace in the respective generational discourses, they have helped the anthropologist to identify different ontologies and how they are embodied in distinctive visions of place and taste where the terroir ideology is reflexively subverted.

Vines over Wines, Reassembling Nature?

If viticulture is the primary focus of environmental and climatic change adaptation, winemaking remains generally marginalized in winegrowers' discourse. Most of the terroir literature on wine production acknowledges the separation between the work of the vine from the process of making wine. In the Côte d'Or, these two areas were historically connected to differently situated bodies of knowledge and actors, with the *vigneron* being attached to the vine and its cultivation while the *négociant* and the oenologist were, and often still are, in charge of the wine fermentation and the aging process in the cellar. As a result of greater access to higher education, a greater number of producers like Jeanine now combine a solid scientific training in agronomy and oenology.

Yet what transpires from Lucien's writings is how the management of uncertainty was until comparatively recently a more holistic and routine driven approach across both viticulture and winemaking. Under the terroir AOC system, the socially emancipated vigneron had to become progressively more resilient as the development of agronomic and scientific knowledge was becoming central to viticultural modernization. For Lucien, temperature control during winemaking was, for example, a real technical achievement, reassuring the wine producer while enabling him to improve the quality of his wines. But it also rapidly became a source of tension for some producers by giving them the "possibility of playing the sorcerer's apprentice and to distort taste through the use of extreme temperature (changing the taste of place or typicity as expression of terroir)." In the case of Lucien, work gave a moral value to his products that he often describes as typical of the AOC. Jeanine, on the other hand, always emphasized the personality of her wines and how care enables her to be recognized in the finished product. In this rapidly changing technical landscape, both the vineyards and the wines were becoming more controllable, thus less uncertain, and when a crisis emerged, the viticultural expert or the oenologist were called to the rescue. Paradoxically, this period of intense modernization of viticulture is described by the older generation as "the true voice of terroir" mainly because of the moral value of labor and level of direct engagement it required.

It was only in the 1990s that a "reawakening" movement of terroir largely focused on viticulture took place, inspired by the emerging organic wine movement. This trend led progressively to the production of a vast and diverse array of organic wines. It is important to note that the broad category of certified organic is not enough to understand the diversity of practices and philosophies (Ascione et al. 2020: 280) that have emerged globally. In the vast transnational movement attached to organic viticulture, Jeanine is, to some extent, the product of her time, and her peripheral position as a wine producer not initially located in the epicenter of the Côte d'Or vineyards, gave her a critical perspective on terroir. Moreover, her level of education and training made her an invaluable informant for the anthropologist as she moves from science to experimentation while being a kind of activist representing what has been termed the "terroir refusal,"[12] a reference to the argument developed by Saurabh Arora and Barbara Van Dyck (2021), who have argued that the refusal of modern industrial agriculture—here incarnated by the terroir conventional ideology—is an act of radical care.

For Jeanine, environmental adaptation is inscribed in the quest for "real" terroirs, stripped away from the technical and chemically intensive intervention with a clear commitment to "working closer to nature." Her problem with the AOC system is that it does not let wine producers express what she sees as "this true natural shifting terroir" and instead insists on fixed practices and fixed taste. Her Facebook profile is orchestrated around this terroir-refusal activism while playing the cards of rootedness and cosmopolitanism. She is one of the rare producers I have met who has expressed ongoing concerns about her workforce and how the workers need to be protected from phytosanitary treatments on site when no other solution can be used to fight certain diseases such as oidium. Equally, she works with the local university climatologist on a number of projects, such as delaying the pruning period to manage the frost: "This year it has been effective to fight frost." Another experiment has been to test the effect of seaweed against heat stress to the plant: "Brown seaweed has always been used as fertilizer. In this case, we use its resistance to stress, which can be transmitted to plants on simple contact. We use it every fifteen to twenty days. We might have to complete by using sulfur or other chemicals in case of strong reaction from the plant."

Unlike Lucien, Jeanine manages uncertainties confidently with the scientific knowledge she has acquired, especially in viticulture but equally in oenology, and despite not working the land directly herself, she emphasizes how managing her team of workers remains a challenge. Yet she is always attending the vineyards with her scientific gaze (Brice 2014). She describes her winemaking as "traditional," but with an emphasis on reducing the use of SO_2 (sulfur dioxide), both during fermentation and in the cellar. Most of her network, unlike Lucien who has remained defined by the village and the AOC syndicate all his life, has been built beyond Burgundy through networks of like-minded producers and consumers, notably in Japan. The importance of viticultural networks in Burgundy has been well documented (Compagnonne 2014), but my ethnographic evidence suggests that individual singularity and bricolage are important characteristics associated with local wine production. Jeanine's market and clients are also believers in her viticultural posture. On several occasions she cited Nicolas Joly, the Loire valley winegrower and leader of the biodynamic wine movement, as an inspiration in the terroir-refusal movement. Moreover, her leading role at local and national level is characterized by her unique positioning between scientific and nonscientific approaches to viticulture at a time where conflicts and tensions are pretty intense among different organically friendly branches of the wine movement and between science and wine production, which are always in tension especially as viticulture is concerned.

Another illustration of the fragmentation of the viticultural realm in relation to the environmental turn and the rise of care as a "terroir refusal" is provided by Clément, the viticulturist cited in the introduction. Attending a climate change conference with him on 8 April 2022, at the local viticulture school, where he received his viticultural training, we discussed some of the changes he wished to implement on his domain. For Clément, the issue of biodiversity and the reintroduction of other plant species around his vineyards is central to the ecological well-being of his vines. The major obstacle he cites relates to the specifications of the AOC Vosne-Romanée, where some of his best plots are located. The minimum density specified by the AOC is set at a very high level and leaves little room for biodiversity: "The vines have a minimum density at planting of 9,000 vines per hectare, with a spacing between the rows which cannot be greater than 1.25 meters and a spacing between feet on a same rank which cannot be less than 0.5 meters."

Trying to find new regenerative solutions, Clément and a few other producers have started to join different groups such as Ver de Terre Production.[13] They have also organized local pruning sessions led by Marceau Bourdarias[14] (slow and careful pruning with a strong emphasis on the care and well-being of the plant, which contrasts with conventional pruning as taught in viticultural schools), as well as attended forestry and biodiversity events. Their thinking has started to snowball, and more domains have joined them in their quest for ecological renewal, although the AOC legal framework is still limiting environmental innovation.

Conclusion

Burgundy offers an original example of how a particular historical and socioeconomic configuration might lead to different engagements and relational mobilization around terroir. Yet this ideology has been increasingly questioned, and environmental challenges are now leading to the interrogation of the foundations of these quality-driven normative rules. Local debates now focus on viticultural practices and reveal the growing heterogeneity of experimental practices and engagement with the environmental shift. Unconventional wines with different tastes produced by a new generation of producers inspired by the environmental turn are seeking to escape the dogmatic definition of terroir and its associated standardization. Building on a wide range of unconventional practices and discourses, which are then mobilized for their own individual ethical engagement with wine production, the market influences a radical rethinking of the relationship between the different components of terroir, especially as far as taste and place are concerned against the broader environmental shift. The taste of place becomes then a place for environmental creativity and debates and what Paxson (2010: 445) has described, in relation to US cheese production, as "reverse engineering" terroir, where producers "think backward from European ideal types" and "create place though environmental stewardship and rural economic revitalization." Unlike the organic tea planters in India analyzed by Kumpf (2020) who use taste to assess soil conditions and climatic changes and to apply organic practices accordingly, wine producers in Burgundy are increasingly adapting through bricolages to climate change. By reinvesting critically and creatively the ideal type of terroir, producers radicalized and polarized their positionings against the conventional and dogmatic framework of terroir, introducing more fluidity and flexibility in the taste of place.

Wine producers are increasingly reflecting on terroir ideology and its monoculture, seeking to reintegrate the plant in their mode of production following three decades of intensive small-scale agriculture. They are, however, equally keen to embrace scientific innovation and experimental creative bricolages that contribute to the production of wine as an artisanal and singular commodity (with the producer's signature). These new orientations could be defined as a combination of the global agrarian, environmental, and social values they seek to engage with through the crafting of their singularization as artists in a market economy. Unlike in Umbria (Ascione et al. 2020), these wine producers cultivate a form of individual singularity enshrined in the market economy of the region and new environmental conversations by contesting terroir while experimenting with sustainability through composite bricolages. When discussing culture and the environment in the light of Malinowski's iconic text "Coral Gardens," the anthropologist Mauro van Aken (2016) has called for the reintegration of futures in our array of ethnographic tools, "not as scenarios of predictions" but as a form of radical refusal that would "perceive, imagine and incorporate the future" in practices in relation to nonhuman agents. The time is ripe for wine producers to go beyond terroir and open new and creative environmental avenues to question ethical ontologies of wine as a global commodity.

Acknowledgments

I would like to thank in particular Guntra Aistara, James Staples, and the editors Anna Colquhoun and Katharina Graf for their generous comments.

Marion Demossier is Professor of French and Social Anthropology at the University of Southampton. She has conducted fieldwork in France, Switzerland, Zambia, New Zealand, and the UK. She is currently writing a book on wine environmental futures and has extensively published on terroir, wine culture, and heritage. She is also interested in ethnography and interdisciplinarity and contributes to the blog Debating Ethnography.

Notes

1. By domain, I refer to the local winery or unit of production that is the norm in Burgundy coexisting alongside the *négociants* (wine merchants). Often it is composed of a house and buildings dedicated to wine production and sale and includes a composite patchwork of vineyards from the surrounding villages. Most domains own a range of plots covering a much wider geographical area than the village in which they are located. The vineyards might include *grands crus*, but also *premiers crus* or AOC villages. For more details, see Demossier (2018: 45).
2. All interlocutors' names are pseudonyms.
3. AOC is short for *Appellation d'Origine Contrôlée* and refers to standards set for wines made in France. There are 363 AOCs for wine and spirits in France, which control everything from how the grapes are grown to what wine varieties are in the bottle.
4. Unlike conventional viticulture, organic viticulture designates a set of agricultural practices excluding the use of products derived from synthetic chemistry. Yet in viticulture the definition of "organic" practices refers to a wide range of technical choices and ideologies, and there is no strict definition attached to it. For further information, see the OIV International Organisation of Vine and Wine: https://www.oiv.int/ (retrieved 11 December 2024).
5. The vineyard area under organic cultivation, and in conversion, is estimated to be around 14 percent of those in Burgundy (150 domains in 2010, but growing), while *biodynamie*, which has become fashionable among the most reputed domains, has gained in popularity (Pineau 2019).
6. The only example I am aware of is attached to the Bordeaux wine region and the use of a specific grape variety more resistant to climate change that was introduced in the specifications a few years ago with the rule of not allowing more than a certain percentage in its use. Any possible demand from the AOC producers requires validation by the governing body called the INAO (the Institut National de l'Origine et de la Qualité). This branch of the French Ministry of Agriculture ensures quality for wine, cheese, and other food products.
7. Vin de France is a designation for table wine from France that has been in use since 2010, when it started to replace the former vin de table category. Vin de France wines may indicate grape variety (for example Chardonnay or Merlot) and vintage on the label, but they are not labeled by region or appellation—they are labeled only as coming from France.

8. Increasingly wine education in agronomy and oenology has become one of the factors of tensions in the circulation of knowledge among the youngest wine producers. According to the most recent INSEE (The National Institute of Statistics and Economic Studies) survey of 2016, levels of education and training have increased across generations, with 35 percent of current wine producers having pursued higher education. For the forty- to sixty-year-olds, nine out of ten have been educated beyond college, with one-third of the total having received a basic standard agricultural level (professional baccalaureate) and three out of ten having pursued their education after the bachelors' degree. The *lycée viticole* (regional viticultural college known as *la viti*) in Beaune remains the point of reference in terms of conventional viticultural training.
9. By conventional I mean a viticulture that combats vine diseases and pests mainly through regular preventative spraying with pesticides without actually controlling the development of diseases or infestation by pests. The nonconventional label covers a wide range of practices that seek to exclude the application of all synthetic chemical pesticides as well as artificially produced fertilizers and herbicides.
10. Sulfur is one of Earth's elements, and its primary use in viticulture is to prevent and control powdery mildew infection, which is one of the most prevalent risks to vineyards. Mildew is a fungus, which can be seen on the leaves or on grape clusters as a white or gray powder.
11. The use of sulfur is key to debates surrounding organic practices, it is permitted for use in organic and biodynamic agriculture. In the vineyard, it is visible through the blue spray used ubiquitously on vines to prevent disease, and in the cellar it is often invisible when added to the vines after fermentation.
12. Her work through the local AOC syndicate, the Burgundy Wine Board, and her letters to the INAO are all testimonies to her activism (Demossier 2018).
13. Agroecological group: https://www.verdeterreprod.fr/ (retrieved 11 December 2024).
14. Rayhana Moalemi's PhD research at the University of Strasbourg (Department of Anthropology) focuses on the study of pruning in Alsace and Burgundy.

References

Arceño, Mark-Anthony. 2022. "Vignerons and the Vines: Mediators of Place-Based Identity in Alsace, France." *Social Anthropology* 30(1): 24–44.

Arora, Saurabh, and Barbara Van Dyck. 2021. "Refusal as Radical Care? Moving Beyond Modern Agriculture." *Development* 64: 252–58.

Ascione, Elisa, Jared Belsky, Mackenzie Nelsen, and Manuel Barbato. 2020. "Cultivating Activism through Terroir: An Anthropology of Sustainable Winemakers in Umbria, Italy." *Food, Culture & Society* 23(3): 277–95.

Barham, Elizabeth. 2003. "Translating Terroir: The Global Challenge of French AOC Labeling." *Journal of Rural Studies* 19(1): 127–38.

Bivar, Venus. 2018. *Organic Resistance: The Struggle over Industrial Farming in Postwar France.* Chapel Hill: The University of North Carolina Press.

Blanc, Emmanuelle, Denis Chartier, and Aurélien Gabriel Cohen. 2022. "Des vivants, des vins: Bricolages polyphoniques." In *Les Esprits Scientifiques: Savoirs et Croyances dans les Agricultures Alternatives*, edited by Jean Foyer, Aurélie Chauné, and Valérie Boisvert, 285–320. Saint-Martin-d'Hères: UGA Editions Web.

Bohling, Joseph. 2018. *The Sober Revolution: Appellation Wine and the Transformation of France.* Ithaca: Cornell University Press.
Boke, Charis. 2020. "Care." In *Anthropocene Unseen*, edited by Cymene Howe and Anan Padia, 71–75. Santa Barbara: Punctum Books.
Brice, Jeremy. 2014. "Attending to Grape Vines: Perceptual Practices, Planty Agencies and Multiple Temporalities in Australian Viticulture." *Social and Cultural Geography* 15(8): 942–65.
Compagnonne, Claude. 2014. "Les viticulteurs bourguignons et le respect de l'environnement." *Revue Française de Sociologie* 2(55): 319–58.
Demossier, Marion. 2011. "Beyond Terroir: Territorial Construction, Hegemonic Discourses and French Wine Culture." *Journal of the Royal Anthropological Institute* 17(4): 685–705.
———. 2018. *Burgundy: A Global Anthropology of Place and Taste.* New York: Berghahn.
Fourcade, Marion. 2012. "The Vile and the Noble: On the Relation between Natural and Social Classifications in the French Wine World." *Sociological Quarterly* 53(4): 524–45.
Foyer, Jean, Julie Hermesse, and Corentin Hecquet. 2020. "Quand les actes agricoles sont au care et au compagnonnage: L'exemple de la biodynamie." *Anthropologica* 62(1): 93–104.
Grasseni, Cristina. 2018. "Understanding Skill, Food and Field." *Interdisciplinary Science Review* 43(3–4): 164–279.
Jacquet, Olivier. 2009. *Un siècle de construction du vignoble bourguignon: Les organisations vitivinicoles de 1884 aux AOC.* Dijon: Éditions Universitaires de Dijon.
Krzywoszynska, Anna. 2015. "What Farmers Know: Experiential Knowledge and Care in Vine Growing." *European Society for Rural Sociology* 56(2) (April): 290–310.
Kumpf, Desiree. 2020. "Organic Taste and Labor on Indian Tea Plantations." *Social Anthropology* 28(4): 789–802.
Lévi-Strauss, Claude. 1962. *La Pensée Sauvage.* Paris: Librairie Plon.
Paxson, Heather. 2010. "Locating Value in Artisan Cheese: Reverse Engineering Terroir for New-World Landscapes." *American Anthropologist* 112(3): 444–57.
Pineau, Christelle. 2019. *La corne de vache et le microscope: Le vin "nature," entre sciences, croyances et réalités.* Paris: Éditions la Découverte.
Van Haken, Mauro. 2016. "'Coral gardens' and their Denials: Culture, Environment and the Uncertainties of the Future." *Anthropologia* 3(1): 90–109.
West, Harry G. 2022. "Terroir Products: A Movable Heritage Feast?" *Review of Agricultural, Food & Environmental Studies* 103(1): 1–27.

CHAPTER 8

Food Producers and Place Brands in Contemporary Japan

Greg de St. Maurice

Encountering *Chiiki Burando* for the First Time

In 2012 I traveled to Northeastern Japan to study how the provenance of agricultural products mattered to Japanese consumers in the aftermath of March 2011's earthquake, tsunami, and nuclear power plant destabilization. The most serendipitous aspect of the trip occurred after the last day of research had ended and I had missed the last train to Tokyo and was stuck in a city I had not intended to visit. Fortunately, I found an inexpensive place to stay. Unfortunately, the room stank of cigarettes, and through the thin walls I could hear someone in the room to my left snoring and the TV in the room to my right. On a whim, I stuffed questionnaires in my bag and dropped by an inviting-looking bar nearby. When I told the bartender why I was in town, he offered to pass out my questionnaires to the other customers. By the end of the night, every single patron in the room had filled one out and spoken to me about their answers.

The most enlightening insight was that while my questionnaire asked specifically about place of origin/provenance (*sanchi*), several respondents in our conversations afterward instead used the word *burando*, the Japanese word for brand. One woman even referred to the word *burando* in her written response, though the word appeared nowhere in my survey. I then realized that the concepts I had been using—*sanchi*, for instance—were not the ones that resonated most with Japanese people when it came to the relationship between food and place.

I subsequently came to understand that *chiiki burando*, often translated as "place brands," are actually quite commonly used in the discourse about food and place in Japan. This incident changed the course of my doctoral research: my dissertation zeroed in on the Kyoto brand—or more accurately, Kyoto's brands—for food and agricultural products. The word *terroir* exists in the Japanese language, but when talking about the relationship between food and place, people use the phrase *chiiki burando* with far greater frequency.

This chapter draws on interviews and participant observation with producers of local agricultural and food products that I have conducted since 2012. It is informed by the field research I conducted in Kyoto, where producers benefit from an existing place brand with great appeal, and Miyagi Prefecture, which has witnessed recent place-branding efforts in which producers played key roles.

Examples like Kyoto vegetables and Kobe beef demonstrate how place names are used to market and sell foodstuffs. Such names imply that merely because the vegetables or beef come from these places or carry their names, they are different and more valuable than similar products that come from places that carry little meaning or are unidentified (though many foodstuffs are differentiated by whether they are domestically produced or imported from abroad).

For Japanese producers, *chiiki burando* offer a flexible means to derive value from communicating to consumers information about the locations that have played a culturally meaningful role in a food's journey. This chapter illustrates the advantages of the proliferation and variety of *chiiki burando* in Japan, namely that there is space for virtually any producer to identify, join, or create a place brand suitable for expressing how place matters to their product. Some producers—and even some of the very producers who have contributed to the creation or strengthening of specific place brands—also see disadvantages and choose to sell their products directly to consumers via informal personal brands. This strategy can entail building onto or strengthening existing place brands rather than separating from them or coming into conflict with them. In the latter part of this chapter, I turn to interviews I conducted with two producers from Miyagi Prefecture: Miura Takahiro,[1] a farmer famous for his *seri* (Japanese parsley), and Aizawa Futoshi, a prize-winning *nori* (a type of seaweed) fisherman.

Place Brands in Japan

Food and place have been linked in Japan for a long time. Seventeenth-century haiku master Matsuo Basho wrote: *yamabuki ya / Uji no hoiro no / niou toki* (Yellow mountain roses / When the ovens at Uji give off / The fragrance of tea leaves) (Shirane 1992: 104). Strikingly, in the original Japanese Basho does not employ the word "tea" or "leaves." Uji was so strongly associated with tea that his audience understood exactly what fragrance the haiku evoked with the mere mention of Uji's ovens.

In Japan, people continue to associate places with specific foods and foods with specific places. Make your way down a grocery store aisle and you will come across items whose provenance is displayed in large print, perhaps even as part of the product's name. In the produce section, you may see signs or labels for Naruto kintoki sweet potatoes (from Tokushima Prefecture), garlic from Aomori, and Arita mikan (citrus from Saga Prefecture). I expect you have heard of Kobe beef, but in Japan, Matsusaka, Tajima, and Hida are perhaps even more famous. Processed foods also advertise the use of place-specific products, from Hokkaido-style instant ramen to popcorn made with soy sauce from Kyushu.

Case studies and analyses from other parts of the world reveal that places and foods with little else in common share certain traits when it comes to the intersection of place branding and food and agricultural products. In Alberta, Canada, Gwendolyn Blue has shown that beef became a dominant symbol for the province and a touchstone for regional identity due to effective government and industry promotion efforts that strengthened following an outbreak of bovine spongiform encephalopathy and a drop in exports (Blue 2008). Stakeholders in the Danish town of Løgstør, meanwhile, turned to place branding as a strategy for reviving the local economy, holding mussels festivals to communicate local uniqueness to outsiders (Blichfeldt and Halkier 2012). Studies such as these have documented efforts to either add value to foods using place as a defining characteristic or to use local foods to increase the appeal of certain places.

What is striking about place brands for food and agricultural products in Japan is their ubiquity and reach. They exist at scalar levels from neighborhood to nation-state, with brands overlapping and even nested within one another. But what is perhaps most distinctive about place brands in Japan is that the term *chiiki burando* is more inclusive and flexible than the term "place brand" is in the English-language literature on place branding.

Based on my fieldwork in Japan, I identify two different but connected types of place brands that draw on two different meanings of the word *brand*. Look up *brand* in the Merriam-Webster dictionary and you will find a series of definitions related to how products or people are perceived, their reputation, and the "aura" they have within a given society. These definitions include: "a class of goods identified by name as the product of a single firm or manufacturer," "a characteristic or distinctive kind," and "a public image, reputation, or identity conceived of as something to be marketed or promoted." These bear similarities with Grant McCracken's discussion of brands as "bundles of meaning" that add value (McCracken 1993). Indeed, in contemporary societies, we distinguish people, places, and things from one another based on distinct impressions or perceptions we have of them in ways that impact their valuation. These are discursively created, shared to a considerable degree, and changeable. Place brand scholars Sebastian Zenker and Erik Braun recognize this in their definition of "place brand," considered a standard one for the field: "a network of associations in the consumers' mind based on the visual, verbal, and behavioural expression of a place, which is embodied through the aims, communication, values, behaviour, and the general culture of the place's stakeholders and the overall place design" (in Braun, Kavaratzis, and Zenker 2013: 109).

In much of the English-language literature place branding is presented as the purview of professional marketers, government officials, and other elites referred to as "place brand managers" or "place authorities," with other residents participating, supporting, or resisting. In contrast, in Japan, a wide variety of actors—including agricultural and food producers—are considered to contribute consequentially to the establishment, promotion, and development of place brands. While the term *place branding* emerged in Japan in the 2000s, after the notion had made headway among European and North American scholars and policymakers, it has clearly evolved differently in the Japanese context.

This is possible because of the sheer diversity and flexibility of place brands in Japan. *Chiiki burando* extends further than the notion of "place brand" used by place-branding scholars in that it also refers to products that carry place names and are associated with those place names (like Kyoto traditional vegetables or Kobe beef, for example). Such usage bears similarities with a second set of definitions for "brand," this time related to trademarks. Merriam-Webster includes the following: "a mark made by burning with a hot iron to attest manufacture or quality or to designate ownership" and "a printed mark made for similar purposes." Producers, marketers, and retailers use indices or symbols—no longer simply printed marks, much less ones left by the application of heat to a surface—to differentiate products and services from like others and add value to them. In institutionalized capitalist economies, individuals, groups, and corporations often seek to obtain legal protection of these brands by formally or legally registering them.

Drawing on these two sets of meanings of the word *brand*—and observations of the use of the word in Japan—I identify two different types of place brands: fuzzy and delineated. "Fuzzy" place brands are the auras and reputations associated with places. These can be cultivated but not regulated, owned, or managed by any kind of formal or legal entity. The use of such place brands is loose, and it is unclear who has the right to use such a place brand and who does not. When people say that Kyoto is a powerful brand, they are referring to this type of place brand. And a great variety of actors in a variety of industries make use of this fuzzy brand. Hence the designation "fuzzy." "Delineated place brands," by contrast, consist of legally recognized or delimited names and symbols that use place as an index to differentiate products for marketing and sales purposes and restrict their use to certain individuals or groups.

Fuzzy Place Brands

"Fuzzy place brands" may lack clear boundaries, but they do not matter less than delineated place brands. Indeed, the scholarship on place branding attests that countries, regions, cities, and even neighborhoods invest in place-branding efforts (Avraham and Ketter 2008). London, Vienna, and West Bengal have hired consulting agency Saffron for help with branding, for instance, while South Africa and Finland have turned to Bloom Consulting for expertise on nation branding.

In Japan the consultants at Brand Research Institute provide similar services and publish yearly rankings for prefectural and municipal brand rankings. Kyoto serves as an example of a strong fuzzy place brand. In Brand Research Institute's 2023 surveys, Kyoto Prefecture and Kyoto City were both ranked number two for brand power in their respective categories (behind Hokkaido Prefecture and Sapporo City). Kyoto City and Kyoto Prefecture score highly in terms of name recognition and appeal because of strong associations with history and tradition, more specifically associations with Buddhist temples, geisha, kimono, and the trope of the "ancient imperial capital." Local government officials, advertisers, tourism industry employees, and other stakeholders nurture this image, and it is one that has been actively cultivated since modern times (de St. Maurice 2018; Breen et al. 2020). There is much more to Kyoto, however: multiple Kyotos exist, including Kyoto City, Kyoto Prefecture, and a past that has more dimensions than simply the legacy of an "ancient imperial city," though that is the fuzzy place brand that Kyoto is often reduced to for marketing purposes.

When marketers in Japan strategically deploy fuzzy place brands, they often include elements related to food and drink. Tourist brochures for Kyoto use photos of seasonal heirloom vegetables, *kaiseki* meals, and frothy matcha in fancy tea bowls. For Osaka City, on the other hand, there are often photos of street food or "soul food"—*okonomiyaki* (often translated as "Japanese pancakes"), *takoyaki* (octopus balls), and the like. These representations tend to obscure the complex and seemingly contradictory aspects of local foodscapes (de St. Maurice 2012).

It is not just that places can benefit from strong associations that exist with certain foods. Community stakeholders in places at different scales are intentionally turning to food as a tool important to their larger place-branding strategies. Berg and Sevón (2014) have found that food is now consciously included as a core element in the branding efforts of cities like Stockholm, and wine journalist Esther Mobley (2022) has analyzed Napa Valley's reliance on the wine industry for its brand. Colquhoun's chapter in this volume illustrates how the Istrian region of Croatia has recently turned to food—specifically olive oil, wine, and ham—as a means of attracting tourists and consumers.

In Japan local governments, producers, and other local stakeholders consciously deploy food to engage in fuzzy place branding. Stakeholders in Ishikawa Prefecture's Oku-noto region, for example, use restaurant *domburi* (dishes—like sashimi or tempura or fried meat—served over rice) that somehow showcase "Oku-noto-ness" to promote the area to tourists (Yoshida 2023). Strategies like advertising campaigns and the organization of local festivals are also adopted by communities in other parts of the world. But others have a particularly Japanese context. The *furusato nōzei* (hometown tax) program, for example, is meant to help localities struggling to meet their needs with a dwindling tax base by allowing them to compete for "donations" of nonresidents' tax money (which would otherwise automatically go to the municipalities where those individuals reside) by offering a choice of gifts from different area specialties. A town or city's ability to communicate a compelling place brand linked to specific products can thus affect its financial health and what services it can provide for its residents.

Negative associations can exacerbate a locality's economic challenges. This was evident in the aftermath of the 2011 earthquake, tsunami, and nuclear power plant accident when the circulation of food products—and people—from Northeastern Japan, but especially Fukushima Prefecture, was restricted (Sternsdorff-Cisterna 2015). Radioactivity does not respect geopolitical boundaries, yet municipal, prefectural, and regional boundaries became indices for safety, risk, and pollution. In fact, research I did at the time (including the fieldwork I mentioned at the beginning of this chapter) showed that while many people associated Northeastern Japan with radiation and risk, Western Japan was perceived as safe and secure.

Delineated Place Brands

The second type of place brand I identify includes legally protected or delimited names and symbols that use place as an index to differentiate products for marketing and sales purposes. I call these "delineated place brands." Geographical indications (GIs) fit into this category, though they do not fit into the definition of "place brand" dominant in the Anglophone place-branding literature. In their European-focused work, for instance, Dentoni et al. (2013: 17) explicitly state that unlike GIs, "place brands do not focus on a specific product but on a wide umbrella of products and services offered by a region."

One reason we see an abundance of place brands, and specifically delineated place brands, in Japan is that several different national systems exist for certifying them. Emerging from the historic link between alcohol and taxation is the National Tax Agency's (NTA) GI program for protecting place brands for alcohol. Recognized categories include *Ryūkyū awamori* (a distilled alcohol from Okinawa made with rice), *Satsuma shōchū* (a distilled alcohol from Kagoshima Prefecture made from sweet potatoes), and *Yamagata sake* (sake brewed in Yamagata Prefecture). Rules restrict the ingredients, production methods, and production sites, and outline the certification process. In documents, the NTA frequently uses the term *regional brand.* For instance, in a brochure that explains the system in English, next to a drawing of a consumer a speech bubble reads, "GIs can be taken as a national guarantee. We can choose regional-brand products which are not imitations" (NTA 2023).

The Japan Patent Office (JPO), meanwhile, oversees a system for what it calls "collective regional trademarks" (*chiriteki hyōji*). As of 2023 the JPO says that it officially recognizes 742 collective regional trademarks with the aim of helping communities protect place brands (Japan Patent Office 2023). Uji tea is one example, and while collective regional trademarks are not limited to food and drink products, they do make up a significant portion of registered items.

The system most recently established by a branch of Japan's national government to recognize place brands is the Ministry of Agriculture, Forestry, and Fisheries' (MAFF) system for GIs. It took effect in 2015, and by the end of 2023, 131 items had been registered. The ministry's English-language explanation of its approach reveals similarities and differences with terroir-type approaches: "In Japan, there are many regional brand products which are high quality and have obtained reputation as a result of unique production methods and natural characteristics of the production area such as climate and soil conditions. The GI Act therefore provides a system that the government protects names of such products as Intellectual Property. The GI Act protects the interests of producers through the establishment of GI protection system, thereby contributing to the sound development of the agricultural, forestry and fishery industries and also to ensure the interests of consumers." The mention of "unique production methods" as well as climatic and geological characteristics is in sync with the way that terroir is often articulated for the purposes of GIs. But the text emphasizes the word *brand* rather than the word *terroir*, a choice that echoes the MAFF's overall approach.

As Staples observes (this volume), GIs are characterized by bureaucracy and the performance of "objective" modernity. Delineated place brands depend on formal systems, including legal frameworks and certification processes. GIs like those for Darjeeling tea or Parma ham as well as trademarks that include place names, like Philadelphia Cream Cheese, are delineated place brands. Groups in Japan's Kyoto Prefecture have registered a dazzling number of products through different frameworks for delineated place brands. Among them are Kyoto traditional vegetables, Kyoto pork, and the Manganji sweet pepper (which originated in the Manganji neighborhood of Kyoto's Maizuru City).

Brands of both types overlap and often nest within one another. In Kyoto in particular there is such a profusion of place brands for food and agricultural products that it seems that such place branding could continue almost infinitely. People use the term *chiiki burando* to refer interchangeably to the sets of associations places carry and also to established product names, including GIs. I differentiate the two for three reasons. First, to emphasize that in Japan GIs can be glossed as brands. Second, to expand the focus of this chapter beyond GIs to fuzzy place brands since (1) they create economic possibilities for individual producers and groups unable or unwilling to participate in delineated place brands, and (2) sometimes consumers prefer delineated place brands and their modern institutionalized authority while other times they prefer products marketed or sold via fuzzy place brands, often at lower prices and through more direct channels. Finally, I differentiate between the two because doing so allows us to recognize patterns in the positioning of place brands vis-à-vis one another.

My use of the term *delineated place brand* is not meant, however, to imply that the borders or boundaries at play are simple, stable, static, obvious things (Green 2018). The local—or locality—or bounded places at any scalar level are fashioned and refashioned and experienced in ways that are imbricated in dynamic sociopolitical contexts (Massey 1990). Consider "Edo Tokyo Traditional Vegetables": this brand name includes two different words designating what some might consider to be the "same" place during different historical periods. This name conjures associations with the locality's legacy as a political, economic, and cultural powerhouse since Edo times, thus drawing connections that articulate a history for what is labeled "traditional." The name also points to a key criterion for eligibility in the program: contemporary Tokyo's much broader boundaries. "Edo Tokyo Traditional Vegetables," like vegetables sold through Kyoto Prefecture's Kyō brand, are a contemporary category created to appeal to contemporary consumers in efforts to support producers within today's prefectural boundaries.

Though place brands for food and agricultural products may be sorted into one type or another, brands in the two categories do not exist at a remove from each other. Fuzzy place brands that resonate with consumers facilitate the creation of economically successful delineated place brands. And delineated place brands for foods that become widely known and highly regarded can help to improve a locale's overall reputation. The relationship between food and place in Japan is co-constituted.

Let's return to Kyoto. People throughout Japan talk about Kyoto as a brand, and, again, it scores highly on brand power surveys. People draw on this brand power to differentiate many kinds of products—not only food and agricultural products—from others in the marketplace. Thus, we have Kyō brand vegetables and collective regional trademarks for Kyō tofu, Kyōgashi (Kyoto sweets), and even Kyoto meat. These are all delineated brands (and to adapt Braun and Zenker's terms, they operate as sub-brands under the umbrella that is the fuzzy Kyoto brand). Companies also use the words *Kyoto* or *Kyō* and associated representative icons for items that are in no way officially registered or legally protected as such. Some of the most striking examples I have come across include coffee said to have the "taste of Kyoto," Kyoto-style ramen, Kyoto ketchup, and even a beef obento box bearing the image of a temple pagoda on the outside wrapper (in spite of Buddhism's valorization of a vegetarian diet).

Nested Place Brands

Where regional and prefectural place brands exist for food and agricultural products, you can often also find municipal and even neighborhood place brands for the same types of products. "Kyoto Traditional Vegetables" has been registered as a collective regional trademark through the Japan Patent Office. The Manganji sweet pepper, a Kyoto vegetable, has also been registered on its own as a Ministry of Agriculture, Forestry, and Fisheries GI. Kyoto vegetables like the Manganji pepper, mizuna, and the Kamo eggplant are also sold via Kyoto Prefecture's Kyō Brand. Kamo eggplant, distinctive for their round shape and their slightly sweet, meaty interior, take their name from the Kamigamo neighborhood in Kyoto City, where they have a history of being grown. Kyoto City certifies Kamo eggplant and other vegetable varieties grown within municipal boundaries via its *Shun* (seasonal) *yasai* (vegetable) program. Not to be outdone, a group of farmers in the Kamigamo area also have their own brand for Kamo eggplant, which uses the location of their fields to generate value. Most people in Japan will associate the eggplant with Kyoto—and specifically Kyoto City, but a small segment of consumers considers the Kamo eggplant from Kamigamo to be of higher quality or more authentic and are willing to pay a premium for it.

Because the Kamo eggplant has not been successfully registered as a GI, farmers outside of Kyoto Prefecture can grow the same variety and call it by the same name when selling it. Indeed, a quick search online reveals farmers across the world who claim to grow varieties of "Kyoto vegetables"—including Kamo eggplant—and companies selling seeds or seedlings. These producers do not benefit to the same degree from the fuzzy Kyoto brand, nor do they profit from the authority and authenticity marking existing delineated place brands for Kyoto vegetables.

Beyond Place Brands: Individual Brands

Brands are often equated with a degree of standardization. An experienced consumer knows what to expect when they enter a Starbucks in a city they have never been to before. Similarly, people expect a Guinness beer or a balsamic vinegar from Modena to taste a certain way. While such standardization may be the expectation or ideal in certain respects, it does not necessarily play out that way in practice. The European Parliament has found that products sold using the same or similar brands in different member countries sometimes contain a smaller amount of the primary ingredient or include different ingredients that are thought of as less healthy, for example (European Parliament Research Service 2017). Such discrepancies may frustrate consumers, but they also cause grief for individuals who provide high-quality products that are mixed with and sold alongside lower-quality products bearing the same brand name.

The attraction of place brands for food and agriculture is such that many local producers want to participate in brand programs to take advantage of the price premium the brands are expected to bestow (as well as a degree of pride resulting from official recognition). Some producers, however, feel constrained by the rules, conformity, or institutionalized distribution routes of delineated place brands (like the younger generation of vintners Demossier writes about in her chapter, this volume). If they feel that their products are superior to those sold via established place brands, they may even be compelled to sell them directly to customers via what is essentially their own smaller, and often individual, brands (which they may explicitly talk about as such). Some Kyoto-based Kamo eggplant farmers opt out of participating in delineated place brands altogether in favor of selling them through their own networks, relying on their individual reputations. Some farmers do both. There are farmers who sell branded produce to outsiders while selling unpackaged, unbranded produce directly to regular customers, for example.[2]

This phenomenon is connected to the popularity of "vegetables with a face you can see" (*kao ga mieru yasai*)—the face being the farmer's. As Aoyama et al. (2016) discovered, images of producers and their farms reassure Japanese consumers about the safety and quality of food products. Whether selling their products in person or online, with the requisite photos, producers who maintain individual brands tend to talk about their products, the land or sea, and the community at a degree of scalar intimacy similar to the cheese producers who are the focus of Grasseni's chapter in this volume. Third-generation *nori* fisherman Aizawa Futoshi, based in Northeastern Japan's Miyagi Prefecture, is a prime example.

Nori, a seaweed of the genus Pyropia, has been consumed in Japan at least since the Edo period (Delaney 2007). It is commonly used to wrap sushi rolls or rice balls (*onigiri*), sprinkled on top of foods like *okonomiyaki* and *chirashizushi*, and incorporated into processed foods like rice crackers and potato chips. Most of the *nori* consumed today is *kuronori*, "black" *nori*, which is cultivated (or "farmed" if you prefer) as opposed to harvested wild.

When I asked Aizawa-san questions about the taste of place for *nori* (which some refer to as *merroir*), he explained that the quality and taste of *nori* depend on where it is from and change from year to year, with weather patterns, ocean current shifts, and the like influencing its flavors. Aizawa-san also emphasized the importance of decisions the producer makes at critical junctures. In 2023 he visited a class I teach and brought two kinds of *nori* for students to sample. The first was one he had harvested in January. While no flavoring ingredients had been added, students remarked at how flavorful the *nori* was. The second had the sealike taste of iodine and a dark reddish-purple hue to it that was especially pronounced when held up to the light. Aizawa-san explained that these second sheets contained two different varieties of *nori*: the *kuronori* that consumers are accustomed to eating and an *aonori* (green nori) that had attached itself and grown with the *kuronori*. While most *nori* fishermen would have eradicated the less desirable *aonori*, Aizawa-san likes to draw out its flavors for some of his *nori*. This, he told us, he does very carefully since the *aonori* can easily overtake the *kuronori*, destroying the intended final product. He is interested in expressing seasonality and place, and the end product is one that is a testament to his preferences and skill.

While he frequently mentions seasonality and place in his talks, he does not use a place brand to sell his *nori*. He sells his highest-quality *nori* via his website (and the remainder to wholesalers at local auctions). He uses his name and refers to it as an "individual brand" (*kojin burando*). When first introduced to me as the producer of "the best *nori* in Japan," he declined the title, saying that there is no "best," that what matters is having a diversity of high-quality *nori* from different places harvested by different people. He told me he believes that an "individual brand" is not about a commodity but rather about the producer, their background, and the knowledge and associations consumers have about them.

Miura Takahiro, a well-known producer of the Japanese green called *seri*, also relies on a personal brand. *Seri* (*Oenanthe javanica*, water dropwort, or Japanese parsley) has been grown in his town of Natori for around four hundred years, I was told. By the late twentieth century, *seri* had become a marginalized local crop that was eaten almost exclusively during the winter holiday season. Miura-san was instrumental in transforming it into an ingredient celebrated as local culinary heritage and eaten in hot pot dishes and new specialties from September through May. His network promoted the consumption of fresh, high-quality, and carefully prepared *seri*, roots and all. His efforts have also benefited the more than fifty households that grow it in Natori today (producing most of the prefecture's *seri*). While Miura-san continues to promote local culinary heritage via social media and events, he sells the majority of his *seri* directly to restaurants and consumers, relying on the reputation he has achieved. One reason he says he does this is that he can monitor the restaurants that use his produce, making sure, for example, that they properly clean *seri* roots before serving them in a hot pot dish. He wants to make sure that local *seri*—and especially his own—maintains its brand power. He does not have such oversight over the quality of what other Natori producers grow or the quality of the dishes that other restaurants using local *seri* serve.

Producers like Aizawa-san and Miura-san have become so well known that they might be seen as the farmer equivalent of celebrity chefs. Miura-san regularly appears on television and in print. He maintains an active social media presence. He has been featured on a national public television series aimed at English speakers and graces the cover of a book written by acclaimed chef Okuda Masayuki about noteworthy farmers in Northeastern Japan (Okuda 2015).[3]

For his part, Aizawa-san leads workshops ranging in size from a few participants to nine hundred or so. In 2022 Aizawa-san led around thirty workshops. He has given talks in Europe, Southeast Asia, and the Pacific. A key turning point in his career, as he tells it, was the realization that setting records for winning awards for best *nori* at a young age—second place at twenty-three and first at twenty-eight years old—did not translate to higher prices for his *nori*. It then sunk in that it was becoming more difficult to make a living as a *nori* fisherman despite technological advancements, new scientific knowledge, and fewer competitors. He came to believe that producers today must do more than simply "produce" and "harvest." He says it is also important that they "communicate," namely that they teach about food production and how it is connected to social and ecological conditions. In his workshops he explains that when agricultural land is transformed into industrial, residential, or urban areas, the amount of nutrient-rich runoff that ends up in seascapes decreases, making it more difficult for those seascapes to continue to support varied algae, plant, and animal life. The loss of agricultural land is a significant reason that *nori* harvests have plummeted. The interconnectedness between people and oceans, land and sea that Aizawa-san discusses bears similarities to the "relational interconnections" between landscapes and seascapes that Aistara zeroes in on in her chapter in this volume.

Conclusion

Place brands have tremendous flexibility in Japan. They are used to talk about and market crab, chicken, miso, and even broccoli. They include both precisely articulated entities (delineated place brands) and ambiguous auras (fuzzy place brands). Place brands are often nested within one another, with individual producer brands coexisting with them too. Friction does of course arise between individuals and groups, but these different types of brands demonstrate surprising symbiosis.

For producers, these conditions offer a degree of agency. While delineated place brands exclude producers who do not meet the criteria for joining, the sheer number of Japanese place brands and the variety of systems for establishing them allows for a considerable degree of diversity and inclusion. Some producers choose to rely on fuzzy place brands or develop their own individual brands instead of participating in delineated place brands.

Japanese producers recognize that they can actively work to create and strengthen place brands. In the fall of 2024 I attended an event in Okinawa for new and prospective coffee farmers. When I introduced myself to producers and mentioned my research on place brands, several of them went beyond expressing interest to stating a need for greater place-branding efforts, even encouraging me to return to give them advice on how to proceed. That place brands resonate with producers as a source of agency does not mean that there is no room for other notions, including terroir. In fact, the event's keynote speaker dedicated part of his lecture to explaining the concept of terroir and relating it to coffee. Just as there is room for many individual brands, fuzzy place brands, and delineated place brands to coexist, there is similarly room for multiple concepts that articulate the complex relationships between place, food, people, and taste in different ways.

Acknowledgments

My sincere thanks to Katharina Graf and Anna Colquhoun for their tireless editorial work. This volume is a testament to their efforts. I'm grateful for the invaluable feedback I received on earlier drafts from other chapter authors, especially

Heather Paxson, Anne Meneley, Cristina Grasseni, and Sarah Czerny. Thank you to James Farrer for inviting me to present this research at Sophia University and to the attendees for their questions and comments, which proved stimulating and helpful. Thank you to Ben Schrager for his suggestions.

Greg de St. Maurice is Associate Professor in the Faculty of Business and Commerce at Keio University. He received his PhD in Cultural Anthropology from the University of Pittsburgh in 2015. His research has appeared in the journals *Gastronomica*, *Japanese Studies*, and *Food, Culture, and Society*, as well as in several edited volumes. Current projects include a study of the transcultural transmission of culinary skills and knowledge in high-end Japanese cuisine and a comparison of place brand formation for different agricultural and food products in Japan. He served as Vice President of the Association for the Study of Food and Society from 2017 to 2022.

Notes

1. I follow the Japanese language convention of writing surnames first. Miura-san and Aizawa-san are well-known producers with a prominent media presence: giving them pseudonyms is not realistic. They have given me permission to use their real names.
2. In Kyoto City, a few farming households continue to engage in *furiuri*, whereby mothers or grandmothers use pullcarts or kei-trucks to make designated stops along predesignated routes, where regular customers choose from seasonal produce, often arranged loosely in baskets or boxes.
3. The location of Miura-san's fields, in Miyagi Prefecture, has meant that relative to farmers in Fukushima Prefecture, his burden in the wake of March 2011's disaster has been comparatively light.

References

Anholt, Simon. 2010. "Definitions of Place Branding: Working towards a Resolution." *Place Branding and Public Diplomacy* 6: 1–10.

Aoyama, Ikuko, Harry Zhu, Shinichi Koyama, Yuji Wada, and Haruo Hibino. 2016. "A Farmer's Image on the Food Package Changes Consumers' Evaluation of Food Safety and Quality." *Shōhisha kōdō kenkyū* 23(1): 47–60.

Avraham, Eli, and Eran Ketter. 2008. *Media Strategies for Marketing Places in Crisis.* Oxford: Butterworth-Heinemann.

Berg, Per Olof, and Guje Sevón. 2014. "Food-Branding Places: A Sensory Perspective." *Place Branding and Public Diplomacy* 10: 289–304.

Blichfeldt, Bodil Stilling, and Henrik Halkier. 2014. "Mussels, Tourism and Community Development: A Case Study of Place Branding through Food Festivals in North Jutland, Denmark." *European Planning Studies* 22(8): 1587–603.

Blue, Gwendolyn. 2008. "If It Ain't Alberta, It Ain't Beef." *Food, Culture & Society* 11(1): 69–85.

Braun, Erik, Mihalis Kavaratzis, and Sebastian Zenker. 2013. "My City—My Brand: The Different Roles of Residents in Place Branding." *Journal of Place Management and Development* 6(1): 18–28.

Breen, John, Maruyama Hiroshi, and Takagi Hiroshi. 2020. *Kyoto's Modern Renaissance: Ancient Capital for Modern Japan*. Folkestone: Renaissance Books.

Che, Deborah. 2006. "Select Michigan: Local Food Production, Food Safety, Culinary Heritage, and Branding in Michigan Agritourism." *Tourism Review International* 9: 349–63.

Delaney, Alynne E. 2007. "The Noriya-san of Northern Japan: An Enduring Coastal Cultural Group." *Asian Anthropology* 6(1): 105–26.

Dentoni, Domenico, Glynn T. Tonsor, Roger Calantone, and H. Christopher Peterson. 2013. "Brand Coopetition with Geographical Indications: Which Information Does Lead to Brand Differentiation?" *New Medit* 10(4): 14–27.

de St. Maurice, Greg. 2012. "Savoring Kyoto: Sensory Fieldwork on the Taste of Place." *Etnofoor* 24(2): 106–22.

———. 2018. "Savoring the Kyoto Brand." In *Devouring Japan: Global Perspectives on Japanese Culinary Identity*, edited by Nancy Stalker, 153–70. Oxford: Oxford University Press.

European Parliament Research Service. 2017. *European Commission Guidelines on Dual Quality of Branded Food Products.* Retrieved 14 November 2023 from https://www.europarl.europa.eu/RegData/etudes/BRIE/2017/608804/EPRS_BRI(2017)608804_EN.pdf.

Green, Sarah. 2018. "Lines, Traces, and Tidemarks: Further Reflections on Forms of Border." In *Political Materialities of Borders: New Theoretical Direction*, edited by Olga Demetriou and Rozita Dimova, 67–83. Manchester: Manchester University Press.

Japan Patent Office, Ministry of Economy, Trade, and Industry. 2023. *Regional Collective Trademark Guidebook.*

Massey, Doreen. 1990. "The Political Place of Locality Studies." *Environment and Planning A* 23(1): 267–81.

———. 2004. "Geographies of Responsibility." *Geografiska Annaler: Series B* 86(1): 5–18.

McCracken, Grant. 1993. "The Value of the Brand: An Anthropological Perspective." In *Brand Equity and Advertising: Advertising's Role in Building Strong Brands*, edited by David A. Aaker, and Alexander L. Biel, 125–39. New York: Psychology Press.

Ministry of Agriculture, Forestry and Fisheries. N.d. Geographical Indication (GI) Act. Retrieved 15 June 2021 from https://www.maff.go.jp/e/policies/intel/gi_act/.

Mobley, Esther. 2022. "Napa Valley Is America's Top Wine Region. But It Has Reached a Turning Point That Could Change Everything." *San Francisco Chronicle*, 27 July 2022. Retrieved 17 June 2024 from https://www.sfchronicle.com/food/wine/article/napa-valley-turning-point-17308313/.

National Tax Agency of Japan (NTA). 2023. "What is the Geographical Indications (GI) for Liquor Products in Japan?" Retrieved 17 June 2024 from https://www.nta.go.jp/english/taxes/liquor_administration/geographical/pdf/04.pdf.

Okuda, Masayuki. 2015. *Tōhoku no sugoi seisansha ni ai ni iku.* Tokyo: Shibata Shōten.

Sekigawa, Yasushi, Yukari Yamada, and Hiroshi Yoshida. 2011. "Regional Promotion by Regional Brand Food Development." *Nagoya Bunri University Journal* 11: 119–27.

Shirane, Haruo. 1992. "Matsuo Bashō and The Poetics of Scent." *Harvard Journal of Asiatic Studies* 52(1): 77–110.

Sternsdorff-Cisterna, Nicolas. 2015. "Food Safety after Fukushima: Risk and Scientific Citizenship in Japan." *American Anthropologist* 117(3): 455–67.

Toyokawa, Sayaka, and Toshio Takagi. 2020. "The Collapse of the 'Myth of Longevity' and the Construction of Alternatives: The Case of the Okinawan Health Food Industry." *Journal of Organization and Discourse* 1(1): 22–29.

Yoshida, Kunimitsu. 2023. "'Localness' in Donburi Rice Bowls in a Remote Rural Area: The Case of Noto Peninsula, Japan." *Research in Globalization* 7(1): 100147.

CHAPTER 9

Shifting Wind, Eternal Earth

Lapsang Souchong, a Foreign Fengtu *Comes Home*

Kunbing Xiao

Introduction

Fengtu (wind-soil/earth) is a Chinese word that expresses how the unique natural environment (land, mountains, climate) and customs and habits of a place contribute to the taste of local food. Although *fengtu* might be translated as "native," "authentic," or even "terroir," teas from the Wuyi Mountains reveal *fengtu* as the more dynamic interaction of human and natural influences, that is, of *feng* and *tu*. This chapter discusses the *fengtu* of two black teas (*hong cha*) from this same region. The first of these is Lapsang souchong, an export tea that was invented by accident and marketed to foreign consumers who were assumed to be less discerning in taste. Yet it was its very market success that built the reputation of the producing region, enhancing its fame as a place of superior tea. The second is Jinjunmei, a black tea that was created for the home market.

By analyzing the case of Lapsang souchong and its later successor Jinjunmei, this chapter introduces the idea of *fengtu* as something more than a tradition rooted in local environment, for it was the foreign legacy of Lapsang souchong that enhanced the prestige of Jinjunmei and the entire growing region. I will ask whether products from the same place that are processed differently and taste completely different still count as local *fengtu*, or whether this "taste of place" is just a marketing strategy.

Fengtu: A Chinese Concept on Local Products and the Evolution of the Meaning of *Feng* (Wind)

Fengtu is a unique Chinese concept referring to the interplay of human and natural environments. Sources from as early as the Yinshang Period (1300–1046 BCE) reveal how *feng* and *tu* were related to natural phenomena and social life. The *Sifangfeng* (four-directions wind) and the interpretation of the relationship between the *Sifangfeng* and the *Sishiji* (four seasonal sacrifices) reflect the Shang people's understanding of the phenomenon, which became an important basis for Yinshang calendars (Feng 1994).[1]

In ancient China the soil was considered "the base of the earth that produces all things" (Xu 2010: 30). *Fengtu* as a concept first appeared in the Spring and Autumn Period (770–476 BCE) and has been mentioned in many Chinese classics. In the *Book of Agriculture* (Wang 1992: 344), Wang ranks croplands and distinctive soils within his native Jiuzhou. Different varieties of crops are associated with specific places separated by mountains and rivers (*feng-qi*), which distinguishes the taste of one place from that of another.

When people talk about agricultural products, *fengtu* is used to describe the unique taste of a place. The *feng* is polysemous: its original meaning of "wind" extends to also include etiquette and customs, habits, and fashion (*fengsu*). *Tu* (soil/earth/land) emphasizes the "local" part. For instance, the terms *tuchan* (local product), *tusheng tuzhang* (locally born and bred), and *tuwei* (local taste) all refer to the native, indigenous, and local. Hence, *feng* gradually shifted its meaning and began to refer to "customs" (human) when in combination with *tu*, while the latter focused on natural influence. Similar to terroir in French culture, *fengtu* claims to be unique to a place.

In imperial China, local specialties were symbolic objects for marginal regions to express their submission and loyalty to the central court. It was a traditional practice to record the local food culture in local gazettes, and to present local specialties as tribute to the royal court. The local gazettes always attributed the superior quality of these foods to the unique *fengtu*, which explains why these foods were chosen as royal tribute. Records of these *fengtu* products are not limited to China but also include exotic tributes from foreign countries. Accounts of foreign food items offered in tribute to emperors of China, methodically recorded into the "veritable records" (*shilu*) of each dynasty, completed this image of the empire and furthermore clarified the political relationship between the imperial realm and its neighbors and trading partners (Swislocki 2009:17).

Although most local specialties in China are defined by their superior *fengtu*, this is not always the case. It is worth noting that the records of imperial tributes throughout the dynasties have in turn contributed to these places becoming famous as places of *fengtu*.

The Transformation of an "Inferior" Tea: Making Lapsang Souchong for the Overseas Market

Tea in China can be roughly divided into six categories, each with distinct processing methods and different resulting degrees of oxidation: green tea, yellow tea, white tea, oolong tea, black tea, and dark tea. The black tea's correspond-

Figure 9.1. The same company sells Lapsang souchong for export and for the hinterland—that is, for domestic consumption. China, 2019. © Kunbing Xiao

ing term in Chinese *hongcha* literally means "red tea." Although there is controversy over the claim, the Wuyi Mountains (Wuyishan) in southeastern China are widely recognized as the birthplace of two of these six teas: oolong and black tea. In terms of geographical distribution, black tea is produced in the upper reaches of the Jiuqu River in the Tongmu Nature Reserve, whereas oolong tea is produced downstream in what is now the Wuyishan Scenic Area. Recent research maintains that oolong tea entered the British market earlier than black tea (Ellis et al. 2015). However, whether the early Wuyi tea (*bohea*) was oolong tea or black tea is not the focus in this chapter. The historical impact of black tea on the British market is much more significant than that of oolong tea. In this chapter I will only focus on the black tea produced in Tongmu: Lapsang souchong and Jinjunmei.

The Tongmu Nature Reserve of Wuyishan is located at the junction of Fujian and Jiangxi Provinces, with an average altitude of one thousand meters. High mountains tower into the clouds on both sides, creating a deep V-shaped canyon acting as a natural defense. Tongmu Village lies at the center of this Nature Reserve. Today, the black tea produced within Tongmu includes two types of tea "invented" in different periods and for different markets: the smoked Lapsang

Figure 9.2. The interior structure of a smoking room for producing Lapsang souchong. China, 2024. © Kunbing Xiao

souchong for the overseas market and the nonsmoked Jinjunmei for the home market.

Lapsang souchong was purportedly first created in the seventeenth century. Although no historical record exists, the local community retains its own lore about the origin of this tea. According to what I have heard in my fieldwork in Tongmu in 2008, the general plot of the story could be concluded as follows.

The Tongmu local community attributes the origin of Lapsang souchong to a series of accidents. One day, during the turmoil of the late Ming Dynasty, a group of soldiers passed through the village of Tongmu in the Wuyi Mountains during the tea-harvesting season. It was getting dark, and the soldiers needed to find a place to stay overnight. A tea-processing factory along the road caught their attention. The factory owners and tea workers had fled to the nearby mountains to hide in advance of the soldiers' arrival, leaving unprocessed tea leaves on the floor of the factory in the rush. The soldiers were very tired, and the fresh tea leaves seemed soft, so they slept on them for one night before leaving early in the morning. Following the soldiers' departure, the tea workers returned to the factory and found the tea leaves dehydrated and turning black due to the body heat of the soldiers. It was no longer possible to dry these leaves according to the regular method. Yet, they did not want to waste them. Therefore, they cut down some locally grown masson pine and dried the tea leaves with a pinewood fire. The tea made in this way looked black and had a smoky flavor. The Chinese market would not appreciate this strange tea, and so the villagers packed the tea and sent it to the nearby Star Village (*Xingcun*) fair and sold it at a very low price. This "special tea" was bought by Dutch merchants and later sold to the British. To the locals' surprise, the smoked tea was much favored by the British, which resulted in an advance order for this tea for the following year at a price two to three times higher than normal. Since then, locals have specialized in producing this black tea for foreign trade.

This narrative about Lapsang souchong underlines that the Western consumers' taste preference is opposed to the Han Chinese, who traditionally drink unoxidized green tea—that is, a tea that local people perceive as inferior is appreciated by overseas consumers. The half-processed green tea that had been slept upon by the army was almost "ruined." From a processing point of view, it actually created a new tea, the oxidized black tea that was quite different from the green tea. Furthermore, they "roasted" it rapidly over the pine fire, which created a new taste—the smoky flavor. Unexpectedly, this "undrinkable" tea was bought by Dutch businessmen, and they were willing to order it again the next year at a price two or three times higher.

Unlike the hybridization or repackaging of local or supposedly "traditional" tastes discussed elsewhere in this volume, Lapsang souchong was created for a foreign market. For example, Garth (this volume) points out that Cubans believe in the "taste of place" that is derived from mixture and hybridity itself rather than tastes that are derived from local cultivation. Lapsang souchong represents something very different. Often considered the earliest black tea, Lapsang souchong was once for the overseas market only. From the Ming Dynasty until very recently, Chinese tea drinkers, especially among the elites, typically the literati in the Jiangnan region, preferred light green tea. Sigmond (1839) pointed out that Bohea (Wuyi black tea) was not widely consumed in its country of origin (China), even among the humbler classes. The taste distinction between the Chinese and the British consumers is somehow still true today. While green tea is a symbol for Chinese gentlemen, the British endowed black tea with an elegant cultural cachet and a complicated drinking method (Chen 2008: 3).

Making Zhengshan (Lapsang), Making "a Place of *Fengtu*"

This is not to say that Lapsong souchong lacks a sense of local *fengtu*. Initially unknown in China, the name of the tea in both Chinese and English itself gradually became known among producers, including nearby rivals who hoped to wedge their way into the market with a cheaper product. A series of legal and administrative actions, including the application for registration as a GI product, transformed the unique *fengtu* of the original tea from a local imagination into a legalized reality. The Chinese name of this tea, *zhengshan xiaozhong*, only partially corresponds to the English name. Souchong, an evident Anglicization of *xiaozhong*, is the name of the specially oxidized tea. The first part is more problematic, since no amount of historical miscommunication could turn the pronunciation of *zhengshan* into Lapsang.[2]

Rather, *zhengshan*, the "genuine mountain range," refers to a place, specifically the Tongmu region. Locals alleged that Tongmu's unique *fengtu* distinguished the *xiaozhong* (souchong) tea grown in the *zhengshan* (genuine mountain) from the one originating from the *waishan* (outer mountain). Local Tongmu tea farmers claim that smoked black tea from Tongmu has a distinctive *longan* fragrance[3] that tea leaves from outside Tongmu do not possess, and that even if the tea leaves grown in the adjacent surrounding area, such as Shaowu, Guangze, and Jianyang, were processed in the same way, they would never be able to produce the same unique fragrance. Tea from the outer mountains can only imitate Lapsang souchong in appearance but will never possess the *zhengshan*'s unique fragrance. Thus, only the smoked black tea produced in the Tongmu region according to the traditional method can be called *zhengshan* (genuine mountain) *xiaozhong*.

However, such an argument is a post hoc romanticization of the tea's origin. The name Lapsang souchong never appeared in local historical records before it became famous in overseas markets. Locals did not give this tea a specific name—they just called it *wucha* (sooty tea) and never mentioned its origins. In the western sources, the terms *Bohea* (*wuyi*) tea and *souchong* often appeared on the purchase lists of the Dutch East India and British East India Companies, but the term *Lapsang* is entirely absent (Xiao 2022). Recent research shows that Lapsang souchong may in fact have been named after Mr. Lap Sing, a Chinese merchant who supplied the East India Company with superior souchong teas as early as 1816. In later records and publications, the name of that particular tea and souchong teas of comparable quality was gradually transformed into "Lapsing" and later to "Lapsang."[4]

The need for defining terminology came from the mid-eighteenth century, when the production of black tea extended into adjoining Fujian and Jiangxi Provinces. Processed in the same way as those from Wuyi, these cheaper teas flooded the market. In 1773 the local county magistrate of Wuyi recorded that angry Wuyi tea producers were instructed to "seize [the fake teas] whenever they see them and prosecute the cases" (Liu 1999). It was from this time that the terms *zhengshan* (genuine mountain) and *waishan* (outer mountain) began to be used.

In 2002 the Wuyishan Municipality in Fujian Province registered Lapsang souchong under the "Registration and Protection of Origin Marks" issued by the General Administration of Quality Supervision, Inspection, and Quarantine (AQSIQ). This designation significantly reduced the statutory scope of "*zheng-*

Table 9.1. The comparison of *zhengshan xiaozhong* in China and Lapsang souchong for international markets. © Kunbing Xiao

	HOME	ABROAD
Name	Zhengshan Xiaozhong	Lapsang Souchong
Focus of Authenticity	Geographical indication (the *fengtu* of Tongmu)	Smokey flavor
Definition (traditional)	The smoked black tea from the Tongmu region	The smoked black tea from the Fujian province or China
Definition (modern)	Two styles of black tea produced in Tongmu: the new method of smoke-free tea; the traditional smoked black tea	The smoked black tea from Fujian province or China. In practice, it is the smoked Souchong produced from Waishan (outer mountain)

shan" from several hundred kilometers to an area of just fifty square kilometers near Tongmu Village. Initially, producers from neighboring regions contended that counties within the larger Wuyishan Nature Reserve should be allowed to use the name, arguing that "Lapsang souchong" served as a collective designation for all high-mountain tea from the region. However, in 2009 the Wuyishan Municipality further solidified its claim by successfully registering the more stringent certification of the Geographical Indication Mark for Lapsang souchong, which was based on the same region delineated in the 2002 AQSIQ certification. Consequently, black tea producers in neighboring counties were required to relinquish the name when marketing their products.[5]

In recent years, the traditional smoking technique used to produce Lapsang souchong has become no longer possible, leading to new techniques and products. Besides the lack of a Chinese market for smoked tea, making the foreign product has encountered a new problem: there is no more masson pinewood available in Tongmu. Since Tongmu is located in Wuyishan National Park and Nature Reserve, cutting local pine trees is now prohibited. For many years, Tongmu tea farmers relied on pinewood purchased from outside; however, in recent years, the entire Wuyishan area has been deeply affected by a devastating forest disease, and the transportation of pinewood has been strictly controlled. Since 2019 the import of pinewood in Tongmu Village has been completely forbidden.[6] In 2022 experts from Fujian Agriculture and Forestry University invented alternative burning sticks to solve this problem, but how can the Lapsang souchong retain its unique *fengtu* when one of the critical factors—being "smoked by masson pinewood"—is missing?

The Birth of Jinjunmei: A New High-End Tea from the *Zhengshan Fengtu*

In 2005 a new high-end black tea named Jinjunmei, a craft variety whose creation blends traditional techniques with innovative production methods, was introduced to the market (DeBernardi and Ma 2022). Within the same geographic production area of Lapsang souchong, this new tea rapidly achieved success in China's tea market and, to some extent, has even managed to overcome the traditional Chinese disdain for black tea drinking. After Jinjunmei was created, more and more domestic consumers developed a preference for black tea, boosting the development of the black tea industry in China.

The origin of this new tea product echoes the myth surrounding the invention of Lapsang souchong. According to the informants I interviewed in Tongmu, including Yan, who was directly involved in the creation of Jinjunmei, the story of its invention is roughly as follows: in 2003 two tea lovers from Beijing, surnamed Zhang and Yan, visited the Yuanzheng Tea Factory in Tongmu Village. As frequent visitors and tea connoisseurs, they asked the factory to produce a fancy single-bud tea for them. Traditionally, Lapsang souchong in Tongmu was divided into grades (first, second, and third) according to the tenderness of the tea leaves. To pursue excellent taste, the Beijing visitors suggested using only tender buds. Considering its high cost, the tea factory did not complete this "special order" immediately, and the "birth" of Jinjunmei was thus delayed until June 2005. Encouraged by the Beijing connoisseurs' perseverance, Liang Junde, the tea master of Yuanzheng Tea Factory at that time, agreed to have a try. They asked tea workers to pick the buds from wild tea plants nearby, and Master Liang personally prepared the new tea by hand. During the processing, given that Chinese customers are not generally fond of the smoky taste, they decided to skip the smoking. The next day, when tasting the newly crafted tea, the Beijing tea lovers found its flavor and fragrance particularly honeyed and pleasing. They proposed to name it Jinjunmei. *Jin*, meaning "gold," refers to its high quality. *Jun* derives from Liang Junde, the master who made the tea, and *mei*, meaning "eyebrow," refers to the shape of the finished tea leaves.[7]

The unprecedented success of Jinjunmei is due to two factors. On the one hand, in the twenty-first century the new middle class emerging in China was aspiring to pursue a quality life, forcing high-status tea connoisseurs into competition for the rarest and finest teas. On the other hand, the smoky taste of Lapsang souchong was always aimed at the export market, and Chinese rarely drank it, while the unsmoked Jinjunmei met the taste preferences of Chinese consumers.

After a series of promotional campaigns by Zhang and Yan and their high-society friends in Beijing, the fresh nonsmoked black tea suddenly became a rare gift and precious commodity among wealthy Chinese, reaching the incredibly high price of more than 10,000 RMB (1,500 USD) per 500 grams, positioning

Jinjunmei as a "high-end black tea for the niche market" and setting a far higher price for it than Lapsang souchong. The reason why Jinjunmei is so expensive is largely due to the scarcity of its *chaqing* (the unprocessed fresh tea leaves). The *chaqing* for Jinjunmei tea must originate from wild tea plants grown in the Zhengshan range between a height of fifteen hundred and eighteen hundred meters. Therefore, the production of Jinjunmei in Tongmu is necessarily limited, and the tea is costly, while the demand for Jinjunmei is increasing. This situation led to the production of counterfeit products that rapidly flooded the market. Similar to Lapsang souchong, Jinjunmei evolved from a specialized *fengtu* product of Tongmu Village into a synonym for any single-bud black tea. Copycat products were soon being produced in large quantities all over China, and all the traditional black tea-producing areas swiftly began to produce a product they sold as Jinjunmei tea. In fact, most consumers cannot discern the uniqueness of *fengtu* by tasting, whereas producers can easily imitate the appearance of single-bud tea leaves.

The process of applying for intellectual protection soon veered into a conflict between private and local interest, embodied in the conflict between trademark and GI. From 2006 to 2013, the Zhengshan Tea Company (Yuanzheng Tea Factory), the earliest manufacturer of Jinjunmei, underwent a protracted six-year process for trademark registration; however, their efforts to register Jinjunmei as a trademark ultimately proved unsuccessful. In March 2007 the Zhengshan Tea Company applied to the State Administration for Industry and Commerce of China for the trademark of the term *Jinjunmei*. In February of that year, other tea companies in Wuyishan also applied. Since this move affected the economic interests of many tea producers, when the State Trademark Office sent personnel to Wuyishan to investigate the Jinjunmei trademark in 2012, a letter of objection to the trademark registration was sent to the State Trademark Office and local governments and media of Fujian Province. The letter pointed out that Jinjunmei is the result of the collective intelligence of the residents of Tongmu and that it originated from the innovation of Lapsang souchong. Jinjunmei black tea, therefore, is one of the GI products of Wuyi Black Tea and cannot be registered as a personal or corporate trademark. Attached to the letter were the signatures and handprints of Tongmu villagers' representatives, as well as manufacturers who disagreed with the registration of the Jinjunmei trademark by individuals or private companies. Ultimately, the Supreme People's Court designated Jinjunmei as a specific type of black tea product.

Although the six-year "Jinjunmei Trademark Dispute" ended with no clear winner, it is important to underline that in fact it was an "internal war" between Tongmu tea factories and did not really involve tea companies outside the region. To some extent, the dispute contributed to increase the legitimacy of Tongmu as the origin of Jinjunmei. The failure to register the trademark further enhanced the semi-mythical status of Tongmu in the high-end consumer's eyes. Just like how, in the past, they emphasized the unique taste of Lapsang souchong, the contemporary producers of Jinjunmei now emphasize that the unmatched quality of tea produced in Tongmu *zhengshan* is due to a unique mix of geographical environment and climatic conditions. In 2015 the national standard for Jinjunmei tea was issued by the ACFSMC (All China Federation of Supply and Marketing Cooperatives). The national standard defines: "Jinjunmei tea is a black tea made from single buds of the high mountain tea trees within the 565 square kilometer Wuyishan Natural Reserve, centered on Tongmu Village, Xingcun (Star Village), Wuyishan, using a unique process . . . with the quality characteristics of golden color, sweet in decoction, sweet and fragrant" (ACFSMC: 2). This national standard actually recognizes Jinjunmei as a GI product.

Conclusion: Shifting Wind, Eternal Earth

In China the traditional belief is that if an agricultural product from a specific region outshines the same product from other areas, it is typically attributed to the superior natural conditions of that place—known as superior *fengtu*. However, this chapter questions this perspective, suggesting that the narrative can be flipped: it is only after a product gains fame that people start crafting the myth of exceptional *fengtu* for that particular region. After all, our experience of taste is deeply shaped by cultural experience, and cultural contexts matter a lot for our perception of the environment (Sutton 2023: 289).

By analyzing tea production practices across time in Tongmu Village of Wuyishan, this chapter challenges and expands upon the Chinese *fengtu* (wind-soil/earth) concept. China's *fengtu* is a rich concept to describe local taste that indicates the shifting bonds between place, people, local custom, and taste. As people widely believe in the irreplaceability of *fengtu*, it sometimes also becomes a tool for branding local products. To distinguish the superior local taste compared to similar products elsewhere, people need to "brand" this place with its unique *fengtu*, thus resulting in related storytelling and value construction (see also de St. Maurice, this volume). In the Dynastic period, the metaphorical royal tribute system between the central court and the periphery, and between China and the foreign markets, was traditionally based on a *fengtu* narrative rooted in local community history. When no written historical records exist, oral history is generally referred to as an even more convenient and flexible approach to "make" *fengtu*. As a cultural concept, *fengtu* shaped the spatial hierarchy of the natural environment. Whether the taste of *fengtu* products is unique or not is not the focus; what matters more is that people (both producers and consumers) believe that the place with *fengtu* produces high-quality products and are willing to pay a premium price for it.

Today, both the smoky Lapsang souchong and the smoke-free Jinjunmei tea from Tongmu are no longer aimed at the European market. This is due to Tongmu's reputation for exceptional *fengtu*, which commands much higher prices for its tea compared to those produced elsewhere in the world. Hence, all the Lapsang souchong teas sold in the international market originate from other regions of the Fujian Province or even out of Fujian; in other words, the smoked teas are products of *waishan* (outer mountain) regions. These are now classified as a variant of Lapsang souchong called *yan xiaozhong* (smoked souchong) that is typically smoked twice (see table 9.1). As one local tea expert explained, "smoked souchong is recognized by craft, while Lapsang souchong is recognized by geographical scope."

From Lapsang souchong to Jinjunmei, the taste of the local tea is continuously changing through time. The particular *fengtu* of Tongmu is not a fixed expression of geographical territoriality but of the politics of ever-shifting nexus of local-global interactions. More specifically, it is the expression of a narrative strategy proposed by Tongmu locals when interacting with consumers at home, in neighboring production areas, and abroad. The birth of Jinjunmei, and the transformation of the former *waishan* (outer mountain) *xiaozhong* (souchong) into the new product of smoked souchong (*yan xiaozhong*) sold overseas, reflects the local repositioning and reconstruction of *zhengshan fengtu*.

Although the literal meaning of *fengtu*, wind and earth, is always reminiscent of a fixed natural environment, to understand China's *fengtu* concept it is probably better to separate the two characters composing this word. "Wind" is not only the wind of nature but also "custom and fashion," which is shifting with the change in people's taste. So even though the *tu* (land/earth), is still in the same place, today's *fengtu* is never the same as in the past.

In today's society, where global development is accelerating, the tensions between the protection of the natural environment and traditional processing techniques, global interconnectedness and the root of local material heritage, and global warming call into question the continuity of *fengtu*. The development of the raw materials and techniques that give products their unique taste is the result of human mobility and exchange, a process that continues to drive the evolution of the taste of any given place today (Feinberg 2020). Therefore, it is not only the "wind" that is changing. Although the physical location (earth/land/territory) has not changed, the soil composition and microenvironment may not remain the same as before in the context of large-scale climate change. Any assumption that there is a fixed *fengtu* is just a market demand for the global dining table and a dream that will never be fulfilled.

Acknowledgments

I would like to thank Jakob Klein, Anna Colquhoun, and Katharina Graf for organizing the workshop "Beyond Terroir" and for their insightful suggestions on this chapter. Many thanks to Gisela Welz, Guntra Aistara, Brandi Simpson

Miller, and other participants in the "Beyond Terroir" workshop for their helpful comments and feedback. Special thanks to Thomas DuBois, who shared his profound insights into Chinese food culture as I was revising this chapter, and to Simone Ricca for useful comments at the early stage and language proofreading. Responsibility for any errors lies with the author.

Kunbing Xiao is Professor of Anthropology at Southwest Minzu University, Chengdu, Sichuan (China). Her research interests include the anthropology of food, sensory anthropology, and cultural heritage studies. Kunbing received her PhD from the Department of Ethnology and Anthropology of Xiamen University, Fujian, China, with a thesis on the Wuyi tea trade in northern Fujian from the seventeenth to the nineteenth centuries in the context of modern globalization.

Notes

1. The Shang Dynasty (1600–1046 BCE) is the earliest dynasty of traditional Chinese history supported by archaeological evidence. Yin-Shang is the last period of the Shang Dynasty according to oracle bone inscriptions unearthed in Anyang and the famous history book, "Shih Chi." Retrieved 25 June 2024 from https://en.wikipedia.org/wiki/Shang_dynasty.
2. Regarding the pronunciation and translation of Lapsang souchong, see Xiao (2019).
3. *Dimocarpus longan*, commonly known as the longan, and the dragon's eye, is a tropical edible fruit. The fruit of the longan is similar to that of the lychee, but less aromatic in taste. It is native to tropical Asia and China. Retrieved 25 June 2024 from https://en.wikipedia.org/wiki/Longan.
4. Johan P. F. Van Mechelen, personal communication, May 2023.
5. AQSIQ is the abbreviation of the General Administration of Quality Supervision, Inspection and Quarantine of the People's Republic of China. According to AQSIQ, the origin of Lapsang souchong is defined as 117°38′6″-117°44′30″ east longitude and 27°41′ north latitude. North latitude 27°41′35″-27°49′00″ has a radius of fifty square kilometers, extending to Masu in the east, Guangdun in the west, Pikeng and Guwangkeng in the south, and Tongmuguan in the north. The souchong black teas produced within this range are Lapsang souchongs, and the others are *waishan* souchongs. In 2010 the scope of "Zhengshan" in the "Zhengshan Xiaozhong Geographical Indication Trademark" was consistent with this definition.
6. For more information, see Xiao (2024).
7. For another statement, Jiang Yuanxun, the owner of Yuanzheng Tea factory, offers different explanations for the origin of the tea name, but many sources confirm the tea is named after Liang Junde. For more details, see DeBernardi and Ma (2022).

References

ACFSMC (All China Federation of Supply and Marketing Cooperation). 2015. *Supply and Marketing Cooperation Industry Standard of the People's Republic of China-Jinjunmei Tea* (GH/T 1118-2015).

Chen, Ciyu. 2008. *Producing Saliva and Quenching Thirst: The Globalization of Chinese Tea.* Taipei: Sanmin Book Company.

DeBernardi, Jean, and Junhong Ma. 2022. "History, Creativity, and Value: The Modern Making of Gold Jun Mei Tea." *Asian Journal of Social Science* 50(3): 195–205.

Ellis, Markman, Richard Coulton, and Matthew Mauger. 2015. *Empire of Tea: The Asian Leaf that Conquered the World.* London: Reaktion books.

Feinberg, Rebecca. 2020. "Uprooting Wine." *Food, Culture & Society* 23(5): 551–69.

Feng, Shi. 1994. "Study on the *Sifangfeng* (four-directions wind) of Oracle Inscriptions." *Journal of Archaeology* 2.

Liu, Qing. 1999. "Pianke Yuxian Ji (A moment of leisure)." In *Classics of Chinese Tea Culture.* Edited by Binfan Chen. Beijing: Guangming Daily Publishing House.

Sigmond, George Gabriel. 1839. *Tea: Its Effects, Medicinal and Moral.* London: Longman, Orme, Brown, Green & Longmans.

Sutton, David E. 2023. "Eating with the Dead Ritual, Memory and a Gustemological Approach to Taste." *Food-Media-Senses: Interdisciplinary Approaches* 100: 289–99.

Swislocki, Mark. 2009. *Culinary Nostalgia: Regional Food Culture and the Urban Experience in Shanghai.* Stanford: Stanford University Press.

Wang, Zhen. 1992. "Nongshu (Book of Agriculture)," In *Dictionary of Economics*, ed. Guangyuan Yu. First published 1313. Shanghai: Shanghai Lexicographical Publishing House.

Xiao, Kunbing. 2019. "What Is the Tea 'Bohea' Popular Overseas in the 18th Century?" *The Paper*, 2 September. Retrieved 27 July 2023 from https://www.thepaper.cn/newsDetail_forward_4048931.

———. 2022. "The Flow of Bohea: The Tea Trade in the Indian Ocean World (Seventeenth to Nineteenth Centuries)." In *Cargoes in Motion: Materiality and Connectivity across the Indian Ocean*, edited by Burkhard Schnepel and Julia Verne, 71–88. Athens: Ohio University Press.

———. 2024. "What's Causing the Lapsang Souchong Tea Shortage?" *Sixth Tone*, 22 February. Retrieved 27 July 2023 from https://www.sixthtone.com/news/1014686.

Xu, Shen. 2010. "Shuowen Jiezi (Analytical Dictionary of Characters)." In *New Shuowen Jiezi*, edited by Zhao Wuhong. Beijing: Popular Literature Press.

PART III

Bodies

CHAPTER 10

Domestic Cooks' Work toward Moroccan *Beldi* Foods in Uncertain Times

Katharina Graf

Introduction

I was about to finish writing fieldnotes in my room on the first floor when I heard someone shuffle across the courtyard of the *riad* (house arranged around a courtyard). The house was otherwise quiet. I decided to have a look. Fatimzahra rested or prayed in her room, but Hajja's door was ajar, her room empty.[1] I found her sitting on the ground in front of a big suitcase in the small *khazin* (storage room). Around her lay jars, plastic boxes, and bags filled with food: olives, spices, dates, coffee, apples, preserved lemons, and more items that I could not identify. I asked Hajja what she was doing, and she began to explain that these foods would be traveling with her to Mecca the following week for the hajj (pilgrimage around the time of 'Id el-kebir, one of the five obligations or pillars of Islam). She listed each item, lifting them visibly for me, then repackaged them for the journey. When she lifted the box with the small preserved lemons, she paused, looked intently at me, and explained, "These are *beldi* lemons."

I had not heard the term *beldi* with respect to food before and enquired. Hajja explained that these are lemons from Taroudant, her *bled* (hometown or village) in the Souss Valley, south of the city of Marrakesh. Usually a woman of few words and gestures, she grew animated as she told me about the lemon trees on her inherited family land: her siblings tended lemon and olive trees for her and sent her a share of the harvest each year, along with other *beldi* food products. She packed them, because she had to have a "taste of home" (*legout dyel bled*) on that month-long journey to Mecca. To make her point and show me another *beldi* product, she lifted the dried black olives that she had packed already. She continued to explain her motivation for every item in the suitcase; many foods were not *beldi*, but she took them because she preferred their familiar taste and quality: "During the hajj I have to eat well, it will be tiring. In Mecca the food is expensive and bad, they sell *whatever* to all the pilgrims. … I know from my last trip to Mecca for the '*omra* [the so-called small pilgrimage, carried out during the rest of the Islamic calendar]."

***

This first encounter with *beldi* foods took place in a very intimate and personal moment, a moment that I could have easily missed. Hajja did not think that this was interesting for my research, yet she evidently cared deeply about some of the foods she processed and packed for her imminent journey. They would keep her tethered to home and strengthen her while traveling to a faraway place; a journey she did not expect to return from.[2] On that day I began to learn how low-income urban Moroccans think, talk, and feel about the connections between food, taste, and place in the context of movement over space and time. While *beldi* is a universal concept to make sense of the taste and place of people and objects across Morocco, definitions of *beldi* foods are situated and differ for every person depending on where they were born and grew up as well as where they temporarily moved and traveled to.

The notion of *beldi* has very practical implications with respect to food. In the absence of reliable quality standards within the national food system, urban Moroccans like Hajja indicate the provenance and taste of food through the notion of *beldi*. *Beldi* (literally of/from the country) denotes food from one's place of origin but also homemade or artisanal food products, and helps low-income cooks to determine food quality from multiple angles. Although geographical origin labels do exist in Morocco, they target foreign markets and are unaffordable for most low-income consumers.[3] Quite like *domaće* ham in Istria (Colquhoun, this volume), real *beldi* food cannot be purchased in a supermarket. As an analytic tool, *beldi* helps us to note the embodied and intimate perspectives of low-income urban Moroccans around the connections between food, place, and taste; a perspective that is often missing from scholarship that still tends to define the "taste of place" in terms of the notion of terroir.

The vignette also points to another crucial dimension of *beldi* foods. For a food product to be considered *beldi*, a lot of invisible knowledge and work is required, from the maintenance of agricultural land and of family connections to planning, processing, preserving, preparing, and (not) serving it. Importantly, this work is not limited to food producers or middlemen; indeed, domestic cooks, usually women, are central to making foods *beldi* and thus good, as Sanders and Simpson Miller (both this volume) show in similar domestic contexts. It is this largely hidden, gendered knowledge and work of indexing and making *beldi* foods in urban contexts that this chapter focuses on. It argues that the place and taste of food are not only produced by food producers, distributors, marketers, or governments but also by domestic cooks, in particular low-income women. Moreover, in the broader context of poverty and economic and environmental decline across Morocco, writing about *beldi* grounds discussions "beyond terroir" in existential debates about food security and the desire to create a sense of certainty in everyday life.

I do so through Hajja's and her daughter Fatimzahra's practices of tasting and placing foods. The thoughts, practices, and feelings invested in *beldi* foods connect them—each a little differently—to the taste and place of their past, their present, and their future. Though idiosyncratic, their experiences and perspectives are also representative of how low-income Moroccans think about and do food, place, and taste, and help us to shed light on the largely hidden domestic work that particularly poor women carry out every day to ensure that the food they provision, prepare, and serve their families is good in a context of latent food insecurity, a perspective that is still missing from accounts focused on terroir in its commoditized forms (e.g., Trubek 2008; Paxson 2013; West 2022). Analyzing how *beldi* foods are produced in this context thus contributes to widening our understanding of the way people meaningfully taste and place foods in order to recreate an intimate, everyday sense of security and control.

For low-income cooks, taste and place—captured in the notion of *beldi*—are important markers of food quality for three connected reasons, which also structure the main part of the chapter. First, *beldi* orients Moroccans in the context of an ever-faster globalizing food market. Second, as an everyday practice based on intimate bodily knowledge, it provides a material and symbolic sense of certainty in the context of movement over space and time. Yet, third, the making of *beldi* foods is simultaneously marked by an acutely felt erosion of livelihoods and a sense of loss of control. While I will introduce, describe, and analyze these dimensions of *beldi* in the three main sections through Hajja's and Fatimzahra's stories, the last point constitutes the core argument of the chapter and moves the debate most obviously "beyond terroir." I will show not only that domestic cooks, via their knowledgeable food practices, are an important group of people who each cultivate and maintain a very intimate taste of place in today's fast-moving world; I will also show how their increasing difficulties of doing so situates urban inhabitants of low income in the broader context of change of a globalizing Moroccan food market that systematically undermines domestic food security.

Studying *Beldi* Practices

Beldi begins with individual people, and so does my methodology. Between September and December 2012 I lived and worked with Hajja and her family as part of a year-long apprenticeship to three different domestic Marrakshi cooks.[4] Between 2016 and 2018 I complemented this fieldwork with ethnographic research with fifteen other low-income families in the cities of Marrakesh and Beni Mellal during a research project on bread (Graf 2024). As opposed to more formalized craft work, the preparation of food is deeply entangled with other daily practices and its apprenticeship much less circumscribed. My methodological approach to studying and learning food preparation, especially my encounter with *beldi* foods, is more aptly described as "participant perception" (Graf 2024): a deeply immersive and multisensory way of participating in everyday life, which embraces the gaps that necessarily accompany such an experienced-based method. Thus, it was often in moments when I was just by chance dipping in and out of food-related activities, in quiet moments as described in the vignette, or in situations where I was tasked with another food-related chore that I encountered *beldi* foods and practices. Indeed, as an embodied and intimate category for foods, people, and places, most of my research participants did not talk much about *beldi* foods; to notice them, I had to learn to perceive their existence and spatial movements through my own multisensory immersion in these women's everyday lives.

Compared to the other families I worked with, Hajja's was slightly better off. Hajja moved to Marrakesh as an underage bride in the mid-1960s and was widowed in the early 2000s. In 2012 only one of her five adult children, Hassan, had a steady wage as a low-income but respectable government employee. Although Hassan fully financed her household, which at the time included herself and her two oldest adult children, Fatimzahra and Mohamed, he mostly lived in his own studio flat in a lower-middle-class suburb of Marrakesh. Like most other low-income families who are not destitute, Hajja and her family would not describe themselves as poor. Indeed, when her husband was still alive, her family fared much better, as the fading beauty of their *riad* in the *medina* (historic city center) testified.[5] Hajja's husband was a local notable (*sherif*) and once a respected figure in the neighborhood. She often reminisced about the early days of their marriage when they hosted lavish meals featuring high-priced Soussi specialties like saffron or argan oil. However, alcohol addiction and poor health contributed to the decline of his car mechanic business and eventually caused his death. He left the family with debts and in perpetual financial insecurity. It is largely thanks to Hajja's origins that the family commanded a vast network of kin relations across Morocco and the diaspora, and thus a stronger social security net than many other families I know. Still, their life stories reflect the socioeconomic and environmental decline that other Moroccans I talked to experienced over the last couple of decades.

Beldi and *Rumi* Foods in a Globalizing Market

To understand the importance of *beldi* as an embodied index of quality, it is necessary to contextualize *beldi* foods in the contemporary Moroccan food system. In the open-air *suq* (market) that most low-income Moroccans frequent for their daily food needs, quality is often unpredictable and unreliable. Except for meat and dairy products, most fresh foods in the domestic market are not subject to any control or national standards (Codron et al. 2004; Amine and Lazzaoui 2011). To the contrary, foods that do not pass the strict quality control in the packing stations for exportation to the European Union or the United States end up on the domestic market (Sippel 2014). For example, Hajja's *bled*, the Souss, is one of the most prominent agricultural regions of Morocco, yet roughly half of the vast amount of fresh fruits and vegetables destined for export do not pass the quality tests; instead, these lower-quality products are sold unlabeled in domestic markets (Sippel 2014: 102). The same happens with respect to seasonality: Morocco produces fresh products like tomatoes or strawberries for the EU market during its offseason. As soon as European producers can supply again, the Moroccan products are no longer admitted to the EU and instead flood the domestic market, pushing down domestic prices and threatening the livelihoods of smaller-scale producers (Boeckler and Berndt 2014). In addition, rainfall and seasonality or transport problems affect the availability and quality of everyday food items. Low-income urban Moroccans are well aware of how these factors impact price and quality (Graf 2015).

Together with its counterpart *rumi*, which means "foreign" and might date back to Byzantine times (*rumi* meaning Roman or Christian, referencing Roman colonialism in Morocco some two thousand years ago), *beldi* slots into this (willful) gap of regulation. It is precisely because it is difficult to define exactly what *beldi* and *rumi* mean, and if and how a product can be labeled one or the other, that the pair is such a useful index in this unregulated context. From an urban perspective, according to ethnobotanist Mohamed el Haouz, there are three regular features of *beldi* foods.[6] First, *beldi* and *rumi* denote origin or provenance, including the specific "ecology of production" (Paxson 2013; West 2013) from the perspective of the speaker. *Beldi* means quite literally from one's village, hometown, or region with no or few middlemen involved in its provision. At the very least, *beldi* indexes foods "from Morocco." *Rumi* indexes food products from another region, from a long supply chain, imported from abroad or simply store bought. Second, the pair indicates mode of production. *Beldi* refers to homemade, artisanal, smallholder, or handmade food production, whereas *rumi* refers to industrial, highly mechanized production or processed foods. Finally, *beldi* denotes a strong or particular taste or flavor, and *rumi* refers to a bland or mild flavor. This includes texture; *beldi* indexes a chewy, crumbly, or less pleasing texture, and *rumi* a smooth, homogenous, and pleasing one.

Despite these fairly widespread features, their meanings and uses vary according to material and social context. In fact, research around *beldi*/*rumi* produces different results depending on where and with whom the research took place (see, e.g., Sarter 2004; Simenel 2010; Zirari 2020; Jonas 2023).[7] Also, as the features of taste and texture highlight, *beldi* does not always index good food, and *rumi* does not automatically mean bad food. Furthermore, not all *beldi* foods embody all three features at once, nor does a *beldi* product always have a *rumi* counterpart (or vice versa). Yet Hajja's *beldi* lemons and olives do: they were produced on her native family's land with artisanal methods, sent to her by her relatives, and she processed and preserved them by hand, as a result of which they developed the favored strong, salty umami flavor. In December 2012 I was able to accompany Hajja on a visit to her hometown, a village in the suburbs of the Souss capital Taroudant. Her relatives showed me around their small farms and fields, some under cultivation, many not due to recurrent drought and lack of investment (figure 10.1).

Importantly, this case reveals that a *beldi* mode of production is not limited to agricultural processes in the rural hinterlands. It includes the domestic production of *beldi* in a connected urban context. In search of a more comfortable life and education for their children, not only Hajja but most of my female research participants in Marrakesh and Beni Mellal had migrated from their native *bled* and continued to cultivate their taste of *beldi* foods away from it (see also Meneley, this volume). In case of a lack of connections due to estrangement, or a lack of foods due to a bad harvest, the next best substitute *beldi* foods could come from the broader native region, the wholesale market in the city or even bought from a shopkeeper so long as he hailed from one's native *bled*. Importantly, through their continuous work to provision, process, and prepare *beldi* foods, migrants reproduced their knowledge and their symbolic connections to the *bled*. This knowledge and work are highly gendered and decidedly lower class. While the knowledge of origin and provenance of foods, of regional ecologies,

Figure 10.1. Lemon and olive trees on the family's land. Morocco, 2012. © Katharina Graf

yearly variations in harvest, changing prices, and the work of maintaining rural kinship ties even decades after migrating to the city is shared equally among low-income men and women, the knowledge and work of processing, preserving, storing, and preparing food in a *beldi* way is predominantly female.

Making *Beldi* Foods in Low-Income Homes

Since Hajja returned from the hajj in mid-November the *riad* was always full. Family members from all over Morocco but especially from Hajja's *bled* honored the newly minted Hajja (honorary name given to returnees from the hajj) with their visit. While every visiting party brought food and drinks as is customary—usually industrially produced sugar cones, milk, coffee, tea, or fresh fruits—as hosts we also prepared lots of meals. My role during that month-long celebration was to shop and process foods. I was not surprised when I saw several new bags of food in the *khazin* one day, which Hajja kept locked with a key that she never took off her necklace. This time, however, Fatimzahra was busying herself in the storage room, getting flour for homemade bread. Upon my enquiry she highlighted that this flour was not your average flour, it was twenty kilograms of *beldi* flour, brought by one of their visiting relatives. Receiving this kind of flour was a rare treat these days, I was told, as were all the other *beldi* products I then spotted: clementine, lemons, and several liters of raw milk. Fatimzahra explained that reduced and unpredictable rainfall as well as decreasing groundwater tables seriously threatened their family's smallholder farming (see also Sippel 2014).

At night on that same day, when temperatures hovered just above zero degree Celsius, I came back to the *riad* from a meeting with a friend when I heard Fatimzahra's electric blender from the not-much-warmer kitchen. I found her in the middle of processing the raw milk I had spotted earlier: with her right hand she held onto the top of her blender, with her left hand she operated the switch, to her right was a casserole filled with something that looked like clotted milk, to her left was a bottle half filled with buttermilk (*lben*) and turned upside down on top of a small bowl and a sieve, yet another white liquid slowly dripped from the bottle into the bowl. When I asked her what she was doing, Fatimzahra pulled out a plate with three little yellow lumps of butter from behind her, "I'm making butter." She explained that it was too cold, and thus the blender had to work harder to churn the milk. She repeatedly switched it on and off because it got too hot; indeed, it smelled of burning plastic.

Finally, she tapped the blender, muttering "poor thing", and decided to clean up and filter the remaining milk through a sieve and into another bottle, entertaining the hope to find some more lumps of butter layered on top in the morning. Nearly finished, Fatimzahra pointed to the casserole with the liquid and introduced it as *ghaib*, a drinkable yoghurt to which she planned to add sugar later. She confessed with a deeply satisfied smile that she had already drank quite a bit of it. It was the first time she seemed genuinely happy and satisfied during these hard-working days following Hajja's return from Mecca. As she walked out of the cold kitchen to go to sleep, she concluded our conversation: "*Beldi* [here meaning homemade] food is simply the best. You know what's in there!" She gestured toward her tummy, rubbed it, and sighed with pleasure. For her, this was food as good as it gets.

***

Although I had spent nearly one hour with her in the kitchen—and had been sharing meals with her and her family for a couple of months already—I was not offered a taste of any of these raw milk products. This was Fatimzahra's very own moment of pleasure, and she had worked toward it. In her case, making *beldi* foods as in this vignette gave her back her agency and sense of being in control of her body and life, both with respect to her subordinate role within the domestic division of labor vis-à-vis her mother and with respect to her inability to purchase more high-priced foods generally deemed healthy, such as fruits or fish. In Hajja's case *beldi* was often oriented toward her past and the life she left behind. Although she often told me about her own practices of hand-rolling couscous grains, ensuring a "better" taste in the resulting dish, she was also adamant that she had "worked much harder back then" and didn't miss this work at all. Most of the times, though, she invoked the *bled* as "her" place marking her roots (*'asl*), her family and land. In the case of her suitcase full of *beldi* foods, Hajja oriented *beldi* toward the future, to the imminent travel as well as her afterlife. Provisioning foods in the *bled* and making *beldi* foods enabled her to reenact her material and symbolic roots and feel a sense of certainty and control in moments of vulnerability, from being a young bride moving to the big city to that of a pilgrim traveling to a holy but unsafe place.

It is important to note that although *beldi* foods were often more expensive, more difficult to provision, and required more work than their *rumi* variants, most cooks carefully considered the trade-offs and often deemed the additional efforts worth it. That real *beldi* products can only be truly cherished by oneself and usually only a handful of other people highlights the immense value that most low-income Moroccans ascribe to it. Thus, rather than indexing simply good or bad foods, the pair has to be understood as a situated and embodied way to define and, crucially, "make" foods good, and doing so allows low-income Moroccans like Hajja and Fatimzahra to create an everyday sense of control in a world of flux.

In other words, the categories depend on context and bodily knowledge; *beldi* does not mean the same thing for everyone and cannot be made by and for everyone. In fact, most middle- and upper-class urban Moroccans would associate

Figure 10.2. Packaged *beldi* bread sold in a supermarket. Morocco, 2017. © Katharina Graf

beldi with a certain rural backwardness and *rumi* with modernity and cosmopolitanism. Notions of "us" and "them" are locating differences across income and class. Rachik's (1997) description of *beldi* and *rumi* furniture and fashion in middle- and upper-income urban homes is suggestive. Whereas low tables and cushions are described as *beldi* or Moroccan, high tables and chairs are described as *rumi* or European. The former tends to be associated with working-class taste, the latter with middle-class tastes and lifestyles.[8] Montgomery (2016) describes a similar association with regards to Moroccan and European dishes: while European or *rumi* dishes such as vegetable creams or pastas are considered to be urban and modern, *beldi* dishes such as meat stews or legume soups are associated with rural foodways and tradition.

At the same time, educated urban professionals who are well versed in European discourses surrounding what Grasseni (2016) calls the "heritage arena" are now "reinventing" (West 2013, Grasseni and Paxson 2014) *beldi* as a Moroccan version of organic (Jazi 2014) or terroir foods (Jonas 2023). The occasional surfacing of labeled *beldi* products in supermarkets, which largely target middle- and upper-income Moroccans, is indicative of this reinvention (figure 10.2; see also Graf 2018). While my low-income research participants, urban inhabitants themselves, were well aware of the above-described derogative meanings of *beldi* and generally refrained from using *beldi* or *rumi* to describe people or index "us" versus "them," they were also disinterested in recent reinventions of *beldi* as an equivalent to organic or local foods. None of my research participants described *beldi* as "organic" or "local."

To the contrary, for my research participants—most of them migrants with rural roots—*beldi* foods materialized and represented a very intimate taste of place that exceeds simplified associations of *beldi* as lower class and resists commodification. The embodied qualities of *beldi* foods may simply be lost to others. As stated above, the products that Fatimzahra produced with the raw milk from her mother's *bled* were not offered to me or any of our visitors. Making and consuming them was as intimate as the notion of *beldi* itself; it was a very personal pleasure crucial to Hajja's and Fatimzahra's sense of security. Outside of certain bodies, certain *beldi* products simply do not make sense. For them, and for countless other low-income Moroccans working to make *beldi* foods every day, *beldi* is not a fixed category or a marketable product but rather a bundle of everyday practices that enable them to locate themselves and others in time and space through tasting and placing foods. The fact that this work was often taking place in quiet and private moments, hidden from others, and that I stumbled upon it by chance rather than being introduced to it more explicitly is indicative of this.

In sum, foods acquire their *beldiness*, that is, their taste and their place, which indicate their goodness, through domestic cooks' knowledge and work. This work begins with the upkeep of social and material relations to the homeland. Regular visits; frequent phone calls about sowing, tending, or harvesting foods on the family land; processing knowledge such as that of preserving lemons or making butter; as well as enacting mutual hospitality are the centerpieces of this work. This work testifies that low-income domestic cooks like them did not assume that food is intrinsically good; it had to be made good. These nuanced meanings and practices associated with *beldi* and *rumi* more generally point to the complex moral economies surrounding Moroccan notions of "us" and "them," traditional and modern or local and global. The pair is contrasting but not necessarily dichotomous, while always being situational and context specific. It is these features of tasting and placing foods and people—including themselves—and the fact that they can be actively made that gives my research participants their sense of security and control in the context of rapid change. So what happens if making *beldi* foods is becoming more difficult?

Beldi Foods in the Context of Decline

With the beginning of the olive harvest in late November, Fatimzahra was regularly on the phone speaking to aunts and cousins, later to acquaintances from other parts of Morocco. She tried to assure a supply of unprocessed olives from the Souss but did not succeed. The trees of her mother's family did not carry any

Figure 10.3. Unused olive press. Morocco, 2012. © Katharina Graf

olives that year, a fact that we confirmed in person during the December visit to the countryside. Indeed, the two olive presses on her family land had remained unused for years, because the harvest had gradually declined to insignificant quantities (figure 10.3). Fatimzahra involved her entire social network to access unprocessed olives to turn them into *beldi* olives herself as she always did; yet after one month of trying via various sources, she gave up, and we bought several kilograms of "normal" (*'adi*) preserved olives in a shop. Of course, the price of olives had nearly doubled in the meantime, thwarting Fatimzahra's efforts to save money by provisioning them via her relatives.

When I later asked her to explain the situation to me, she replied, "It was the Americans' fault." From one of her acquaintances near the city of Beni Mellal, an olive producer, she found out that American buyers had come to Morocco to buy unprocessed olives, because "abroad" the harvest had not been good that year.[9] She mentioned that fresh Moroccan produce fetched a higher price when sold abroad and that, to make matters worse, this also drove up domestic prices. Whereas Hajja lauded the technological changes that eased some of her daily workload and seemed resigned to watching the world globalize, Fatimzahra was angered by what she described as a "sell-out" of Moroccan food products to wealthier foreigners like myself. She tirelessly pointed this out to me whenever her work to identify and make *beldi* foods bore no fruits.

***

Fatimzahra's failure to find and make *beldi* olives further showcases the work invested in making *beldi* foods and relates it to broader social, material, and environmental changes in Morocco. Especially from the perspective of younger low-income Moroccans, the work to make *beldi* foods is symptomatic of a degrading economy and environment (see also Demossier, this volume). These developments are real and the result of a historically dualist approach to agriculture. Since at least the times of the French Protectorate (1912–56) and cemented in the 2008 Green Morocco Plan (GMP), the Moroccan government has favored the industrial production of resource-intensive cash crops for export over more environmentally adapted smallholder farming for the domestic market (Swearingen 1987; Akesbi 2014). Given the potential that origin labeling has for political control and economic extraction (as Caldwell shows in the case of Russia, this volume), it is not surprising that a major aim of the GMP is the implementation of GIs across a wide range of modernized and resource-intensive commodities, which contribute to the degradation of the Moroccan environment in favor of foreign currencies and to the detriment of national food security and food sovereignty (cf. Akesbi 2014). As a result, the Moroccan food market is well integrated into the global market, with a fast-growing range of standardized food products destined for export, while smaller producers and subsistence farmers like Hajja's family are marginalized and driven out of business (cf. Sippel 2014). As described above, when fruits and vegetables unfit for export are discarded and enter the unregulated domestic market, the latter serves as a shock absorber for the highly competitive global market (Boeckler and Berndt 2014), resulting in unpredictable availabilities, poor quality, and price deformations in the domestic market. In this context, *beldi* foods are increasingly hard to come by.

The vignette provides a glimpse of the difficulties that low-income Moroccans—rural and urban—face in provisioning, preparing, and consuming foods that are tasty, healthy, and meaningful to them. Low-income women like Fatimzahra invest a lot of work in sourcing and preparing *beldi* foods, yet in the ever-more globalized Moroccan market context, they grow increasingly frustrated at their inability to do so. In combination with the previous vignettes, this last vignette highlights how deeply low-income Moroccans care about placing and tasting foods and how difficult this work is becoming. Fatimzahra's problems in sourcing and processing olives into *beldi* olives are not only about reconnecting her and her family back to their *bled*, tethering them to their origins in the agricultural countryside, nor are they only about recreating a taste of their past in the present and for the future, but they also express more existential difficulties of living well and exerting agency and control in the context of globalized poverty. For poverty is not simply the absence of money but also of water and land, and of social relations; a truly poor person is one without *'asl* (roots, origin). Not being able to make and eat *beldi* foods is thus both a bodily felt sense of loss of control and a daily reminder of one's marginal, seemingly forgotten position in an unequally globalized world.

Conclusion

Hajja's suitcase full of *beldi* and non-*beldi* foods on the way to Mecca at once materializes and symbolizes the importance of placing and tasting foods for low-income Moroccans like her. She packed her life and everything it symbolized, where she is coming from, who she is, and where she might be going. At the very least, the recounting of Hajja's and Fatimzahra's taste of place demonstrates that understanding the materially and socially constructed connections between food, place, and taste requires attending to peoples' and foods' movements over space and time (and many more actors, see for instance Pope and West, this volume). Of course, it is impossible to describe the many social, material, and environmental changes that mark the lives of Hajja and Fatimzahra in the space of one chapter. Yet, each vignette provided snapshots of the shifting connections between people and their meaningful practices of tasting and placing foods and people.

All the vignettes highlight the breadth of the largely invisible work that domestic cooks and urban consumers do to make foods *beldi* and thus good for them; seemingly small practices like packing and transporting homegrown and home-preserved lemons to faraway places, making and drinking *ghaib*, or sourcing and processing a few kilograms of *beldi* olives. The first vignette about *beldi* lemons highlighted how *beldi* could be dubbed "my taste of place": an embodied and intimate marker of food quality, which still serves as widely shared index for placing people and products across Morocco, particularly in contexts of migration and movement. The next vignette about processing raw milk demonstrated that through the knowledgeable work of provisioning and making *beldi* foods, domestic cooks gain a sense of control in a highly uncontrollable and volatile market context and life more generally. The last vignette, on trying and failing to provision olives, embeds the work of placing and tasting foods in the broader context of globalization and poverty. Taken together, the vignettes demonstrate not only how sourcing and making *beldi* foods is an intimate bodily practice but also how the work of maintaining relations, knowledge, and taste of and for these foods is also constrained by problematic agricultural policies that favor export production over domestic food sovereignty. And, of course, these two things are also closely connected.

Ultimately, *beldi* as told through Hajja and Fatimzahra is a story of gradual decline and of loss, evoking common themes across a world marked by migration, environmental degradation, repeated financial crises, and rising levels of poverty.

At the same time, this chapter reminds us that the persistence of the concept of *beldi* and of *beldi* foods today is also owed to the knowledge and continuous work of women like Hajja and Fatimzahra who, in making *beldi* foods against the odds, reproduce not only the taste and place of foods that matter to them but also themselves and other disenfranchised people in this context. In other words, to understand the past, present, and future of people and their places and tastes "beyond terroir," it is worth attending to less visible actors such as domestic cooks and their everyday work to make good food in an increasingly unequal world.

Acknowledgments

I would like to thank my research participants for their tireless efforts of explaining the notion of *beldi* to me. It is not an exaggeration to say that without them this chapter—and this book—would not exist. Of course, I am also immensely grateful for the many years of exchange on the topic with Anna Colquhoun as well as the valuable input from the other authors over the last two years of this book project. I am also grateful for the feedback from our two peer reviewers.

Katharina Graf is a social anthropologist based at Goethe University Frankfurt, Germany. Her research interests range from food, gender, and family to bodily knowledge, generational change, as well as global markets, food security, science and technology, and citizenship. She has recently published *Food and Families in the Making: Knowledge Reproduction and Political Economy of Cooking in Morocco* (Berghahn, 2024). She received her PhD in Anthropology and Sociology from SOAS University of London.

Notes

1. All names used in this chapter are real names, in accordance with interlocutors' consent.
2. Dying during the hajj is considered an honorable death for elderly Muslims. Although Hajja was in her mid-sixties, no one in her family expected her to die during the journey. Yet, symbolically, all family members parted from her as if they were seeing her for the last time. Her safe return, one month later, was thus celebrated accordingly.
3. The Moroccan government has actively encouraged the production of geographical indication (GI) products since the early 2000s (Lambarraa-Lehnhardt, Ihle, and Elyoubi 2021).
4. I have known the family since 2007 when Fatimzahra taught me *darija*, the Moroccan Arabic dialect.
5. In 2019 Hajja sold the near-crumbling *riad* to a European neighbor and, together with Fatimzahra, bought a small purpose-built apartment near Hassan's flat.
6. He was the only person I asked about *beldi* foods who defined its broad characteristics abstractly. All other interview partners related to *beldi* from their own embodied perspective and emplaced positionality.

7. If considering *beldi* exclusively from a rural perspective, it is less surprising why it might be described as a terroir-like concept. Simenel (2010) even argues that rural Moroccans accord more value to their terroir than rural societies in France. However, as soon as a person or foods travel (including the ethnographer), the notion of terroir quickly loses its analytical capacity to explain relations between people, foods taste, and place in Morocco.
8. Associations of taste with class are commonplace across class-divided societies. Based on Bourdieu's notion of class distinction in French society, Wilk (1999) provides a useful comparative perspective on how tastes for certain foods—for example, lobster—were linked to colonial-era class identities in Belize.
9. Indeed, see Butler 2013.

References

Akesbi, Najib. 2014. "Which Agricultural Policy for Which Food Security in Morocco?" In *Seasonal Workers in Mediterranean Agriculture: The Social Costs of Eating Fresh*, edited by Jörg Gertel and Ruth S. Sippel, 167–74. London: Routledge.

Amine, Abdelmajid, and Najoua Lazzaoui. 2011. "Shoppers' Reactions to Modern Food Retailing Systems in an Emerging Country: The Case of Morocco." *International Journal of Retail & Distribution Management* 29(8): 562–81.

Boeckler, Marc, and Christian Berndt. 2014. "B/ordering the Mediterranean: Free Trade, Fresh Fruits and Fluid Fixity." In *Seasonal Workers in Mediterranean Agriculture: The Social Costs of Eating Fresh*, edited by Jörg Gertel and Ruth S. Sippel, 23–35. London: Routledge.

Butler, Julie. 2013. "World Olive Oil Production Drops by a Quarter, Council Predicts." *Olive Oil Times*, 11 March. Retrieved 6 June 2024 from https://www.oliveoiltimes.com/business/world-olive-oil-production-drops/33212.

Codron, Jean-Marie, Zouhair Bouhsina, Fatiha Fort, Emilie Coudel, and Aurelie Puech. 2004. "Supermarkets in Low-Income Mediterranean Countries: Impact on Horticulture Systems." *Development Policy Review* 22(5): 587–602.

Graf, Katharina. 2015. "Beldi Matters: Negotiating Proper Food in Urban Moroccan Food Consumption and Preparation." In *Halal Matters: Islam, Politics and Markets in Global Perspective*, edited by Florence Bergeaud-Blackler, Johan Fischer, and John Lever, 72–90. London: Routledge.

———. 2018. "Cereal Citizens: Crafting Bread and Belonging in Urbanising Morocco." *Paideuma* 64: 244–77.

———. 2024. *Food and Families in the Making: Knowledge Reproduction and Political Economy of Cooking in Morocco*. New York: Berghahn.

Grasseni, Cristina. 2016. *The Heritage Arena: Reinventing Cheese in the Italian Alps*. New York: Berghahn.

Grasseni, Cristina, and Heather Paxson. 2014. "Introducing a Special Issue on the Reinvention of Food: Connections and Mediations." With Jim Bingen, Amy J. Cohen, Susanne Freidberg, and Harry G. West. *Gastronomica* 14(4): 1–6.

Jazi, Salima. 2014. "Les valeurs de consommation bio et 'beldi' au Maroc." *Revue Marocaine de Recherche en Management et Marketing* 9–10 (Janvier-Decembre): 209–23.

Jonas, Joana. 2023. "Being Beldi: The Value and Prospects of the Rif Terroir." *Anthropology of Food* 17: online. URL: https://journals.openedition.org/aof/14137.

Montgomery, Mary. 2016. Personal communication, 6 June. London.

Lambarraa-Lehnhardt, Fatima, Rico Ihle, and Hajar Elyoubi. 2021. “How Successful Is Origin Labeling in a Developing Country Context? Moroccan Consumers’ Preferences towards Local Products.” *Sustainability* 13: 8433.

Paxson, Heather. 2013. *The Life of Cheese: Crafting Food and Value in America*. Berkeley: University of California Press.

Rachik, Hassan. 1997. “Roumi et beldi: Reflexions sur la perception de l’occidental à travers une dichotomie locale.” *Égypte/Monde Arabe* 30–31: 293–302.

Sarter, Gilles. 2004. “Entre beldi et roumi: Préférences des consommateurs urbains et production de poulets au Maroc.” *Cahiers Agricultures* 13: 75–78.

Simenel, Romain. 2010. “Beldi/roumi: Une conception Marocaine du produit de terroir, l’exemple des Ait Ba’Amran de la région de Sidi Ifni.” *Hespéris-Tamuda* 45: 167–76.

Sippel, Ruth S. 2014. *Export(t)räume: Bruchzonen marokkanischer Landwirtschaft*. Bielefeld: Transcript.

Swearingen, Will D. 1987. *Moroccan Mirages: Agrarian Dreams and Deceptions, 1912–1986*. Princeton, NJ: Princeton University Press.

Trubek, Amy B. 2008. *The Taste of Place: A Cultural Journey into Terroir*. Berkeley: University of California Press.

West, Harry G. 2013 “Appellations and Indications of Origin, Terroir, and the Social Construction and Contestation of Place-Named Foods.” In *The Handbook of Food Research*, edited by Anne Murcott, Warren Belasco, and Peter Jackson, 209–28. London: Bloomsbury.

———. 2022. “Terroir Products: A Moveable Heritage Feast?” *Review of Agriculture, Food & Environmental Studies* 103(1): 1–27.

Wilk, Richard. 1999. “‘Real Belizean Food’: Building Local Identity in the Transnational Caribbean.” *American Anthropologist* 101(2): 244–55.

Zirari, Hayat. 2020. “Entre alimentation (*makla*) et nutrition (*taghdia*): Arbitrages et réinvention au quotidien des pratiques alimentaires en contexte urbain.” *Hespéris-Tamuda* 55(4): 385–407.

CHAPTER 11

Culinary *Mestizaje*

On the Making of an Authentic Cuban Taste of Place

Hanna Garth

Introduction

In his celebrated 1940 essay, *Cuban Counterpoint*, Fernando Ortiz, Cuba's most famous anthropologist, defined the ajiaco as "a native dish," a Cuban stew consisting of different tubers that combined to symbolize the Cuban people.[1] A proper Cuban *ajiaco* is made by slowly boiling cuts of meat with these starchy root vegetables. According to Ortiz, Amerindians supplied the corn, potatoes, taro, sweet potatoes, yams, and peppers. Spaniards added squash and other tubers, while Chinese people added spices, and African people contributed ñame, a tuber similar to a yam, along with their culinary taste. For Ortiz, the *ajiaco*[2] was a metaphor for Cuban culture as an ongoing identity process that is "open to hybridity, heterogeneity, and hyphenation" (Pérez Firmat 1987: 14). The analogy represents the coming together of Natives, Africans, and Spaniards, among others, to create Cuban society. The key to the *ajiaco* metaphor is that as the ingredients are brought together to make the soup, they do not lose their original identity but, rather, mix together to create something with a new and different flavor; also, new ingredients can always be added. They do not "melt" together but comingle to create something unique while maintaining their individual constituency. The ideology of *mestizaje*, racial and cultural mixing, has a long history in Latin America and the Caribbean. Beyond Cuba, Caribbean societies have long been complex, modern, heterogeneous societies (Khan 2001, 2004; Trouillot 2003). Caribbean understandings of identity and historical consciousness are rife with constructs of hybridity, both in scholarly analysis and everyday interpretation. Aisha Khan claims that "'mixing' is among the most persevering of cultural themes in most Caribbean and Latin American countries" (2004: 3).[3] Ortiz suggested that Cubans themselves are "a *mestizaje* of kitchens, a *mestizaje* of races, a *mestizaje* of cultures, a dense broth of civilization that bubbles on the stove of the Caribbean" (1940: 165–69). The forms of *mestizaje*, the social and biological mixture of European colonizers, enslaved African people, and local native peoples that took place under the colonial plantation system were crucial for establishing Cuban cuisine. In this chapter, I focus on the process and practices of culinary mixing as central to the creation of a particularly Cuban set of flavors, dishes, and cuisine.

Building upon Ortiz's *mestizaje* and Khan's arguments about the persistence of "mixing" as a framework for understanding the Caribbean more broadly, I draw in this chapter on ethnographic examples and literature to make sense of how Cubans on the island understand and debate the concepts of taste of place and authenticity with respect to Cuban food (Trubek 2008; Trubek and Bowen 2008). I build upon the theorization of mixture in the Caribbean to illuminate the complexity of the practice of mixing in the production of taste of place on and off the island. As Cubans on the island face ongoing food scarcity during recent economic crises, some call into question whether the foods they consume are "real" Cuban foods, and if not, how that relates to what it means to be Cuban (Garth 2020). Given this crisis of identity, I argue that Cubans' ongoing historical definition of themselves and their cuisine as a mixture allows for an adaptable taste of place. Furthermore, this sense of Cuban taste of place also extends to Cubans living in the diaspora as they continue to create authentically Cuban flavors while displaced from the island. For Harry West (2022: 1), much of the scholarship on terroir misunderstands the centrality of movement and mixing to human life; instead "terroir asserts that certain foods must be grown in certain places by particular people to be real, and to be the best foods—in terms of taste, of livelihood provision, or of environmental sustainability." Building on West's critique I bring together examples from Cuba that offer a wide-ranging understanding of taste of place on the island and for Cubans in the diaspora. Given the context of Cuba, theorizations of terroir and taste of place must have the capacity to hold very contradictory elements that are part of contemporary political and economic contests without a clean resolution.

Based on ethnographic research carried out in Santiago de Cuba between 2008 and 2019, this research took place during a period of political and economic transition for Cuba. During this research ingredients for "traditional" Cuban dishes were often scarce or prohibitively expensive, forcing Cuban households to "invent" other kinds of dishes, or eat things they did not consider to be "real" food to get by (Garth 2020). Unlike in Ortiz's *ajiaco*, the ingredients for these meals do neatly match with the ancestral origins of Cubans; they come from all over the world, and sometimes it is not even possible to pinpoint where they come from at all. But to the people eating these meals, the food is still "Cuban food." Given these circumstances, debates about terroir and taste of place are relevant for understanding how Cubans define and redefine authentic cuisine during periods of change.

Specifically, to unpack how the concept of *mestizaje* is enacted in everyday life beyond classic dishes like the *ajiaco*, I focus on the *sofrito*, a mixture of sauteed vegetables, herbs, and spices that constitute the aromatic base of many sauces, as the quintessential base not only of the traditional stew but also as the central feature that renders many other dishes Cuban or "authentically" Cuban. To make this case I focus on Ortiz's finer point that, unlike the melting pot, the ingredients and people do not melt in his metaphor, but mix. That is, they retain elements of their original character, and it is specifically the taste, smells, textures, etc. that emerge when they come together that matters in a process of *mestizaje*. Building on ethnographic cases, I argue that the embodied cultural practice of creating the perfect mixture of ingredients is central to how Cubans understand taste of place. This embodied practice of creating specific cultural flavors complicates our understandings of terroir and taste of place when it involves mixing together ingredients that come from all over the globe to create a local taste of place. Given the ways in which taste of place is produced in the Cuban context, the culinary skills of household cooks are essential to the production and maintenance of taste of place both on the island and in diaspora (see also Graf, this volume). For many Cubans the process of making a sofrito from scratch with their embodied knowledge is linked to ideas of "traditional" food preparation and contrasted to seasoning mixes like Sazon Completo, which can be used to achieve similar flavors without the traditional techniques. On the other hand, Cubans also invoke ideas of terroir, though I have never heard the term used in Cuba, as they conceive of foods grown locally as imbued with the flavors of struggle and sacrifice for Cuban independence, literally from blood shed on the land. Terroir here is simultaneously linked to freshness and the ability to eat produce at peak ripeness, which is in contrast to the taste of place of the 60 to 80 percent imported foods in the Cuban diet. To underscore this point, I analyze Cuban reflections on the consumption of fresh cane juice and the making of *hallacas*, a local version of tamales. However, to understand Cuban taste of place we must move beyond what is grown on the island and even beyond what is consumed on the island. The Cuban sandwich as consumed in South Florida offers a key example of taste of place consumed off the island, or in exile.

In this chapter I bring together a wide variety of seemingly contradictory understandings of taste of place to illuminate the complex notions of "authentic," "real," or "traditional" Cuban cuisine. Although Cubans use the language of authenticity, anthropologist John Jackson's understanding of sincerity is more fitting for my analysis. Sincerity is not about authentication of what is "real" or not, but instead sincerity is "a trait of the object's maker," which "presumes a liaison between subjects—not some external adjudicator" (2005: 15). Respecting Cuban interests in authenticity, my own focus is on the ways in which shared social meaning is derived from embodied practices and agreed-upon categories. I show that, given the colonial and postcolonial context, taste of place in Cuba necessarily derives from ingredients that come from all over the globe, not the local territory. Secondly, I show that it is the act of mixing, specifically the embodied and sensory practices of cooking, and the national myths surrounding mixing as an essentially Cuban characteristic that are central to the processing of ingredients from all over the world to create the specifically Cuban taste of place. Furthermore, a distinguishing characteristic of the Cuban consumers' experience of sincerity is that it is not always grounded in the production (agriculture or local hunting and trapping) process.

Contextualizing Cuban Cuisine

Before colonization Cuba was inhabited by Ciboney- and Taino-speaking Arawaks and Caribs. Tainos inhabited the eastern half of the island; Ciboneys remained in the West. Under Spanish colonial rule most foods were imported from Spain, and the local economy was based on agricultural production for export. In the early 1500s enslaved people were brought from Africa to labor on sugar and coffee plantations. While Spanish settlers maintained culinary traditions and imported foods from Spain, enslaved Africans cultivated a different set of food consumption habits more akin to those developed in their countries of origin. Yams were a key African contribution to Cuban cuisine. The *conuco*—the planting plots traditionally used by the Taino—was the name given to small plots of land that enslaved people used for their own food cultivation (Ortiz 1985). Because Tainos were the only agriculturalists on the island before conquest, it is believed that the cultivation of these plots began in eastern Cuba (Esquivel and Hammer 1988). Typical crops included maize, yuca (cassava/manioc), sweet potatoes, taro, squash, beans, fruits, spices, and sugar cane for making *guarapo* (fresh cane juice). Arawak-Carib food preparation techniques included slow cooking meats over green wood grills called *brabacots*, which translated to Spanish as *barbacoa* and English as *barbeque* (Opie 2008: 3).

The forms of *mestizaje* that took place under the colonial plantation system were crucial for establishing Cuban cuisine, and they also laid the groundwork for the formation of Cuban nationalism after independence from Spain on 1 January 1899. The US military occupation of Cuba that began immediately upon independence from Spain was the start of over fifty years of strengthened ties between Cuba and the United States. During this time the United States had an overwhelming commercial influence on Cuba, and American products could be easily found at stores throughout the island. Through the early 1950s about one-quarter of Cuba's national income came from the sugar industry, which accounted for 80 percent of all Cuban exports. Cuba was economically dependent on a single crop and a single consumer, the United States. It was this circumstance that erupted into the 1959 Cuban revolution and shaped the agricultural and economic policies of post-revolutionary Cuba (Benjamin et al. 1984).

The food system established through colonialism and into the first decades of independence all came to an end after Fidel Castro and the 26 July movement took over the island on 1 January 1959. Cuba's food-rationing system, still in place today, was officially established on 12 March 1962. Every Cuban is eligible for a ration card, with which they can purchase basic food items. The ration is commonly referred to as *la libreta*. Prices are heavily subsidized, but households must still pay a small amount for the rationed food. The items included in the ration fluctuate with national scarcities and surpluses.

The Cuban socialist food and agriculture systems were established with heavy investments from the Soviet Union and the Council for Mutual Economic Assistance (Comecon). During the period of Soviet material aid in the 1960s, 1970s, and 1980s, Cubans grew accustomed to products imported from the Soviet bloc, such as canned meats and desserts. In the 1990s, because of the collapse of the Soviet Union, Cuba plummeted into a period of economic hardship that the state called the "Special Period in Time of Peace." Agricultural inputs decreased abruptly, as did the food imports that had formed the basis for Cuba's food system since the 1960s. Cuba's food system radically changed; many food products became scarce, and those that were available were difficult for average Cubans to access due to their increased prices. To deal with the food shortages, the state attempted to introduce new foods into the Cuban diet, including soy and other vegetable proteins, which were substituted for meat and dairy. Most of the Cubans I have worked with are deeply dissatisfied with these changes (Garth 2020).

Making Cuban *Sofrito*: Taste Making, Placing Taste

A Cuban *sofrito*, a sauté of onion, garlic, peppers, cilantro, cumin, and oregano, forms not only the base of the *ajiaco* but also that of at least half of all Cuban dishes in my estimation. The making of the perfect Cuban *sofrito* is all about the timing and the senses. It begins by adding oil to the pan; for most Cuban households that I worked with this would be soy oil, from Brazilian soy processed into oil at the local processing plant. One knows when the oil is the right temperature by the sound. While I was accustomed to flicking a bit of water into hot oil, to listen for the sizzle indicating readiness, the Cubans I worked with just knew by the sound of the oil itself that it was time to add the onion. Usually thrown in all at once, the onions are likely to be locally grown or at least domestic to Cuba. For the *sofrito* the cooking of the onion is an essential step. The key is to soften the onion and begin to brown it but not burn or caramelize it. Stirring regularly, the cook uses sight, sound, and smell to know that it is time to add the garlic, also likely locally grown. The sensory assessment repeats, and the peppers are added, a smaller pepper with a thinner skin, known to me as Italian kitchen peppers, Italian sweet peppers, or frying peppers, they are far less bitter than bell peppers. The peppers would have been purchased at a local market, likely grown locally, definitely grown domestically. Either thinly sliced or diced, the peppers are cooked well, until they are so soft that they blend into the onions and become indiscernible. After this step, in my observation, practices differed across households, but this way of adding the first three ingredients of the *sofrito* was nearly ubiquitous.

In my years conducting ethnography in Cuban households, I have watched the making of a Cuban *sofrito* hundreds of times. But I only had a few occasions to reflect on the *sofrito* with my interlocutors, one of whom was Pati. In 2008 I sat down with Pati as she made Cuban-style spaghetti for her family. At the state market she had purchased peppers, onions, garlic, and oil to make the *sofrito* base of the meat sauce. She started the water to boil for the noodles, peeled the onions and garlic cloves, and then chopped them along with the peppers. After waiting for the oil to heat in the pan, she added in the chopped vegetables one by one, letting it all come together just so before adding the tomato sauce and a healthy splash of vinegar, a pinch of salt, pepper, and Cuban oregano. She cooked it over low heat, stirring as she talked to me. She explained to me it was in "how the ingredients are mixed" that made the spaghetti Cuban, as opposed to some other kind of spaghetti. She noted how important the *sofrito* was to make the spaghetti *Cuban*, in that when you slowly cook the onion, garlic, and oil, the flavor that results is not simply a combination of the three ingredients, but rather, when they come together in a particular way, their flavor is unique, which makes the "authentic" Cuban version of a more generalized cuisine.

Like the Italian American meatball, the Cuban *sofrito* is just one of a type where the global variations "seem inexhaustible" (Weiss 2022). Indeed, there is the Puerto Rican *sofrito*, Mediterranean *sofrito*, the Italian *sofrito*, and many more.[4] What makes the Cuban *sofrito* particularly Cuban then? Pati's understanding of what makes it authentically Cuban is derived from a very particular social, cultural, and historical practice, which has been taught to her across generations of Cuban household cooks, but also must be adapted to the changing conditions on the island as the scarcity of ingredients in general and uncertainty about what will be available in the markets in recent years requires Cubans to adapt and "invent" with their food (Garth 2020; see also Wilk 2006). Pati's practice of creating a Cuban spaghetti is derived from a particular kind of embodied expertise, which is "dependent on inculcating a capacity for discernment" (Grasseni 2004; Weiss 2011; see also Graf, this volume).

There will always be shortages of ingredients, but Cuban household cooks will still attempt to combine foods in just the right way to approximate Cuban flavors. For Pati and many of my research participants it is the way in which the ingredients come together that makes a dish particularly Cuban, not necessarily a specificity of ingredients. For instance, I have seen households make a *sofrito* without onion, without garlic, without peppers when any one ingredient is scarce. Of course, the tipping point of when there are too few required ingredients to still call it a *sofrito* must exist but has gone undefined by the families I have worked with. In the case of the *sofrito* then, taste of place is not about the consumers' ability to discern the origin and quality of the ingredient; rather, it is about the household cook's embodied, sensory skills to produce certain flavor profiles through mixing (see also Graf, this volume). Authenticity, often glossed in Cuba as "real" food, as Pati invokes in the case of Cuban spaghetti, is a social construct that is often tied to the ways people identify with particular histories, nostalgia, longing, and desire. But the Cuban case reveals that the ways people use concepts of authenticity and sincerity as a social and cultural process of meaning making vis-à-vis nostalgia and tradition may shift with other contemporary social, economic, or political conditions.

In contrast to homemade *sofrito*, the use of Sazon Completo, a Maggi brand seasoning mix, offers an interesting case to think through importation to Cuba and taste of place. Across comparative settings, Maggi seasonings in West Africa, and others like Vegeta seasoning powder in former Yugoslavia, have been incorporated into cooking to approximate the flavors of fresh herbs, spices, and vegetables. The Cuban households I studied regularly used Sazon Completo, although they always said using fresh or dried herbs and spices was preferable and tried to only use seasoning mix when they did not have enough or the right combination of herbs and spices. Sazon Completo is imported; the Maggi brand, owned by Nestlé, has offices all over the world, and their products come from dozens of countries. Based on my interviews, Cubans tend to think that their Sazon Completo comes from Venezuela.[17] Although not ideal, Cuban household cooks who use Sazon Completo to flavor their food still told me that the meals they cooked with it were authentically Cuban and made of "real" Cuban flavors.

Although the act of deeming a cuisine authentic or not is fraught and of debatable importance, authenticity and sincerity as constructs are still taken up and enacted by consumers and producers alike. Goods and services may be used and purchased, but individual meaning making can radically differ from consumer to consumer, from producer to consumer, and across time and space. Enactments of sincerity certainly draw on the past as well as present contingencies but are also articulations of food futures and hope. Like Weiss's (2012) consumers of local pork products, the ways Cubans define authentic food or reject foods as "not real" is deeply entangled with how they connect to imagined pasts and envision themselves living an authentic life in the present and future. Contrary to Heather Paxson's Wisconsin artisan cheesemakers who are "unfettered by tradition or concern for authenticity" (Paxson 2010: 446), the Cuban families detailed here are extremely concerned with scrutinizing what counts as authentic, even in the context of centuries of culinary innovation and cultural mixture.

While local production is not required to produce taste of place, many Cubans do prefer fresh, seasonally grown local produce. For many Cubans on the island, sincerity lies in the ways in which consumers define it, accept it, or reject it, and it is enacted in the process of food preparation and the labeling of something as "real" or "not real/fake/whatever appears" (Garth 2020). In this context, unlike Cavanaugh and Shankar's (2014) analysis of "producer-based claims of authenticity," Cuban household consumers are able to retain a great deal of control over local definitions of sincerity and the ways it is enacted in daily life. Cuban consumers can base the ways foods are imbued with identities upon their own cultural imaginary and local definitions of sincerity in order to assign the boundaries of "real" Cuban food. For meals like "Cuban" spaghetti, it is the particular process of bringing the ingredients together that makes them sincere "Cuban" versions of a more generalized cuisine. Cuba's history of importation and *mestizaje* is precisely what allows for "new foods" to be readily integrated into Cuban cuisine.

Place Making and Tasting Place

If process and technique are what make an authentic *sofrito*, and the use of Sazon Completo does not render a dish inauthentic, how do Cubans make sense of the value of local ingredients in producing taste of place? In Ortiz's telling, traditional Cuban dishes are derived from a mixture of new and old-world ingredients that create *criollo* (creole) cuisine. Colonial-era Cuban cookbooks included many creole dishes, such as *ajiaco*, *arroz blanco criollo*, with ingredients such as *boniato* (sweet potato), *plátanos* (plantains), and *malanga* (taro). The connections between Cuba's struggle for independence and idealized authentic ingredients came through in Maria Isabel's reflections on making *hallacas*, a local version of tamales made of fresh corn.[5] She stated: "What is most important is that our food is grown here on the *Oriente* soil—[that refers to the eastern part of the island], which is so fertile with a history—with our history—of the blood and the *lucha* [struggle] of our African, French-Haitian, and Cuban ancestors and years of *lucha* and victory that give the corn grown in the region with a sweeter flavor and juicier kernels."

For Maria Isabel, part of the authenticity of the dish lies in her romanticized view of the relationship between ecology and history. She envisions herself, the corn, and the nation as growing out of the same soil, fertilized by the blood of her ancestors. Maria Isabel's understanding of taste of place is more in line with notions of terroir as taste derived from the particular mix of minerals, microbes, soil and water types, air, wind, and the symbiotic potential of nearby forms of life, including in this case human blood (Tsing 2015; West 2022; Zee 2022). Importantly, her sense of terroir is linked to bloodshed and a diverse group of people making territorial claims on a land that was never theirs. In her reading, the blood that seeped into the soil in the violent struggle for land is what makes the corn and the triumph so sweet. Her understanding of terroir is grounded in the fact of human movement, a concept that Harry West argues "troubles" the common understanding of terroir.

Related to these ideas of taste of place, on a particularly hot day one August I made a stop with my moto driver Ariel at a roadside stand selling freshly harvested sugar cane juice when he asked, "Would you mind if we stop for some *guarapo*?" I said I did not mind, and he purchased two cups of *guarapo de caña*, one for each of us. *Guarapo de caña* is a juice made from freshly squeezed sugar cane. At this stand a man stood in the back, pushing cane stalks through a press that released a slow trickle of liquid, to which he added water and put into a bucket with a huge block of ice. *Guarapo* is to always be served as cold as possible. As we drank our first two cups, Ariel took a deep sigh of relief. The drink felt extremely cold as we drank with the sun low in the sky. He then purchased two more cups for us and explained that he and "*Los Cubanos*" in general believe that *guarapo* has a capacity to transform the body from an overheated and exhausted state. It produces a shock that rushes through the body, scaring away fatigue and awakening the wiltedness of the body in Cuba's summer heat. He said he could feel the heat-induced swelling of his body go down after the second cup.

Though in some ways troublingly essentializing, the cases of local corn and *guarapo* show that a particular nexus of embodied meaning, historical contexts, and the forms in which food is consumed can be used to elicit embodied responses and generate specific connections to ideologies of Cubanidad and patria. This nexus is conceived by Cubans on the island as a particular kind of taste of place. Although the vast majority of food consumed in Cuba today is imported, similar to the historical and embodied connections found in these cases, Cubans understand their cuisine as having a "taste of place" derived from the process of mixture, movement, and hybridity itself. While there is a broad understanding of taste of place as inextricably linked to hybridity and movement, there is at the same time an appreciation and reverence for fresh ingredients, from local sweet corn to freshly squeezed cane juice, imbued with another kind of "taste of place" that is attuned to freshness and peak ripeness. Even if contradictory in some ways, these two approaches to taste of place are often held simultaneously as essential to taste of place.

Maintaining Taste of Place in Exile

In *The Cuban Sandwich: A History in Layers*, authors Andrew T. Huse, Barbara C. Cruz, and Jeff Houck (2022) ask how the Cuban sandwich became a nostalgic symbol for displaced people. Dating back before the socialist revolution, thousands of Cubans have fled the island first under the regime of Fulgencio Batista and then under Fidel Castro. Many fled to South Florida and specifically Miami, which has the largest community of Cuban exiles in the world. There they quickly established Cuban restaurants, grew Cuban ingredients in their gardens, and imported tropical fruits and vegetables from nearby islands to create Cuban food in exile. Huse, Cruz, and Houck (2022) trace the origins of the Cuban sandwich, the Cubano, from upper-class cafés in Havana to the working-class snack of factory workers on the island before the socialist revolution. Then, as if the sandwich ceased to exist on the island, they follow the life of the Cubano in South Florida and beyond. The combination of sweet ham, Cuban-style roasted pork, Swiss cheese, heated in a sandwich press to the exact point where the warmed meat juices combine with gooey cheese, pickle brine, and mustard along with the perfect crunch of freshly baked Cuban bread creates a dynamic flavor profile like none other.

While Cubans on the island eat sandwiches regularly, it is rare to have all of the ingredients at once that are necessary to create the synergy of flavors for the perfect Cubano. In South Florida though, all these ingredients are readily available. The traditional Cuban sandwich has taken on a life and set of meanings off the island. At the same time, sandwiches consumed on the island, often with only ham, or only ham and cheese, rarely with pickles or mustard in my experience, has become something to merely fill the belly. A ghost of what it once was, the Cubano has slowly lost its cultural significance as a delicious, highly sought after Cuban snack on the island.

Like the Cubano, *ropa vieja*, the name of a dish that literally translates to "old clothes," made of shredded beef, became a delicacy rarely consumed in Cuban households on the island. Preparing *ropa vieja* begins with a *sofrito*—oil, onions, peppers, and garlic with cumin, oregano, paprika, tomato paste, and a dash of wine or cooking vinegar. Tomatoes are added to the sauce for *ropa vieja*. This forms the base of the sauce that the shredded beef is served in. The beef, usually flank steak, is either slow cooked or prepared in the pressure cooker with a mojo sauce. Mojo is a garlic-forward sauce made with olive oil, orange juice, lime juice, minced garlic, cumin, oregano, white pepper, and salt. Once the beef is tender and shredded it is added to the tomato *sofrito* base. *Ropa vieja* is served over white rice often with a side of stewed black beans.

During my research over the course of a decade I only observed *ropa vieja* prepared once in a household on the island. In 1963 Fidel Castro made slaughtering a cow without government permission a punishable crime. Cattle ranchers and dairy farmers were highly scrutinized and investigated if any of their flock died. Cubans joked that killing a cow, which could come with a sentence of up to fifteen years in jail, was worse than killing a human in the eyes of the government. During my research, beef was rarely consumed, and it was referred to by my research participants as *carne de no se habla* (the meat we do not speak of); they were scared to mention beef for fear that it might lead to them being investigated. At the same time, black market beef was probably the most sought after and most important black market food product during my research. When purchased on the black market, it was most often found as ground beef rather than steaks. *Ropa vieja* has become a rare delicacy on the island (Moon et al. 2022).

Despite the inaccessibility of beef on the island for the last sixty years, *ropa vieja* persists as a quintessential traditional Cuban dish because it is still commonly consumed among the Cuban diaspora. Serving *ropa vieja* is practically required for a Cuban restaurant in Miami to be considered authentic. This situation demands an analysis of taste of place that extends beyond the bounds of the nation-state in a case where access to necessary ingredients for traditional, authentic recipes is only possible away from the dishes' place of origin (for issues with taste of place and displacement/migration see also Caldwell, Meneley, and Sanders, all this volume). For many Cubans in the diaspora and on the island, it is more common and easier to create "real" Cuban food off the island away from contexts of scarcity.

The decline of *ropa vieja* and the Cubano on the island juxtaposed with their thriving existence in exile poses a challenge to ideas of terroir and taste of place. These foods and the flavors associated with them are Cuban, and consumers continue to think of these dishes as traditional Cuban dishes. But scarcity of ingredients has rendered the "real" traditional versions of these dishes impossible on the island where they originated and continue to be tied. In these cases, authenticity and taste of place are still grounded in "an imagined historical connection with recuperated cuisines and tastes" of "home" while living in exile (Weiss 2012: 614). If we maintain that these dishes in exile retain a Cuban taste of place, then that requires what Harry West (2022) has called the "denaturalization of terroir," whereby links between people, place, and foods are no longer static and durative. The Cuban case offers a clear situation in which not only was the notion of Cuban food established from the mixture of many people and ingredients that originated elsewhere, but also the cuisine and its people continue to produce a sincere Cubanness off the island as well.

Conclusion

The foods outlined in this chapter that participants demarcate as specifically Cuban, as "our" food, incorporate a conscious reflection on how these foods relate to Cubanidad. In the case of Cuban food, the dishes that are seen as specifically Cuban are not unique to Cuba—we find rice and beans, tamales, tubers and pork dishes all over the Caribbean and much of Latin America. The Cuban cuisine that was established after independence from Spain was originally constituted by mixture and movement, it was understood as part of a hybrid and ongoing process defining tradition, meaning, and value. On the island where most ingredients are imported, though notions of freshness and flavor might favor foods grown locally, few traditional Cuban dishes could come together without ingredients grown elsewhere. In addition to mixture and movement as a central component of traditional Cuban taste of place, the Cuban cook's embodied ways of knowing the pacing of bringing ingredients together on the stove or over an open flame are also central to the creation of specific flavors that form the basis of "authentic" Cuban cuisine. Mixture, movement, and embodied practice are also central logics for understanding how the most "real" or authentic versions of a Cuban dish might be produced in exile as in the case of *ropa vieja* or the Cubano. The case of Cuban food reveals how much meaning making around taste of place and authentic or "real" Cuban food takes place in the household kitchen rather than at the level of the producer or the point of purchase, as might be the case in the meaning of terroir in European contexts. In the case of Cuban food, the history of mixing people and ingredients as well as the ongoing geopolitical contexts of migration and exile necessitate a more expansive and adaptable understanding of taste of place that can be sincerely produced on and off the island in the hands of household cooks.

Acknowledgments

I would like to thank all of my Cuban interlocutors for sharing their lives with me. I am grateful to comments from Lee Cabatingan, Erin V. Moore, Malavika Reddy, and Mrinalini Tankha on early drafts, as well as the close commentary of Jakob Klein and Brandi Simpson Miller. I thank the editors, all of the other authors in this volume, and our peer reviewers for their comments and steadfast work in stewarding this volume.

Hanna Garth is a sociocultural and medical anthropologist specializing in the anthropology of food. She is Assistant Professor of Anthropology at Princeton University with affiliations in African American Studies, and the Program in Latin American Studies. She published the book *Food in Cuba: The Pursuit of a Decent Meal*, and coedited the volume *Black Food Matters: Food Justice in the Wake of Racial Justice*.

Notes

1. In this same piece, Ortiz (1940) defends tobacco, which he aligns with Cuban nationalism, and criticizes sugar, which is aligned with imperialism and world exploitation of Cuba. Derived largely from that of Cuban national hero José Martí, Ortiz's perspective on nationalism influenced his view that the capitalist sugar economy was not inevitably global. Ortiz thought globalism to be artificially imposed, caused by a lack of regulation within Cuba.

2. Cuban *ajiaco* is similar to a dish called *sancocho* in Colombia, Ecuador, Peru, Costa Rica, Panama, and the Dominican Republic. In Cuba the word *sancocho* refers to household food scraps used as pig feed.
3. In other parts of Latin America *mestizo* and *mestizaje* are by Indigenous ancestry, whereas in much of the Caribbean *mestizaje* is simply used to connote racial mixing. It is loaded with colonial and contemporary aspirations to improve Caribbean society by whitening the population, with the goal to diminish Africanness in terms of phenotype as well as cultural expression. Khan also notes the different forms of Caribbean mixing as *callaloo* (Trinidad and Tobago), *creolite* (Martinique), *embranquecimento* (Brazil), and *mestizaje* (Mexico and Cuba) (2004: 3).
4. A group of scholars has even broken down the bioactive compounds in the Mediterranean *sofrito*; see Vallverdú-Queralt et al. (2013).
5. All names of people are pseudonyms in accordance with standard anthropological ethics.

References

Benjamin, Medea, Joseph Collins, and Michael Scott. 1984. *No Free Lunch: Food and Revolution in Cuba Today.* Princeton: Princeton University Press.

Cavanaugh, Jillian R., and Shalini Shankar. 2014. "Producing Authenticity in Global Capitalism: Language, Materiality, and Value." *American Anthropologist* 116(1): 51–64.

Eckstein, Susan, and Timothy Wickham-Crowley. 2003. *What Justice? Whose Justice? Fighting for Fairness in Latin America.* Berkeley: University of California Press.

Esquivel, Miguel, and Karl Hammer. 1988. "The 'Conuco': An Important Refuge of Cuban Plant Genetic Resources." *Die Kulturpflanze* 3: 451–63.

Garth, Hanna. 2020. *Food in Cuba: The Pursuit of a Decent Meal.* Stanford: Stanford University Press.

Grasseni, Cristina. 2004. "An Apprenticeship in Breeding Aesthetics." *Social Anthropology* 12(1): 41–55.

Huse, Andrew T., Barbara C. Cruz, and Jeff Houck. 2022. *The Cuban Sandwich: A History in Layers.* Gainesville: University of Florida Press.

Jackson, John L., Jr. 2005. *Real Black: Adventures in Racial Sincerity.* Chicago: University of Chicago Press.

Khan, Aisha. 2001. "Journey to the Center of the Earth: The Caribbean as Master Symbol." *Cultural Anthropology* 16(3): 271–302.

———. 2004. *Callaloo Nation: Metaphors of Race and Religious Identity among South Asians in Trinidad.* Durham: Duke University Press.

Moon, Krystyn R., Jennifer Rhode Ward, José Vazquez Rodriguez, and Jorge Foyo. 2022. "Food Access, Identity, and Taste in Two Rural Cuban Communities." *Gastronomica* 22(1): 66–78.

Opie, Frederick. 2008. *Hog and Hominy: Soul Food from Africa to America.* New York: Columbia University Press.

Ortiz, Fernando.1940. *Contrapunteo cubano del tabaco y el azúcar.* Havana: Jesús Montero. [English trans: (1947) 1995. *Cuban Counterpoint: Tobacco and Sugar.* Translated by Harriet de Onís. Durham, NC: Duke University Press.]

———. 1985. *Nuevo catauro de cubanismos.* [New basket of Cubanisms]. La Habana: Ediciones de Ciencias Sociales.

Paxson, Heather. 2010. "Locating Value in Artisan Cheese: Reverse-Engineering Terroir for New World Landscapes." *American Anthropologist* 112(3): 442–55.

Pérez Firmat, Gustavo. 1997. "A Willingness of the Heart: Cubanidad, Cubaneo, Cubanía." *Cuban Studies Association Occasional Papers*: Paper 8.

Sanderlin, George, ed. and trans. 1971. *Bartolomé de las Casas: A Selection of His Writings*. New York: Knopf, 63–65.

Trouillot, Michel-Rolph. 2003. *Global Transformations: Anthropology and the Modern World.* New York: Palgrave MacMillan.

Trubek, Amy B. 2008. *The Taste of Place: A Cultural Journey into Terroir.* Berkeley: University of California Press.

Trubek, Amy B., and Sarah Bowen. 2008. "Creating the Taste of Place in the United States: Can We Learn from the French?" *GeoJournal* 73: 23–30.

Tsing, Anna. 2015. *The Mushroom at the End of the World: On the Possibility of Life in Capitalist Ruins.* Princeton: Princeton University Press.

Vallverdú-Queralt, Anna, José Fernando Rinaldi de Alvarenga, Ramon Estruch, and Rosa M. Lamuela-Raventos. 2013. "Bioactive Compounds Present in the Mediterranean *Sofrito*." *Food Chemistry* 141(4): 3365–72.

Weiss, Brad. 2011. "Making Pigs Local: Discerning the Sensory Character of Place." *Cultural Anthropology* 26(3): 438–61.

———. 2012. "Configuring the Authentic Value of Real Food: Farm-to-Fork, Snout-to-Tail, and Local Food Movements." *American Ethnologist* 39(3): 614–26.

———. 2022. "Cuisine of Economy, Cuisine of Excess: Materializing Value in Culinary Practice." *Journal of the Royal Anthropological Institute* 28(4): 1309–25.

West, Harry G. 2022. "Terroir Products: A Movable Heritage Feast?" *Review of Agricultural, Food & Environmental Studies* 103(1): 1–27.

Wilk, Richard. 2006. *Fast Food/Slow Food: The Cultural Economy of the Global Food System.* Lanham: Altamira Press.

Zee, Jerry. 2022. *Continent in Dust: Experiments in a Chinese Weather System*. Berkeley: University of California Press.

CHAPTER 12

Food, Place, and Personhood in South India

The Limits of Terroir

James Staples

Introduction

Gongura (*Hibiscus cannabinus L*)—a tart, leafy green vegetable—features a lot in my fieldnotes and memories from the years I have spent in coastal Andhra Pradesh, South India. It was on my first trip there, in 1984, that villagers told me that the vegetable was known as *Andhra matha* (Andhra's mother): a kind of material metonym for the state and the Telugu-speaking people who lived there. Although the leaves grow in other hot countries as well as in other Indian states, the plant is likely indigenous either to India or Saudi Arabia (Mishra, Dash and Das 2018: 2534). It also plays a particularly pertinent role both in Andhra cuisine and in Telugu identity. I soon learned that telling people of my love of *gongura patchidi*—a spicy, sour pickle that was present at every feast and accompanied most other meals—was a surefire way of establishing rapport. Even the demeanor of a gruff police official, who had hardly glanced up from his desk as he processed my application for residency during an eighteen-month research trip from 2005 to 2006, changed entirely when I told him, in response to a casual question about what I liked about being in India, that *gongura patchidi* and *gongura pappu* (pigeon peas cooked with *gongura*) were among my favorite things to eat. I will never know for sure if it sped up approval of my application, but it certainly led to an animated and much friendlier conversation about the joys of Andhra cuisine: he no longer treated me as an outsider.

In the valedictory speeches sometimes made by the elders to mark my various departures from the community where I conducted the bulk of my fieldwork,[1] they often made reference to the fact that, remarkably for a foreigner, in their view, I could eat like they did, with my penchant for *gongura* specifically referenced. It was an appreciation of local food that tied me most closely to those I worked with in Andhra Pradesh and Telangana: it helped to establish me as an honorary Andhra *wallah*, one of them as opposed even, sometimes, to other Indian people from neighboring states.

***

This chapter is not specifically about *gongura*, although *gongura* is certainly part of the story it tells. I begin with it here because, on the face of it at least, my interlocutors' ideas and feelings about *gongura* and other local delicacies appear to resonate well with the French notion of terroir—the taste of a place—that this volume interrogates. Although *gongura* does grow elsewhere, nowhere else, to my knowledge, is either the vegetable, or the dishes made from it, quite so closely associated with a people and a place. A distinctive ecology—tropical, with loamy, well-drained soil and up to ten inches of rain a month in the growing season[2]—combines with agricultural practices and culinary skills fine-tuned over generations to render *gongura* something heralded by my interlocutors as a unique aspect of Andhra culture and, therefore, constitutive of themselves as particular kinds of persons vis-à-vis those of other states. But there are also important differences that framing local foods in India in this way gloss over, and which point to the conceptual limitations of terroir, at least in the senses appropriated by international bureaucracies to serve global trade.

Terroir, understood as a universal, bureaucratic category, arguably flattens out and thus limits anthropological understanding of the relationships between food, place, and personhood in South India and elsewhere. As West (2022; and this volume) argues, conventional understandings of terroir also assume that the relationship between product, people, and place—what he terms the "terroir triad"—are static and durable, when, as ethnographic studies regularly testify, all three are in constant flux. If place, as Raffles puts it, is always "in that flow of becoming" (2002: 185), how can it also be framed as inherently fixed? A notion as complex and as fluid as place requires more nuanced tools to illuminate it.

The issue is not only a conceptual one, however. Terroir also "renders invisible a variety of conflicts" (Beriss 2019: 63) that are implicated in the associations that agricultural products come to have with peoples and places. The histories that frame links between product and place are often obscured, and the workers whose labor has been essential in making those products—like the migrant labor vital to the successes of Darjeeling tea plantations (Besky 2014)—"are often hidden behind the genteel image of the land owners" (Beriss 2019: 63). Assertions of terroir might also be deployed tactically as a way of making claims to disputed land—something the Israeli wine industry, for example, has arguably done in the Golan Heights (Handel et al. 2015; Kastrinou et al. 2021; see also Meneley, this volume). Terroir, in these contexts, can become a tool of the powerful rather than protection for local producers.

In the following, I begin by sketching out some background on how terroir, and the legal protection offered by geographical indications (GIs), have been mobilized by major producers in India. This will offer a comparative basis from which to consider the relationships articulated by my interlocutors in coastal Andhra Pradesh and Hyderabad between people, food, and place. Those whom I worked with over the years, although from comparable poor economic backgrounds, did not constitute a homogenous block of consumers. There were differences, for instance, between coastal Andhra villagers and the city dwellers I worked with in Hyderabad (Staples 2020: 68). The latter were more dependent upon, and had greater access to, industrially produced foods than those in rural contexts, who generally had everyday access to a narrower range of foods, but more that were traceable to their origins, often growing some of their own food. Other, cross-cutting distinctions in what people ate were marked by gender, caste, class, generation, and community affiliation. In terms of the latter, for example, younger people were more likely than their older peers to consume (or desire) foods considered international, such as Chinese-style noodles or pizza.

Despite these differences, however, there were also broad similarities in what my interlocutors considered food (Staples 2020: 68). For most, rice was the centerpiece of two main daily meals,[3] accompanied by side dishes crafted from local vegetables and legumes, flavored from a common palette of spices. Those who marked their relative cosmopolitan sophistication or aspirations to middle-class identity by also consuming foods beyond this menu—such as cauliflower Manchurian from food carts in provincial towns or fast food from international chains in the city—nearly always saw these latter preparations as add-on items to what was considered proper food.

In comparing the logics of terroir and GIs to those of local consumers, I argue that these should not be seen simply as two sides of a familiar binary opposition, with local ideas categorized as "traditional" and grounded in "culture," and those expressed through the globalized idioms represented by the bureaucratic category of GIs as "modern" and universal. Considering the two intersecting logics alongside one another is also useful because it offers ways of thinking beyond such stark dichotomies.

Geographical Indications in India

Geographical indications (GIs), a category created by the World Trade Organization (WTO) to protect products with terroir, are place-based names, recorded in GI registries, "that convey the geographical origin, as well as the cultural and historical identity, of agricultural products" (Bowen and Zapata 2009: 108).[4] In contrast to terroir, which is oriented inward toward locality, GIs are oriented outward, as international markers of quality.[5]

In 1999 Darjeeling tea became India's first GI, giving the product legal protection as the "intellectual property" of, in this instance, the Indian government (Besky 2014). In India, applications for GIs—which any legal entities, including producer associations and state governments, can apply for[6]—are managed by the Geographical Indications Registry, a government-established authority. Once awarded, GIs offer authorized products domestic and international protection. Basmati rice–growing regions, along with over 350 other placed-based products, have subsequently joined the country's list of GIs, which are often framed as a kind of resistance against the impact of placeless food production systems (Bowen and Zapata 2009). Or, as the Indian government phrases it, GIs help "protect reputations carefully built up and painstakingly maintained by the masters of that region . . . traditionally handed over from one generation to the next for centuries."[7] GIs might prevent, according to this logic, traders from other parts of the world from appropriating the distinctive qualities of, for example, basmati rice or Darjeeling tea and claiming them as their own.

If the fact that the term comes from the WTO is insufficient warning of the possible tensions between local, artisan-based food production, on the one hand, and the global export trade the WTO promotes, on the other, there are a number of specific examples in the literature that highlight such paradoxes. Besky's ethnography of Darjeeling tea plantations, for instance, documents how the GI for Darjeeling tea, and the marketing it enables, sanitizes the labor conditions of seasonal, migrant tea workers as "craft," and the industrial plantations, inherited from British colonialism, as "gardens" (2014: 109). Such sanitation is profitable for plantation owners; less so for local agricultural workers. Nor does a GI necessarily ensure a better quality product for consumers. In the Istria region of Croatia, for example, "Istrian ham"—a product with a GI—is often compared unfavorably by local consumers with *domaće* (homemade) ham (Colquhoun, this volume).[8] Moldovan winemaking villagers similarly compare the "good" taste of their homemade wines with the "bad" taste associated with the international award-winning wines of a local winery (Ana 2022).

The paradox, then, is that while GIs are often presented by those applying for them as being about preserving tradition and protecting artisan skills and livelihoods, they also facilitate transnational capitalism, often to the exclusion of the small-scale farmers and producers whose rights they theoretically protect. GIs might thus be understood, following Bruno Latour (1991), as a kind of acultural, globalized system for classifying what are assumed to be the fixed cultural attributes of products made in particular places. Latour drew a distinction between what has been constructed as the "West" and the "Global South." The former, he suggests, classifies the latter as having "culture," while the West perceives itself and its institutions as modern and, therefore, to exist outside or beyond culture. As such, through scientific knowledge, Latour argues that the "West" has distinguished itself both from its own premodern past and from those parts of the world that remain anchored in locally specific "culture." Thought about in these terms, GIs might be considered to provide modern, objective ways through which local connections between places, people, and products might be understood, in contradistinction to how those relationships might be experienced and understood on the ground in local contexts.

GIs are thus part of a bureaucratic system of legal certification and verification, which enables the global marketing of qualities simultaneously said to be anchored in particular places. GIs on basmati rice, for example, have been used to prevent farmers from regions, such as rice producers in the state of Madhya Pradesh (Mishra et al. 2018), from marketing their product as basmati, while large-scale producers (equipped, as the website of one company with the GI certification describes it, "with innovative technology and expert hands") dominate the market.[9] In short, authenticity, for GI-registered products, is based not just on quality as judged by those who consume it (like those I worked with) but by modern, scientific apparatus: statutory definitions, verifications, and bureaucracies, including the Indian government's Agricultural and Processed Food Products Export Development Authority (APEDA).

In the next section I shift away from these official, globalizing categories to consider the significance that those I worked with drew between food, place, and identity.

Food, Place, and Person in South India

If we take the premise of Val Daniel's (1987) classic ethnosociological account of Tamil people in South India seriously, we accept that the food and drink that Hindus consume—and with it the place from which it comes—shapes not only their physical bodies but also their moral substance. We are what we eat not only in the mundane sense envisaged by nutritionists but also in terms of who we are as persons. Place and personhood are inextricably linked. We thrive on rice grown from the land of our *ur*—the place from which we come, rendered in English by my interlocutors as "native place"—because we are also "of" that place: the two things match. Eating particular foods, grown in particular places, helps people to maintain their "substance codes" (Daniel 1987: 186), a term coined by McKim Marriott (1976: 110) to recognize that, in contrast to Western philosophical traditions, in India (and, for that matter, much of the world)[10] social actors are seen as inseparable from their actions. By this logic, in addition to thriving on food grown in our *ur*, we might also fall sick when we consume the food or water of another place, because it is less compatible with our substance (Staples 2016: 79). While ethnosociological accounts aimed at highlighting ontological differences might well have overdrawn the distinction between Western and non-Western (or, more specifically, Hindu) persons, the broader point of Daniel's Marriott-inspired analysis still holds true for many of those I encountered in villages in South India: "where" sustenance came from in relation to "who" ate it mattered.

For example, on a week-long cycle rally with a dozen village men a few years ago, taking us across state borders into Tamil Nadu, several of my companions complained of stomach upsets caused by the changes in drinking water en route. This was not because it was contaminated, they stressed, but because it was unsuitable for their bodies. In the terminology of the ethnosociologists, it did not match their "substance codes" (Marriott 1976: 110). Still more complained, among ourselves if not directly to our hosts, about the quality of Tamil Nadu rice we were fed on arrival in our final destination compared to that grown in Andhra. Not only were the individual grains too short and fat, so less suitable for soaking up the liquid elements of the accompanying dishes, but they also, I was told, lacked flavor. Like the water, the change in rice also unsettled stomachs. There were several things at play here, not all of which were related to precisely where the rice had been grown, although that was important. For one thing, feeding people foods deemed to be of low quality could itself be seen as insulting, with refusal to accept such food a potential strategy for reasserting one's identity and dignity—something I saw used to productive effective in other fieldwork contexts (Staples 2008).

At the same time, choices made around what foods to take and what not to take, and over which foods are acceptable and which are not, also play a central role in defining personhood. My fellow cyclists were not only implicitly complaining about the rice and those who had prepared and offered it when they shared their critiques; they were also asserting their identities as Andhra (or Telugu) people, in this case in contradistinction to Tamil people, despite their geographical proximity. Unlike products for export granted GIs, for my interlocutors (in common with those of Colquhoun, this volume, in Croatia), *who* consumed locally produced food was as important as *where* that food was produced.

To offer another example, local chickens, raised within the village by one's neighbors—like the fruit and vegetables from one's own land—were nearly always heralded as better quality than those purchased outside. In part this was because such chickens had the authenticity officially associated with GI foods: there was less opportunity for them to have been tampered with or fed what were glossed as "chemicals" or "hormones," and their successful rearing relied on locally acquired skills and knowledge. In having been raised on the same soil as those consuming them, the chickens provided meat that was already well-aligned to the consumers bodies. But it was also because local chickens, unlike the white, plumper broiler hens reared en masse in ever larger chicken farms—the "global chicken" of Dixon's (2002: 164) description—were considered indigenous to India.

Opinions on this, it should be noted, were not homogenous. Ramaswamy,[11] who ran a shop selling chicken—slaughtered at the point of sale—in the market closest to where I conducted fieldwork, was insistent when I interviewed him in 2017 that the broiler hens he now sold tasted better than their predecessors, and that the tenderness of their flesh made them more suitable than country birds for dry fried chicken, *pakoras*, and for the Chinese-style preparations that were sold as popular snacks from stalls in the bazaar. Part of this, of course, was positive marketing on his part. Broiler hens, after all, were cheaper to produce and thus more profitable. But his commentary also points to a tension between preferences for foods deemed local and the alternative desire—expressed by some of my interlocutors, particularly those under forty—to express cosmopolitan sophistication through knowledge and consumption of what they saw as foreign foods. Eating in the local town at food joints like Rock Starz, which emulated international food chain restaurants like Kentucky Fried Chicken, enabled diners—at least among their peer groups—to distinguish themselves from others as modern (Staples 2020: 123).

This points to the understanding that while locally produced foods were generally seen as better for local bodies, local people were themselves differentiated from one another—not only along caste and communal lines, which I will come to shortly, but also in relation to generation and, importantly, class. Aspirational middle-class bodies, or at least the identities self- and other-ascribed to those bodies, might thrive on cosmopolitan preparations—from pizza to noodles—which situate them on an imagined global stage. While this certainly nuances the claim that local is always better, this did not necessarily represent a contradiction for my interlocutors. Snacks—including the "foreign" preparations described here—were considered different to "food," the usually rice-based meals consumed at home. This is a point well illustrated by the fact that many people I knew in the village considered it acceptable to consume such items, but never rice-based meals, during weekly religious fasts. One could, therefore, justify eating pizza or noodles bought from outside the home, while insisting that the rice and water of one's *ur* was vital for maintaining one's health.

The kind of industrially produced food served in places like Rock Starz or purchased from supermarkets had benefits beyond conveying the sophistication necessary for cultivating middle-class identities, however. As with commercially packaged foods elsewhere (see, e.g., Kjaernes, Harvey, and Ward 2007; Bergeaud-Blackler, Fischer, and Lever 2015), mass-produced goods from outside could sometimes generate reassurance and trust (Staples 2020: 55). Several rural women told me, for example, that packaged milk from a commercial dairy in the local town was considered safer to that purchased from neighboring buffalo owners: the plastic packets in which the former was sealed communicated a level of hygiene (different from, but often blurred into, ideas of ritual purity). Milk from a neighbor, unless you really trusted them, could always be watered down, and accusations of such practices were commonplace. It was for this reason, after all, that milk sellers traditionally took their cow or buffalo directly to the buyer, milking her in front of the customer so it was clear that the milk was not being contaminated (see, e.g., Raman's memoir of food in 1950s Madras, 2011: 167). Likewise, I was often advised by my village neighbors to buy my spices prepackaged and branded rather than, as they would, loose in the market. At least I would know, people said, that they were not "duplicate," the English word commonly deployed to denote fakes or willfully contaminated goods.

My point here is that while unprocessed foods rooted in the locality—grown in the soil or from the animals that grazed on what grew there—were considered better quality, and more aligned to the bodies of those who consumed them, they did not come risk free. For someone like me, who, despite having acquired some local tastes (and the cultural capital that came with that), was rooted in another place and likely lacked the embodied skills to judge quality, the potential risks were sometimes seen as outweighing the potential benefits. Hygiene, from the perspective of village friends of all ages who took an interest in my welfare, was more important than ritual purity or "substance code" for a Western body like mine, which, by implication, was seen as cosmopolitan, more akin to—but still different from—what were perceived as urban middle-class Indian bodies.

It was not just a case of matching "where" (and who) food came from with the consumer, however; different "types" of food were also compatible with different kinds of local bodies. Food considered "heating"—such as onions and garlic—might be compatible with people from "hot castes" (Daniel 1987: 186) but were potentially health threatening when consumed by members of "cool castes." Such classificatory systems, however, are highly contingent and changeable (cf. Staples 2008). According to Daniel's fieldwork, buffalo milk is considered "hot" by Telugu Brahmins of Kalappur but cooling by Parayar caste members of the same village (Daniel 1987: 186; Staples 2016: 79). The importance of particular qualities of foods also varied according to season, with cooling foods that were considered essential in the summer being riskier to consume during the winter. In my own research on the politics of meat consumption in India, there were numerous comparable examples of people explaining that the meat of particular animals—such as that of the water buffalo for some of my Dalit interlocutors, or of cow beef for Muslim consumers—was more or less suitable for particular bodies, as well as in particular seasons (Staples 2014, 2020). In addition, children might be less vulnerable to ritual pollution from food than their elders (Cantlie 1981; Caplan 2008; Donner 2008), while widows (and women more generally) might need to exercise extra caution in managing the risks of excess heat because of its potential to inflame bodily passions (Lamb 2000). In short, it was not just where the food came from that was important but who ate what and when. Understanding food in India thus goes beyond the neatly bounded terroir triad of product, place, and skills: it also requires knowledge of how those factors intersect with different consumers across changing contexts.

Nevertheless, regionality was important to those I worked with. Produce such as the local Baganapalle mango and the Guntur chili pepper (both of which had

GIs, even though no consumers I knew had ever referenced that fact) or *gongura* (which did not, but as noted above, was more significant in defining a local identity) was always compared favorably with the food of "outsiders." In part this was to do with the short chain between production and consumption, which, in village contexts, was often as short as the walk to the kitchen garden. In the same way that observing the milk being pumped directly from a cow's udders ensured that the milk was not being doctored, eating food grown in one's own soil also avoided risks of external contamination. But, like GI-identified products, it was also about the "distinctiveness" of, say, a particular type of mango as compared to other mangoes grown elsewhere. They were considered better, not just because they were objectively better but because they were intertwined with one's own personhood. This connection was not just to do with the literal connection that people and food are said to have through the soil of their natal homes but also about the pride that one might take in the positive qualities associated with their place or region—something that even I, as an outsider, was not immune to.

I recall, for example, a light-hearted argument I was drawn into in a coffee house during an academic conference in Kolkata back in 2004, in which my Bengali discussant was decrying Andhra cuisine as "all fire and no taste." I felt duty bound to defend the fare that my interlocutors held so dear, critiquing Bengali food (as my Telugu friends did) as "too sweet and not sufficiently spicy." Although my Andhra identity was an adopted one, at that moment of defending its culinary traditions I surprised myself at the strong sense of belonging I had developed—not so much to a fixed physical location but certainly to a group of people associated with a place and the cultural practices and artifacts that helped define them. Local varieties, and the dishes that could be prepared with them, were central to emplacement.

Worth noting here, too, is that the associations people had to a place were sustained, and in some ways made stronger, when they had migrated elsewhere (see, e.g., Vallianatos and Raine 2008: 356), a point illustrated by the fact that defending Andhra cuisine was more important in Kolkata than it was in the village. For Telugu people in the diaspora—the largest number of whom are in North America—types of food and how they are prepared in these contexts seem more significant than the auditable provenance of ingredients that terroir demands. I did know of at least one mother who sent family in the United States food that had been prepared by her own hand, however, and the fact that a parcel courier's office in the local town displayed special rates for delivering pickles and sweetmeats overseas suggested she was not alone in this.[12] But when products were not easily sent from home, they could sometimes be locally sourced: online blogs, for instance, share recipes for *gongura pappu* and *patchidi* from locations as far away as Silicon Valley and Singapore,[13] while a restaurant in Sunnyvale, California, to take just one example, offers such Telugu specialties as Rayalaseema goat *vepudu* and *gongura* boneless chicken biryani.[14] Place here is not restricted to the geographical boundaries of Andhra Pradesh and Telangana, although the existence of those locales—imagined or concrete—is essential for the re-creation of those places elsewhere.

Finally, back in coastal Andhra, people's positive associations with local foods were also often bound up, as for their peers in the diaspora, in nostalgia. In their case, though, it was not nostalgia for an imagined homeland but for a past when food tasted better. Decades ago, I was told by older villagers, there were fewer agrichemicals—or "medicines," as people referred to them—used to produce vegetables. Carrots, friends said, really used to have the flavor of the *matti*—the earth, the Telugu word closest to the French *terroir*—and required less seasoning to make them palatable (Staples 2020: 72, 73), a trope also common elsewhere in India (Gold 2015: 552–53; Gupta 1998: 2–4). Likewise, chickens that were home reared over a six-month period rather than the six weeks it took to get a modern broiler to the pot gave them the chewiness and depth of flavor that older people, in particular, longed for. And although none of my informants referenced the expensive organic foods marketed in affluent urban areas, they nevertheless expressed a preference for produce they considered more natural; the very kinds of produce that GIs and the concept of terroir were meant to protect and promote. What terroir elides, however, is the understanding that the distinctive ecologies it documents are not static but, as my interlocutors were well aware, liable to change over time and in response to other factors.

Conclusion

A key limitation of the terroir concept, at least in the senses it has been invoked in relation to global trade, is that it fixes place, as well as the people and the products produced there, in both space and time. Local perceptions of place in relation to food, on the other hand, are far more fluid, nuanced, and contingent. In drawing out the apparent contradictions between my interlocutors' understandings and experiences of taste and place and those embodied in the notions of terroir and GIs, however, I am conscious of the danger of reasserting a "tradition" versus "modernity" dichotomy, with classical South Asian ideas about the body and person—as well as the more nuanced notions expressed by those I worked with—conceived of as "traditional" and context specific, and those that relate to GIs and/or the marketing of products as "modern" and global. Such a split risks allowing universalizing categories—paradoxically placeless even as they are applied to specific places—to sideline those deployed by people in everyday life.

Such a split is avoidable, however. The Latourian thinking I invoked earlier pushes us to conceive of terroir and GIs not as neutral and universally applicable but, like "development" itself (Gupta 1998), as artifacts of a positioning every bit as cultural as the variable categories deployed by my interlocutors. Thought about in this way, terroir might be understood as a kind of standardized template for classifying and valuing agricultural products, one that has emerged out of particular historical processes and which is aligned to a particular set of capitalist logics. Indeed, one of the problems of approaching terroir and the bureaucratic systems set up to protect it in international trade as objective ways of understanding the links between people, place, and product is that it also obscures the political (mis)uses of such classifications in the ways outlined earlier in this chapter. Framing terroir as a culturally specific means of classification, however, renders it potentially comparable with, rather than opposed to, the various South Indian ways of understanding the relations between people, place, and foods that I outlined in the second part of the chapter.

In particular, my examples (in common with others in this volume, e.g., those from Ghana and Morocco in the chapters by Simpson Miller and Graf) demonstrate that to the triad of producer, place, and product, a fourth dimension—that of the consumer—also needs to be factored into an understanding of how food and place are intertwined. Consumers, here, are not a homogenous mass, differentiated only by their willingness to appreciate products with terroir, but are themselves uniquely linked to places in ways that render their bodies more or less compatible with particular foods at different times. Along with their individual "substance codes," people's consumption is also shaped by caste, gender, and community identities, as well as by class and class aspirations, and seasonality. These multiple considerations intersected with a more general affiliation to place that manifested itself in preferences for particular foods and preparations, such as the *gongura patchidi* I introduced in my opening vignette, often against the dishes of other places. Shared references to regional allegiances marked by food also enabled, when it was strategically useful for people to do so, the bracketing of other divisive identities, such as those rooted in caste or religion.

For my interlocutors, place was physical and portable—rather than anchored to geographical boundaries—in the sense that it was considered literally embodied in the people who emerged out of it and, less tangibly, carried also in memories. Like terroir foods, the local foods of those I lived with, considered important to their shared identities, were also connected to the skills and knowledge required to produce them, but they additionally demanded tacit knowledge and appreciation of those foods' regional significance and history on the part of cooks and consumers. It was those shared sensibilities—whether in the village, the city, or the diaspora—that drew together the connections people made between place, food, and their identities. The fact that I knew about *gongura* and its local importance was enough, in certain contexts, to link me to my Andhra friends and their place in the world. Official designations, like those afforded by GIs, were conceived of as the tools of powerful producers, well beyond their reach and, in any case, irrelevant to their everyday consumption. The relationship my interlocutors described between food and personhood, however, also extended well beyond considerations grounded in place: issues of risk and trust, bodily compatibilities, time, gender, caste, and class were all intricately entangled with the connections made between food and place in ways that an enquiry limited to terroir alone could not accommodate.

Acknowledgments

A big thank you to Anna Colquhoun and Katharina Graf, both for organizing the original workshop at which I presented the paper on which this chapter was based, and for their constructive, nurturing approach toward bringing this volume together. I am grateful, too, to the other workshop participants, many of them published in this volume, for their valuable feedback, both at the workshop itself and in response to reading subsequent drafts.

James Staples is Professor of Social Anthropology at Brunel University of London, coeditor of the journal *Medical Anthropology*, and cohost of the podcast *The Migration Menu* (www.themigrationmenu.com). He is author of numerous articles and three books, including *Sacred Cows and Chicken Manchurian: The Everyday Politics of Eating Meat in India* (2020), and is currently engaged in research on British South Asian restaurants in West London.

Notes

1. I have been visiting my field site—a self-run leprosy colony and the surrounding area—since 1984, officially undertaking research there from 1999. This has included multiple visits to South India, including PhD fieldwork in 1999–2000, and sixteen months, split between the village and Hyderabad (now capital of Telangana state) from 2005 to 2006. Targeted fieldwork on food was undertaken in 2016 and 2017, building on copious references to food and eating in my field notes from previous visits.
2. Jagdish, "Gongura Farming (Roselle); Cultivation Practices," Agrifarming, last updated 9 December 2023, https://www.agrifarming.in/gongura-farming-roselle-cultivation-practices (retrieved 7 March 2025).
3. Which is itself a change ushered in by the Green Revolution of the 1960s, prior to which rice had to be supplemented by finger millet and sorghum (Staples 2020: 72; see also Frankel 1971; Gupta 1998: 2–4; Chaudhuri 2005).
4. Under the Indian Geographical Indication of Goods (Registration and Protection) Act 1999.
5. I am grateful to Marion Demossier (personal communication) for pointing out this important distinction between terroir and GIs.
6. Office of the Controller General of Patents, Designs and Trade Marks, Department for Promotion of Industry and Internal Trade, Ministry of Commerce and Industry, Government of India, "Frequently Asked Questions (FAQs)," https://ipindia.gov.in/faq-gi.htm (retrieved 25 October 2023).

7. Ibid.
8. See also Graf, this volume, on the comparable Moroccan notion of *beldi*.
9. India's KRBL, the world's largest rice miller, provides 30 percent of domestic basmati rice and 25 percent of the export market, having expanded with substantial overseas investment.
10. Marion Demossier (personal communication) notes, for example, that some French wine consumers also express not only a preference for the wine of their local region but also their inability to digest wines from elsewhere.
11. All names used in this chapter are pseudonyms.
12. David E. Sutton writes similarly about food packages sent from Greece to family members in the diaspora to help overcome the sometimes painful sense of disjunction experienced by people separated from food and foodways that help define home (Sutton 2001: 77-78).
13. Swasthi's Recipes, "Gongura," https://www.indianhealthyrecipes.com/?s=gongura (retrieved 17 March 2023).
14. Sankranti Indian Cuisine, "Catering Details," http://sankrantimenu.com/#menu (retrieved 17 March 2023).

References

Ana, Daniela. 2022. *Wine Is Our Bread: Labour and Value in Moldovan Winemaking.* New York: Berghahn.

Bergeaud-Blackler, Florence, Johan Fischer, and John Lever, eds. 2015. *Halal Matters: Islam, Politics and Markets in Global Perspective.* London: Routledge.

Beriss, David. 2019. "Food: Location, Location, Location." *Annual Review of Anthropology* 48: 61–75.

Besky, Sarah. 2014. "The Labor of Terroir and the Terroir of Labor: Geographical Indication and Darjeeling Tea Plantations." *Agriculture & Human Values* 31: 83–96.

Bowen, Sarah, and Ana Valenzuela Zapata. 2009. "Geographical Indications, *Terroir*, and Socioeconomic and Ecological Sustainability: The Case of Tequila." *Journal of Rural Studies* 25: 108–19.

Cantlie, Audrey. 1981. "The Moral Significance of Food among Assamese Hindus." In *Culture and Morality: Essays in Honour of Christoph von Fürer-Haimendorf*, edited by Adrian C. Mayer, 42–64. Delhi: Oxford University Press.

Caplan, Patricia. 2008. "Crossing the Veg/Non-veg Divide: Commensality and Sociality among the Middle Classes in Madras/Chennai." *South Asia: Journal of South Asian Studies* 31(1): 118–42.

Chaudhuri, Sabuj Kumar. 2005. "Genetic Erosion of Agrobiodiversity in India and Intellectual Property Rights: Interplay and Some Key Issues." *Patentmatics* 5(6). Retrieved from http://eprints.rclis.org/7902/1/Patentmatics_June_2005.pdf.

Daniel, E. Valentine. 1987. *Fluid Signs: Being a Person the Tamil Way.* Berkeley: University of California Press.

Dixon, Jane. 2002. *The Changing Chicken: Chooks, Cooks, and Culinary Cuisine.* Sydney: University of New South Wales Press Ltd.

Donner, Henrike. 2008. "New Vegetarianism: Food, Gender and Neo-liberal Regimes in Bengali Middle-Class Families." *South Asia: Journal of South Asian Studies* 31(1): 143–69.

Frankel, Francine R. 1971. *India's Green Revolution: Economic Gains and Political Costs.* Princeton: Princeton University Press.
Gold, Ann. 2015. "Food Values Beyond Nutrition." In *The Oxford Handbook of Food, Politics, and Society*, edited by Ronald J. Herring, 545–67. Oxford: Oxford University Press.
Gupta, Akhil. 1998. *Postcolonial Developments: Agriculture in the Making of Modern India.* Durham: Duke University Press.
Kjaernes, Unni, Mark Harvey, and Alan Warde. 2007. *Trust in Food: A Comparative and Institutional Analysis.* Basingstoke: Palgrave Macmillan.
Handel, Ariel, Galit Rand, and Marco Allegra. 2015. "Wine-Washing: Colonization, Normalization, and the Geopolitics of Terroir in the West Bank's Settlements." *Environment & Planning A: Economy & Space* 47(6): 1351–67.
Kastrinou, A. Maria A., Salman Fakher El-Deen, and Steven B. Emery. 2021. "The Stateless (Ad)vantage? Resistance, Land and Rootedness in the Israeli-Occupied Syrian Golan Heights." *Territory, Politics, Governance* 9(5): 636–55.
Lamb, Sarah. 2000. *White Saris and Sweet Mangoes: Aging, Gender, and Body in North India.* Berkeley: University of California Press.
Latour, Bruno. 1991. *We Have Never Been Modern.* Cambridge: Harvard University Press.
Marriott, M. 1968. "Caste Ranking and Food Transactions: A Matrix Analysis." In *Structure and Change in Indian Society*, ed. M. Singer and B. S. Cohn, 133–72. Chicago: Aldine.
———. 1976. "Hindu Transactions: Diversity without Dualism." In *Transactions and Meaning: Directions in the Anthropology of Exchange and Symbolic Behavior*, edited by Bruce Kapferer, 109–42. Philadelphia: Institute for the Study of Human Issues.
———. 1990. *India through Hindu Categories.* London: SAGE.
Mishra, Subhrajyoti, Dilip Kumar Dash, and Arun Kumar Das. 2018. "South Indian Leafy Vegetable Gongura (Hibiscus sabdariffa L.) as an Important Medicinal Herb: A Review." *Journal of Pharmacognosy and Phytochemistry* SP1: 2534–38.
Narsing Rao, G., P. G. Prabhakara Rao, K. Balaswamy, and D. G. Rao. 2011. "Preparation of Instant Tomato Pickle Mix and Evaluation of Its Storage Stability." *International Food Research Journal* 18: 589–93.
Raffles, Hugh. 2002. *In Amazonia: A Natural History.* Princeton: Princeton University Press.
Raman, Parvathi. 2011. "'Me in Place, and the Place in Me': A Migrant's Tale of Food, Home and Belonging." *Food, Culture & Society* 14(2): 165–80.
Staples, James. 2008. "'Go On, Just Try Some!' Meat and Meaning-Making among South Indian Christians." *South Asia: Journal of South Asian Studies* 31(1): 36–55.
———. 2014. "Civilising Tastes: From Caste to Class in South Indian Foodways." In *Food Consumption in Global Perspective: Essays in the Anthropology of Food in Honour of Jack Goody*, edited by Jakob A. Klein and Anne Murcott, 65–86. New York: Palgrave Macmillan.
———. 2016. "Food, Commensality and Caste in South Asia." In *The Handbook of Food and Anthropology*, edited by Jakob A. Klein and James L. Watson, 74–93. London: Bloomsbury.
———. 2020. *Sacred Cows and Chicken Manchurian: The Everyday Politics of Eating Meat in India.* Seattle: University of Washington Press.
Sutton, David E. 2001. *Remembrance of Repasts: An Anthropology of Food and Memory.* Oxford: Berg.
Vallianatos, Helen, and Kim Raine. 2008. "Consuming Food and Constructing Identities among Arabic and South Asian Immigrant Women." *Food, Culture and Society* 11(3): 355–73.

West, Harry G. 2022. "Terroir Products: A Movable Heritage Feast?" *Review of Agricultural, Food & Environmental Studies* 103(1): 1–27.

Zhang, M., N. S. Hettiarachchy, R. Horax, A. Kannan, A. Praisoody, and A. Muhundan. 2011. "Phytochemicals, Antioxidant and Antimicrobial Activity of Hibiscus Sabdariffa, Centella Asiatica, Moringa Oleifera and Murraya Koenigii Leaves." *Journal of Medicinal Plants* 5(30): 6672-6680.

CHAPTER 13

To *Chop* Means to Eat

The Cosmology of Taste in Ghanaian Foodways

Brandi Simpson Miller

Introduction

This chapter is a historical account of *chop*, a term that illustrates the importance of a gendered division of labor to the making of not only food but also place, taste, and people. *Chop* offers up an understanding of how women, in their role as producers and reproducers of ethnic social identity, have historically maintained layered sets of embodied relationships to food and to place. This chapter seeks to demonstrate that gender relations were inseparable from *chop*'s meanings in relation to place, ethnicity, and cosmology. *Chop* offers a new set of questions and conceptual tools, based on the gendered aspects of place making, with which scholars may ground their understanding of how food is linked in forming people and place.

Chop meant (and still means) proper food, and I will employ it here as a tool for exploring foods taste, texture, and emplacement both in historic Ghana and today. A close exploration of the concept of *chop* and West African foodways has not been investigated in the existing historical literature. *Chop* related to the common meal format of a starch and its accompanying soup, both of which were composed of local regionally specific ingredients. *Chop* and its origins in local ecology, agricultural practices, processing, and culinary skill allowed people to distinguish themselves from their neighbors and to define their social relationships. However, *chop*'s true value lies in its connection to local cosmology, which in this context is used to highlight how people made sense of the universe—their place in it—and was intertwined with the concept of a divine presence embedded in the landscape. *Chop*, or proper food, gave people the ability to secure a claim to the local landscape that was renewed with each meal, and that ensured the fertility of the region and the women who inhabited it. A versatile concept that incorporated migrations, trade, and changing economic organization into evolving ethnic identities, the concept of *chop*, as relayed in numerous origin stories, was founded upon a gendered division of labor that can be traced back several centuries in the historical record.

Development of the Term *Chop*

The earliest known use of the noun *chop* is in the seventeenth century, developing from the Hindi word *chaap*, meaning, imprint, seal or brand, or instrument for stamping. The word may have formed from the sound associated with its use. The word *chop* then is a consequence of the British Empire's expansion into the Indian subcontinent, where merchants and civil servants traveling from British India to other outposts of the empire spread the word (Purchas 1905; Lim 2016). By the early nineteenth century the word *chop* came to mean "trademark," as well as something that was first rate (Greene's Dictionary of Slang n.d.).

In Nigeria in the early twentieth century, the word *chop* made a distinction between local and foreign food—local food being composed of locally produced, culturally significant starchy staples such as yam, millet, maize, and cassava:

> "food" n. can be as S[tandard] E[nglish], but most commonly applies to starchy staples; "let us go chop food," "let us go and eat a full meal," "I need food, not snacks," "We have food but no soup." (Blench 2005: 10)

> "continental" a. describes non-Nigerian food of vaguely European type. (Blench 2005: 6)

In both Nigeria and in Ghana, to "*chop* small" or "small *chop*" came to mean the consumption of snacks, not starchy staples. Only local, "heavy" food was considered *chop* (Osseo-Asare 2002: 49–57). James McCann observed that regardless of the ecological region, most cooking in West Africa was based upon starches that imparted a feeling of fullness: "Starches are … bland. Yet they provide an essential factor of texture, shape, and bulk that frames other components of a meal and is in fact the defining feature of the culinary culture" (2009: 33). The most desirable quality of proper food was the ability to satiate hunger and to provide a feeling of fullness. Also, as proper food was eaten with the fingers and was usually swallowed, not chewed, the presence of a pleasing smooth and heavy texture of both the soup and starch was essential (Osseo-Asare 2002; La Fleur 2012: 123). In Ghana the texture of the food was and still is integral to the taste of food and important to it being considered "proper." It was the embodied daily labor of women in the processing of starchy staples that produced proper food: "Just as daily food labor was a task of the body, the use of technological objects such as a grinding stone, a garden hoe, a fishing basket, or a cooking pot was a sensorial and embodied experience. Women's quotidian actions and gestures were purposeful and drew together their environmental and technological expertise" (Twagira 2021: 4).

Cultural memory is performative, and the dissemination of culture often happens via daily bodily practices such as food preparation (Counsell 2009). Women's bodies served as a conduit through which meaning was made from foodstuffs. In the context of Ghana (or as it was known in the late nineteenth and early twentieth centuries, the Gold Coast) women's embodied food-preparation skills and knowledge, through the use of tools such as grinding stones or mortars and pestles, served to transmit cultural knowledge via the texture of the starchy staple.

The word *chop* was not found in common usage in Ghana until the very late nineteenth and early twentieth centuries. In the nineteenth century, the Twi word *di* or *dzidzi* was commonly used to mean to eat, to have the usufruct of, to possess, or to live a luxurious life. It also meant to have sexual intercourse with, to practice onanism, or to masturbate (Christaller 1933: 83). Generally, for those using a mortar and pestle to process starchy staples, the pestle represented the male part. For fufu eaters especially, "pounding fufu" was used as a metaphor for sexual intercourse. Thus, the cooking of food by a woman for a man definitively signified a sexual relationship that is still extant (Allman and Tashjian 2000: 60; Clark 2014: 51). "Cooking in the south is still a fundamentally private act with connotations for marriage and/or sexual liaison" (McCann 2009: 129). The overall material "tasting" of women's work was also about more than just place. It engendered sexual relations between men and women.

In twentieth-century Ghana, the word *chop* began to be used in a similar fashion to *di* or *dzidzi*, both as a noun (meaning food) and as a verb (to have sex with) (Robertson 1984). The word *chop* came to replace *dzidzi* after British colonization and the establishment of extractive industries in the early twentieth century: "The sexual connotation of cooking also applies to commercial sources of the type of food served at evening meals. Informal restaurants serving these heavy meals to patrons of ordinary incomes are called chop bars. Many are perfectly respectable, but the suspicion persists that the chop bar proprietor or her assistant provides sexual services along with the evening meal, as a wife does" (Clark 1989: 326–28).

Here we have the meaning of the word *chop* that blends food and sex and situates it in the context of capitalist colonial enterprises between 1890 and 1919 in industries such as palm oil production and gold extraction. Mechanized mining and railway towns, situated in places in which there were no densely inhabited settlements, attracted a heavily male labor force and created a demand for sellers of cooked food and retailers of alcohol (Akyeampong 1996: 48, 101). *Chop* bars filled that need by selling indigenous heavy—that is, local—foods. Operated by women in urban areas, at rest stops, and near markets in rural areas, *chop* bars were customarily patronized by men who benefitted from the labor of women who were producing multiple regional dishes from across Ghana to satisfy migratory workers.

Figure 13.1. Cooks at the University of Ghana prepare lunch. Ghana, 2014. © Brandi Simpson Miller

Place and Ethnic Identity

Chop was, and still is, proper food that is structured by the microclimate. Regional and ethnic differences in Ghanaian cooking were (and still are) generally reflected in the starchy staple produced in a particular region.[1] New starchy staples could be adopted provided they grew well in the region and the texture of the older staple could be replicated. For example, when maize was introduced in the sixteenth century, local coastal women developed varieties that would suit their microclimate and their processing methods of grinding and fermenting (La Fleur 2012: 90–95). It is in this way that new starches were slotted into the repertoire of regional foodways and became *chop*.

The space and adaptation of new starchy staples into the local repertoire reflected change over time in how both *chop* and regional ethnic identities evolved. Much like other ethnic groups on the coast, the Ewe history was a tale of exodus (Simpson Miller 2021: 56). This exodus began in Benin in the late sixteenth century, through present-day Notsie in Togo, to southeastern Ghana. Beginning in 1679 the coastal Ewe received the first wave of what would be successive migrations of refugees fleeing conflicts from the expanding Akwamu state on the west side of the Volta River. Ewe speakers became early adopters of cassava as a foodstuff to cope with the waves of refugees escaping the slave trade. In towns physically separated from the mainland, they lived on the other side of the lagoons and mangrove swamps of the coast. Sandy soils were not capable of supporting traditional millet production, so the Ewe turned to cassava, which they named *agbeli*, or "there is life" (Agbodeka 1997: 97; La Fleur 2012: 167).

The fleeing of the Ewe people is still commemorated each year at the Ayiza or Hogbetsoso harvest festival on the coast. Hogbetsoso is from the Ewe *hogbesotsoza*—*hogbe* (meaning homeland, in this case Notsie), *tsotso* (meaning exodus), and *za* (festival) (Bosman 1967: 300–301; Venkatachalam 2015: 152). Both the major festival commemorating their flight to safety and the commentary of contemporary observers tell us that the Ewe relied heavily upon cassava as a major part of their survival strategy during the seventeenth century. Thus, cassava became a marker of general Ewe ethnic identity.

Clashes over Christian commensality customs in missionary schools revealed the connection between regional foodways, social boundaries, and ethnic identities, and clarified the role of women in maintaining them. Institutions such as the Presbyterian Training College at Akropong in Akwapim, founded in 1848, provided exposure to both foreign and regional foodways and identities. Built to produce teacher-catechists, it drew students from every region. To limit contact from outside caterers and the young women who worked for them as food deliverers, and to establish the practice of commensal meals, the college replaced them with a staff of male cooks from Liberia. This caused a strike that shut down the seminary. Students objected to Kru men as cooks because they were unfamiliar with local dishes. The Kru men were charged with failing to use the proper techniques to produce the correct texture of starchy staples. For example, the Kru cooks did not take the necessary care with the sorting and preparation of cassava before cooking it, resulting in boiled cassava of varying textures (Miescher 2005: 79–80).

The origin, gender, and technique of the cooks were not the only objections, however. "Akan students objected to the preparation and the choice of cassava as a staple dish, since this root crop was considered 'food for pigs' and other ethnic groups, especially for 'Ewes'" (Miescher 2005: 79–80). Here food intersected with gender, authority, and the maintenance of ethnic boundaries. The Kru men lacked the authority to produce *chop*. Local Akropong women knew which starches to prepare for different ethnic groups, and they possessed the embodied techniques of *chop* preparation that would produce the desired texture. Only the local women had the requisite knowledge and authority to replicate *chop* for the students. The strike was a success—the Kru men were dismissed and replaced with local women, and students were allowed to purchase their own food in town on Wednesdays. This incident highlighted the power of regional starchy staples to define ethnic identity, which is tied to place.

The Akropong student strike also firmly identified women as makers of place, producing appropriate *chop* to ensure social reproduction. Scholar and writer

Figure 13.2. A resident of Accra near Makola Market gives a *fufu* cooking demonstration in her courtyard. Ghana, 2014. © Brandi Simpson Miller

Psyche Williams-Forson encountered this in her own experiences as a partner to a Ghanaian man, indicating that this concept of women as makers of place is durable: "Although unspoken and certainly debatable, it seems that my ethnicity and not my cooking skills were called into question. Anything I cooked that was a non-native food was usually eaten without hesitation. This is not to say that all the kinfolk who participated in our culinary network cooked to his liking—hardly—but the absence of my direct cultural knowledge in how to cook this cuisine was an issue" (2010: 450). As an American, Williams-Forson lacked the authority to prepare *chop*. Therefore, it is not just that proper *chop* is cooked by a woman. The woman needs to be equipped with an embodied understanding of the requirements to replicate *chop*.

Beginning in the late nineteenth century when the Gold Coast was transitioning to a cash economy, the transformation of starch into heavy food was the woman's work, while the man's job was to supply her with "*chop* money"—the funds to prepare the cooked dinner (Christaller 1881: 76; Blench 2006: 12). In the contemporary parlance, the woman would be called the *chop* master—the one who purchased the food and set the menu (Blench 2006: 12): "Traditional maternal and paternal roles show a parallel division, with mothers providing use values and fathers exchange values. Both parents contribute to the support of the children, but the mother contributes vegetable foodstuffs, usually homegrown until recently, while the father contributes meat, fish and salt, all widely traded in precolonial times" (Clark 1989: 325). Not only did the husband provide *chop* money, but he also was able to exchange *chop* money for cooked food, which created other social bonds and obligations. Women became obligated to assist the husband in the marketing of his business. If he was a fisherman, she would help him to sell or process his catch. The husband likewise had obligations to his wife to assist with expenses for their children, such as the payment of school fees, or to help with clearing the farm before planting (Fortes and Fortes 1936: 9; Field 1940: 64). However, the biggest obligation borne by a woman was the preparation of proper food for a husband, a testament to her having spent her time in a wifely fashion. The nature of proper food—its mode of preparation, the demand that the woman spend time procuring the ingredients, the care with which those ingredients were prepared, and the requirement that the meal be served in a timely manner—epitomized the wife's obligation to the husband and the meaning of *chop* that is extant to this day (Clark 1989: 326; Simpson Miller 2021).

Chop and Social Relationships

Chop retained a special status in the role of social reproduction, centered as it was on the division of labor within a marriage (Allman and Tashjian 2000: 60; Clark 2014: 51; Simpson Miller 2021: 249). At table women typically served men first, and men customarily ate with other men, while women and children ate together. At times boys would eat in the company of men, although in a separate age group that shared the same bowl. Older men typically got the best of the food prepared in terms of portion and amount of protein. In contrast, for a woman's social inferiors, any type of food would do, provided it aligned with the requirements of ethnic taboos (Perregaux 1906: 23–24). Essentially, it was the woman's responsibility, through the cooking, processing, and serving of *chop*, to create and recreate, maintain, and reinforce gender, age, and social hierarchies, as well as ethnic identities and religious taboos.

It was with the Basel Mission Girls' Boarding Schools in the 1860s that tensions boiled over around traditional relational dependencies and the social role of women as breadwinners and nourishers of their progeny. It was the custom for students to purchase and cook their own food with funds provided by their mothers. Alternatively, students' mothers would provision them directly by having food delivered. This individual provisioning ensured that students were observing their ethnicities' food taboos. To facilitate this observance, students tended to eat with their peer group, which was defined by one's age and ethnic/geographic origin. The custom of eating in similar age and ethnic groupings preserved the appropriate social distances. In 1860 the Girls Institute at Abokobi, just north of Accra, decided to require communal meals. Although commensality was more efficient, it violated peer group eating norms and prevented the observation of food taboos, which students found extremely objectionable. Not only was the revocation of peer group eating at issue, but the disregard for social ideas about dependency was problematic. Local custom dictated that slaves were only to be compensated with food and clothing. Food slaves received did not observe their ethnic taboos but the taboos of their enslavers, signifying a loss of their previous ethnic identities. The schools' attempt to provide food for students by sourcing it, cooking it, and serving it to them was akin to reducing the students to slave status, which the mothers found offensive (Sill 2010; Simpson Miller 2021: 171). Students went on strike until the preexisting meal arrangements were restored.

Gold Coast locals had access to local food, the trade of which underpinned their economy and whose preparation and consumption signaled their social identity and rank. Additionally, it was the mother's role to provide properly cooked food for her progeny. The school was applying pressure on these relational dependencies in trying to provide food for students and requiring commensality. Controversy in new institutions, such as missionary schools, demonstrated that local foodways still underpinned social relationships. The woman's role as the provider of food for dependents, local commensality customs, and continued observation of food taboos indicated that local ways of eating and ideas of consumption endured during and after the transition to the legitimate commercial trade after the British abolition of the slave trade in 1807 (Sill 2010; Simpson Miller 2021: 171–72).

The two institutional strikes discussed in this chapter illustrate the point that *chop* as a foodview resisted changes in its application, even as the Christian faith was being adopted in the nineteenth century. It was the food itself, in combination with the cooking labor performed by women, that made the people. The concept of *chop* signified the labor that created social relationships and marked social distinctions such as dependencies, age grades, and class. The taste and texture of the regional starchy staple and soup made place and people, as well as the place itself making taste.

Chop and Cosmology

Origin stories illuminated gendered social roles and instructed people on what was wholesome and appropriate to eat. They also informed one of the ways in which cooking was a woman's sacred duty (Reindorf 1895: 268; Huydecoper 1962: 74; Fischler 1988: 285; Clark 1989; Kyei 2001: 126; Miescher 2005). The Asante, whose empire lasted from 1701 to 1901, related an origin story that clarified people's relationship to food and to one another. A worm bored its way up to the surface at Asante Manso (now a sacred grove) and led seven men, several women, a leopard, and a dog out of the earth. The dog left and came back with fire in its mouth. Food was laid upon the fire, and the dog was fed with the food to ascertain whether it was fit for consumption. The dog grew fat upon this food, and as it grew fat, men came to eat cooked food (Rattray 1923: 21–24). Gendered relationships were made clear by the phrase "As it grew fat, the men came to eat cooked food." This part of the myth helps us to understand that it was the men who came to eat the cooked food first, and by omission, the women were doing the cooking and ate after the men were served (Simpson Miller 2021).

The duty and obligation of women to make *chop* as outlined in the Asante origin story was reinforced by religious precepts that tasked women with supporting both social and sexual reproduction through their cooking. The Asante believed that there was an element supplied by the man that they called the *ntoro*. It was this *ntoro* or "spirit" that mingled with the blood or *mogya* of the woman, enabling conception and molding the embryo in the womb. As the Asante were (and remain) matrilineal in organization, the mother's blood in this context was synonymous with the child's clan or *abusua*. Every child was then supposed to have within him, or her, two elements: the male *ntoro* or spirit, and the clan or *abusua* blood transmitted by the mother: "From the day on which a woman marries she makes her husband's *ntoro* taboos her own, for if she did not she would risk offending his *ntoro* and seriously interfering with conception and birth" (Rattray 1927: 51–52). The obligation to observe her husband's *ntoro* taboos to ensure conception was foundational to the division of labor in marriage. The woman was responsible for avoiding the processing and serving of food that would be "hateful" to her husband's *ntoro*. *Chop* in this case would be proper food that observed the *ntoro* taboos of one's husband. A man's food needed to be from a specific place and prepared in such a way that the ancestors would approve of it and grant him and his family blessings. Women then supported men in their endeavors to remain ritually pure to ensure the continued good fortune of the family.

The requirement that it be women who produce *chop* bestowed upon them an authority that rendered them simultaneously powerful and dangerous. There was (and still is) a fervent belief in witchcraft and the transmission of harmful substances through food. A witch could only kill a person from her own clan, and the conclusive evidence among the Akan that one was a witch was the discovery of *bayt kukuo* or a witch's cooking pot (Rattray 1927: 30). The fear of poisoning was a factor that needed to be confronted in women's role as communal cooks. To manage the danger of communal eating during festivals, trusted holders of women's chieftainships prepared the *chop* (Goody 1973: 3). Communally consumed *chop* was an alchemy, an incantation that bound up the clan and fortified the tie between the dead, the living, and the yet to be born. Only trusted women would be positioned to regulate the ritual communal consumption of staple starches.

While it was the woman's responsibility to honor taboos to ensure propagation, and to fortify the connection between the living, the dead, and the unborn, the highest responsibility for communicating with ancestors through the embodied act of cooking rested with men. Men prepared *chop* when it came to honoring ancestors or ghosts: "Caretakers of the royal grave or mausoleums (*barimfo*); they are also the cooks for the royal ghosts and tend the graves, or coffins, and the burial quarters which it is their duty to keep in repair. … The food they prepare for the spirits on ceremonial occasions is given by the chief himself, but the *barimfo* give the usual daily ration of yams or rice and water" (Rattray 1927: 116). In other words, men were (and still are) responsible for cooking for, feeding, and managing ancestors and intercessors, who often lived in nature. For example, in the northern regions, the dominant tree species were locust bean (*dawadawa*) and shea (*Parkia biglobosa*). Further north, the baobab (*Adansonia digitata*) was also found (Blench 1999: 21–26). Although seeds of the African locust bean were considered a women's crop, their access to this sacred tree was mediated by the local chiefs and often male land users. These trees were considered sacred as they served as homes for spirits. At the same time, these trees were vital to the local foodways, producing protein and oil that were foundational to the cuisine in this region. The seeds were an essential ingredient to soup and had medicinal value. *Dawadawa* trees were traditionally managed by an earth priest or *tendaana* and could only be harvested or cut with their permission (Lelea et al. 2022: 31).

Close ecological management is vital in savanna areas, and the *tendaana* served this function. The following northern origin story relates the appropriate way that each gender connected with the Supreme Being who lived in the sky: "The Kassena relate that in the beginning, the sky was close to the ground. An old woman was about to cook, but the sky was in the way, so, in her temper, she cut off a piece and made it into soup. The sky, angered, went away to its present place" (Cardinall 1920: 23). Thus, in this story we learn of the centrality of soup to the diet of people in the far north, the role and character of "woman," and her responsibility for alienating the Supreme Being (O'Connell 1962). Like the Asante origin story, this story made clear the role of women in cooking *chop*, and of men like the *tendaana*, who were responsible for managing and repairing the relationship between humans and the local god, Tongnaab. The *tendaana*'s propitiation of Tongnaab ensured the fertility of the land and of women in the Tong Hills and its broader savanna hinterland. Local gods like Tongnaab lay at the heart of a complex ritual system that included overlapping rites for ancestors and for the earth (Allman and Parker 2005: 105, 154). This connection to the fertility of land and of women was of paramount importance and demonstrated how food and food practices actually brought about the land and its fertility rather than the soil making the food.

The initial appeal and continued maintenance of the relationship with the local god(s) was central to the claim upon the region where a people group settled, as this Sukpe example from east of Accra demonstrates:

> As a priest, Lomo-weir's function was to read the will of local gods and spirits, and appeal to them for assistance. A priest was also charged with the establishment and maintenance of shrines for this purpose. Food was the most common sacrifice at these shrines. Lomo-weir would have observed ritual while hunting and preparing food, in sacrifice and thanks to local deities. In a place and time where sin was equated with the neglect of deities, iniquity itself could be expunged, and land ownership was established, by the offering of food sacrifice. Thus, good food was contingent upon observances of the moral and ethical dimensions of the local spiritual landscape. (Simpson Miller 2019)

Thus, propitiating the deities with local food that was pleasing to the god(s) was essential for maintaining the claim upon the land. In point of fact, local foods and food practices constructed the land and its fertility. Women participated in this important work by cooking these same local foods at festivals and by preparing food for their husbands, brothers, and fathers that would be agreeable and satisfying to the local gods.

Conclusion

When researching and traveling to Ghana over a period of three years, I was never offered local food. People actually expressed surprise when I demonstrated knowledge of, or interest in, the local foods. I am guessing this was because, as a foreigner, I was not invested in the local ritual landscape that *chop* represented. I did not have a claim to land I needed to reinforce, I was not concerned with reproducing a lineage, and I did not need to distinguish myself from my immediate neighbors. I could not be placed through the local food, so there was no need to offer it to me. *Chop* still persists today as a foodview that bolsters connection to the land. Most Ghanaians who work in the city keep a farm outside the city or a home in their village that they either visit frequently or staff with relatives who continue to produce starchy staples.

Chop helps us to explore how food, culinary traditions, and their connection to location shaped individuals and their diverse social interactions. *Chop* in Ghana concerned itself with historical evolution, ethnic differences, social hierarchy, cosmology, sexual reproduction, and migration and trade. Although Ghanaians appreciated and valued food grown in certain regions and understood these particular foods' connection with a regional quality, the commodification of local starchy staples does not make sense in this specific context. The daily cooking of (or the abstention from) local foods that were pleasing to local gods and clan totems reinforced the claim to a particular piece of land, framing and fashioning the identity of the people inhabiting that region. The embodied knowledge women built up over generations of how to grow, process, cook, and serve their starchy staple was reinforced in their cosmology. The relationship between food, place, and personhood was revealed in the concept of *chop* as it reflected historical migration, conflict, and centuries of trade as the adoption of new foods, which can become *chop*, demonstrate. *Chop* is exculpatory of historical context as it connects the living, the dead, and the yet to be born in a deliberate establishment of space through the gendered division of labor.

Chop is a unique concept, extant, and specific to Ghana. As *chop* was rooted in doctrine describing the natural order of the universe and expressed in gendered practices, *chop* encompassed change and subsumed it, marking taste as a component of the divine landscape. The concept of *chop* moves our thinking beyond terroir in its resiliency, adaptability, and its capacity to accommodate and reflect the experiences of people and where they find themselves as they migrate, seeking refuge and fruitfulness in new landscapes.

Acknowledgments

I am deeply grateful to the editors, Anna Colquhoun and Katharina Graf, for their thoughtful guidance and oversight throughout the development of this chapter. Working with them, as well as others from the SOAS Food Studies Centre, has been a truly rewarding experience. Their expertise and dedication to this project reflect the vibrant intellectual community fostered at SOAS University of London, and I am honored to have collaborated with such talented scholars. I would also like to express my heartfelt gratitude to my supervisor and mentor, John Parker, whose patience, insight, and encouragement have been invaluable in shaping my work.

Brandi Simpson Miller is a social historian of West Africa whose research investigates the history of food, cooking, and eating from the seventeenth century to the present day. She holds a PhD from SOAS University of London and an MA in World History from Georgia State University. Her publications include the monograph *Food and Identity in Nineteenth and Twentieth Century Ghana: Food, Fights, and Regionalism*—part of the Palgrave Food in a Globalizing World Series. Currently she is Assistant Professor of History and the Assistant Director of the Lane Center for Social and Racial Equity at Wesleyan College in Macon, Georgia.

Note

1. Generally, yam is associated with ethnic Akan people from the central forested region, cassava with Ewe from the southeast, maize with the Gã people in and around Accra, and millet with people from the Northern Region.

References

Acquah, G. A. 1957. *The Fantse of Ghana: A History.* Hull: Hull University.
Agbodeka, Francis. 1997. *Handbook of Eweland: The Ewes of Southeastern Ghana.* Vol. 1. Accra: Woeli Publishing Services.
Akyeampong, Emmanuel. 1996. *Drink, Power, and Cultural Change: A Social History of Alcohol in Ghana, c. 1800 to recent times.* Portsmouth: Heinemann.
Allman, Jean, and John Parker. 2005. *Tongnaab: The History of a West African God.* Bloomington: Indiana University Press.
Allman, Jean Marie, and Victoria B. Tashjian. 2000. *"I Will Not Eat Stone": A Women's History of Colonial Asante.* Portsmouth: James Currey.
Besah-Adanu, Courage, Aske S. Bosselmann, Lise Hansted, and Peter K. Kwapong. 2019. "Food Origin Labels in Ghana: Finding Inspiration in the European Geographical Indications System on Honey." *Journal of World Intellectual Property* 22(5–6): 349–63.
Blench, Roger. 1999. *Natural Resource Management in Ghana and Its Socio-economic Context.* London: Overseas Development Institute.
———. 2005. "*A Dictionary of Nigerian English.*" Retrieved 5 December 2023 from https://www.rogerblench.info/Language/English/Nigerian%20English%20Dictionary.pdf.
———. 2006. "*'Observers Are Worried': A Dictionary of Ghanaian English,*" 12 January. Retrieved 5 December 2023 from http://www.rogerblench.info/Language/English/Ghana%20English%20dictionary.pdf.
Bosman, William. 1967. *A New and Accurate Description of the Coast of Guinea.* London: Cass and Co.
Cardinall, A. W. 1920. *The Natives of the Northern Territories of the Gold Coast: Their Customs, Religion and Folklore.* London: Routledge.
Christaller, J. G. 1881. *A Dictionary of the Asante and Fante Language Called Tshi.* Basel: Evangelical Missionary Society.
———. 1933. *A Dictionary of the Asante and Fante Language Called Tshi: With a Grammatical Introduction and Appendices on the Geography of the Gold Coast and Other Subjects.* Basel: Evangelical Missionary Society.
Clark, Gracia. 1989. "Money, Sex and Cooking: Manipulation of the Paid/Unpaid Boundary by Asante Market Women." In *The Social Economy of Consumption*, edited by Henry J. Rutz and Benjamin S. Orlove. Lanham: University Press of America.
———. 2014. "From Fasting to Fast Food in Kumasi, Ghana." In *Food Consumption in Global Perspective: Essays in the Anthropology of Food in Honour of Jack Goody*, edited by Jakob A. Klein and Anne Murcott, 45–64. Basingstoke: Palgrave Macmillan.
Counsell, Colin, and Roberta Mock. 2009. *Performance, Embodiment, and Cultural Memory.* Newcastle upon Tyne: Cambridge Scholars.
Douny, Laurence. 2014. *Living in a Landscape of Scarcity: Materiality and Cosmology in West Africa.* New York: Routledge.
Field, Margaret J. 1940. *Social Organization of the Gã People.* Accra: Crown Agents for the Colonies.
Fischler, Claude. 1988. "Food, Self and Identity." *Social Science Information* 27(2): 275–92.
Fortes, Meyer. 1970. *Time and Social Structure and Other Essays.* London: Athlone Press.
Fortes, Meyer, and S. L. Fortes. 1936. "Food in the Domestic Economy of the Tallensi." *Africa* 9(2): 237–76.

Greene's Dictionary of Slang. n.d. *First Chop.* Retrieved 5 December 2023 from https://greensdictofslang.com/entry/rdbcdqa.

Goody, Esther N. 1973. *Contexts of Kinship: An Essay in the Family Sociology of the Gonja of Northern Ghana.* Cambridge: Cambridge University Press.

Huydecoper, W. 1962. *Huydecoper's Diary: Journey from Elmina to Kumasi 28th April 1816–18th May 1817.* Legon: University of Ghana.

Kyei, Thomas E., Jr. 2001. *Our Days Dwindle: Memories of My Childhood Days in Asante.* Portsmouth: Heinemann Educational Books.

Kuuwaabong, G., H. Egelyngand, and J. Yaro. 2015. "Identifying the Potential of Ghana 'Pona' Yam for Geographical Indication (GI) Labelling." In *Tropentag 2015 Book of Abstracts: Management of Land Use Systems for Enhanced Food Security: Conflicts, Controversies and Resolutions,* ed. E. Tielkes, 588. Göttingen: Cuvillier Verlag. Retrieved 5 December 2023 from https://www.tropentag.de/2015/abstracts/full/801.pdf.

La Fleur, James D. 2012. *Fusion Foodways of Africa's Gold Coast in the Atlantic Era.* Leiden: Brill.

Lelea, Margareta Amy, Lydia Madintin Konlan, Rashida Chantima Ziblila, Lara Elena Thiele, Araba Amo-Aidoo, and Brigitte Kaufmann. 2022. "Strategies to Promote Sustainable Development: The Gendered Importance of Addressing Diminishing African Locust Bean Resources in Northern Ghana's Agro-Ecological Landscape." *Sustainability* 14(18).

Lim, Lisa. 2016. "Where Does the Word 'Chop' Come from?" *Post Magazine.* Retrieved 5 December 2023 from https://www.scmp.com/magazines/post-magazine/article/1996080/where-does-word-chop-come.

McCann, James C. 2009. *Stirring the Pot: A History of African Cuisine.* Athens: Ohio University Press.

Miescher, Stephan. 2005. *Making Men in Ghana.* Bloomington: Indiana University Press.

O'Connell, James. 1962. "The Withdrawal of the High God in West African Religion: An Essay in Interpretation." *Man* 62: 67–69.

Osseo-Asare, Fran. 2002. "'We Eat First with Our Eyes': On Ghanaian Cuisine." *Gastronomica* 2(1): 49–57.

Perregaux, Edmond. 1906. "Chez Les Achanti." *Société Neuchâteloise de Géographie* 17(7): 387.

Purchas, Saumel. 1905. *Haklutyus Posthumus* 4. Glasgow: James McLehose and Sons.

Rattray, R. S. 1923. *Ashanti.* Oxford: Clarendon Press.

———. 1927. *Religion and Art in Ashanti.* Oxford: Clarendon Press.

Reindorf, Carl Christian. 1895. *History of the Gold Coast and Asante.* Basel: Missionsbuchhandlung.

Robertson, Claire C. 1984. *Sharing the Same Bowl? A Socioeconomic History of Women and Class in Accra, Ghana.* Bloomington: Indiana University Press.

Sill, Ulrike. 2010. *Encounters in Quest of Christian Womanhood.* Leiden: Brill.

Simpson Miller, Brandi. 2015. "Food and Nationalism in an Independent Ghana." MA diss., Georgia State University, Atlanta. Retrieved 5 December 2023 from https://doi.org/10.57709/7182591.

———. 2019. "The Moral and Ethical Aspects of Gold Coast Foodways." *Gastronomica* 19(1): 111–12.

———. 2021. *Food and Identity in Nineteenth and Twentieth Century Ghana: Food, Fight, and Regionalism.* Cham: Palgrave MacMillan.

Tait, David. 2018. *The Konkomba of Northern Ghana.* New York: Routledge.

Tuomainen, Helena Margaret. 2006. “Migration and Foodways: Continuity and Change among Ghanaians in London.” PhD diss., Warwick University, UK.

Twagira, Laura Ann. 2021. *Embodied Engineering: Gendered Labor, Food Security, and Taste in Twentieth-Century Mali*. Athens: Ohio University Press.

Venkatachalam, Meera. 2015. *Slavery, Memory and Religion in Southeastern Ghana, c.1850–Present.* Cambridge: Cambridge University Press.

Williams-Forson, Psyche. 2010. “Other Women Cooked for My Husband: Negotiating Gender, Food, and Identities in an African American/Ghanaian Household.” *Feminist Studies* 36(2): 435–61.

PART IV

Imaginaries

CHAPTER 14

Terroir in Future Tense?

Gender, Taste, and Emplacement in an Age of Borders

Charlotte Sanders

Introduction

If tastes of place are conceived as universally enduring and immutable relationships between people, place, and food, then how might displacement strain this understanding, as connections between people and place become extraordinarily, and often permanently, disrupted? As geographic and economic constraints make sourcing ingredients grown via "traditional" means in places of origin impossible for many displaced people, how might their creative responses to these obstacles challenge normative indexes of food quality, value, or authenticity that have largely dominated taste-place literature through the concept of terroir (see Graf and Colquhoun, both this volume)? This chapter explores the food practices—sourcing, cooking, and consuming—of Sudanese women in Portsmouth, a port town in the south of England, to illuminate the more expansive and co-constitutive understandings of taste and place that emerge when contexts of displacement are centered.

In Portsmouth, border policies, economic limitations, and travel restrictions have made it increasingly unfeasible to source food grown in Sudan. Through ethnographic description, I explore how Sudanese women have negotiated food immobility as they continue to prepare and share Sudanese food in Portsmouth, employing various creative innovations across ingredients, recipes, preparation practices, and cooking methods. The vignettes elucidate the value of food for my interlocutors beyond the dominant indicators of quality evoked by terroir, illuminating the ways in which global political economy, uneven border policies and practices, and alternative indexes of care and community play key roles in producing more flexible evaluations of "good" Sudanese food for my interlocutors in Portsmouth. Taking seriously Sudanese women's food practices also pushes beyond terroir's commonplace key actors—namely landscapes and ingredients—to think about the roles of bodies, affects, social relations, and imaginaries in producing new tastes of place, but also new senses of place through taste. This underscores taste and place as not predetermined but, rather, emergent through women's everyday efforts.

In addition, food flexibility in Portsmouth does not only provide a fresh perspective on the relationship between people, food products, and place—in West's phrasing, the "terroir triad" (2022: 7)—but also on the sense of time, or temporality, at work in these food innovations, particularly as practices undertaken in diaspora. While terroir conventionally emphasizes heritage and tradition in assigning value to food, the labors of my interlocutors reach instead toward new connections to and through taste (that is, productions of the future). As I show, these include novel relations with place—Sudan and Portsmouth—and new constellations of community, between those who have arrived in Portsmouth from different regions in Sudan. Beyond the preservation of a traditional "taste of place," I argue that Sudanese women's food practices instead present food as a potentially radical gendered mechanism for future-making (remaking "people" and "place"). I also add a different perspective to the focus on "nostalgia" in scholarship on food in diaspora (Mannur 2007; Parveen 2016), even when nostalgia is put forward as a potentially generative practice for rebuilding presents and futures (Hage 2010).

In highlighting how food projects produce new possibilities for emplacement, I am inspired by the work of historian and Black feminist theorist Tina Campt, whose study of Black diasporic histories in Europe put forward "futurity" as a conceptual frame for giving political meaning to the "quiet" and "quotidian" practices through which futures are aspired toward in conditions of profound uncertainty; "futures that do not yet exist, but must" (Campt 2014, 2017). As attempts to "live the future now" Campt sees these often unacknowledged practices as a "politics of prefiguration" in the everyday (Campt 2017), a term first defined by Carl Boggs to refer to the aspiration of political movements to embody in the present "those forms of social relations, decision-making, culture, and human experience that are [the movement's] ultimate goal" (Campt 2017: 120; see also Raekstad and Gradin 2020). Refocusing attention away from formal political movements, Campt challenges in particular the masculinist logics that trivialize domestic or women's work and deny the importance of the everyday to the production of futures. Instead, Campt situates these everyday practices as gendered "registers" (2017: 9) of struggle; determined ways in which conditions of possibility are remade in the ruins of displacement, dispossession, disposability.

In this chapter I draw upon Campt's insights to shift focus from the past to the future in analyzing the value of food, and to challenge the invisibilization of women's labor, domestic space, and informal daily practice in terroir discourse, which takes for granted place (and taste) as already existing rather than constantly made and remade by multiple actors, including women in their homes. This framing also supports my analysis of how taste is constrained by global inequalities and border practices and a locus of resistance in contexts of displacement. As such, through Campt and others this chapter seeks to contribute to a feminist and race-critical perspective on the (geo)politics of terroir (Handel et al. 2015; Monterescu 2017). In laying out these claims, the chapter also sits in fruitful conversation with the work of other authors in this volume. I reference these points of dialogue throughout.

Eating Sudanese Style in Portsmouth: Procurement, Preparation, and Relational Emplacements

As I began research in 2015 my interlocutors were busily preparing for Ramadan. The fasting month heralded numerous opportunities for social events, including weekly *iftar* gatherings where community[1] members congregated to break their fast together. Especially at Ramadan, individuals expressed their desire to eat Sudanese food, and women would guard Sudan-sourced ingredients for use during this month. While this was true for fasts broken in private domestic spaces, it was particularly so for meals shared in the public forums of community gatherings. While women would remark that dishes "tasted better" when made with Sudanese ingredients, their descriptions of their importance to a successful Ramadan meal would far more frequently hinge on embodied effects, and affective and/or mnemonic capacities; the ways that such ingredients made them feel "fuller" or more "nourished," and how they reminded them of sharing *iftar* meals with loved ones, neighbors, and other extended kin prior to displacement.

In figure 14.1 Munira[2] displays her *abreh*, awoken from its hibernation in a Tesco carrier bag tucked away in her kitchen cupboard to prepare the cold drink with which she will later break her fast. The thin *abreh* flakes, made from fermented sorghum with added sugar and spices, are mixed with water and ice until the flakes dissolve, making a refreshing drink consumed throughout the year but most often during Ramadan. *Abreh*, Munira explained, is cherished for its nourishing qualities; its blend of sweet and savory replenishes depleted blood sugar levels, and with an accompanying date forms an aperitif. Unavailable locally, Munira's *abreh* flakes had been painstakingly sourced from Sudan, requiring significant logistical labor. As a Darfuri refugee without access to international travel—neither money nor travel documents—Munira could not travel to Sudan. Instead, as many other Darfuri women, she sourced her ingredients via women who hailed from Khartoum, whose visa statuses (often spousal) and financial means allowed for trips to visit family. Darfuri women would arrange for a family member in Darfur, West Sudan, to transport their ingredients to Khartoum, North Sudan, where they would be dropped off at the family home

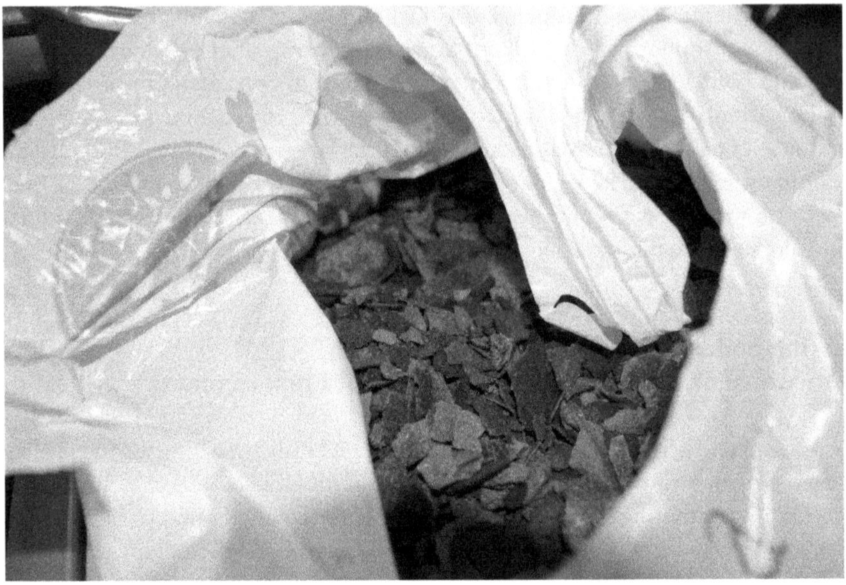

Figure 14.1. Munira presents her *abreh*, which she had stored in her cupboard in anticipation of the fasting month of Ramadan. Portsmouth, 2015. © Charlotte Sanders

of a woman who would shortly be visiting from Portsmouth. The visitor would then transport the ingredients to Portsmouth for distribution.

Considering the decades-long genocidal conflict in Darfur, its effects on the local economy and local infrastructures (including phoneline accessibility), and that Darfur is over one thousand kilometers away from Khartoum, organizing this was no mean feat. Yet Munira articulated the importance of *abreh* to her Ramadan practices as about its ability to create feelings of belonging. While this was in part about her extended kin network in Sudan, *iftar* gatherings also made clear that sharing this drink together enabled the formation of new kinships in Portsmouth, as I later elaborate. While it was ideal for *abreh* to be sourced from childhood villages in Darfur, it was not essential, and women would compromise on the origins of ingredients by accepting the less logistically challenging option of food products grown in Khartoum. At times, however, even this compromise raised obstacles, as transporting ingredients from Sudan to Portsmouth had become somewhat of a business enterprise for women from Khartoum, who would charge up to thirty pounds a kilo for their transportation services.

Some weeks after visiting Munira, I arrived at the home of Nadima, another woman from Darfur unable to return for almost twenty years. For Nadima, the most treasured ingredient in her kitchen cupboard was ground beef, produced in the local area in which she had grown up, and where the meat would be laid

Figure 14.2. *Aseeda* accompanied by *it-tagaliya*, a sauce made using ground beef. Portsmouth, 2015. © Charlotte Sanders

out in the sun to dry before being ground into powder form. Ground beef was a key ingredient to a sauce, *it-tagaliya*, that Nadima made to accompany *aseeda*, as shown in figure 14.2. Again, *aseeda*, with its accompanying sauces, was a central dish in the repertoire of (particularly, Darfuri) women because of its alimentary qualities. Both the dough, made from millet flour and water served traditionally in a semicircle shape, and the meaty sauce it was served with were considered key to a healthy body. As Nadima said, "Maybe you can eat pizza, pasta, fish, but if you eat *aseeda* your body will always be strong." For Nadima, this remained the case even as millet flour was mostly replaced in Portsmouth by a mix of plain and self-raising flour.

This dish's capacity to sustain the body made it particularly crucial for maintaining health during the month of fasting, but, again, *aseeda* was not only valued for its embodied nutritional effects but also for its affective potency. Similar to *abreh*, women considered *aseeda* to engender constellations of connection, translocal—that is, to loved ones in various locations across Sudan—but also local in Portsmouth. Indeed, *aseeda* was by nature a dish to be shared, served in its semicircle shape—traditionally in a woven dish like the one seen in the image below, taken in Nadima's kitchen—with numerous hands reaching in to pull apart chunks of dough used to scoop up the surrounding sauce. Sharing food, Nadima explained, allowed her to recall, but also to relive and rebuild moments of eating with loved ones under the tree that stood outside her childhood home. *Aseeda* and sauce made possible mnemonic, present-tense, and future-tense connections. For Nadima, *aseeda* was a key dish through which she enjoyed the relational opportunities available to her in Portsmouth—with her husband, and with friends and new arrivals whom she invited to her home to eat. Nevertheless, despite the significance of *aseeda* to her physical and social well-being, Nadima had grown tired of the need to pay women from Khartoum to source her ground beef.

As others, Nadima sometimes articulated the hefty transportation charges levied by women from Khartoum to be an opportunistic means to make money, and symptomatic of the uneven experiences and accesses to capital in the community (as in Sudan) between more affluent, educated, documented, and resourced women from Khartoum/the North, and women from Darfur in the West. Indeed, Darfur and Darfuris have experienced devastating levels of economic, social, and political marginalization, as well as direct state violence widely recognized as genocide. While this violence has been constructed as a conflict between Sudan's "African" and "Arab" populations, its roots are situated squarely in British colonial policies during its occupation of Sudan (1899–1956),[3] which encouraged uneven development and distributions of resources between the northern "center" and its peripheries, including Darfur (see Sharkey 2008; Vaughan 2015; indeed, this also led to the secession of South Sudan in 2011; see Sefa-Nyarko 2016). As Nadima herself confessed, prior to arriving in Portsmouth she had considered that Northern Sudanese supported government actions in Darfur, and it was only her friendships in Portsmouth that had shown her otherwise. Yet tangible class, racial, and mobility inequalities remained between women in Portsmouth, both in regard to the resources they arrived with and the ways that those resources had enabled them to build particular sorts of lives in the city.

Nevertheless, it was also the case that carrying cargo like ground beef posed risks. Arriving in the UK carrying meat products such as ground beef—but also milk-based products and other ingredients that were sought after in Portsmouth, including nut butter and honey (darker in color than honey produced in the UK, and with unique medicinal properties)—was an illegalized act, even carrying the possibility of prosecution. As Fatima—a key distributor to her frequent returns—explained, carrying these products required numerous strategies of subterfuge, such as hiding ground beef beneath the lining of her suitcase. Importantly, these border restrictions are not universal but targeted at particular groups of moving people.[4] Thus, in Portsmouth, the ability to incorporate oneself into the regime of value encapsulated in "terroir" is imposed upon by a border regime that unevenly polices the movement of food across transnational space, as well as the classed and racialized constraints of economic and travel restrictions more broadly.

These restrictions, legal, logistical, and financial, provide the context for the scene I encountered as I walked into Nadima's kitchen that morning, as seen in figure 14.3. Frustrated with the growing impossibility of sourcing ground beef from Darfur, Nadima had begun to hone a method for drying out meat purchased locally at any one of the city's numerous halal butcheries. Nadima had settled on hanging the meat out on a string, held in place by her kitchen cupboards and suspended over her hob to maximize heat resources. Despite the relative lack of sun in Portsmouth compared to Darfur, Nadima had toyed with the idea of hanging the string up outside her kitchen window in the outdoor passageway, but as she was relatively new to the block, she had decided that this might risk jeopardizing cordial relations with new neighbors. Nevertheless, Nadima was proud of the technique she had landed upon, and hopeful that the process would yield appetizing results. She was also well aware of the potential for selling her ground beef to others in her situation.

Nadima's creative response to the constraints she faced in sourcing ingredients was far from an isolated occurrence. Instead, playing with procurement and preparation methods to recreate Sudanese dishes was commonplace among my interlocutors. Figure 14.4 shows *kisra* pancakes, laid out on Hanifah's plate as Amira prepares a burger for her daughter. In Sudan, but particularly in Darfur where

Figure 14.3. Nadima hangs her meat out to dry above the hob in her kitchen as part of an effort to circumvent the logistically and financially taxing process of sourcing dried meat powder from Sudan. Portsmouth, 2015. © Charlotte Sanders

Figure 14.4. Women gather together with their children in a local play park during the school summer holidays. While children eat beef hamburgers from their paper plates, women share *kisra* pancakes from porcelain plates. Portsmouth, 2016. © Charlotte Sanders

kisra is most habitually eaten, *kisra* is made with a specific flour—*dukhun*—that gives the pancakes a taste described to me as "sour, but still a little bit sweet." In Sudan, I was told, the hot climate means that the flour and water mix takes only a few short hours to sour as desired. In Portsmouth women had found they had to leave the mixture to ferment for much longer, preferably days, and often in a large Tupperware container in a kitchen cupboard. They had also perfected the method of always adding new mixture to already fermented leftovers to best recreate the sour taste evocative of the *kisra* prepared and shared in Darfur.

Beyond ingredient preparation, cooking methods had also changed in Portsmouth (for a comparative case, see Graf 2024). For many Darfuri interlocutors, this was down to the marked change of gas and electricity as the central elements for cooking, which prior to their arrival in Portsmouth most women had not experienced in their childhood or marital homes. As Raghda described, arriving at a flat in Portsmouth without space for fire cooking had remained one of the foremost moments of dislocation in her life trajectory. Keen to impress her new husband, Raghda had been moved to tears by her reliance on a technology she had never used before, the oven, to feed her husband and their visitors on one of her first evenings in the city. For Raghda, the realization that she would need to learn how to cook dishes using an oven and hob (and to learn so from her new husband) had felt a devastating and insurmountable task, which disrupted her access to one of the primary means at her disposal for embodying herself as a gendered and relational subject: her ability to nourish others.

Just as women learned how to cook *aseeda* on a gas or electric hob, they had also found new ways to produce *kisra* pancakes, which in Darfur had been prepared on a hot plate sat atop burning coals. A chance discovery of a plug-in pancake and crepe maker, in the middle aisle of the local LIDL supermarket, had provided new possibilities for women to produce *kisra* in the city, alongside the use of an old plastic card (debit, credit, library) as the best means to smooth out the mixture on the plate to ensure that the pancakes were as thin as possible, Sudanese style. Like new ingredients and preparation methods, new cooking methods spread like wildfire among women, traveling across the physical and virtual spaces that made up the local Sudanese community, spaces that women played a central role in building (on social media, see also Czerny in this volume). In the months after my visit to Nadima, when she had introduced me to her embryonic method for producing ground beef in her kitchen, other women also began attempts to hone the technique. Raghda had discovered that hanging the meat behind her fridge hastened the drying-out procedure, due, she suspected, to the "gas" the fridge emitted throughout the day and night.

While my interlocutors readily admitted that dishes could not taste the same in Portsmouth, this did not demotivate them. Instead, what mattered most was that these dishes could be made at all, crucial as they were to the forging and maintenance of relational connections in the city. As Garth also notes (this volume), while dishes may not have been "ideal," they were also not "inauthentic." Instead, authenticity came not from the origin of ingredients, but the act of sharing techniques and final results, making taste a relational process rather than a "property" (see also Colquhoun, this volume). Indeed, women would frequently state that when they were eating alone—if their husbands were out, particularly if working night shifts—they were more inclined to eat "British" foods (in fact, pizza, pasta, and so forth) as far quicker and easier forms of bodily nourishment than more intricate Sudanese dishes. What Sudanese foods offered went beyond the satiation of physical need, and beyond evaluations of "taste" in the organoleptic sense (that is, quality assessed through flavor and smell). Instead, quality was inferred from food's affective and relational capacities; in enacting a gendered sense of self in caring for others (and being cared for) and in making possible a shared experience of alternative belonging, not reductively to "another" place but as suspended across translocal and local landscapes of inhabitation: of being Sudanese in Portsmouth.

Care and Community

While my research focused on the experiences of women, I became acquainted with men. Across our interactions, both would articulate a sense of Sudanese distinction in Portsmouth that hinged upon a Sudanese ethics of care, and the primacy of community. Rather than being homogenizing characteristics of a Sudanese "culture," these articulations were often offered against a perceived absence of care and community locally (Portsmouth) and nationally (UK), diagnosed by my interlocutors as entrenched in the individualist logics of capitalism.[5] More broadly, life in Portsmouth was described as isolated and isolating, and this was considered an issue of systemic proportions that diminished the lives of all residents. Nonetheless, this analysis was undoubtedly shaped by everyday and structural experiences of racial exclusion, which shaped consistently negative experiences of accessing housing, employment, social belonging, and social support, as was the focus of my broader doctoral research. In this difficult present, more caring and interdependent futures took on a particular salience. For my interlocutors, the impetus for a Sudanese Community as an organized political space was to ensure the maintenance of collective well-being for all members, old and especially new. Indeed, one of my first invitations to join a community event, alongside the *iftars* of Ramadan, was to a wake that had been financed and catered in less than twenty-four hours (in line with Islamic conventions for burial) by the collective efforts of the community.

While this care often manifested in financial and logistical support from men, for women it manifested in the sourcing and provisioning of food, whether at large-scale events or smaller, more informal gatherings at one another's homes. Of the latter, these frequently involved hosting local single asylum-seeker men, who had arrived displaced from Darfur. Sometimes it also involved sending meals packaged in Tupperware. Throughout the course of my fieldwork, whatever event occurred in a community member's life—whether birth, loss, moving into a new home, or visiting relatives—it would be responded to by women with the provision of food, and more specifically, Sudanese food Portsmouth style. For women, Sudanese food held the capacity to animate gendered expressions of care, and the labor involved in reproducing dishes despite constraints signified the value placed in the relationship with, and well-being of, another. Sudanese food was not always crucial to everyday life but was absolutely crucial to moments of care and community, such as celebrations, bereavements, and ritual gatherings. Just as in other contributions to this volume, the politics and poetics of taste in these encounters moved beyond gustatory or organoleptic evaluations (see Jung; Grasseni; Graf, all this volume)—measured in relation to equivalents in Sudan itself—to a more expansive embodied, affective, and social experience. This experience certainly involved the senses—not only taste and smell but also touch—but transcended them too.

The effects of these moments in relation to community were both affective and practical in nature. Sharing information about sourcing, preparing, and cooking food, as well as, of course, eating food together, brought people together in ways that allowed for the sharing of wider information, advice, and resources. These conversations also tangibly impacted the livability of everyday life. Through food-related conversations, friends were made from strangers, and these topics were often at the core of the lively discussions that occurred among women at informal and formal community gatherings, where complementing one another on a dish well done would also serve to produce and maintain affective bonds. A key significance of food was its ability to re-create Portsmouth as place, a resource for producing spaces in which possibilities for living, and living otherwise, became more thinkable. Food did not gesture to the past but toward the possibility of a future beyond multiple and variant (some individual, some shared) experiences of disorientation, loss or exile, and exclusion.

These outcomes gain an additional layer of meaning when considering the different imaginaries of Sudan as place, and of "Sudanese" as a political and moral community, present in Portsmouth and Sudan. As introduced above, this is not only about the geographical distance of the regions from which members in Portsmouth arrived, but also about the material and symbolic inequalities that have emerged from the country's history of colonial occupation. Alongside Darfuri women who previously understood the genocide in Darfur to be supported by their compatriots in the North, women from the North also admitted to concealing their new friendships with Darfuri families from kin in Sudan, as they would be considered inappropriate. As such, there was clear potential for racial hierarchies to impose themselves upon the community in Portsmouth, with divisory effect. Yet for community organizers and members alike, displacement demanded new visions of belonging and had provided access to information that had prompted collective reflection as to the politically constructed nature of regional antagonisms.

While imperfect, what had been achieved in the community by the Spring of 2016 when my fieldwork began was already remarkable. Later, as tensions in Sudan rose with the civil unrest of 2018–19, community members from the North and the West stood together each Sunday at Portsmouth's town hall in solidarity with protestors in Sudan, chanting against the regime and its genocidal violence in Darfur, as seen in figure 14.5. Yet while attention is often drawn to moments of spectacular protest, the foundations for this collective action had been laid across the course of years in more subtle ways, and in large part through the Community's consistent formal and informal efforts to (re)build a new sense of Sudanese belonging through facilitating spaces of gathering. As in other diasporic contexts (D'Sylva and Beagan 2011; Parveen 2016; Lin et al. 2020; Cassidy and El-Tom 2021), women had played a key—if not the key—role in manifesting this new vision, through their organizing and catering efforts across community

Figure 14.5. The Sudanese Community gathers every Sunday at the city's town hall to stand in solidarity with those protesting political violence in Sudan. Portsmouth, 2019. © Charlotte Sanders

events, but also more broadly through their efforts to connect with one another, which, as I have detailed, always involved some provision of food.

Whether hosting one another at home or working together to cater a community event, the sharing of culinary knowledges also involved learning together across Northern and Western expertise, which in subtle but important ways had begun to reform imaginaries and materialities of Sudanese cuisine. As seen in figure 14.6, community events such as the weekly *iftar* gatherings would see *aseeda* (top right and typically eaten in Darfur), being served alongside *falafel* (center left and most often consumed in the North), being shared by one and all.

As exchanging food and recipes across regions became an increasingly ubiquitous practice, horizons for what it meant to "eat Sudanese" were undergoing visible transformations, as women from the North took tips from those from Darfur about how best to make *aseeda* and *kisra*, and women from Darfur learned how to add spinach to their *baamiya* (made usually only with okra in Darfur) or to bake cakes like the *basbousa* seen in figure 14.7, typically associated with Egyptian cuisine, and made by oven. Indeed, in an interesting inversion to the setting

Figure 14.6. Cling film is removed from pots and plates as community members prepare to eat. As each person brings a dish to share, the central table now features traditional food from different regions of Sudan, eaten together. Portsmouth, 2020. © Charlotte Sanders

of charges for carrying food products to Portsmouth, women like Nadima (from Darfur, and whose ground beef production I introduced earlier) would also make *kisra* pancakes for women from the North to purchase, such was the growing demand.

Food and Futurity in Portsmouth

This chapter has attended to the novel perspectives that displacement might contribute toward a more dynamic understanding of the possible relationships between people, food, and place. Through ethnographic description, I have sought to challenge terroir's conceptual capture of this far more vibrant conversation, bringing into view the presence of alternative indexes of "taste" (food quality or value beyond the gustatory or organoleptic), alternative experiences or configurations of "place" (as complex, emergent, and both cartographic and imaginary), and alternative understandings of the relation between "taste" and "place" (as co-constitutive, rather than a unidirectional production of taste through place) in the world. This has also drawn greater attention to the meaning of time in the

Figure 14.7. *Basbousa* cake, brought along to a summer picnic by Hanaan, a woman who—as Nadima, aforementioned—had not used an oven prior to her displacement from Darfur, and had learned to make *basbousa* in Portsmouth. The plate rests upon a rug brought to the park to be sat on. Portsmouth, 2021. © Charlotte Sanders

production of tastes of place, shifting focus from preserving place as heritage, toward food products and practices as involved in continuous productions and reproductions of place (see also Grasseni, this volume).

If the value of food is reduced to its ability to conjure tastes of place as bounded, immutable, and fixed, it becomes difficult to perceive the continued investment in Sudanese food in Portsmouth. I suggest instead that for my interlocutors the value of food was most centrally located in its capacity to engender new imaginaries of place and of place in the world, enabling new constellations of community and new cartographic and affective experiences of both Portsmouth and Sudan as places. Regarding the former, food provided a crucial mechanism for community building in Portsmouth and, thus, through which spaces for living otherwise were conjured from experiences of isolation and exclusion. Food as an act of caring was also an important means for reorienting and reconstructing relational experiences of self, in the aftermaths of displacements that had indelibly disrupted networks of kinship and neighborly belonging. Regarding the latter, sharing recipes and dishes in Portsmouth between Darfur, Khartoum, and elsewhere also led to shifting horizons of Sudan as place, as well as "Sudanese" as a political and moral community, in ways that challenged, in turn, racial hierarchies and exclusions. In turning attention from the past to the future, and thinking with Tina Campt's theorizing of "futurity," I am inspired by the possibilities that flow from considering my interlocutors' practices of procuring, preparing, and sharing food in Portsmouth as a gendered register of struggle, which attends to the deep rupture of displacement by producing in the present conditions of possibility for future emplacement. Their practices necessarily challenge static understandings of place—as well as binaries of "here" and "there"—precisely because they gesture toward senses of place in the world that "do not yet exist, but must" (Campt 2014, 2017).

While Sudanese women's food practices are ethnographically specific, they also share much with other contexts and scholarship, within this volume and without. In their aspirational mode, taste becomes a malleable resource for feeling out new possibilities for living in and in relation to place, as well as in relation to others. As Graf and Colquhoun also argue in other contexts (drawing on the work of Paxson 2013), food in Portsmouth forms a resource for (re)"making a life" that feels rich and meaningful. For my interlocutors, this project may be inspired by previous and contemporary places of inhabitation but is nevertheless not reducible to an either/or. Instead, the places to which tastes refer are not yet precisely known, emergent in a continuously co-constitutive relationship to taste as food practices shift and mold. Food certainly provides a means to "tether" self and selves to "home" (see Graf, this volume; see also Abranches 2014), just as this home is not geographically fixed but multiple and evolving, affective and cartographic. Again, that Sudanese women did not always eat Sudanese food but would alone or with their children enjoy "British" food, which they also invested energy in learning how to cook, is testament to the irreducibility or multiplicity of "home" in material and imagined modalities of human experience.

Just as Graf describes in Morocco, Garth in Cuba and its diaspora, Staples in South India, and Simpson Miller in her historical analysis of *chop* in Ghana (all this volume), this chapter has challenged the terroir focus on producers, formal processes, and food production, illuminating instead the roles of cooks, women, consumers, and informal and domestic spaces in producing and reproducing tastes of place. Beyond landscapes and ingredients, this chapter has also highlighted bodies, social relations, affect, and imaginaries as actors whose effects on taste-place relations should be taken seriously. Similarly, in challenging terroir from the vantage point of displacement, the impact of both border regimes (see also Klein, this volume) and global inequalities have brought to the fore the impossibility of universal relationships between taste and place, as both engender multiple constraints that govern not only the capacity for the physical mobility of bodies across borders but also the mobility of objects that engender embodied, affective, and relational connections to place, including food (see Mintz 2008).

Pointing toward the political economies that shape access to particular horizons of taste, I have worked to illuminate the contemporary (geo)politics of terroir (see also Brawner 2021: 225; Handel et al. 2015; Monterescu 2017) within what critical migration scholars have referred to as "the age of borders," as well as the possibility of deploying terroir as a diagnostic of power, which reveals its embeddedness in multiple matrices of power, here most principally race, class, and gender. Of course, further work remains to be done in producing a robust feminist and race critical challenge to terroir theory (and, indeed, practice).

Nevertheless, what Sudanese women's food practices in Portsmouth make clear is that even as cartographies of both inhabitation and belonging are governed in evermore carceral ways for the global majority, these forms of border policing are also, as West suggests, provoking novel relationships to place, which contest essentialist understandings of place, as well as "relations between product, people and place [as] static and durable" (2022: 7). Instead, they show how just as border power constrains, food products and practices also form a crucial conduit for resistance to border power itself, as getting creative with food challenges border policy, cartographic logics, and nationalist discourse. Again, thinking about both power and resistance insists upon Sudanese women's food practices in Portsmouth as political acts, which are responding to and redrawing multiple social, political, cartographic and moral boundaries, not least toward more socially just futures beyond racial violences in Sudan.

In 2018, at the height of the protests in Sudan, which would later lead to the overthrowing of the regime, then-president Omar al-Bashir attempted to blame the growing civil unrest on "Darfuri rebels," drawing upon and deepening the decades-long exclusion of Darfuris from the imagined community of Sudan. In Portsmouth, after decades of careful community building and weeks of formal protest at the local town hall, women were overjoyed when protestors across Sudan were heard chanting in response: "You arrogant and racist man! All of this country is Darfur!"[6]

Conclusion

Beyond an understanding of terroir that centers heritage, tradition, and a bounded sense of place, this chapter has explored what displaced Sudanese women's everyday food practices in Portsmouth might reveal about the relationship between people, food products and emplacement as a future-orientated project, in which food is involved in an emerging relationship to place. Notions of terroir which understand the value or quality of food in relation to geographical provenance clearly rub up against the realities of life for displaced populations as border policies and practices as well as financial constraints impose upon the ability to procure food products from "countries of origin." In this chapter, I have centered Sudanese women's food practices in Portsmouth to contribute to broader scholarship that considers terroir as a diagnostic of power, and to provoke further interest in feminist—and race critical—analyses of terroir. Most of all, I have sought to enunciate the meanings of food and food products in Portsmouth beyond the nostalgic, the organoleptic, and the logic of "authenticity," instead pointing to the value of food as situated in its affective and aspirational capacities, underscoring the place of food products in materializing new imaginaries of belonging—relational and ecological—and enacting a particularly Sudanese ethics of care in the city, which is also remaking Portsmouth itself.

Acknowledgments

This research was only made possible by the generous investments of time and energy from my interlocutors over the course of years. I thank them for their continued support and interest in my research. I am also grateful to the ESRC's PhD Studentship that funded this project, and to my colleague Dr. Jakob Klein for encouraging me to return to the project with a fresh interest in how food shaped and was shaped by displaced Sudanese women's lived experiences. Finally, I thank my coauthors and the editors of this volume for their invaluable feedback and understanding throughout the writing process.

Charlotte Sanders is Lecturer in Anthropology at SOAS University of London, where her teaching and research moves across and between the anthropology of borders, migration, and diaspora, with attention to issues of gender, race, and colonialism. Charlotte is Deputy Chair of the SOAS Centre for Migration & Diaspora Studies, and a founding partner of the Housing, Migration and Health (HoMH) Lab. Charlotte's research has been published in journals including *The Journal of International Women's Studies*, *Sociological Review*, and *The Journal for Cultural Analysis and Social Change*, and her first monograph is forthcoming with Bloomsbury.

Notes

1. In this text I sometimes capitalize *community* and sometimes do not. When I capitalize, I do so in reference to the organized social group of the Sudanese Community as a more top-down community-building effort, and when I do not I refer to the emerging community in the more everyday grassroots sense.
2. Pseudonyms are used throughout this chapter to protect participants' identities, and some minor identifying details have also been modified to the same end.
3. Technically, the British mandate in Sudan was a shared enterprise between Britain and Egypt, the Anglo-Egyptian Condominium. However, in practice the structure of the

agreement left the British in full control over the territory and its inhabitants (see Abd Al-Rahim 1969: 29–31).

4. The policing of food movement reflects and (re)produces ideas about purity and contamination (Douglas 1966) that are both racialized and racializing in their drawing of boundaries around political and moral communities. Interestingly, in Border Force informational resources uneven distributions of food policing are justified by reference to the potential for food products to carry "pests and diseases," citing the 2001 and 2007 outbreaks of foot-and-mouth disease as an example (Gov.uk 2016) even while the 2007 outbreak was found to have been caused by a laboratory leak in Surrey, UK (see Cottam et al. 2008). In addition, despite claims that Brexit would increase scrutiny over the arrival of food products from the EU, this has not been reflected in official government guidance to date (see Gov.uk 2024).
5. Perhaps the most memorable quote of my fieldwork in this regard came from Hanaan, a woman in her seventies from Khartoum. Hanaan told me, "Charlotte, I pray to Allah every day that Jeremy Corbyn will come," referring to the socialist politician who was leader of the Labour Party from 2015 to 2020.
6. In Sudanese Arabic: يا عنصري ومغرور! كل البلد دارفور!

References

Abd al-Rahim, Muddathir. 1969. *Imperialism and Nationalism in the Sudan: A Study in Constitutional and Political Development, 1899–1956.* Oxford: Clarendon Press.

Abranches, Maria. 2014. "Perceptions of the Country through the Migration of City-Grown Crops: Guinean Food in Bissau and in Lisbon." In *Food between the Country and the City: Ethnographies of a Changing Global Foodscape*, edited by Nuno Domingos, José Manuel Sobral, and Harry G. West, 127–42. London: Bloomsbury.

Brawner, June. 2021. "Domesticating the Taste of Place: Post-Socialist Terroir and Policy Landscapes in Tokaj, Hungary." In *Politics and the Environment in Eastern Europe*, edited by Eszter Krasznai Kovacs, 211–34. Cambridge: Open Book Publishers.

Cassidy, Tanya and Abdullahi Osman El-Tom, eds. 2021. *Moving Meals and Migrating Mothers: Culinary Cultures, Diasporic Dishes and Familial Foodways.* Ontario: Demeter Press.

Gov.uk. 2016. *Bringing Food Products into the UK.* Retrieved January 2024 from https://assets.publishing.service.gov.uk/media/5fdce8c28fa8f5148ebf4182/Bringing_food_into_the_UK_leaflet.pdf.

———. 2024. *Bringing Food into Great Britain.* Retrieved January 2024 from https://www.gov.uk/bringing-food-into-great-britain.

Campt, Tina. 2014. *Black Futures and the Practice of Fugitivity.* Presentation for Barnard Centre for Research on Women. Retrieved January 2024 from https://www.youtube.com/watch?v=2ozhqw840PU.

———. 2017. *Listening to Images.* Durham: Duke University Press.

Cottam, Eleanor M., Jemma Wadsworth, Andrew E. Shaw, Rebecca J. Rowlands, Lynnette Goatley, Sushila Maan, Narendar S. Maan, Pater P. C. Mertens, Katja Ebert, Yanmin Li, Eoin D. Ryan, Nicholas Juleff, Nigel P. Ferris, John W. Wilesmith, Daniel T. Haydon, Donald P. King, David J. Paton, and Nick J. Knowles. 2008. "Transmission Pathways of Foot-and-Mouth Disease Virus in the United Kingdom in 2007." *PLoS Pathogens* 4(4): e1000050.

D'Sylva, A., and B. Beagan. 2011. "'Food Is Culture, but It's Also Power': The Role of Food in Ethnic and Gender Identity Construction among Goan Canadian Women." *Journal of Gender Studies* 20(3): 279–89.

Douglas, Mary. 1966. *Purity and Danger*. London: Routledge.

Graf, Katharina. 2024. "Cooking with(out) Others? Changing Kitchen Technologies and Family Values in Marrakech." *Journal of North African Studies* 29(4): 575–600.

Hage, Ghassan. 2010. "Migration, Food, Memory, and Home-Building." In *Memory: Histories, Theories, Debates*, edited by Susannah Radstone and Bill Schwarz, 416–27. New York: Fordham University Press.

Handel, Ariel, Galit Rand, and Marco Allegra. 2015. "Wine-Washing: Colonization, Normalization, and the Geopolitics of Terroir in the West Bank's Settlements," *Environment & Planning A: Economy & Space* 47(6): 1351–67.

Lin, Hsien-Ming, Ching Lin Pang, and Da-Chi Liao. 2020. "Home Food Making, Belonging, and Identity Negotiation in Belgian Taiwanese Immigrant Women's Everyday Food Practices." *Journal of Ethnic Foods* 7(29): 1–18.

Mannur, Anita. 2007. "Culinary Nostalgia: Authenticity, Nationalism and Diaspora." *MELUS* 32(4): 11–31.

Mintz, Sidney. 2008. "Food and Diaspora." *Food, Culture & Society* 11(4): 509–23.

Monterescu, Daniel. 2017. "Border Wines: Terroir across Contested Territory." *Gastronomica* 17(4): 127–40.

Parveen, Razia. 2016. "Food to Remember: Culinary Practice and Diasporic Identity." *Oral History* 44(1): 47–56.

Paxson, Heather. 2013. *The Life of Cheese: Crafting Food and Value in America*. Berkeley: University of California Press.

Raekstad, Paul, and Sofia Saio Gradin. 2020. *Prefigurative Politics: Building Tomorrow Today*. Cambridge: Polity Press.

Sefa-Nyarko, Clement. 2016. "Civil War in South Sudan: Is It a Reflection of Historical Secessionist and Natural Resource Wars in 'Greater Sudan'?" *African Security* 9(3): 188 210.

Sharkey, Heather J. 2008. "Arab Identity and Ideology in Sudan: The Politics of Language, Ethnicity, and Race." *African Affairs* 107(426): 21–43.

Vaughan, Chris. 2015. *Darfur: Colonial Violence, Sultanic Legacies and Local Politics, 1916–1956*. New edition. Suffolk: Boydell & Brewer.

West, Harry G. 2022. "Terroir Products: A Movable Heritage Feast?" *Review of Agricultural, Food and Environmental Studies* 103(1): 1–27.

CHAPTER 15

British-Born Chinese Restaurateurs and the Reinvention of Chinese Cuisine

Jakob A. Klein

Introduction

In March 2022 I interviewed chef Andrew Wong and Dr. Mukta Das in the A. Wong restaurant in Pimlico in London's West End. Andrew is the head chef and proprietor of the establishment, which was awarded a Michelin star in 2017 and two stars in 2021. Mukta, an anthropologist, works with him as a researcher and menu developer. In response to a question about English school dinners, suggested to me by students I had consulted in preparation for the interview, Andrew brought up A. Wong's version of the custard bun, (C.) *lausaabaao*,[1] a Hong Kong dim sum classic:

> This whole idea of British affinity to custard, now that is very culturally specific, when you talk to any Brit about custard, they automatically think about school dinners. But that isn't something that transfers through internationally. So, when we made custard buns, *lausaabaao*, traditionally, it's meant to be quite salty, quite grainy, and that's the way it's supposed to be.[2] . . . I made the decision to play on this kind of British affinity with custard and modify the dish. And that dish, I never thought in a million years, but actually it has ended up becoming one of the most popular dishes on the menu, and I think that is because it taps into this Britishness and that at the same time it's very much still a dim sum, so people still see it as this dish that travels across this cultural bridge of Hong Kong and Britain in a kind of, like, fluid way. (Interview with Andrew Wong and Mukta Das, 21 March 2022)

A. Wong's custard buns resemble peaches, a Chinese symbol of longevity. They are filled with a creamy, English-style custard, made with the yolks of duck eggs rather than the more commonly used chicken eggs. With their "fluid" move-

Figure 15.1. A. Wong's "steamed duck yolk custard buns". London, 2022. © Jakob A. Klein

ment between Hong Kong and Britain, they reflect A. Wong's culinary ethos. The restaurant's menu is presented as indisputably Chinese, in that it "celebrates Chinese food heritage, historical recipes, and kitchen craft evolved over 4,000 years."[3] At the same time, the A. Wong restaurant takes a creative approach to Chinese traditions, introducing tastes and textures that reflect its London location and Andrew's own experience of growing up in Britain.

This is not so much (or not only) a question of adapting Chinese cooking to the British palates, but about encouraging diners to enjoy A. Wong's food as Chinese *and* British. While promising to deliver food that is delicious, Andrew and his team also challenge culinary boundaries, nudging guests and observers to critically reflect on the relationship between taste, people, and place. In this chapter I situate A. Wong's attempt to create a Chinese restaurant cuisine that simultaneously conveys tastes and memories of China and Britain in the context of changing contours of Chinese migration, restaurant cuisines, and identities.[4]

In this volume Sanders reveals how displaced Sudanese women in Portsmouth rebuild senses of belonging through everyday food practices. My concern is also with migration, food, and belonging in contemporary Britain, but through the lens of a public-facing restaurant cuisine and a longer-established immigrant community. I explore the ways in which Andrew Wong and other British-born Chinese restaurateurs who grew up in the catering trade reinvent Chinese restaurant foods to raise the status of Chinese cuisines and, by extension, of Chinese people. "Belonging" in this context is less about the sourcing and sharing of food to create connections, as in Sanders's discussion, and more about gaining public "recognition" (cf. Taylor 1994) for the contributions of Chinese immigrants to modern Britain and for their fluid identities as both British and Chinese.

These projects of culinary reinvention and recognition come up against "authenticity," that is, notions about what is genuine cuisine and what is not. Can Chinese food that reflects British tastes or memories of London school canteens be "real Chinese food"? Are restaurant foods made by Chinese and other immigrant communities now constitutive elements of British cuisine and national identity, comparable to the Cuban culinary *mestizaje* discussed in Garth's chapter in this volume? Or is "real British food" grounded in local produce and regional cooking (Edwards 2019)? Is culinary authenticity inevitably underpinned by terroir-like ideas that fix connections between people, place, and taste as "tradition"? Or can actors in "culinary fields"—assemblages of chefs, reviewers, diners, award bodies, and others involved in the cultural production of restaurant cuisine (Farrer 2019; Lane and Opazo 2022)—redefine authenticity around fluid mobilities and personal reinterpretations? In conversations, Andrew Wong has expressed an exasperation with "authenticity," and I am similarly skeptical of its usefulness as an analytical tool. However, it is a pervasive value in British and other culinary fields (Lane and Opazo 2022), difficult for either of us to ignore. My interest here is thus in the "politics of culinary authenticity." How is it deployed and defined? Who decides what is "real Chinese food" or "real British food" and under what conditions?

The extent to which Chinese restaurateurs are recognized for their contributions to modern British culture and gain the authority to redefine culinary authenticity is often connected to their entry into the higher echelons of culinary fields. As sociologist Krishnendu Ray (2016) discusses in a North American context, non-European immigrant restaurateurs have struggled to achieve this, as they are expected instead to serve up "ethnic" cuisines at affordable prices. As Ray points out, this has been challenged in recent years. In Britain, too, cooking styles associated with its large immigrant communities, including Indian, West African, and Chinese cuisines, are gaining recognition in "high-end" culinary fields (Lane and Opazo 2022). Nevertheless, British-born Chinese chefs attempting to raise the status of their Chinese restaurants and redefine Chinese cuisine face several challenges. To contextualize these, I turn now to the history of Chinese migration and restaurant cuisines in Britain.

Chinese Restaurants and Cuisines in Britain

Between the late 1950s and the 1990s, Chinese restaurants and takeaways became a prominent feature of Britain's culinary landscape. A key driver was large-scale immigration, principally of Cantonese speakers from Hong Kong but also of Chinese from Southeast Asia. Catering became one of the main sources of employment for Chinese settlers, even though the majority had little or no experience running or working in restaurants prior to migrating to Britain. Compared to other postwar immigrant groups, Chinese settlement in Britain was highly dispersed, driven by the immigrant entrepreneurs' search for new markets for Chinese prepared food (Watson 1977; Song 2015). Small family-run eateries were established in cities, suburbs, and small towns throughout the country. In the early 1950s there were perhaps thirty-six Chinese restaurants in Britain (Benton and Gomez 2009: 116). By 1998 there were nearly eight thousand Chinese catering establishments, including five thousand takeaways (Benton and Gomez 2009: 130).

Most Chinese restaurants and takeaways during this period adapted their offerings to British tastes and meal structures, at prices that were affordable to a wide range of consumers. The "British Chinese" cuisine they developed resembles, and presumably was informed by, "American Chinese food" (Chen 2014), with menus featuring chop suey and chow mein, sweet-and-sour pork, and egg fried rice. Dishes often considered to be representative of British Chinese cuisine (even if versions can be found elsewhere, too) include "crispy fried duck," a variation on Peking duck, with the duck being deep-fried rather than roasted, typically served with pancakes, spring onions, cucumber, and hoisin sauce. "Sweet-and-sour pork balls" are battered, deep-fried, and covered in a thick sauce. "Sesame prawn toast," normally listed on menus under "starters," is made with slices of white bread coated in a batter of minced prawns and egg whites, sprinkled with sesame seeds, and deep-fried. Clearly, deep-fried dishes feature heavily in British Chinese cuisine. Most Chinese takeaways serve chips (chunky fries) with curry sauce or gravy. Many had previously been fish-and-chip shops (Watson 1977), and Chinese families often continued to serve deep-fried fish, along with other "English dishes" and "curry dishes," to borrow menu categories from a Chinese takeaway near my home in a small town in southeast England.

From the perspective of Chinese immigrants, British Chinese cuisine was food for "foreigners," shunned in principle, if not always in practice (cf. Cho 2010). In some towns and cities, more upmarket, sit-down restaurants offered British Chinese favorites alongside dishes that might have been more acceptable to Chinese diners, such as steamed fish, stir-fried green vegetables, and Cantonese-style roast duck and roast pork (cf. Lu and Fine 1995). By the mid-1960s, Hong Kong-style teahouses and restaurants targeting Chinese immigrants were being established in Chinatowns in London and other metropolitan centers, on weekends attracting Chinese from around the country and even from mainland Europe (Watson 1977). Such restaurants also interested adventurous, non-Chinese diners. Dim sum and other Hong Kong–style Cantonese foods became popular among urban restaurant-goers. A few notable restaurants, such as Memories of China, which was opened in London in 1980 by the Fujian-born, former Republic of China diplomat, gourmet, and cookbook writer Kenneth Lo, sought to educate British diners about Chinese gastronomy, rooted in "real" regional cuisines. More commonly, restaurants managed culinary expectations and ethnic boundaries with the help of mixed menus—an English-language menu appealing to British palates, and a Chinese-language menu (and off-menu items) for Chinese customers.

Since the 1990s, new waves of Chinese immigrants and sojourners have arrived in Britain from around mainland China and Southeast Asia, speaking a variety of Chinese dialects and other languages. Compared to the postwar Chinese migrants, the majority of whom had working-class and often rural backgrounds, these more recent arrivals include many more middle-class professionals, investors, students, and tourists. While the Chinese restaurant scene had been dominated by Cantonese-inflected British Chinese dishes and, to a lesser extent, Hong Kong–style Cantonese foods, these new migrants and sojourners have stimulated the proliferation of Chinese restaurants offering diverse cuisines from mainland Chinese regions and cities, including Sichuan, Hunan, Dongbei (Northeast China), Xi'an, Shanghai, and Xinjiang, not to mention establishments specializing in Taiwanese, Singaporean, Malaysian-Chinese, and other cuisines developed by Chinese-speaking communities outside mainland China (Dunlop 2019). Since around 2021, "tea cafés" (C. *chahchaanteng*) and other Hong Kong–style eateries have opened in the wake of a new wave of large-scale migration from Hong Kong. Ranging from simple noodle bars and cafés to upmarket restaurants and transnational, fast-casual dumpling and hotpot chains, many of the new regional Chinese restaurants cater primarily to the palates of Chinese and East Asian customers.

They also attract cosmopolitan diners, of various backgrounds, in search of "real" Chinese food. The word "authentic" and its Chinese equivalents (M. *didao*, *zhengzong*) are regularly printed on menus, storefronts, and websites. According to the website of one London restaurant, the Sichuan, head chef Zhang Xiaozhong "is renowned in the world of Sichuan cuisine. . . . His lifetime of expertise and passion will bring authenticity, indulgence and delicate flavours to the food."[5] In Swansea, Gigi Gao named her restaurant "Gigi Gao's Favourite Authentic Chinese" (Rayner 2022). This reflects not only the importance of authenticity as a value in Britain's culinary field but also the centrality in Chinese culinary cultures of terroir-like notions linking taste, people, and place (see Xiao, this volume). As in North America (Liu 2015), the authenticity of Britain's Chinese restaurants has primarily been presented and judged in relation to their faithfulness to Chinese regional and local cuisines.

The explosion of "authentic" Chinese regional cuisines has done much to enhance the reputation of Chinese restaurants in Britain's culinary field (Dunlop 2019). At the same time, these establishments have created new competition for the existing British Chinese restaurants and takeaways, which by the 1990s were facing a crisis, with closures brought about by labor shortages, by educated children leaving the catering trade for more prestigious occupations, and by competition from fast-food chains and the supermarkets' expansion into ready-made "ethnic" foods (Benton and Gomez 2008: 129–31). In Britain's now diverse Chinese restaurant scene, conventional British Chinese food has often come to stand for "fake Chinese," as in a recent review by critic Grace Dent, who pans a "pan-Asian" restaurant in these words: "It's the sort of food invented for British people that you used to get at a Cantonese restaurant in Braintree in 1994" (Dent 2024: 23).

All this does not mean that British Chinese establishments have fallen out of favor with British eaters. Outside of metropolitan centers and university towns, in places like Braintree, they remain the prevalent style of Chinese catering. Nevertheless, having once been virtually synonymous with "Chinese food," eateries serving British Chinese fare must often adapt to compete with the new, "authentic" regional Chinese and Southeast Asian cuisines—one of my local takeaways has added "ma po to fu" (M. *mapo doufu*, a classic Sichuanese dish), "wok grilled Beijing dumplings," "chicken Szechuan style," and "Thai style dishes" to their menu. As I discuss in the next section, the array of sophisticated restaurants serving diverse regional cuisines, run by restaurateurs and chefs trained in China, Taiwan, and Southeast Asia, pose a particular challenge for British-born Chinese seeking to reenter the catering trade.

"Modernizing" British Chinese Cuisine

In an interview, Andrew Wong reflected on what it meant to him to be awarded a second Michelin star in 2021:

> *Wong*: It really felt like it was an award for *us* as a community, we were breaking new ground. . . . A guide which predominantly is French-centric is . . . looking for a way of connecting their new market, which is Asia, to existing demographics of people in Europe and North America, through the medium of food. And I think the fact that they have chosen us to do this . . . I think means a lot.
> *Klein*: So, when you say this was important for "us as a community" . . . what community are you referring to?
> *Wong*: It's probably not the random mainland Chinese community which is coming into London . . . it is very much the old-school original Chinatown community . . . and it's also this second-generation Chinese community like myself and a lot of my peers, who've gone to university, gone into different professions to make their own mark and their own space within their own industries and a lot of the time, what they're grappling against is their own identity towards themselves and how the UK perceives their ethnicity and their culture. . . . As a restaurant, what we do is we give people, we give the community the idea that times are changing. . . . My grandfather used to say, "You will never be

> accepted, you are a Chinese, just give it up." . . . And we're highlighting this through apparent excellence now, you know, I'm very glad to be a part of it. (Interview with Andrew Wong, 25 October 2022)

Andrew Wong is part of a new wave of British-born Chinese restaurateurs, whose parents or grandparents ran takeaways and restaurants. These new restaurateurs often hold university degrees and have had experiences in other professions before starting their own restaurant businesses. Some, including Andrew, have been formally trained in cooking schools with an emphasis on European gastronomy. Like Andrew, many seek to make use of their cultural and economic capital to "modernize" or "elevate" their Chinese menus to establish themselves in the fast-casual and high-end sectors of Britain's culinary field. Andrew is not alone in explicitly linking his individual business strategies to a project of cultural recognition. For example, Cardiff-born Larkin Cen explained to a journalist that his motivation for setting up a restaurant stemmed from a feeling that "Chinese food was underrepresented, with lots of negative connotations and a complete lack of understanding when it comes to the skill involved" (Anonymous 2022a).

Andrew's generation of restaurateurs is not the first to attempt to raise the status of Chinese cuisine, but, unlike their predecessors, they grew up in Britain and came of age at a time when Chinese in the country increasingly were demanding to be seen and heard. Sociologist Miri Song (2015) has discussed how Chinese were represented in British discourses as a hardworking, quiescent, model minority, who kept their heads down in the face of racial discrimination. However, since the mid-2000s, British-born Chinese have developed a distinctive, British Chinese identity and have rejected the "model minority" label (Song 2015; see also Yeh 2014). In some contexts, for example, in response to anti-Asian racism during the COVID-19 pandemic, this "Chinese consciousness" may extend to other Chinese and even East and Southeast Asians living in Britain. In others, as suggested in the interview with Andrew, British-born Chinese with roots in the postwar migration from Hong Kong and Southeast Asia distinguish themselves from more recent migrants, especially those coming from mainland China.

For British-born Chinese chefs seeking to raise the status of Chinese cuisine while also marking their own distinctiveness and unique contributions to modern Britain, building on the British Chinese cuisine that they grew up with in their parents' catering businesses might seem an obvious move. Indeed, they typically lack the culinary capital needed to compete in Chinese regional styles with Chinese-born and trained chefs. However, British-born chefs may be ambivalent about British Chinese food, aware of the desire among many Chinese to dissociate themselves from the stigma attached to "the takeaway" (Yeh 2014). While some British food writers may recall family meals of Chinese takeaway food with fond nostalgia (Dunlop 2021), for those who grew up "behind the counter," memories of the takeaway can be bittersweet, tainted by feelings of marginalization and episodes of racist abuse (Hui 2022). Further, chefs may be reluctant to celebrate the foods served to cultural outsiders and viewed in Chinese families as sweet and unhealthy in contrast to the nourishing, comforting Cantonese foods shared among kin (Hui 2022: 54-57). And, not least, given the value in the British culinary field placed on "authentic" regional Chinese cuisines, serving Chinese food "invented for British people" may not go down well among culturally Chinese and cosmopolitan diners and critics.

British-born Chinese restaurateurs have approached the question of British Chinese cuisine in different ways. Despite championing the skills of the Chinese takeaway (Anonymous 2022a), Larkin Cen's three Woky Ko restaurants in Bristol (two of which closed in 2022) avoid serving British Chinese foods in favor of "pan-Asian" offerings: "You won't find chicken balls or egg fu yung on the menus of Woky Ko. What you will find are Taiwanese style bao buns, Japanese Katsu and signature Chinese chow mein.[6] Woky Ko's dishes focus on authenticity, provenance and quality with a slight modern twist."[7]

In contrast to Cen, Henry Yau and his WowYauChow restaurants in Manchester fully embrace the "British Chinese" label on their menus, shopfronts, and logo. In a media interview, Yau defines their style as "Chinese casual dining" and claims that they have a "disruptive" approach to Chinese food, taking foods familiar from takeaways, and serving them in small portions with drinks, "almost tapas style," in a "more modern environment" (Anonymous 2022b). The offerings are described on their menus as "Chinese Comfort Food"—the fact that the menu is in English only suggests an appeal to mainstream British rather than Chinese notions of "comfort food." This is risky in a city like Manchester, with its large population of Chinese immigrants and students. Indeed, a few years after launching the business in 2018, Yau invited a Hong Kong chef to one of his restaurants to offer a few dishes—listed in both Chinese and English—that reflected "flavours and styles typically enjoyed by the Chinese community."[8]

Despite their differences in approach to the possibilities and constraints afforded by British Chinese food, both restaurant groups seek to "modernize" Chinese food while avoiding portraying their establishments as representatives of specific Chinese regional cuisines. And both are keen to present themselves not just as "modern" but also as "authentic." In both cases, "authenticity" is centrally defined by reference to the personal biographies of the restaurateurs as British-born Chinese with roots in the catering trade. A passage from their (now defunct) website describes Woky Ko as "the culmination of Larkin's experience as a chef as well as the childhood spent growing up in a traditional Chinese takeaway."[9] WowYauChow even contains the owner's family name, Yau, in the name of their restaurants. The website states: "The story of WowYauChow is one of great authenticity as Henry comes from a long line of family run Chinese eateries, both past and present. Working with and developing old family recipes,

Henry has enjoyed exploring his roots whilst embarking on the next stage of the journey with Chinese food."[10]

As suggested by this quotation from the WowYauChow website, establishing authenticity in terms of their biographies as members of immigrant families in the catering trade is key to attempts by Yau and Cen to assume the authority to "modernize" or "disrupt" Chinese food. Andrew Wong goes even further in putting himself at the center of his restaurant's culinary innovations.

"A. Wong's Chinese Food"

> I am not an expert in Chinese food, I am an expert in A. Wong's Chinese food . . . So what is A. Wong's Chinese food? A. Wong's Chinese food is my interpretation of Chinese food through its fourteen international borders, through its three thousand years, but also through my own lens. (Interview with Andrew Wong and Mukta Das, 21 March 2022)

In contrast to the more "casual dining" styles and price points of Yau's and Cen's restaurants, A. Wong is very much part of London's "high-end" scene. A tasting menu in 2022 was two hundred pounds per person, three hundred pounds with wine pairings. The emphasis on the head chef's own vision is typical of, or even required by, this segment of the culinary field. The foundation of "A. Wong's Chinese food" reflects the food Andrew grew up with at home and in his family's and other London Chinese restaurants—Hong Kong–style Cantonese cuisine, with a particular emphasis on dim sum, and some Sichuan delicacies reflecting influences from his Sichuanese paternal grandmother. Over time, A. Wong has increased the number of dishes based on Chinese regional cuisines and historical dishes from around China. As suggested in the quote above, Andrew takes an interpretative approach to these dishes. For example, the "Shanghai steamed dumplings," rather than served in the conventional way, with vinegar on the side for dipping, are injected with ginger-infused vinegar and garnished with pickled tapioca pearls. In discussions, Andrew has impressed upon me that he seeks to combine his interpretive approach with great respect for the culinary traditions on which he draws. As stated on the restaurant's website, "his cuisine is an intuitive expression of tradition, authenticity and craft."[11]

The A. Wong menu evidently does not center on "British Chinese" food like Henry Yau's. But nor does Andrew try to excise these elements from the menu in the fashion of Larkin Cen. On the topic of "crispy aromatic duck," Andrew explains: "We have it on the menu because we are a British Chinese restaurant. . . . We're not a Chinese restaurant per se. We're a Chinese restaurant in an international gastronomic city. That is a very defining difference."[12] Clearly, like Yau and Cen, Andrew celebrates his background in the British Chinese catering trade.

The "A" in the name of the restaurant is an homage to his parents, Annie and Albert, who on the same site as A. Wong once ran Kym's Chinese Restaurant, an upmarket establishment catering mostly to non-Chinese customers, including tourists and MPs coming over from the nearby Houses of Parliament.

Another British Chinese classic on the menu is "sweet and sour chicken." Like other dishes, Andrew puts his own spin on it. A. Wong's "sweet and sour chicken" is prepared with smoked meat, Thai basil, and candied walnuts. He explains his reasoning behind adding the dish to the menu: "We are in London! If we can translate a dish like sweet-and-sour chicken in a way that it's . . . memorable and it allows people to connect with what they used to eat. . . . And at the same time, I still manage to keep myself happy by creating it in a way which I think is testing the gastronomic technique and stuff—then why not?" (interview with Andrew Wong, 25 October 2022).

In short, as suggested by the "custard bun" example at the beginning of the chapter, "authenticity" at A. Wong emerges not just from fidelity to specific regional cuisines but through the connection to Andrew's skill and imagination and his own life experiences, which include growing up in London and its Chinese restaurant trade, training in European fine dining, an academic education in chemistry and anthropology, links to Hong Kong, and culinary travels in China. Moreover, not only are his dishes meant to tap into his own memories or those of Chinese customers, but, like Henry Yau, he is also interested in connecting to the memories of his non-Chinese customers—at least if he "can still manage to keep himself happy."

As mentioned, the extent to which A. Wong succeeds in defining itself through the vision of its head chef is connected to the role given to the chef-auteur in the high-end, "modernist," transnational culinary field (Farrer 2019). Andrew's authority to take on this role is established in the culinary field through reviews and accolades, including from Michelin—A. Wong being the first Chinese restaurant outside Asia to be awarded two stars. He explains that the first Michelin star was crucial in legitimizing the restaurant's innovative approach to Chinese cuisines. This attracted a new clientele from Britain and overseas, including East Asia, described by Andrew as the kind of people who visit high-end European gastronomic restaurants, who were now enticed to go to a Chinese restaurant and "not expect that Chinatown experience" but instead "come into the restaurant with that mindset of gastronomic celebration."[13]

However, while Andrew points to the possibilities afforded by Michelin recognition, his take on Chinese cuisine, often juxtaposing different regional styles or drawing on techniques and ingredients familiar from European gastronomy, are nevertheless not always accepted by customers, despite his stated attempts to always be respectful of the traditions he is drawing on. This skepticism is especially widespread, Andrew explains, among Chinese customers, who are split down the middle. For them, "We are essentially that Marmite":[14]

> One half will be like, thank you Andrew for helping our cuisine, for celebrating it in a different light, so that Westerners look at our cuisine differently. The other half are like: "We think you are a rip-off, we think you are average, and we think you are conning people." . . . It's taken a long time for me to accept that as a restaurant we will never be able to satisfy that crowd, because they carry so much baggage with them before they come through the door. I can't change that. . . . My cuisine now is something where part of it is grounded in the past, in tradition, and another one is about looking forward. And because there's a side of the cuisine, which is grounded in tradition, everyone who wants to be nasty about our cuisine pounces on that side of stuff. So, they'll be like, oh, your take on the soy chicken[15] is this or is that. It is only because they have a reference point in soy chicken. . . . If you go to the Fat Duck[16] you either like it or you don't, you don't go "I've had a better steak [elsewhere]." You don't go to the Fat Duck to eat steak—you eat at the Fat Duck to eat the Fat Duck's food. (Interview with Andrew Wong, October 25, 2022)

Becoming established in the world of "fine dining" attracts an international set of elite diners, including many from East Asia. This enables and requires Andrew and his team to do novel things with Chinese foods, be these associated with Chinese regional styles or British Chinese restaurants. It also produces challenges, in particular vis-à-vis culturally Chinese customers and their expectations of flavors, ingredient combinations, meal and menu structures, and costs. Clearly, despite the increasing openness of Britain's culinary field to "non-core high-end cuisines" (Lane and Opazo 2022), immigrant restaurateurs entering this domain still must cope with many customers' expectations that they perform to more rigid definitions of authentic "ethnic" cuisine—which in the Chinese case means place-based, regional traditions. Creating a cuisine that is emplaced in both China and Britain and moves fluidly between the two is no easy feat. It involves accommodating diverse expectations and memories and doing a complex balancing act between, in Andrew Wong's words, being "grounded in tradition" and "looking forward."

Conclusion

Chinese in the diaspora have well-documented practices of "improvising" cuisine, adapting their traditions to shifting conditions, including available ingredients and, for those in the catering trade, to diverse customer tastes, food rules, and expectations (Wu 2002). In some settings, such as Cuba (Garth, this volume) and Peru (Siu 2025), these improvised Chinese cuisines have become constitutive elements of "creolized" cuisines and national identities. In others, such as Britain and North America (Cho 2010; Chen 2014), they have been more clearly separated from dominant cuisines, at least conceptually, both among Chinese communities and in mainstream discourses. In such contexts, improvised Chinese restaurant cuisines have acted as a buffer, separating "real" from "fake" Chinese foods. In Britain, establishments targeting Chinese customers and culinary cosmopolitans, not least those restaurants opened by newer arrivals from the Chinese-speaking world, define themselves through contradistinction to British Chinese restaurants, reinforcing the idea that the latter serve "fake" Chinese food for "foreigners."

Separations between "real" and "fake" Chinese food invoke ideals of culinary authenticity, which hold that local and regional Chinese cuisines can be reliably stable even as they travel and are adapted to new settings. Yet in China, regional Chinese cuisines are not timeless traditions. Nor are they necessarily imagined to be, at least not entirely. For example, in Guangzhou, Cantonese chefs distinguish their cuisine from those of other places through claims about its openness to overseas cooking methods, flavors, and ingredients, as well as through ideas about unchanging flavor profiles and other transhistorical characteristics (Klein 2007). Notions of authenticity that rely on terroir-like, essentialized connections between people, place, and taste highlight one aspect of Chinese culinary regionalism but obscure the mixing and innovation that are an inherent and sometimes celebrated dimension of all cuisines.

Notions of authenticity as the timeless taste of place may be useful assets for new arrivals from China purveying regional Chinese cuisines, but they pose a challenge for British-born Chinese restaurateurs attempting to "modernize" and raise the profile of Chinese cuisine in the country of their birth. Among the latter, their catering knowledge and skill are often profoundly shaped by their labor and other lived experiences in the British Chinese eateries owned by their parents and grandparents. If British Chinese food is inherently "inauthentic," then how can it be used as the basis for culinary and wider cultural recognition? As we have seen, while some restaurateurs avoid British Chinese food, others attempt to transform it into trendy, casual dining, tapping into a British nostalgia for "Chinese comfort food," even at the risk of alienating Chinese customers.

One strategy for resolving the problem of authenticity, adopted to different degrees by Cen, Yau, and Wong, is to redefine it in terms of their life experiences of growing up in the immigrant Chinese catering trade. This allows them to highlight their distinctive connections and contributions as British Chinese over two or more generations, and at times to differentiate themselves from more recent arrivals, the "random mainland Chinese community." As Sanders points out in her chapter, there are temporal dimensions to migrants' strategies of emplacement and "home-building" (Hage 2010) through food. For many Chinese immigrants in the postwar period, serving up Chinese food adapted to British customers was crucial to home building, by creating a stable livelihood. So too, in a different way, were attempts to maintain Hong Kong Cantonese, Chinese-Malaysian, and other cooking traditions in their domestic commensality. For the second and third generations of Chinese in Britain, home building may also involve attempting to transform the catering work of parents and grandparents into a form of cultural capital, heritage, and public recognition, amplifying British Chinese voices and enhancing feelings of belonging. Here, the past being used as a resource in home building is thus associated with collective memories not just of East and Southeast Asia but also of Britain.

Convincingly redefining authenticity in this way is not a foregone conclusion. Andrew Wong's apparent success in his attempts to do so is inseparable from his recognition in the domain of fine dining. By redefining Chinese food as "A. Wong's food," an interpretive take on Chinese regional and British Chinese cuisine based on the chef's own life experiences, visions, and skill, Andrew and his team have sought to develop a menu that moves fluidly between Hong Kong and London and speaks to the memories and tastes of both British and Chinese customers. As we have seen, his attempts to redefine authenticity and enhance the recognition of Chinese cuisine in Britain have not gone uncontested, particularly among culturally Chinese customers, be they British-based or those visitors from East Asia, who may be attracted to the restaurant by its Michelin-backed position in the transnational culinary field (Farrer 2019). For these diners, as Andrew says, the A. Wong restaurant and their reinvention of Chinese cuisines are "Marmite"—embraced by some, reviled by others.

Acknowledgments

I am deeply indebted to Andrew Wong and Mukta Das, without whom this chapter would not have been possible. The chapter has benefited immeasurably from detailed feedback from Anna Colquhoun and Katharina Graf. I have also received many valuable comments from participants in the 2023 Beyond Terroir workshop, from members of the Nkumi writing group, and from fellow panelists and a discussant at the 2022 conference of the International Society for the Study of Chinese Overseas.

Jakob Klein is Senior Lecturer (Associate Professor) in the Department of Anthropology and Sociology at SOAS, University of London. He is Deputy Chair of the SOAS Food Studies Centre and co-convenes a master's program in the anthropology of food. Klein's research explores the culture and politics of Chinese food, mostly in the People's Republic of China. He is the coeditor of *The Handbook of Food and Anthropology* (Bloomsbury Academic, 2019), *Ethical Eating in the Postsocialist and Socialist World* (University of California Press, 2014), and "Consumer and Consumed: Humans and Animals in Globalising Food Systems" (special issue of *Ethnos*, 2017).

Notes

1. Cantonese (C.) words are transliterated using the Yale system. Mandarin (M.) words are rendered in pinyin. I have left out tone diacritics.
2. *Lausaabaao* translates as "flowing sand bun," suggesting a grainy filling. The custard filling in the A. Wong bun is silky smooth and runny.
3. A. Wong Dim Sum Lunch Menu, May 2022.
4. The discussion is based on preliminary research conducted since 2022 in preparation for a larger, collaborative project. It draws on two recorded interviews and several informal discussions with Andrew Wong, visits to the A. Wong restaurant, restaurant reviews, media interviews, and restaurant websites and menus.
5. http://www.thesichuan.co.uk/ (retrieved March 2024).
6. Popular in British Chinese and other diasporic Chinese restaurant cuisines, various versions of chow mein (from the Cantonese *chaaumihn*, meaning "stir-fried noodles") can be found throughout China and the Chinese-speaking world.
7. https://www.wokyko.com/larkin-cen (Retrieved 18 October 2022, website now defunct).
8. https://www.wowyauchow.com (retrieved 17 October 2022).
9. https://www.wokyko.com/larkin-cen (retrieved 18 October 2022, website now defunct).
10. https://www.wowyauchow.com (retrieved 17 October 2022).
11. https://www.awong.co.uk/about-chef-andrew-wong (retrieved 20 October 2022, page no longer available. For a similar wording, see "About Chef Andrew Wong" on https://www.awong.co.uk/).
12. Interview with Andrew Wong, 25 October 2022.
13. Interview with Andrew Wong, 25 October 2022.
14. Marmite is a salty sandwich spread, made with yeast. In British popular culture it stands for something that is either loved or loathed.
15. Served at A. Wong "with ginger oil and Oscietra caviar wrap" (A. Wong Dim Sum Lunch Menu, May 2022).
16. Heston Blumenthal's "modern British" restaurant, with three Michelin stars.

References

Anonymous. 2022a. "Larkin Cen: Woky Ko." *Great British Chefs*. Retrieved 18 October 2022 from https://www.greatbritishchefs.com/chefs/larkin-cen.

Anonymous. 2022b. "'We Want to Disrupt Chinese food'—Meet Henry Yau of Alty's Wow Yau Chow." *Confidentials—Manchester*. Retrieved 23 October 2022 from https://confidentials.com/manchester.

Benton, Gregor, and Edmund Terence Gomez. 2008. *The Chinese in Britain, 1800–Present: Economy, Transnationalism, Identity*. Basingstoke: Palgrave Macmillan.

Chen, Yong. 2014. *Chop Suey, USA: The Story of Chinese Food in America*. New York: Columbia University Press.

Cho, Lily. 2010. *Eating Chinese: Culture on the Menu in Small Town Canada*. Toronto: University of Toronto Press.

Dent, Grace. 2024. "This Is the Sort of Food That Was Invented for British People." *The Guardian Feast* 327 (27 April): 22–23.

Dunlop, Fuchsia. 2019. "The New Chinese Revolution." *Observer Food Monthly* (15 September): 36–41.

———. 2021. "How the British-Chinese Takeaway Took Off." *Financial Times Magazine* (19 March).

Edwards, Jason. 2019. "'O, the Roast Beef of Old England!' Brexit and Gastronationalism." *Political Quarterly* 90(4): 629–36.

Farrer, James. 2019. "Red (Michelin) Stars over China: Seeking Recognition in a Transnational Culinary Field." In *Culinary Nationalism in Asia*, edited by Michelle T. King, 193–212. London: Bloomsbury.

Hage, Ghassan. 2010. "Migration, Food, Memory, and Home Building." In *Memory: Histories, Theories, Debates*, edited by Susannah Radstone and Bill Schwartz, 416–27. New York: Fordham University Press.

Hui, Angela. 2022. *Takeaway: Stories from a Childhood behind the Counter*. London: Trapeze Books.

Klein, Jakob A. 2007. "Redefining Cantonese Cuisine in Post-Mao Guangzhou." *Bulletin of the School of Oriental and African Studies* 70(3): 511–37.

Lane, Christel, and M. Pilar Opazo. 2022. "Collaboration and Cooperation in Cultural Fields: Non-core High-End Cuisines in Global Cities." *Food, Culture & Society* 25(5): 847–74.

Liu, Haiming. 2015. *From Canton Restaurant to Panda Express: A History of Chinese Food in the United States*. New Brunswick: Rutgers University Press.

Lu, Shun, and Gary Alan Fine. 1995. "The Presentation of Ethnic Authenticity: Chinese Food as a Social Accomplishment." *Sociological Quarterly* 36(3): 535–53.

Ray, Krishnendu. 2016. *The Ethnic Restaurateur*. London: Bloomsbury.

Rayner, Jay. 2022. "Gigi Gao's Favourite Authentic Chinese, Swansea: 'A Fabulous Creation'—Restaurant Review." *The Guardian* (July 31). Retrieved March 2024 from https://www.theguardian.com/food/2022/jul/31/jay-rayner-restaurant-review-gigi-gao-swansea-a-fabulous-creation.

Siu, Lok. 2025. "Chifas: How Chinese Food Became a Peruvian National Treasure." In *Modern Chinese Foodways*, edited by Jia-Chen Fu, Michelle T. King, and Jakob A. Klein, 253-69. Cambridge: The MIT Press.

Song, Miri. 2015. "The British Chinese: A Typical Trajectory of 'Integration'?" In *Chinese Migration to Europe: Prato, Italy, and Beyond*, edited by Graeme Johanson, Narelle McAuliffe, Massimo Bressan, and L. Baldassar, 65–80. Basingstoke: Palgrave Macmillan.

Taylor, Charles. 1994. "The Politics of Recognition." In *Multiculturalism: Examining the Politics of Recognition*, edited by Amy Gutmann, 25–73. Princeton: Princeton University Press.

Watson, James L. 1977. "The Chinese: Hong Kong Villagers in the British Catering Trade." In *Between Two Cultures: Migrants and Minorities in Britain*, edited by James L. Watson, 181–213. Oxford: Basil Blackwell.

Wu, David Y. H. 2002. "Improvising Chinese Cuisine Overseas." In *The Globalization of Chinese Food*, edited by David Y. H. Wu and Sidney C. H. Cheung, 56–66. New York: RoutledgeCurzon.

Yeh, Diana. 2014. "Contesting the 'Model Minority': Racialization, Youth Culture and 'British Chinese'/'Oriental' Nights." *Ethnic & Racial Studies* 37(7): 1197–210.

CHAPTER 16

"Good Wine" (*Dobro Vino*) and the Social Imaginary of Place

Wine Quality Debates in the Bulgarian Wine Industry

Yuson Jung

Introduction

In the global wine market, terroir, a concept rooted in the French wine tradition and commonly understood as "the taste of place," exemplifies an imagined connection of place and wine (e.g., Trubek 2008; Demossier 2011; West 2022). It is premised on the idea that distinctive environmental elements such as the vineyard's soil, seasonal patterns of rain and sunshine, the slope and orientation toward the sun, and the particular grape variety chosen for cultivation in that vineyard affect the wine and give it its distinctive taste (West 2013: 211). Although this idea can make the human element rather invisible, it includes people and their knowledge which harness the environmental elements and turn them into traditional practices (Black 2013; West 2022).

According to Trubek (2008), terroir is a food-centered worldview produced by a particular history of social practices in France over the past two centuries. Taste here becomes an important quality and characteristic of a given place. The cultural authority of this concept in the wine world has made it a hegemonic discourse and practice for validating a wine's value—especially its premium quality—by privileging a particular manifestation of locality in the globalized wine world (Jung 2014).

For Tzvetan,[1] a veteran Bulgarian winemaker, the terroir as a quality standard bears relevance only for the category of "fine wine," which expresses a place-based distinction that can be tasted.[2] By this, he is referring to flavor characteristics of a wine, such as minerality, which supposedly reflects the geological conditions where the grapes are grown, as well as a "typicity"[3] that winemakers harness in the winemaking process to reproduce identifiable wine characters in gustatory terms. The gustatory is part of the five physical senses (taste, smell, sight, hearing, touch) in the Western model (Sutton 2010), and refers to the sensory perception primarily through the mouth (tongue).[4] Yana, another Bulgarian winemaker, explained terroir in terms of the gustatory difference between a fine Cabernet Sauvignon from Napa Valley and one from northwestern Bulgaria. In other words, the different terroirs of Napa and northwestern Bulgaria produce different tastes of the same varietal.

Here is an example of a popular representation regarding the connection of terroir and "fine wine" that points to the imaginative power of place and its quality validation through the taster's palate. A scene of the popular documentary film *SOMM* (2012), directed by Jason Wise, is particularly telling: the film is about the wine professionals' rigorous training process to become a master sommelier (a professional credential) by taking an exam that is notoriously difficult to pass. This scene[5] demonstrates particularly well how terroir manifests itself in gustatory terms for these wine professionals, and how it serves as a key quality standard in the wine world.

In the film, two wine professionals, Ivan and Ian, are blind tasting to identify the wine in terms of geographical origin, varietal, and vintage. While Ian is tasting the wine and describing it in terms of its sensory descriptors (color, dryness, smell, such as fruit or flower, or even tennis ball, etc.),[6] he narrows down the geographical locales of the wine he is blind tasting: "From the New World, high-quality producer, Riesling . . . must be Clare Valley Riesling, possibly 2009." In going through the taste evaluation process in meticulous detail, he is able to identify the wine correctly in terms of its geographical origin and varietals based on his trained palate of the gustatory discernment of the terroir—that of Clare Valley, Australia. In other words, a fine wine is identifiable through gustatory discernment based on its placed-based identity. The assumption here is that the experience of wine is mediated through the physical senses.

"Taste," however, does not only refer to the physical sensory experience even in the context of food. It can include ideas such as tradition, heritage, connection to land, work, self-sufficiency, and temporality (see also Colquhoun, Grasseni, or Meneley, all this volume; see also Graf 2022). It can also be inferred from memory (Seremetakis 1994) and can contribute to place-making projects (Weiss 2011). As such, the "taste" of a place can combine physical and nonphysical senses such as affective, emotional, and temporal ones, all contributing to the social imaginary of a place.

Terroir has a particular purchase for premium-quality wines, as the example from the *SOMM* film shows, and supports winemaker Tzvetan's point. Demossier (2020) argued that terroir was essentially a legal and ideological system that provided fixed and predictable framing of taste in the wine sector, taste here referring to the gustatory experience of typicity of a place. The authoritative power of the terroir idea has contributed to the valuation of a constructed locality and the creation of a wine hierarchy.[7] This wine hierarchy is based on the wine's quality, which is often quantified through an evaluation process where wines are scored according to criteria, including how well it expresses a given locality (e.g., elite wines from Bordeaux or Burgundy score high in wine evaluation by wine experts at tasting events). Hence the normative understanding in the wine industry that terroir wines are "good wines" (*dobro vino*).

Some Bulgarian wine professionals, such as winemakers, wine technology workers in industrial wineries, wine merchants, and wine journalists, argue, however, that terroir wines are not the only "good wine" that demonstrate a wine's connection to its place of origin. This raises the question of what other quality valuation standards allow for a wine to demonstrate its connection to a place, and how Bulgarian wine professionals construct the salient place of taste differently. It thus speaks to this volume's aim to explore the contexts in which the terroir concept is relevant, irrelevant, or contested, as well as how different social actors conceptualize and practice the relationships between food, taste, place, and people, and what consequences ensue from such practices.

It also raises the question of how a wine manifests itself in sensory terms beyond the gustatory that can contribute to producing a social imaginary of a place, connecting intrinsic values of a food commodity to the environment (both natural and cultural) where it was produced. How do Bulgarian wine professionals articulate the place-based identity of their wines in sensory terms beyond the hegemonic terroir discourse?

In this chapter I focus on the quality debates in the Bulgarian wine industry to understand the construction of a place-based identity of Bulgarian wines. I am particularly interested in understanding the invisible standards for categorizing and evaluating wines in sensory terms that evoke the social imaginary of a place, and also shape its perception simultaneously. After discussing the wine valuation standards and practices in the Bulgarian wine industry since the socialist era, I examine three different articulations of "good wine" by Bulgarian wine professionals working in industrial production (wineries A and B), boutique production (winery C), and a relatively midsize production (winery D), to show how they locate quality in relation to place in sensory terms that contributes to producing and reproducing Bulgarian wine values as a place-based commodity.[8]

Wine Valuation in the Bulgarian Wine Industry

As arguably one of the oldest wine-producing countries in the world, Bulgaria built a large, highly industrialized, and export-oriented wine sector during state socialism as a wine-producing specialist of COMECON (the economic alliance of Soviet allies; an average of 60 percent of the total production was exported). When socialism collapsed in 1989, the wine industry faced multiple challenges, including the widely accepted international hierarchy of wine-producing countries through which Bulgarian wines then became evaluated and marketed. This wine hierarchy placed wines reflecting a particular locality, demonstrated through gustatory discernment (terroir), on the top. In comparison, the socialist wine industry did not engage in quality discussion based on this hegemonic terroir practice. But as their high export ratio shows and people who worked in the industry mention, it offered "good wines." Bulgarian wines were deemed as having "good/high quality" (*dobro/visoko kachestvo*), competitive in the international wine market and recognized by their geographical origin, namely as Bulgarian wine, though not identified in terms of a particular region in Bulgaria (like Burgundy in France, for instance).

For Bulgarians, winemaking is part of a cultural patrimony, a key cultural heritage, and the socialist state capitalized on this tradition when it developed the wine industry starting in the late 1960s, especially during the 1970s and 1980s. The state-owned wine industry had its own implicit and explicit wine categories and standards for valuation. For example, red wines industrially produced in large quantities in state-owned wine plants were privileged for the export market as there was more demand for it. Bulgaria had a reputation for its good-quality reds.

During that time in the Bulgarian wine industry, wines were not categorized by their geographical origins—meaning, where the grapes were grown in Bulgaria was not relevant for wine valuation.[9] Instead, wines were categorized based on grape varietals (Merlot and Cabernet Sauvignon, for instance, or their native grape varietals, such as Mavrud and Gamza). Typicity in this context was understood as imparting the typical flavor characteristics of the varietal without assuming any connection to a particular place (vineyard or region) where the grapes came from. This understanding did not include any human element, such as the winemakers' role in harnessing the natural elements of the environment where the grapes were grown.

Wines were also categorized according to the export-worthy quality. The veteran winemakers, those who have worked in the Bulgarian wine industry since the state socialist times (1980s), explained to me the quality standards largely in two ways: one was that the wine had no technical flaws (e.g., from faulty fermentation or storing processes) and that it tasted balanced (not too acidic or too sweet/fruity), making it "very/easily drinkable," especially for international consumers. Another way they explained wine quality was in terms of the quality of their native grape varietal found only in Bulgaria, such as the case with the most iconic native varietal Mavrud or the broad-leaf Melnik, which was known to be Churchill's favorite wine. The quality of these native varietals imparted "unique Bulgarian flavors" that were appreciated abroad. Wines that did not meet these quality standards remained for the domestic market.

The standards for categorizing wine and validating its quality changed since the socialist system collapsed in the 1990s. The Bulgarian wine industry had to adapt to an increasingly competitive global wine market. There the geographical origin expressed in gustatory terms, namely the hegemonic terroir discourse and practice, was an important quality standard that affected a wine's standing in the hierarchy. Many Bulgarian wine professionals were compelled to engage with this notion of terroir in order to carve out a good standing for Bulgarian wines, which reflected the power dynamics in the globally sanctioned wine hierarchy. The terroir discourse and practice also show how the authoritative and globalized wine knowledge plays an important role in Bulgarian wine professionals' engagement with the categorization and evaluation of wines (Jung 2014). At the same time, it raises the question of whether there are spaces where this hegemonic quality standard of terroir bears little meaning, allowing room for different quality standards to partake in the valuation of wine and its connection to a given place. In other words, can one imagine a place through wines in sensory terms that seemingly do not exhibit terroir in any gustatory sense?

Can Industrial Wines Be Good Bulgarian Wine?

In a former state-owned wine plant, winery A in northwestern Bulgaria, in early winter 2008, a worker, Mitko, was disgorging, which is a part of the traditional champagne-making process to remove crown caps and lees, and adding dosage, the topping of sugar-added wine, before finally corking the bottle. When I marveled at his deft skills of disgorging, he sighed and said, "This is nothing," referring to the quantity (only five hundred bottles) he was working on with two other colleagues: "We used to produce over two million bottles of champagne annually, and exported them to the Soviet Union. They were good wines in high demand! . . . Gone . . . those days are gone." Mitko's comment here points to how the high demand of large quantity validates a wine's quality.

These nostalgic sentiments often referred to what some Bulgarians (such as Mitko) perceived as the "successful days" of the quantity-oriented socialist wine enterprise before "the crooks in the market economy destroyed it all." This quantity-oriented production, however, is not only a hallmark of socialism. In fact, the artisanal-based boutique wineries that we so often associate with the "wine landscape" (Demossier 2020) and premium quality wine production are globally only responsible for about 20 percent of the entire wine production, according to Tzvetan. The rest of the wine is an outcome of industrial production. While the quality of the sparkling wines produced in the industrial wine plant where Mitko worked may not be considered "premium" quality according to the global wine hierarchy sanctioned by wine experts, its "goodness" was connected to the place where they were produced. As Mitko said, they were famous as the producer of "good-quality Bulgarian Champagne" (*dobro kachestveno bulgarsko shampansko*).

Winery B, located in the eastern part of the Thracian Valley, was another former wine plant and was perceived by some foreign industry professionals and

Bulgarian professionals as having transformed itself successfully as a capitalist business. Its production is geared toward the mass market, resulting in millions of tons of wines both for export and domestic markets. They have the largest market shares in Bulgaria's restaurant sector, according to the head winemaker, Krassimir. It is one of the most common wine brands one comes across when eating out in Bulgaria. The aesthetics of the winery (inside and outside) refutes any romanticized notion one associates with a chateau-like winery surrounded by vineyards. According to Tzvetan and John (Tzvetan's colleague, an American oak barrel exporter), whom I accompanied during a visit, and who have had decades of experience in the wine industry (Bulgarian and global), pointed out that this was typically what an industrial winery looked like around the world.

There were ten winemakers employed in this winery, and their work resembled that done by *tehnologs* (the official title of winemakers trained to oversee the entire industrial wine production) during the socialist time, in the sense that where the grapes came from was not as important as producing consistent and good-quality wine. Krassimir said that he was proud of his wine quality that is highly drinkable and, most importantly, consistent from year to year. He pointed out that he did not pretend that his wines were the best, but he was continuing the legacy of the Bulgarian wine industry with a reliable and large-scale production of quality wine—"good wine." By emphasizing how the wine quality has improved compared to the socialist era, he had no qualms in relating Bulgaria's wine heritage to industrial production. The "taste of place," for him (like it was for Mitko from winery A), was in the broadest sense—wine made with grapes grown in Bulgaria. But he also pointed to the technical skills of the industrial winemakers like himself, modern production facilities of the industrial winery, as well as the industrial tradition that they continue. These different dimensions played a role in a wine's taste, indicating that the "place" salient to the wine's taste can be constructed differently. This is why he shrugged his shoulders when I asked him whether he worried about climate change affecting the taste of wine. He added that they were skilled and experienced enough to make wine of consistent quality that could be sold abroad and domestically—something that the consumers would always search for.

According to Tzvetan, Krassimir's wines were indeed "good" ("enjoyable to drink") but not something that an expert taster could identify in a blind tasting through a place-based terroir identity. For these larger industrial producers, terroir was an elusive concept, and wine was conceived as an industrial endeavor, and a mass-produced commodity that heavily relied on human intervention. It was not about harnessing natural conditions that leads to distinctive products connecting to the place (microregion) and identified through an intrinsic gustatory evaluation. Place constructed through the notion of terroir was not how people like Krassimir related to taste and quality. According to Krassimir, mass-produced and therefore cheap(er) in this case does not necessarily mean poor quality (see also Besky 2020 on the quality debates in the tea industry). One of the wine labels of this winery B did have the word *terroir* on it, but when we asked what that meant, Krassimir shrugged his shoulders and said with a smile: "It's from the Bulgarian soil—a helpful marketing tool . . ."

His attitude echoed other wine professionals in Bulgaria, all of whom professed terroir knowledge but treated it more like a foreign concept rather than something that resonated with their practice. Their pride as winemakers was based on their ability to produce large quantities of "good wine" and continuing the Bulgarian winemaking heritage in such a capacity. Interestingly, Krassimir's stance regarding his industrially produced wines may point to a sustainable practice in light of the environmental shift that drives debates on viticultural practices in Burgundy, for example, where terroir and typicity are contested by a new generation of winegrowers (Demossier, this volume).

This practice suggests potentials for a different quality standard other than terroir that can valorize the connection between a wine and place. As Besky (2020: 280), following Tsing (2015), argues, "Quality . . . while easily invoked as a universal good, does not index a uniform set of experiences or values." It should therefore be understood as an experimental undertaking. Rather than being intrinsic, quality is produced, and a good wine in this context is produced by skilled Bulgarian winemakers using grapes grown in Bulgaria. The grapes are processed in modern facilities with high technical skills for industrial production, following decades of industrial heritage. Wine quality does not only need to be produced through connoisseurship that expresses place-based distinction in gustatory terms (as implied in *SOMM*). For Krassimir, the seemingly generic (or nondiscerning) taste of an industrially produced wine does not preclude it from generating a connection to a given place. The social imaginary of place here is perhaps more accessible and affordable as a shared experience among wine producers and consumers. Such an approach allows them to partake in the construction of quality and the reproduction of Bulgaria's wine heritage, of which industrial production is also a part.

The Construction of Place and Wine Value

In promotional videos of different world wine regions, a camera often takes the viewer through an impressive panoramic view of the wine landscape, which includes vineyards, wineries, and close-ups of grapes. Rarely do the videos include humans, but the manicured landscape clearly reflects human intervention. Bulgarian wine professionals, too, promote their wines through evocative imagery connecting place and taste, certainly conjuring up a social imaginary that reproduces the hegemonic terroir discourse and practice. In 2020 one of my key interlocutors, Yana, a veteran winemaker trained under the state socialist wine

Figure 16.1. Vineyard nestled by the ancient rocks in northwestern Bulgaria, 2013. © Yuson Jung

industry, agreed to her Bulgarian distributor's plea to create a video that shows the stunning panoramic view of the region where her vineyards nestle.

Yana and Tzvetan were old colleagues and co-owned the boutique winery C in northwestern Bulgaria until Tzvetan's untimely passing. This region is particularly known for its ancient and distinctive rock formations, although few people even in Bulgaria relate the region to vineyards, let alone distinguish the wine produced there in distinctive gustatory terms.

Yana and Tzvetan's vision was anchored in terroir that led them to create a new vineyard by these ancient rocks. Although the larger region has always cultivated vines and produced wine, their vineyard was the first commercial vineyard in the area. In the video, similar to promotional videos of world-renowned wine regions, the viewer is led through the humbling panoramic natural landscape with idyllic sounds of the wind, leaves, and insects—indeed a complex sensory field of synesthesia (Sutton 2010) to which one gets emotionally drawn—leading to the vineyards and to the winery where Yana explains her vision. The viewer is compelled to imagine the taste of place as Yana pours a glass of wine against the backdrop of the incredible rock formations. The sounds in the vineyard and around the winery also contribute to the imagination of the wine and its connection to the place.

Their wines won critical acclaim from global wine experts, indicative of their success based on the sanctioned gustatory standard of expressing discernable difference. But to such niche producers from a marginal wine country, the external recognitions were insufficient in putting the terroir of northwestern Bulgaria on the global wine map. Yana and Tzvetan were strong advocates of terroir wines because they believed their wines reflected a typicity found in grapes of this particular microregion, which they discovered as experienced winemakers and intensively studied for over two decades, first as negociants and later as winery owners. Visits by renowned global wine experts, for example, validated their premium wine quality by recognizing minerality—a key terroir indicator—in their wines. Yet these experts had not tasted all wines from the region, nor from different places of Bulgaria, to draw a meaningful connection to the notion of terroir even though they acknowledged terroir potential.

This is why Yana mentioned that "our wines are incredible, discernable from the terroir of our vineyards, and we have a lot of fans who enjoy our wines and express how they sense a strong connection to our place [region]. . . . But will we ever gain world recognition as a [wine] region, with our distinctive place-based identity—will people remember us as part of the terroir of the Bulgarian northwest connected to the taste of our terroir?" She wondered how meaningfully their wine's terroir can be translated to the globally sanctioned wine world. While terroir practice is very important to her, she recognized the gustatory-privileged standard is only meaningful to wine consumers engaged with the hegemonic practices of connoisseurship, and to global wine experts who can provide the external validation through their authoritative knowledge (like the judges in international wine competitions, for instance). To achieve a collective identity based on a regional typicity that is expressed in gustatory terms, and to have such connection "naturalized," an individual winemaker's vision needs to be embraced and advocated by a larger collective effort and recognized by authoritative wine experts. This is because terroir is a cultural, and not a natural, phenomenon, as numerous food scholars in this volume have demonstrated (see also Paxson 2013; Besky 2014; Weiss 2016).

Achieving a terroir-based identity as a wine region and being evaluated according to the gustatory standard is not so straightforward, especially if a given wine industry and wine culture were not organized in such a way. Yana and Tzvetan once submitted their wine to the Decanter World Wines Award in the UK, an internationally reputable competition. They received a bronze award and were the first Bulgarian winemakers to achieve this accolade. It was an exciting accomplishment but ultimately did not result in better sales—domestically, in the UK, or elsewhere globally—nor did it help elevate their wine status in the global wine hierarchy. In fact, they learned about the less visible standards that are being used for quality validation.

For example, in the Decanter wine competition, the criteria for judging, and its award system, are first organized geographically. The wines are judged by experts (e.g., masters of wine and master sommeliers) who are certified professionals put through rigorous training, including the gustatory discernment of wines. This geographical category can be as narrow as a microregion within a country—such as is the case with many French viticultural areas (think Champagne or Bordeaux); or it can be broader, such as "North, Central and Eastern Europe," which points to the implicit wine hierarchy. Simply put, the nonelite or newly emerging wine regions do not have a historically cultivated typicity that can be broken down into a more micro level according to global wine experts organizing these competitions. There is no system in place that would allow the wines from nonelite places to even be recognized as terroir wines. There are few trained wine experts who would be able to blind taste and identify a Bulgarian wine from the northwestern region based on its typicity, for example. Other evaluative criteria in the competition include grape, style, vintage, and "price band" (ranging from entry-level retail price of under ten British pounds to over fifty British pounds, six categories).

According to these established standards, then, Yana and Tzvetan's wine was evaluated with other wines from the "North, Central and Eastern Europe" category from the same retail price band (under ten British pounds), but not against established wines from France or Italy that may be priced at under ten British pounds. Generally due to labor cost differentials, Eastern European wines could often be a better "bargain" (better value for price), making the "price band" an ambiguous standard. The bronze medal recognized their wine as "good wine" from North, Central and Eastern Europe, but not necessarily as terroir wine from northwestern Bulgaria. Tzvetan pointed out how these international competitions essentially lose meaning for marginal producers, because they are pegged in this broad geographical category and arbitrary price category, neither of which will have tangible outcomes for elevating the place-based quality status of their Bulgarian wines expressed in gustatory terms in a globally sanctioned wine hierarchy. Their wine quality may deserve a terroir distinction, meaning their wines could reflect the taste of their particular vineyard where the grapes come from, but under the current system and standard, they are not categorized as premium-quality wines, and therefore their specific terroir is not considered.

For Yana and Tzvetan, the visual and auditory aspects manifested in the promotional video are actually not important for the taste of their wine. But Yana acknowledged that for their wine consumers, domestic and abroad, these other sensory appreciations could be meaningful in helping them both place and taste their wines. While the hegemonic wine valuation may privilege the gustatory based on a particular construction of place, there are other quality standards expressed sensorially that connect a wine to a place. In addition to physical senses of the look and sound in the video, the viewer is also able to infer a mood or vibe, namely an affective sense, or an emotional sense, all of which can contribute to a sensorially grounded social imaginary of a place. This does not mean that the gustatory has no role in evaluating "good wine"—rather, wine's taste may not be salient only through the terroir standard, and a place-based wine identity can be expressed and valued through different quality standards beyond the gustatory.

The Social Imaginary through Heritage Stewardship

The notion of cultural heritage or patrimony is often central in the origin stories of new winery owners, essentially Bulgarians who joined the wine sector as new wine producers only in the past decade. Winery D, for instance, was built by a wealthy machine manufacturer and is located in the foothills of the Rodopi Mountains at the western end of the Thracian Valley. During our visit with Tzvetan and John, the winery owners Ivan and Dessi (a husband and wife team) proudly described how the area was where the ancient Thracians, the supposedly talented first winemakers in the world, had created their first capital. The land around there, Dessi continued, "simply had the Bulgarian soul," by which she meant that the wines produced from the grapes there imparted a special taste. One could sense the Bulgarian soul in the wine.

They considered themselves as good stewards of this land and the cultural heritage of winemaking, and wanted to demonstrate the "Bulgarian soul" through their wines. The winery was considered midsize in scale (capable of processing

Figure 16.2. Vineyard in the Thracian Valley near the Rodopi Mountains in southern Bulgaria, 2013. © Yuson Jung

three thousand tons of grapes) and focused more on the domestic market rather than export. Like many Bulgarian wineries, it, too, was supported by an EU subsidy for rural development. The vineyards and winery were the basis of the owners' larger mission of turning the entire area into a new tourist destination to showcase the ancient history and heritage.

While the business thrived on producing "good wine," its primary mission appeared to be not so much making profit from winemaking as being part of a developing heritage industry, including agrotourism, of which winemaking was an important element. They were upholding the romanticized ideals of reconnecting with the ancient land and continuing its cultural legacy by cultivating new vineyards in the area. In their case, this was not an area where the socialist wine enterprise (*vinprom*) had any direct legacy. Instead, winemaking was a new enterprise for this particular area, driven as much by the goals of rural development and heritage preservation as by the wine business itself (similar to Grasseni's case, this volume). They therefore embraced the idea of terroir, using the term occasionally to market their wine, not so much as a quality standard for distant wine connoisseurs but as a means for associating their wines with a particular ancient place, which could then be "sensed" by visitors to the region as part of their experience of distinctive local heritage. The sensory experience here included an emotional and temporal one, evoking a connection to the past through a social imaginary of place.

Unlike Yana and Tzvetan, Ivan and Dessi did not articulate terroir front and center as a key quality standard for their wines. Their head winemaker Peter was trained under the socialist system and was respected for his talents, but he was rather vague about how a new and young vineyard could already show a place-based identity through its grapes. After tasting their wines, Tzvetan and John thought they were good, but did not think that the wines in this winery reflected a place-based identity that could be identified in blind tasting. They did not detect any minerality either. They also thought this kind of orientation and mission as perhaps the stewards of Bulgarian heritage (natural and cultural) could make the winery here more sustainable and adaptable to the changing environment by continuously reinventing itself. The idea of "good wine" in this winery related to their evocation of the ancient land through multiple sensory terms (including the sensing/feeling of the Bulgarian soul and connection to the ancient past) and promotion of wine as part of the broader heritage industry here. Regardless of whether the sensory experience they reference is just a marketing strategy, the evocation of a place in emotional and temporal sensory terms points to a different way to connect wine and place, and articulate quality.

This way of connecting wine and place actually resonates well in Bulgaria, as the beloved cultural heritage and tradition of homemade wine demonstrates. Homemade wine (*domashno vino*) indexes a certain kind of value grounded in locality and is often expressed in sensory terms, without privileging the gustatory. For instance, Valyo, who worked for the industrial winery A and continued to produce homemade wines himself, put it as the following: "We always have homemade wine to be sure that we have it. It is what I have always done with my father, my grandfather, and now I am doing it with my son. It is a tradition. We connect to our land directly with our hands—we work our land, we pick the grapes, process them, and put them in our barrel. . . . It may not be what the experts call the best wine, but it is good wine. This is our culture, our heritage." This sentiment is commonly expressed in Bulgaria even though fewer people actually work the land.

During harvest season in the fall, one frequently sees plastic and wood barrels being washed and people getting them ready for the new harvest and producing homemade wine in many villages and provincial towns across the country. My Bulgarian interlocutors repeatedly expressed how making their own wine allowed them to "feel or sense" the connection to their land and ancestors. Wine's quality articulated as "good wine" here manifests again through an evocative social imaginary around the wine heritage, connecting people to their lands through the winemaking practice. The "goodness" in this social imaginary includes many physical sensory dimensions but does not privilege the gustatory imparted from the product. Here the wine's taste perception is something anticipated and inferred from the look, sound, and smell of the place that is not registered necessarily through climatic or geological conditions of the soil. More importantly, it includes emotional and affective senses, such as the feel/mood/vibe of a shared memory (firsthand and imagined) around the winemaking practice.

Like Valyo's reasoning of why homemade wine is "good," the winery D owners saw their winery as an element of helping people (both Bulgarians and foreign visitors) learn about the ancient land and cultural heritage, and used this vision for making "good wine" from their place. A wine's quality and its place-based identity does not always derive from terroir-discernable taste in the gustatory sense. The social imaginary of a place that a wine evokes is complex and multisensory (including both physical and nonphysical sense) and does not always need to privilege the gustatory through connoisseurship.

Conclusion

For many Bulgarian wine professionals, wine quality debates are intimately linked with the legacy of their highly industrialized and export-oriented wine industry from socialist times, which was a successful industrial endeavor capitalizing on Bulgaria's rich nature and winemaking tradition. Furthermore, the tremendous development since socialist times is a great source of pride for them, which led to global recognition of premium quality wines. Wine categories and quality standards are meaningful to them because they validate their wines' values. In the categorization and evaluation of wines globally, terroir has been a hegemonic quality standard that privileges the gustatory-mediated social imaginary of a place. The concept of terroir constructs "place" in a particular way based on climatic and geological conditions, along with humans' ability to harness them to express "the taste of place." Place, just like taste, is socially and culturally constructed, and as such they are both flexible. For Bulgarian wine professionals, the salient place of taste can be constructed differently and expressed in sensory terms without privileging the gustatory. Terroir is not the only quality standard showing the connection of wine and place.

Ultimately, it is important to recognize to whom a place-based food identity matters and why. The Bulgarianness of the wines that Bulgarian winemakers produce is not a fixed taste. Rather, it is constantly produced, and this process includes continuously engaging with creating and recreating a social imaginary of Bulgarian wines inclusive of regional diversity (particularly for premium-quality fine wines expressing terroir). Quality is not an exclusive domain for only wines in the top category ("premium quality"). Even the so-called generic table wines (which can include both homemade wines and industrially produced wines) can be good wines manifesting their locality. This is so because the social imaginary of place does not exclusively derive from a gustatory experience and is constructed beyond the demarcation of microregions that is premised in terroir ideologies. Taste can be expressed in multisensory terms, including both physical and nonphysical senses such as affective, emotional, and temporal senses. The link between wine, people, and place is continuously made and remade, and quality is produced in this process. The social imaginary of place is constituted in multisensory terms as a process, and beyond the intrinsic connection to spatially demarcated microregions.

Acknowledgments

Special thanks to the editors Anna Colquhoun and Katharina Graf for their tireless commitment to this project. Their constructive comments and those of many colleagues in this volume have been stimulating and greatly appreciated. As always, my deepest gratitude to my inspiring longtime interlocutors in the Bulgarian wine industry. All shortcomings in the text are mine.

Yuson Jung is Associate Professor of Anthropology at Wayne State University in Detroit, Michigan. She is the author of *Balkan Blues: Consumer Politics after State Socialism* (Indiana University Press, 2019), and coedited *Ethical Eating in the Postsocialist and Socialist World* (University of California Press, 2014, with Jakob Klein and Melissa Caldwell). Focusing on issues of globalization, consumption, food politics, postsocialism, and entrepreneurship, she has conducted ethnographic field research in Bulgaria and in Detroit. She is currently completing a book project on the cultural politics of the Bulgarian wine industry. She received her PhD in Anthropology from Harvard University.

Notes

1. All names of my interlocutors are pseudonyms.
2. For a more detailed discussion of taste and the anthropology of the senses in the context of the terroir discourse, see Jung (2014).
3. This term is an English translation of the French word *typicité*, which is used in wine tasting to describe whether a wine reflects its varietal origins (Teil 2012; see also Grasseni, this volume, who uses the Italian word *tipicità*). It is also translated sometimes as "typicality" (Oxford Wine Encyclopedia). In the French AOC (*Appellation D'Origine Contrôlée*) system (which recognizes the geographical origin of a wine), it is used by French wine professionals when granting the AOC certificate to a specific wine (Demossier 2011, 2020: 78).
4. Strictly speaking, "taste" in the gustatory sense is also affected by its smell and look. My Bulgarian interlocutors used the term *vkusovi*, which is the literal translation of the gustatory.
5. https://youtu.be/yFcsWyq2QO8?si=wPyOq67Byx901xPq (the scene appears between 00:07:52 and 00:09:18).
6. Wine professionals sometimes use the term *organoleptic* to refer to the holistic taste experience, which includes taste, color, smell (aroma), and mouthfeel (texture) of wine. Organoleptic evaluation of wine taste and its quality essentially uses four out of the five physical senses (all but the sound). It is a specialized term that could be understood in terms of synesthesia (the union of senses), but unlike synesthesia, it relies on the Western sensory models of registering taste experience passively rather than considering how sensory experience can be actively created between people (Sutton 2010: 218).
7. The popular Japanese manga series on wine, The Drops of God, by Tadashi Agi, first published in 2004, and translated globally, demonstrates the hegemonic terroir discourse of the wine world particularly well.
8. The chapter is based on ethnographic and archival data from my longitudinal fieldwork in Bulgaria (2007–23, intermittently), with an ethnographic focus in the Belogradchik area in northwestern Bulgaria, visits to wineries across Bulgaria, and engagements with wine professionals in the cities of Sofia and Plovdiv.
9. See Ina (2022) for a similar history in Moldova.

References

Besky, Sarah. 2014. *The Darjeeling Distinction: Labor and Justice on Fair Trade Tea Plantations in India*. Berkeley: University of California Press.

———. 2020. *Tasting Qualities: The Past and Future of Tea*. Berkeley: University of California Press.

Black, Rachel E. 2013. "*Vino Naturale*: Tensions between Nature and Technology in the Glass." In *Wine and Culture: Vineyard to Glass*, edited by Rachel E. Black and Robert C. Ulin, 279–94. London: Bloomsbury.

Demossier, Marion. 2011. "Beyond Terroir: Territorial Construction, Hegemonic Discourses and French Wine Culture." *Journal of the Royal Anthropological Institute* 17(4): 685–705.

———. 2020. *Burgundy: A Global Anthropology of Place and Taste*. New York: Berghahn.

Ina, Daniela. 2022. *Wine Is Our Bread: Labour and Value in Moldovan Winemaking*. New York: Berghahn.

Graf, Katharina. 2022. "Taste Knowledge: Couscous and the Cook's Six Senses." *Journal of the Royal Anthropological Institute* 28(2): 577–94.

Jung, Yuson. 2014. "Tasting and Judging the Unknown Terroir of the Bulgarian Wine: The Political Economy of Sensory Experience." *Food & Foodways* 22(1–2): 24–47.

Paxson, Heather. 2013. *The Life of Cheese: Crafting Food and Value in America*. Berkeley: University of California Press.

Seremetakis, C. Nadia. 1994. *The Senses Still: Perception and Memory as Material Culture in Modernity*. Boulder: Westview.

Sutton, David E. 2010. "Food and the Senses." *Annual Review of Anthropology* 39: 209–23.

Teil, Genevieve. 2012. "No Such Thing as Terroir." *Science, Technology & Human Values* 37 (September): 478–500.

Trubek, Amy B. 2008. *The Taste of Place: A Cultural Journey into Terroir*. Berkeley: California University Press.

Tsing, Anna. 2015. *The Mushroom at the End of the World: The Possibility of Life in Capitalist Ruins*. Princeton: Princeton University Press.

Weiss, Brad. 2011. "Making Pigs Local: Discerning the Sensory Character of Place." *Cultural Anthropology* 26(3): 438–61.

———. 2016. *Real Pigs: Shifting Values in the Field of Local Pork*. Durham: Duke University Press.

West, Harry G. 2013. "Appellations and Indications of Origin, Terroir, and the Social Construction and Contestation of Placed-Named Foods." In *The Handbook of Food Research*, edited by Anne Murcott, Warren Belasco, and Peter Jackson, 209–28. London: Bloomsbury.

———. 2022. "Terroir Products: A Movable Heritage Feast?" *Review of Agricultural, Food & Environmental Studies* 103(1): 1–27.

CHAPTER 17

Intimacy at Scale

Sovereignty as Political Temporality

Cristina Grasseni

Introduction

This chapter looks at local ways of making sense of cheese, and the role of cheesemaking in place making. My ethnographic case focuses on Val Taleggio, a mid-mountain valley in Lombardy (northern Italy). Here, small-scale local cheese production is celebrated in ways that fit a discourse of locality. This discourse underlines the significance of place for developing and nurturing affects and practices of belonging. I call a discourse of intimacy and sovereignty the way in which my interlocutors use—among others—keywords such as *dreams*, *future*, *passion*, *commitment*, *handmade*, *sustainability*, *biodiversity*, *tradition*, *heritage*, *community*, and *territory*, as we will see from an ethnographic testimony. I will argue that this semantics of *territorio* goes far beyond conventional terroir considerations of microclimate, soil condition, and production techniques. I use ethnographic examples to show that claiming a special link to *territorio* is a deliberate performative, political, and rhetorical act. An enhanced conceptualization of *territorio* reveals assumptions about heritage, other species, and future-making, which far exceed commercial and technical considerations.

My interlocutors in the field—cheesemakers and cheese *affineurs* of Val Taleggio—understand their ambition of building a sustainable future for their broader community as a political responsibility qua entrepreneurs. Among their key choices in this direction is the strategy to maintain a local scale of their maturing operations by keeping their cellars in the valley while exporting. Connecting globally with networks of dairy excellence and connoisseurship, this practice produces a discourse of governance of the local landscape and territory. The vernacular notion of *territorio* (territory; cf. Counihan 2019) is often used in conjunction with *tipicità* (translated as "typicity," or "typicality" in Ceccarelli et al. 2013). I argue that these are fluid semantic, discursive, and performative imaginaries. Looking for the meaning of *territorio* forces us to include reflections on future-making, as local entrepreneurs must do in the face of climate change, global market consolidation, and depopulation in mountainous regions. This exceeds simply bearing responsibility for the quality and taste of a commodity and expands into a broader futuring exercise. Reflecting on my ongoing collaboration with the cheese entrepreneurs of Val Taleggio, I contend that this responsibility analytically repositions not only notions of terroir and territory, but also of intimacy, belonging and sovereignty.

Tipicità and *Territorio*

As Elizabeth Barham sums up: "Historically, terroir refers to an area or terrain, usually rather small, whose soil and microclimate impart distinctive qualities to food products. The word is particularly closely associated with the production of wine. A terroir can be identified, for example, as one that produces a *grand cru*, or a particularly excellent wine. It can also be said that a certain wine has a *goût*, or taste, of its particular terroir" (2003: 131). However, the semantics of terroir, which has especially informed discussions of food, place, and taste in American scholarship about Europe (Laudan 2004; Trubek 2008), does not fit the multiple and diverse specificities of European locations, histories, and debates. Terroir has been taken as an objective link between taste and place due to (micro)climate, soil condition, cultivation, production techniques, and traditions. The historical establishment of this linkage in particular regions has been scrutinized and debated, particularly in the case of wine. Scholars and professionals know that terroir is the result of a process of construction of lineage and authority to serve commercial competition (Ulin 1996). In the Italian case, *tipicità* similarly captures the local polemics and dilemmas around (dairy) excellence and heritage. To claim traditional status (*tipicità*) for one's cheese, especially through a link to its territory (*territorio*), is a deliberate, performative, political, and rhetorical act to add value rather than an attempt at describing a state of things (Grasseni 2017).

In my field site, Lombardy, terroir (in French) does not play any role in the vernacular or professional language of heritage cheesemakers, even though the cheesemakers I interviewed travel to international fairs, have clients abroad (including in France), and produce advertising material in multiple languages (including French). *Tipicità* and *territorio* instead appear regularly and have different weight according to the audiences one wishes to address, ranging from urbanite foodies to ethical consumers. Among the latter, unlike in Northern and Western European countries, a dairy-based diet is still largely unchallenged by sustainability concerns. Vegan trends are minoritarian, and unlike, for example, in the Netherlands, the unsustainable byproducts of intensive dairy farming (such as an accumulation of nitrates in the soil and water) are completely lacking from the political landscape and public debate. On the contrary, dairy-based diets are seen as a healthy provision of proteins for those not eating meat (see Czerny, this volume). Rather, in a context characterized by a diverse geographical landscape and historical transhumant traditions, how, where, and which cheese (and in which season) is made is culturally meaningful.

For example, preference for mountain cheeses in northern Italy goes hand in hand with the high value they represent not only economically but also ecologically and demographically. In fact, marginal rural areas such as upland communities are costlier to cultivate and maintain for pastures and woods. Transport and logistics are expensive in these hardly well-connected localities. Additionally, mountainous areas are critically depopulated. Neo-rural "return migration" involves the Italian mountainous regions (Corti 2007; Pérez-Vitoria 2015). Young, educated entrepreneurs invest in these relatively cheap and remote areas, with the intention of repopulating abandoned villages and salvaging what little is left of the domesticated alpine ecology where natural resources such as woods, mines, caves, streams, and pastures were tidily and systematically combed by often overpopulated villages just a couple of centuries earlier (Da Lezze 1596; Mitterpacher 1784; Jacini 1882), and well into the twentieth century.

This weighs heavily on the discourse of *territorio*, its meaning and performance. In the French context, terroir has been mobilized beyond wine and beyond producers themselves to craft a discourse of locality supporting not only the AOC market but territorial development in the broader sense (Demossier 2020 and this volume). *Territorio* is often used to underlie the importance of local communities of practice to stimulate both extant and neo-rural local economies (in the expression *economie di territorio* for example). However, the discourse of intimacy and sovereignty signified by the use of the word *territorio* can also make use of other keywords such as *patrimonio* (heritage) and *tipicità*—also within the framework of a broad reference to tradition—to do the same semantic work. With the following ethnographic examples, I hope to show how this is—like all semantic work—situated and flexible, as it targets a variety of audiences (professional and lay, vernacular and international) with multiple tools (such as marketing, design, and rhetoric). I will argue that this semantic work is part of a broader discourse of intimacy and sovereignty, namely a temporal framework for meaning-making that uses the past to help envisage a future worth living, and a moral economy of place that underlies the local scale and frame of reference of any attempt at crafting a future.[1]

Field Interlocutors as Articulate Peers

My first ethnographic example comes from an unlikely place, namely an academic venue. Figure 17.1 was taken during my book presentation of *The Heritage Arena* (2017) at the Royal Anthropological Institute in London, which, planned

Figure 17.1. Adele Arrigoni Ravasio introduces her enterprise's Manifesto. London, 2022. © Hanine Habig

in 2019 for 2020, had been postponed almost three years due to COVID-19. The person sitting at the table next to me, Adele Arrigoni Ravasio, is co-presenter. Adele is probably the most prominent cheese merchant in the tiny valley of Val Taleggio today, being heir to casArrigoni, a medium-size enterprise of affineurs in Val Taleggio, which spearheaded the Consortium for the Protection of Strachítunt cheese PDO (Protected Designation of Origin), of which I tell the story in my book. Her mother, who does not speak English, has come to witness the event.

Using this vignette and calling it ethnographic allows me to reposition anthropological scholarship as adjacent to one's interlocutors (or "para-ethnographic," Holmes and Marcus 2006). In other words, it invites reflection on the viewpoint of those research participants who capably address multiple audiences, in different languages, in diverse contexts. Our conversations with often equally highly educated research interlocutors, who bear real-life responsibilities to their communities, enterprises, and peers, allow both us and them to reflect on intimacy and sovereignty.

It is the first time in many years of research on and around cheese that I share the stage on a par with a so-called research participant. I feel it is unavoidable and enriching, since my interlocutor from the field speaks the language in which we present, has read my books (in Italian and English), and has shared many reflections with me, in full knowledge of our different takes and stakes on and around Val Taleggio. She has involved me in several initiatives, and I in turn have made suggestions that might have made some difference (hopefully positive) to how she took some decisions about her enterprise, her valley, and her life.

She uses different language choices today, in London, speaking to a (semi) academic audience as my peer rather than to the publics I heard her speaking to in Italian. For example, she mentions tradition, whereas in the contexts and language addressing professional publics, such as the international Cheese Award competitions for which Adele is a registered judge, she would be more precise, talking about texture, aroma, and taste, and the details of cheesemaking techniques (including temperature, rennet, salt, and materials). Today she presents herself as an entrepreneur who tells the story of her cheese. *Storia* in Italian covers many areas: it means the history supported by documents and recorded in archives and published sources, the oral history, gathered by ethnographers and scholars from vernacular interlocutors and published as local history and ethnology, but also the "stories" one tells. These are true family stories passed down through the generations—thus overlapping with oral history—but also narrations, fables, and myths. Telling a story is a moral act of witnessing, honoring past generations, but also a fabulation and a performance, with some rhetorical license. She takes this license today when she talks about "tradition" tout court.

Her slides, introducing her family enterprise, emphasize the landscape of Val Taleggio as a picturesque enclosure, characterizing it as "my valley" (figure 17.2).

This evocative visual backdrop also articulates a significant semantic framework: "my valley" is connected to "dreams, future, passion, commitment, handmade, sustainability, biodiversity, tradition, heritage, community, territory." The photograph also contains an important detail: the "We are here" signpost, with

Figure 17.2. PowerPoint slide. © Adele Arrigoni Ravasio

the crest of casArrigoni and its altitude (823 meters above sea level). By adding that, Adele operates a powerful act of self-reference, by which she asserts location and scale as important elements of her business. *Territory* evidently plays a part in this indexical framework, but only as one of the many other keywords Adele employs to articulate the connection between people and places.

Crucially, this slide is about the connection one can make with Val Taleggio "as entrepreneur," namely through the dynamics of economic systems, and capitalist systems at that. So yes, it is about making money, but as Adele underlines, it is not exclusively about that. In her speech, she explains she is committed to "things inside and around the company": "I am exactly from this place. . . . My company is based in the valley, in the village. The mountains all around is exactly where our cheesemakers do the summer transhumance. . . . These cheeses are really linked with the people in these places. They are capable of activating dynamic economic systems. Of course I am there to make money. But in the process we hire people, we are there, we keep the place alive. Money is important and cheese is important but there are other things we are committed to that are around and inside the company."

In this territorial cosmology, one grasps both origin (transhumance) and evolution (dynamic economic systems) of Val Taleggio as the only frame and scale of reference possible for her unfolding as a person and as a businesswoman. Her intimate connection to this place is not a given but can be kept alive only through the economic and ecologic practice of grazing this land, milking these cows, and making this cheese. And selling it. Indeed, this is about "making a life and a living" (Paxson 2013: 6, 33). But a further important dimension to this discourse of intimacy is the political one, a sovereignty that finds both its mandate and its justification in the local scale and temporal dimension of her enterprise ("we are here, we keep the place alive") and yet has the ambition to shine and project itself in global conversations and (economic) exchange: "Mine is a family business of which I represent the third generation. . . . A company that has worked for forty years to protect all the things we are. . . . What I have inherited is a unique tradition. . . . I have a special goal, that is protecting and carrying on this long tradition of cheeses. . . . We aim to deliver these beautiful cheeses to the world, to let people all over the world be close to us and share this huge heritage."

This temporal dimension not only looks back but extends to the future, and it does so with a problematizing look. Will it also be possible to craft cheese in this same way in the future? Or, tout court, is it still possible to craft a future for this valley? "What I do in my company is try to understand if and how the breeders, the family, the valley, the economy can still survive in this present moment. Small and medium companies like mine have been bought by huge conglomerates from France, the Netherlands, Germany (I can think of five just in the last six months). So we need to find a space and occupy it. . . . Otherwise we miss a good business opportunity, but I will also see my place die."

Adele's solution is consciously one of reinvention, namely a malleable and creative approach to *tipicità*: in the following lines, she finds her own reasoning around a notion of "tradition," which she sees as intrinsically woven with material culture and skill, something that is handed down through learning, from skilled practitioner to skilled practitioner:

> So I am trying to identify a language of the present moment and address people of the modern age and time and make this heritage accessible to them and reach out to them in a modern way. So today this is a different meaning of cheese than the one my ancestors saw. To them this was survival. Today we see how the market and the economy have brought on devastating industrialization. I see consumers who are losing knowledge of what cheese has to be like, to be good. . . .
>
> I think it makes sense to continue the tradition, not for nostalgia and romanticism. . . . Tradition means to be able to make something higher in quality. It is the tradition that produces excellent results. Industrialized technology is not capable of obtaining the cheeses you will taste in a few minutes. Tradition is not something we are able to substitute now with modern tools. . . .
>
> We are trying to be part of this modern world balancing tradition and innovation, balancing what my mum gave me with what we can do in modernity. We continue to age our cheeses in wooden boxes wrapped in cotton, but we spend a lot of money to control the hygiene of these materials and surfaces. 90 percent of [the] industry uses plastic. We age our cheeses in underground cellars we built twenty years ago, they are made of cement because it is the closest thing to aging in rock caves. We brush our cheeses by hand just like our ancestors did. And we keep making raw milk cheese not because it's just traditional, but because it is completely different. It is good.

This engagement with milk quality and cheese taste speaks to belonging and political will, through a discourse of intimacy and sovereignty: "Our tradition needs to evolve and adapt, we are open to discuss in our village, we are involved as citizens, we are deeply involved in the consortium for Strachítunt. It's more than just running a company and paying your bills. So we take a lot of risks and we are open and listen to you for advice, for inspiration."

From this series of quotes one takes away a clear understanding that producers are not enchanted by a reified vision of tradition any more than anthropologists are, and that Adele understands territory as much more than a technical and objective relationship between a natural context, a traditional technique, and a culinary end product (as happens in terroir discourse). Importantly, one also takes away the message that priority goes to a sense of future-making, of community reproduction, and of survival in an economically and normatively adverse context, whose global dimension both intensifies the challenge and offers opportunity.

Shaping Past and Future

This ambition is uniquely articulated, in the case of Adele's casArrigoni, in the company's Manifesto.[2] The first pledge one finds when consulting it online is that "at casArrigoni we declare ourselves responsible for a history." This is the history of the "transhumant breeders" of Val Taleggio, "forefathers" who "for centuries have carried out the practice of moving cow herds from the mountains to the plains and back," "creating the modern dairy context" of northern Italy.[3] Among the key points referenced in the Manifesto we find an analytic understanding, factor by factor, of what Heather Paxson (2010) has termed the "ecology of production." This is specified by keywords, each represented by a dedicated icon. Territory features as being "settled in the mountains" as an enterprise, and by conducting cattle to graze on "summer pastures." An additional three icons and relevant caption make a detailed case for exclusionary choices such as: using raw milk (as "keepers of raw milk," they do not pasteurize milk); not using exogenous starters (qua "supporters of molds"); and keeping only Brown cows (which, despite aggressive progeny-breeding, are still more adapted to mountainous terrain than Friesian cows). Three further icons articulate the small-scaled and traditional management of the cheese-maturing ecology, through "manual and artisanal processing," the "use of natural and traditional tools," such as pinewood crates and cotton sheets, in "natural aging cellars" (shown in figure 17.3).

Molds develop thanks to the porous surfaces of these underground cellars' walls and floors. Perhaps the reinforced cement does not strike us as traditional as mountain caves would. But notice the wooden crates and cotton cloth used to line the cheeses. Scrubbing and brushing is done by hand, following HACCP hygiene protocols. These stubborn compromises are not only implemented but also, importantly, visualized, articulated, and defended. In sum, a lot of linguistic and visual packaging surrounds these "natural aging cellars," as well as the "manual and artisanal procedures," using "traditional natural tools," that take place daily in them. It's a give and take, a compromise between modernity and tradition.

Tradition remains an anchor point for this Manifesto, but it is embraced not for its own sake, and certainly not for the sake of a naïve understanding of authenticity (Grasseni 2023), but in the full knowledge that it needs constant reinvention (Grasseni 2017), while the bottom line of "good" taste cannot be let go of. Stressing the importance of quality milk and "good" cheese, Adele in her speech laid out the criteria for her choices: what can or should change and what can or should remain the same? Aging cheese should remain in wooden boxes and cotton, because they are important to cheese texture. On the other hand, when it comes to improving milk quality, one can fully embrace techno-scientific improvements, for example through repeatedly sampling for cell count in the milk to monitor bacterial presence, or through the introduction of ration-giving robots that distribute fodder to the cows regularly over the day, and in accordance

Figure 17.3. CasArrigoni cellars. Lombardy, 2022. © casArrigoni

to their dietary needs, thus facilitating an optimal metabolism and gut health (and thus milk quality).

I argue further that this consciously performative celebration of the valley's cheese-making as unique for its *tipicità* and *territorio* can be considered a claim to self-determination, a form of sovereignty. In the face of global competition, material and technological change, and risk and uncertainty, this claim comes across not only in casArrigoni's materials but also in more broadly encompassing events and marketing sources. For example, Val Taleggio's Strachítunt PDO features among the local heritage cheeses representing "Bergamo European capital of cheeses" at Bergamo's cheese expo Forme. Here, and among Italian professional circles, the most prominent talk is of dairy excellence (*eccellenza casearia*), for example, in conjunction with *tipicità* evidencing pedigree, ancestry, and lineage. This symbolic language evidences the scale and temporality at which mountain cheese is being projected: with its nine cheeses with a PDO, including Strachítunt, the association the Cheese Valleys claims for Bergamo the imaginary title of "European capital of cheeses,"[4] projecting by analogy Bergamo's cheeses onto national and international diplomacy and national history. A further edition of the same international cheese expo, Forme, taking place in Bergamo every October since 2017, visualizes future-making through the temporalization of traditional shapes and forms of mountain cheese. The rarefied design introduced on occasion of the October 2021 edition of *Forme Future* (future forms), and further developed in the subsequent editions, visually enunciates the ambition to address present and future challenges (including the post-COVID-19 scenario for heritage marketing) through both heritage and creativity, addressing past, present, and future.[5] These scales and temporalities are political, in the sense that they strive to project possible futures and invite to think and deliberate which acts and strategies are necessary in order to realize them.

Successful entrepreneurship includes standing one's ground and finding one's place in the market, exploiting all the available discursive and communicative means, including professional design. This new global proximity also employs a language of diversity, shifting one's marketing in terms of accessibility to a broader public, potentially international, less versed in the intricacies of geographic denomination and culinary distinction, but more broadly interested in questions of sustainability (which locally translates in the possibility of continuing long-term settlement in mountain communities).

Prefiguring, envisaging, and realizing that opportunity is more than economic practice. It is intimately felt as a form of civic duty and communicated as a political act. Beyond producers and consumers, beyond regulators and traders, and also beyond mere citizens, here the entrepreneur is a sovereign. Legitimacy for this political role is drawn from the intimately felt responsibility for the valley's future and the sheer fact that—more than others—the sovereign entrepreneur is positioned to have the means and the opportunity to make a difference to that future—also to the benefit of (but not necessarily in consultation with) others. In this sense, this sovereignty is all but democratic. It is Machiavellian in the original sense of the term: according to Machiavelli, hereditary circumstances or military or conjunctural fortune give the prince the "occasion" (1891: 209) and thus the duty to operate—with a measure of discretion—for the good of one's country (1891: 365). What defines one's country is, today as it was in sixteenth-century Italy, debatable. But everything we learned so far indicates that in this case it is "my valley." In this discourse of intimacy and sovereignty, successful entrepreneurial activity is enacted as a form of civic, political, and economic practice that is exercised to the benefit of, and under the scrutiny of, one's intimately defined community of practice. This community is at once professional, gustatory, and territorial—and has very little to do with terroir. Through the creative construction of meaning and value around local resources, cheese entrepreneurs assert themselves as political actors inasmuch as they assume the responsibility of crafting futures for "their" valley. As with every negotiation about futures, what is key to this form of sovereignty is finding viable margins. At the same time, it renegotiates a certain image of the past as traditionally unchanged. In the next section I focus on what is left out of this self-representation.

The Compromises of Future-Making

In November 2020 a Bergamo-based mountaineering magazine published this photograph of one of the higher pastures where Strachítunt was made during my fieldwork in the summers of 1997 and 1998, at around two thousand meters in altitude. The photo was taken by a local photographer around 5:00 a.m. on 27 August 2020 and donated to the president of the Strachítunt consortium (Fig. 17.4).

The scene is portrayed from higher up, so that the scenic crevasse in the background is visible—a view one does not get from the hut. This photograph provides "a grammar and, even more importantly, an ethics of seeing" (Sontag 1977: 77), which, applied to transhumance practice, suggests "what is worth looking at and what we have a right to observe." It offers a picturesque, cinematic view that does not match the phenomenology of a "sentient body" (Gieser 2014), which includes, for example, the diesel generator one needs to illuminate the milking shed. This view from nowhere shapes the social imaginary of commodities in its lack of concrete materialities (such as the smell of diesel or the fatigue of milking every dawn and dusk).[6]

Crucially, this ideal view, once published in November, took license with reality also because milking on this station was discontinued, in fact, the very summer after this photograph was taken. Weighing up risks, costs, and benefits, it is simply no longer worth it for the dairy farmers to move their lactating herds up there, just to graze an extra two or three weeks. Firstly, one needs to be lucky to find the right weather to enjoy those weeks at such altitude, due to the unpredictability of seasons caused by climate change. Secondly, these Brown breed cattle are, after all, the product of progeny breeding. They are

Figure 17.4. Alpe Piazzo. Lombardy, 2020. © Marco Mazzoleni, courtesy of Alvaro Ravasio

worth several thousand euros each just in terms of their genetic line and would not have shelter in case of hail or thunderstorm, thus risking their health or even their lives. Thirdly, this station is just too remote—logistically speaking—to drive with tractor and motorbike an extra twenty minutes up dangerous and uncomfortable mountain trails in order to pick up and take down the cheeses made here. The lower station lies right on a walking trail, is serviced by a fountain, has recently been renovated, has a cellar and a little shop corner, and is even equipped for tourist accommodation! These, in sum, are the reasons my field hosts of twenty-five years ago succinctly articulate for me when I almost reproach them, for having abandoned their late father's favorite grazing station, where I lived with him during my first fieldwork. "It's not abandoned"—is their sober answer. "It is just not lived in." It is being grazed by not-yet-lactating young heifers, who do not need as much monitoring and human presence as milking cows. It is the practice of milking and making cheese on this location that has been discontinued.[7]

Everything about this conversation highlights the give and take, the compromise and the constant triaging to achieve the best effect with the least reasonable expected risk or loss (of stock, of pasture, of grazing days, of fuel, of customers). Not only affineurs but also dairy farmers actively deliberate how to best synergize available environmental and economic resources, which include their own time and well-being, as individuals and as family units, as well as that of their livestock. This congeals in a fluid and negotiable strategy, one intimately interlinked with what they call *territorio*—which includes the landscape, the pastureland, the regional economy, the human resources, the local species, the reservoir of skills they can tap into, their history and ancestry, and their own future.

Another aspect of the contemporary dairy economy of Val Taleggio that is absent from the visual representation that local producers choose to give, whether in glossy magazines or in marketing design, is the reliance on migrant workers. However, casArrigoni is adamant during interviews that half of its manual labor workforce is Senegalese, and that the same holds for other affineurs in the valley. These workers do not feature in the visual and discursive representations of intimate belonging, nor do they find themselves (just like all other residents of the valley) in the pivotal decision-making position of the "sovereign" entrepreneur. Like many locals who do not appear in the picture, they do not actively contribute to the envisioning of the valley's future. It is the job of the entrepreneurs to articulate the margins for such compromise to the target audience, adjust tones and fill in the details, focusing on one aspect while silencing another. The resulting precarious compromise we get is the ongoing process of packaging and repackaging, articulating and arguing, rethinking and re-expressing, correcting, and recalibrating the message.

Conclusion

The fluid semantic, discursive, and performative exercise of intimacy and sovereignty we have analyzed is a complex affective, political, and temporal construct. Adele is adamant that this construct needs articulating "in modern words," as the semiotic and conceptual tools that terms like *terroir* or *tradition* offer have been depleted and are exposed to novel challenges. One of the ways she tries to find the right words is by visualizing them, through the icons that we have seen in her Manifesto. This is a designer's product and a marketing tool, but it also does the profoundly important work of place making and future-making. With an ethnographic vignette and the analysis of visual sources, I have shown the reasons for which the exercise of this intimate sovereignty is problematic because of its privilege and its silences, but also how it is constantly open to reinvention, including in conversation with anthropologists.

Elsewhere I explained how to claim traditional status (*tipicità*) for one's cheese is a deliberate performative, political, and rhetorical act, a strategy to add value rather than a description of a naturalized state of things (Grasseni 2017). When Adele invokes and evokes "my valley" in addressing the Royal Anthropological Institute in London, she provides a defining indexical framework for this political act. "My valley" is the cosmological beginning and end of moral economy. It does not denote just a territory but a place where one can imagine a future. The words used to articulate the cosmology of cheese sovereignty are situated and negotiable, subject themselves to reinvention (Grasseni 2017). *Eccellenza* (*casearia*) or (dairy) excellence pitches *tipicità* to the discerning (global) markets of heritage cheese. Different vocabulary is used with diverse international audiences of cheese tasters, merchants, artisans, and gourmands. The language of excellence and distinction is used in the world of food journalism, chefs, gourmands, Slow Food, among others, and requires ambitious geopolitical positionings (as visualized in marketing materials). PDO certification can be used to brand the distinction of Strachítunt, but this does not guarantee a future. Beyond terroir, *territorio* is situated within a discourse of political temporality and intimate belonging that requires negotiating the right scale of action, vis-à-vis local traditions and vis-à-vis the global market.

Cheese entrepreneurs in Val Taleggio go "beyond terroir" in many ways. Through the business of selling cheese as a commodity with a particular making and a desirable quality, Adele is also engaging in civic responsibilities and political place making. Her future-making project for the valley continuously negotiates social, material, and semantic practices (including compromises, silences, polemics, and dilemmas). Her conscious reflection and strategic use of taste-place concepts also includes conversations with other practices and disciplines, including with anthropologists. In her self-determination as an entrepreneur, she exercises a privileged form of sovereignty over one's future, one's territory, one's scale of economic but also political action, making future also on behalf of a broader and diverse community of residents, and indeed over their past and future, too.

Acknowledgments

I wish to thank my generous peer readers, in particular Marion Demossier, Heather Paxson, Greg de St. Maurice, Katharina Graf, and Anna Colquhoun. This chapter was developed in the framework of the ERC-funded project *Food Citizens?* (Grant agreement 724151).

Cristina Grasseni is Professor of Cultural Anthropology at the Institute of Cultural Anthropology and Development Sociology of Leiden University, the Netherlands. She has published on food heritage (*The Heritage Arena*, Berghahn 2017), food activism (*Beyond Alternative Food Networks*, Bloomsbury 2013), and visual anthropology (*Audiovisual and Digital Ethnography*, Taylor and Francis, 2023; *Skilled Visions*, Berghahn, 2007). After completing her ERC-funded project *Food Citizens? Collective Food Procurement in European Cities*, she is developing a project on *Crafting Futures*, a comparative ethnography of "new craft" in advanced-capitalist consumer cultures.

Notes

1. My argument focuses here on globally valued commodities such as Taleggio PDO or Strachítunt PDO (comparable to the Burgundy wines studied by Demossier 2020). A local economy continues to run in parallel "under the radar," including homemade *stracchini* for self-consumption and unpretentious local distribution through village market stalls and word of mouth (cf. Colquhoun on *domaće*, this volume). However, this artisanal production does not contribute toward an *economia di territorio* (namely it does not create jobs locally).
2. Online at https://www.casarrigoni.it/en/azienda#manifesto (retrieved 11 December 2024).
3. Transhumance is the practice of driving herds in an itinerant way from lower stations to higher stations. In the case of contemporary Val Taleggio, it is limited to the *alpage*, namely a summer stationing in higher pastures of the same valley (Grasseni 2021; cf. Jacini 1882).
4. https://www.letresignorie.eu/eventi/ (retrieved 3 December 2023). Bergamo competed to become European capital of culture in 2019 but failed. After the COVID-19 pandemic, Bergamo and Brescia together were nominated Italian capital of culture for 2023: https://bergamobrescia2023.it/en/ (retrieved 11 December 2024).
5. See for example the 2021 edition of Bergamo cheese expo Forme: https://progettoforme.eu/dairy-culture-and-civilisation-forum/ (retrieved 11 December 2024).
6. As underlined by several authors in this volume, among others Simpson Miller, Staples, Sanders, Colquhoun, and Graf, sentient experiences are key to conceptualizing the "taste of place," with and beyond terroir.

7. This is my own rendition of a conversation with the dairy herders who use the pasture in figure 17.4, during the conference "Strachítunt: Synergies and Strategies for an Ethical Future of the Territory" on 19 and 20 November 2022 in Val Taleggio.

References

Barham, Elizabeth. 2003. "Translating Terroir: The Global Challenge of French AOC Labeling." *Journal of Rural Studies* 19(1): 127–38.

Ceccarelli, Giulio, Alberto Grandi, and Stefano Magagnoli, eds. 2013. *La typicité dans l'histoire: Tradition, innovation et terroir / Typicality in History: Tradition, Innovation, and Terroir.* Brussels: Peter Lang.

Corti, Michele. 2007. "Quale neoruralismo?" *L'Ecologist Italiano* 7: 168–86.

Counihan, Carole M. 2019. *Italian Food Activism in Urban Sardinia: Place, Taste, and Community.* London: Bloomsbury.

Da Lezze, Giovanni. 1596. *Descrizione di Bergamo e del suo territorio.* 2nd ed. 1988. Bergamo: Provincia di Bergamo/Lucchetti Editore.

Demossier, Marion. 2020. *Burgundy: The Global Story of Terroir.* New York: Berghahn.

Gieser, Thorsten. 2014. "Enskillment Inhibited: 'Industrial Gardening' in Britain." *Journal of the Royal Anthropological Institute* 20(1): 131–49.

Grasseni, Cristina. 2017. *The Heritage Arena: Reinventing Cheese in the Italian Alps.* New York: Berghahn.

———. 2021. "Italian Cheese in the Global Heritage Arena." In *The Cultural Politics of Food, Taste, and Identity,* edited by Stefan Ayora Diaz, 73–85. London: Bloomsbury.

———. 2023. "Crafting Futures through Cheese-Making in Val Taleggio." *Gastronomica* 23(1): 51–64.

Holmes, Douglas, and George Marcus. 2006. "Fast-Capitalism: Para-ethnography and the Rise of the Symbolic Analyst." In *Frontiers of Capital: Ethnographic Perspectives on the New Economy,* edited by Marcus Fisher and Greg Downey, 34–57. Durham: Duke University Press.

Jacini, Stefano. 1882. *Atti della Giunta per la Inchiesta Agraria. Volume VI, Tomo I, Fascicolo I.* Rome: Forzani Tipografi del Senato.

Laudan, Rachel. 2004. "Slow Food: The French Terroir Strategy, and Culinary Modernism." *Food, Culture & Society* 7(2): 133–44.

Machiavelli, Niccolò. 1891. *Il Principe.* Edited by L. Arthur Burd. Oxford: Clarendon Press.

Mitterpacher, Lodovico. 1784. *Elementi d'Agricoltura: Pubblicati per ordine del Regio Governo.* Milan: Imperial Monistero di S.Ambrogio Maggiore.

Paxson, Heather. 2010. "Locating Value in Artisan Cheese: Reverse Engineering Terroir for New-World Landscapes." *American Anthropologist* 112(3): 444–57.

———. 2013. *The Life of Cheese: Crafting Food and Value in America.* Berkeley: University of California Press.

Pérez-Vitoria, Silvia. 2015. *Manifeste pour un XXIe siècle paysan.* Arles: Actes Sud.

Sontag, Susan. 1977. *On Photography.* New York: Delta Books.

Trubek, Amy B. 2008. *The Taste of Place. A Cultural Journey into Terroir.* Berkeley: University of California Press.

Ulin, Robert. 1996. *Vintages and Traditions: An Ethnohistory of Southwest French Wine Cooperatives.* Washington: Smithsonian Institution Press.

Afterword

Thinking, and Becoming, Beyond Terroir

Heather Paxson and Brad Weiss

The discipline of anthropology has long grappled with the challenge of developing theoretical forms while simultaneously grounding these concepts in concrete phenomena. Is kinship, for example, an empirically observable domain of human life; one model of relationship-making; or an ideological claim, only present in specific times and places, about the value of shared "blood" or genetic inheritance? Are rituals the ceremonial practices by which humans punctuate a collective temporal order, the communicative dimension of all social activity, or merely the artifact of utilitarian models of cultural life (that is to say, what remains after all "practical" activity has been accounted for can only be a "ritual")? The notion of terroir, glossed as "the taste of place," presents a similar conundrum. Is terroir best understood as a very specific attribute of viticultural performance; a cultural category of perception (perhaps one developed to evaluate precisely said viticultural qualities); or a framework for articulating the material connection between histories, modes, and techniques of food production and the communities of consumers who appreciate these goods?

The undoubted generativity of terroir as part of the anthropological tool kit over the last generation surely owes a great deal to this capacious ambiguity. It is appropriate that we offer a reflexive appraisal of this practice-cum-theory since—as the chapters in this collection clearly suggest—the limits and contingencies of terroir as a general model are also strikingly clear. In each of our own ethnographic studies of "local" food production in the United States, with artisan cheesemakers in Heather's case (Paxson 2013) and pastured pork producers in Brad's (Weiss 2016), the importance of terroir to communities of producers as well as consumers was something that we noted, but also noted as something less than self-evident or settled. For some American cheesemakers, terroir was a potential property of their wares to be "reverse engineered," revealed, as it were, by paying attention to environmental stewardship in their dairying and cheesemaking activities and by asking, "What production is suited to this land?"—and then drawing attention to these distinctive material conditions in their marketing

(Paxson 2010). Similarly, pig farmers and pork purveyors alike hoped to "educate" their clientele about the values and character of "the local," highlighting ecological, communitarian, and species-specific (allowing pigs to express their "pigness" as a method of livestock husbandry) virtues that curious customers might come to discern in pastured pork (Weiss 2016). In each instance, a taste of place is less something that is readily and spontaneously perceived even by the most observant of connoisseurs than it is an aspirational category, one that might inspire both producers and eaters to greater heights of "good" (Jung, this volume) or "real" food, prized as a means of creating if not preserving the sort of "places" imagined to be a wellspring of shared values and virtues.

The very idea of a "taste of place" is necessarily built out of a conjunction of complex concepts. Taste itself is a perception and a judgment, a material set of properties and the cultivated capacity of an inquisitive subject. Place, too, is less a delimited location in space than a range of possibilities from which actions and events, undertaken by human and nonhuman agents alike, might unfold (Casey 1996). This productive ambiguity (terroir as an ethnographic category and as a generalizable model; or, terroir as a quality in the product and terroir as a goal toward which to aim one's efforts) is what motivates our reassessment and suggestions in this afterword. Where the volume itself is structured around the range of locations where terroir-related claims are sited—lands, laws, bodies, imaginaries—here we take an alternative pass through the chapters' case studies to call attention to the range of analytical moves that take us beyond terroir: disentangling place from territory; approaching the borders and boundaries between places as semipermeable thresholds; and emphasizing food's capacity to remake (and not just represent) worlds. Thinking "beyond" the taste of place allows us to build on the problematics of making and eating, now well described across a range of fields, while seeking out alternative ways of imbuing the locales we inhabit with distinctive (often destabilizing) qualities, and grounding perception in the world.

Places Beyond Territory

When scholars and connoisseurs articulate the relevance of terroir, they generally make the assumption—sometimes quite naively, but often in rather nuanced ways—that sensory perception is (somehow) an expression of a material set of localized conditions. Whether that locality is characterized as a microclimate, a geologically distinguishable substratum, or a longstanding community of practitioners that inhabit these locations, place is pinned almost inevitably to geographic position: it can be located on a map. But the more we know about how food and all that attends to it—from craftsmanship to gastronomy—is made and assessed, the less inevitable this connection appears. In part, the characterization of "place" now widespread in uses of terroir suggests the resilience of certain objectivist framings of time and space, framings that betray the Enlightenment commitment to supposedly underlying truths that are only subject to subjective "interpretation" after the fact (Casey 2013). Hence, "space" is a physically observable external object, a set of known coordinates, which can then be modified (within limits) by the various modes of practice through which people inhabit "it," and so demarcate and define "places." Like the divide between nature and culture now called into question by so much ontological turning, this notion of place—whether as a set of material limits, or a thoroughly culturalist order of relations—subtends a dualism that restricts the possibilities of what place and place making might offer. An alternative perspective, one supported by the work presented in this volume, suggests that anthropology and allied fields can draw out more than the way that localities format practice, but can further illustrate just how activity—such as preparing and serving "homemade" foods (Colquhoun; Graf; Sanders), or replicating the specific texture and feel of "proper" food (Simpson Miller), or creating new food products that concretize the natural-cultural advantages of a particular locale (Xiao)—can formulate and format the places in which they go on (Merleau-Ponty 1962; Munn 1986; Weiss 1996).

Although terroir is frequently used as a descriptor of the ways that food is an expression of place, it can equally be characterized as the ways that place is an expression of food. Gastronomic worlds are full of place making and place-claiming. An approach to taste and place that takes such an orientation reveals (as many of the chapters here do) that our sense of "place" need not be thought of as ineluctably geographical. Place is power that precedes territory. It need not be sought only in specific geographic zones, but in an array of place-making operations that create the horizon of the world (Lefebvre 1991). By putting place making (and the transformation of place, as discussed below) at the center of our concerns with food, we can further an understanding of the many ways that places come into being and become knowable.

Bodies, for example, are foundational to the creation of place. Above and beyond the fact that bodies are located in space and occupy situated positions, they are also perspectives from which activities emerge and events arise, and "into which" social processes, practices, histories, relations, and political economies are sedimented. Bodies and place are deeply interconnected, each constituting the other as such; it is impossible to imagine (except in the abstract) places without bodies, or bodies unmoored from places. This mutual grounding of body and place is expressly articulated in James Staples's recognition that human well-being in South India is grasped as the proper "fit" between bodies and places, a fitness confirmed through moral substance that co-constitutes people and places. "Place was physical and portable," he writes in this volume, "it was considered literally embodied in the people who emerged out of it" (213). In this way suitable foods are appropriate to suitable bodies. So, too, the textural qualities of *chop*, which Brandi Simpson Miller reveals to be a quality with tremendous perceptual and material potential. The capacity to reproduce the textural form as a dimension of the taste of starchy foods, their *chop,* by Ghanaian women who prepare these daily staples is an embodied skill that further links up cooks (and by extension, eaters) to the lineages of which they are a part. Ancestral forces that protect the living and assure the reproduction of the lineage are also (and not surprisingly) concerned with the physical experience and activity of sexual intimacy. In each of these embodied ways, *chop* materializes connections among generations past, present, and future, and grounds them, as well, in the fertile fields where starchy cassava flourishes (Simpson Miller). Hanna Garth's account of the efficacy of *guarapo* as a sweet and icy cold drink beloved by *los Cubanos* also speaks to the ways bodies register deep historical connections, in her case to the labor of sugar plantation, sweat, and enslavement—but *guarapo* can also provide a respite from these burdens, reappropriating the potential of sugar through the reinvigorated Cuban body. Each of these cases (and others, including Colquhoun's account of making, sharing, and eating *domaće* cured pork, and Graf's demonstration of the links between embodied knowledge and cooking skill in Morocco) exemplifies the capacity of the active, eating body to recast the qualities of place through an encounter with food.

Another category from the study of "local worlds" that is repeatedly evoked by food producers and consumers alike is home. Here again, home need not suggest a geographical or regional specificity—*domaće* (homemade) cured pork is a clear illustration of this point; rather, as Anna Colquhoun notes, *domaće* connotes home as "a set of social relations that are at once economic and moral" (this volume: 119). Home is clearly a "place," if perhaps one that is imagined or aspired to. It takes up a position, offers an orientation to the wider world, and so makes mere spatial forms into a place. Home can be literally anywhere, not bound to a concrete location. Home both is constituted by and always has consequences for relationships—for family and kinship, for domesticity, for household economy. Home cooking and domestic food production are often meaningfully gendered examples of labor. Perhaps above all, home is a familiar locality to and from which people come and go, a place from which social cohorts stand in relationship to their peers, each of whom occupies their "own" home. In this sense, home is a spatial position, but also a reflexive and a mobile one—an origin for moving and dynamic engagement. As Katharina Graf tells us, "*beldi* [the Moroccan sense of "homemade" as well as "local"] foods are situated and differ for every person depending on where they were born and grew up as well as where they temporarily moved and traveled to" (this volume: 174). This is exactly what *domaće* also traces, and what Sudanese meat traveling to and through Portsmouth is (Sanders)—as well as, perhaps, what *nostrano* (our local), also reflecting a scaled-up feeling of home, resists in remaining wedded to a shared place. Still, "the production of *nostrano* is an ongoing achievement, as the in-group it indexes is large, complex, and dynamic" (Cavanaugh 2023: 30). In all these ways, an emphasis on "home" as a quality both recognizable and desirable further demonstrates the deterritorialized character of place making in food matters.

After all, it is precisely when people experience a loss of connection to geographical place owing to migration or exile—or when they lose direct access to land in the face of roadblocks or border enforcement (Meneley)—that the generational preservation of practical, embodied foodmaking knowledge gains heightened significance (de Silva 1996; Sutton 2000; Mankekar 2002), and bodies become home places. It is little wonder that grandmothers—so often repositories of both loss and nostalgia, generational passage, as well as heritage—figure frequently in the accounts collected here.

Borders and Boundaries as Thresholds

Thinking "beyond terroir" means recognizing the impossibility of territorially bounding what is meaningful about the place of a food. By inviting us to picture, smell, hear, and even savor smuggled Sudanese beef strung up to dry in a migrant woman's kitchen in Portsmouth, England (Sanders), the *mestizaje* of "traditional" Cuban dishes that embody a tension between aspirational self-sufficiency and the reality of a global food system rooted in slavery and colonial exploitation (Garth), the songs and microbes circulating around Devon's apple orchards (Pope and West), or the comfortably familiar cuisine of diasporic Chinese restaurants (Klein), chapters in this collection remind us that foods and recipes, no less than peoples and cultures, continue, as ever, to move and meld. As cheese refiners in Italy's Val Taleggio told Cristina Grasseni, following decades of rural outmigration and depopulation, "no heritage foods would exist in Italy without migrant labor" (2023: 53). Borders need not be walls; they are also thresholds. And yet, as we are also reminded in these chapters, not all foods—and not all peoples—enjoy the same freedom of mobility.

Charlotte Sanders's observation, for example, that Sudanese beef is subject to confiscation at the border of the United Kingdom, whereas beef from countries of the European Union is permissible, is consistent with why, in Croatia, Colquhoun tells us that the planned "Istrian sausage" Protected Geographical Indication (PGI) would permit the use of pork from across the EU: in each case, economic protectionism must also contend with meat's propensity to harbor harmful viruses (such as foot-and-mouth disease or African swine fever) that, if released into the food chain, might infect and undermine national livestock industries. Food safety regulation of animal products enacted by both import restrictions and hygiene standards embedded in geographical indications thus share a concern with controlling "what circulates and how" (Bingham and Lavau 2012: 1591). The "disease geometry" of biosecurity, as Hinchliffe et al. (2013: 532) put it, is commonly "understood as practice of demarcating and shoring up borderlines" by determining and enforcing who and what can and cannot pass through.

And yet, the futility of attempts to fully wall off "healthy" bodies and populations from microbiologically "unhealthy" ones has been widely noted and, indeed, widely experienced throughout the COVID-19 pandemic. In the United States, the Food and Drug Administration's (FDA) response has increasingly been to "move the border away," as one food industry professional said to Heather. Not only must food producers the world over register with the FDA before their goods can be offered for importation into the States, US-based importers must now be able to verify that their international suppliers meet hygiene and safety standards set by US agencies (in addition to their own governments' requirements). By externalizing the border as a regulatory threshold, US market regulation enacts a kind of culinary imperialism, imposing standards that would "clean up" ostensibly "dirty" agricultural industries and foodmaking practices in other parts of the world (Paxson 2019). Offshoring of this variety superimposes the "place" of US sovereignty onto the territory of compliant would-be food exporters. Although of a different imperial order than the "terroirism" of what Lissa Caldwell in this volume names Russian culinary colonialism—in which "Russian foods, sensory experiences, and bodies have been made by ingesting local, domestic products, by transforming foreign foods into local foods, and even by seizing and claiming foreign foods as rightful national patrimony" (this volume: 92)—here, too, the global hierarchies of political and economic power are unmistakable.

At the same time, the homogenization pushed by hygiene and other safety standards operates in tension with the heterogenous ideal concretized in Protected Designations of Origin (PDOs) and other appellation schemes that promote international appetite for other people's "local" foods in the first instance. Regulated global markets inescapably reframe the "taste of place" by moving from localized, subjective ideals based on proximity and patrimony (*beldi*, *domacé*, *nostrano*, *nash*)—of being embedded "in" place—to a more objectivist typicality "of" place (terroir, *fengtu*). As such, PDOs can be viewed as "thresholding projects" (Paxson 2023) aimed at shoring up distinctions between the very places that "typical" products are today encouraged to traverse as commodities. As Simon Pope and Harry West suggest of the revival of cidermaking rites in Devon, UK, "boundedness" may be realized "through repetitive acts of demarcation that render visible the very shifts and movements on the land that such practices seek to forestall" (this volume: 54). Such boundaries are not only commonly breached by microbial, plant, animal, and human mobilities; they are continuously redrawn. Sometimes, as with Italian Taleggio or Istrian ham, the negotiated rules of a PDO designed to be compliant with EU hygiene standards and scaled for international markets bears scant resemblance to what Gisela Welz has described, for Halloumi, as the "gendered subsistence activity" (2015: 97) behind their namesakes of previous generations.

After Italy's celebrated Taleggio cheese "won" an expansive PDO that invites industrial fabrication well beyond the bounds of Val Taleggio itself, that valley's artisan cheesemakers came together to reinvent a more distinctive cheese, Strachítunt, in such a way as to promote the culinary status and economic interests of Val Taleggio as a place. In Strachítunt's strategically designed PDO guidelines, Grasseni writes, it was "the (non)treatment of milk that allows redrawing boundaries: raw milk worked at milking temperature (*a munta calda*) cannot travel far because it cannot be refrigerated, cannot be pasteurized, and cannot be reheated according to the protocol. This bound ecology also redefines its craft" (2023: 53). Although the fermentation time of raw milk may bound the territorial scale of cheesemaking: "Paradoxically, this hyperlocal protocol of production calibrates Strachítunt to a 'global hierarchy of value' (Herzfeld 2004): disdaining scaling up, keeping production niche, and commending a premium price for this distinction" (Grasseni 2023: 54).

The transnational trade in place-designated foods is rife with such paradoxes. Among France's most iconic cheeses is the delicately aged Valençay, whose AOC (France's version of PDO) rules stipulate that it must be made from unpasteurized goat's milk. To be permissible for import into the United States, however, cheese must be either made from pasteurized milk or aged for a minimum of sixty days at a temperature no less than thirty-five degrees Fahrenheit. In its country of origin, raw-milk Valençay may be sold as young as the eleventh day of maturation (Dumont 2016); by sixty days it would be overripened to the point of inedibility. How, then, can Valençay cheese be found (as it is) in upscale American markets? Thinking beyond terroir, enterprising French dairies have formulated especially for US export a version using pasteurized milk. Just as AOC Valençay (*au lait cru*) cannot be sold in the United States, what is available as "Valençay" in the United States cannot legally be sold by that name in the country of its manufacture (or elsewhere in the EU). In navigating both US safety standards and French AOC standards, Valençay had to become multiple, effectively redrawing the encounter between "Valençay" and the regulatory body of the United States.

Such creative maneuvers are surprisingly common. To offer one more cheese example, in order to get around an especially high US tariff and low quota on imports of classic Dutch Gouda, the Dutch dairy giant Uniekaas invented Parrano™, described as a Dutch cheese "with an Italian temperament."[1] Parrano™ is made following a procedure similar to Gouda but with the addition of adjunct bacteria cultures that give it a flavor reminiscent of Parmesan. The modification warrants a registered trademark, allowing it to enter the United States under a more favorable tariff rate. The very idea of Parrano™, or of Valençay *frais* (made with pasteurized milk)—not to mention the vegan cheese/cheez made by fermenting nut-based "milks" of which Sarah Czerny writes—is well beyond terroir in that the "place" of these mobile, explicitly commercial comestibles is an assemblage of sovereign regulations and entrepreneurial adjustments to customary practice that in turn redefine their "tastes." The quiet ubiquity in the market of such heterotopic goods puts into perspective the lengths to which food purists must go to insist upon what Roberta Raffaetà (2021) has called the "utopia" of "an ideal alignment between nature and culture" imagined to be found in a food "truly" typical of and embedded in a local place. And why, for some, that ideal seems worth striving for.

Remaking Worlds, Remaking Taste

Despite its clear limitations, the concept of terroir, as a heuristic, can also articulate a useful vision of how agricultural products, no less than the bodies that ingest them, are semipermeable to their environments. As much as this may be celebrated—most famously in wine—it can also sound an alarm. When pregnant eaters are warned against consuming tuna and other top-predator fish for fear of mercury poisoning, we would do well to query how and why heavy metals became part of their material (though hardly "natural") composition (Mansfield 2011; Probyn 2016). In drawing attention to talk of the possible taint of tear gas spoiling the quality of Palestinian olive oil, Anne Meneley suggests that adverse conditions of a disordered political climate can register off-flavors in locally made foods. In such ways, the force of "the world" writ large can pull food substances beyond the logic of terroir: changes in the environmental conditions of agricultural production—drought, heat, fire, flooding, warfare, pollution—can lead to the development of flavors, odors, and colors in agricultural products that exceed thresholds of expectation and thus register as being "off." Burgundian winegrowers have taken note, as Marion Demossier tells us in tracing a discursive shift "from terroir to viticultural bricolage" in their framing of the relation between taste and place. Juxtaposing Demossier's observations with Yuson Jung's account of the Bulgarian wine industry, it would seem environmental crisis is pressing the economic center of European winemaking (France) to resemble its periphery (Balkans), inverting expectations of a global hierarchy of value (Herzfeld 2014).

Similar to how Nadia Seremetakis (1994) famously pointed to the loss of taste—or rather, the loss of a particular taste (in her case, the disappearance of a local variety of peach from Athenian markets)—as an index of globalization's homogenizing pressures, the "taste of contamination" points critically to place gone awry, whether owing to violent conflict, the toxic legacy of industrial agriculture and industry, or anthropogenic climate change. "Wildfire Loaf," an art exhibit by the Center for Genomic Gastronomy,[2] which Heather and Katharina viewed at the MIT Museum in Fall 2022, invited just such contemplation: "Making a Wildfire Loaf is about capturing the taste of place when wildfires are on the rise. How do wildfires affect the smell, taste, texture and microbial diversity of sourdough bread?" How do food industries respond when valued elements of an

Figure 18.1. "Making a Wildfire Loaf." Exhibit by the Center for Genomic Gastronomy at the MIT Museum. Massachusetts, 2022. © Heather Paxson

"environmental assemblage" of taste are no longer reliably "typical" to a place owing to the erratic conditions of a warming climate?

In the winegrowing and winemaking counties of Northern California, Brad found that agricultural extensions officers, laboratories, and vineyard management companies are all deeply concerned with the effects of smoke on winemaking. "Smoke taint," as the phenomena has been coined, is seen by some as evidence for why more heat-tolerant grape varieties should be grown across Napa and Sonoma Counties—or, alternatively, perhaps winegrowing operations should relocate to the still-temperate climes of British Columbia. Taking to heart the opportunistic origins of Lapsang souchong tea as related by Kunbing Xiao, Napa winegrowers, as another strategy, might seek out an export market for the exotic flavor of smokiness. Indeed, many winemakers have already done something like this. Leaning on the strength of what Greg de St. Maurice would call Napa's "place as brand," they blend "tainted" harvests and cheaper, unaffected grapes into their wines, assuming that less-sophisticated drinkers (who make up the majority of consumers) will not be able to discern fire's effects on wine purchased from the corner grocery store.

In all these ways and more—as place is reconfigured through national and supranational regulatory control, globalized markets and diets, military occupation, and climate catastrophe—tastes are also redefined, sometimes adapted to new conditions, sometimes pursued across distinctly different terrain, and sometimes simply lost altogether.

If off-flavors and discordant tastes can call attention to the disordering of places, what "political" effort is required for typicality to persist? Grasseni joins her cheesemaking interlocutors in asking precisely this question: what conditions will be necessary not only to allow artisan producers to be able to make recognizably *tipicità* products using (some) traditional methods while also complying with contemporary hygiene and other regulatory standards, but also for the *territorio* of Val Taleggio to persist economically, more or less as itself, without giving in to the temptation to sell out to game-changing Northern European conglomerates? In Latvia, Guntra Aistara finds by asking similar questions that the productive ecologies of coastal foodscapes are merging land and sea, terroir and *merroir*, and thereby reintegrate the local economy that Soviet state socialism had segregated into distinct fishing and farming taskscapes. As Grasseni writes, "the ongoing reinvention and rearticulation of place-based foods . . . goes beyond a simplistic evocation of authenticity and squarely addresses local needs of future-making" (2023: 51; see also Grasseni and Paxson 2014).

Rewriting terroir "in future tense," as Sanders puts it, commercial foodmakers across varied cultural and culinary contexts continue to invest in the promise that, taken together, proper stewardship of ecological and social relations, devotion to craft, entrepreneurial ingenuity, and savvy branding will be able to sustain or create desired places and sustainable worlds. The politics and policies that such efforts entail are as situated as the tastes at stake in their undertaking, especially when the ideology of terroir continues to serve, too, as a "form of political dominance, aggression, and even violent ethnic cleansing" (Caldwell, this volume: 103; see also Meneley, this volume). The core themes we have identified in this chapter—more expansive ways of imagining "place," the prominence of movement especially across borders of many kinds, and new material conditions wrought by environmental change that have in turn generated new tastes—all speak to the instability of what are assumed to be objectified features of food, location, and community. It is clear that some of these instabilities have been extremely disruptive and pose challenges that require concerted collective efforts to address. But rather than seeing such disruptions as necessarily exemplifying what has been lost, we might also think about what these new conditions make possible. As the fixity of categories, boundaries, and communities are unsettled, we might look to the kinds of opportunities that this creates, opportunities for new perspectives to emerge, and new modes of participation to be established. If we seize these opportunities, the politics that make the future may yet have a chance against the many challenges of the present.

Acknowledgments

We thank Anna Colquhoun and Katharina Graf for inviting us to be part of this volume, and of ongoing conversations.

Heather Paxson is William R. Kenan, Jr. Professor of Anthropology at the Massachusetts Institute of Technology. She is the author of two books, including *The Life of Cheese: Crafting Food and Value in America* (California, 2013), and the editor of *Eating beside Ourselves: Thresholds of Food and Bodies* (Duke, 2023). Her current research investigates the practical and semiotic work of moving perishable foods, beginning with cheese, across international borders.

Brad Weiss is Professor of Anthropology at William & Mary. The author of four books, Professor Weiss has carried out fieldwork and archival research in rural and urban Tanzania, producing scholarship on rural social transformation, popular culture, and the implications of the commodity form in (post)colonial contexts. He engaged in a multisited ethnographic project for over a decade in North Carolina, publishing the award-winning book, *Real Pigs* (Duke, 2016). Professor Weiss is currently studying the implications of climate change, heat events, and catastrophic wildfire for winemakers in Northern California.

Notes

1. "Parrano," Cheese.com, https://www.cheese.com/parrano/ (retrieved 11 December 2024).
2. https://genomicgastronomy.com/.

References

Bingham, Jim, and Stephanie Lavau. 2012. "The Object of Regulation: Tending the Tensions of Food Safety." *Environment & Planning A* 44: 1589–606.

Casey, Edward S. 1996. "How to Get from Space to Place in a Fairly Short Stretch of Time." In *Senses of Place*, edited by Steven Feld and Keith H. Basso, 13–52. Santa Fe: SAR Press.

———. 2013. *The Fate of Place: A Philosophical History*. Berkeley: University of California Press.

Cavanaugh, Jillian R. 2023. "Authenticity and Its Perils: Who Is Left Out When Food Is 'Authentic'?" *Gastronomica* 23(1): 28–37.

de Silva, Cara. 1996. *In Memory's Kitchen: A Legacy from the Women of Terezín*, plus sample recipes. New York: Rowman and Littlefield.

Dumont, Morgane. 2016. "Valençay." In *The Oxford Companion to Cheese*, edited by Catherine Donnelly, 746. New York: Oxford University Press.

Grasseni, Cristina. 2023. "Crafting Futures through Cheese-Making in Val Taleggio (Northern Italy)." *Gastronomica* 23(1): 51–64.

Grasseni, Cristina, and Heather Paxson. 2014. "Introducing a Special Issue on the Reinvention of Food: Connections and Mediations." With Jim Bingen, Amy J. Cohen, Susanne Freidberg, and Harry G. West. *Gastronomica* 14(4): 1–6.

Herzfeld, Michael. 2004. *The Body Impolitic: Artisans and Artifice in the Global Hierarchy of Value*. Chicago: University of Chicago Press.

Hinchliffe, Steve, J. Allen, S. Lavau, N. Bingham, and S. Carter. 2013. "Biosecurity and the Topologies of Infected Life: From Borderlines to Borderlands." *Transactions of the Institute of British Geographers* 38: 531–43.

Lefebvre, Henri. 1991. *The Production of Space*. Translated from the French by Donald Nicholson-Smith. Malden: Blackwell Publishing.

Mankekar, Purnima. 2002. "'India Shopping': Indian Grocery Stores and Transnational Configurations of Belonging." *Ethnos* 67(1): 75–97.

Mansfield, Becky. 2011. "Is Fish Health Food or Poison? Farmed Fish and the Material Production of Un/Healthy Nature." *Antipode* 43(2): 413–34.

Merleau-Ponty, Maurice. 1962. *Phenomenology of Perception*. London: Routledge.

Munn, Nancy. 1986. *The Fame of Gawa: A Symbolic Study of Value Transformation in a Massim (Papua New Guinea) Society*. Cambridge: Cambridge University Press.

Paxson, Heather. 2010. "Locating Value in Artisan Cheese: Reverse Engineering Terroir for New-World Landscapes." *American Anthropologist* 112(3): 444–57.

———. 2013. *The Life of Cheese: Crafting Food and Value in America*. Berkeley: University of California Press.

———. 2019. "'Don't Pack a Pest': Parts, Wholes, and the Porosity of Food Borders." *Food, Culture & Society* 22(5): 657–73.

———. 2023. "Introduction." In *Eating Beside Ourselves: Thresholds of Foods and Bodies*, edited by Heather Paxson, 1–28. Durham: Duke University Press.

Probyn, Elsbeth. 2016. *Eating the Ocean*. Durham: Duke University Press.

Raffaetà, Roberta. 2021. "Microbial Antagonism in the Trentino Alps: Negotiating Spacetimes and Ownership through the Production of Raw Milk Cheese in Alpine High Mountain Summer Pastures." *Current Anthropology* 62(S24): S323–32.

Seremetakis, C. Nadia. 1994. "The Memory of the Senses, Part 1: Marks of the Transitory." In *The Senses Still: Perception and Memory as Material Culture in Modernity*, 1–18. Chicago: University of Chicago Press.

Sutton, David E. 2000. "Whole Foods: Revitalization through Everyday Synesthetic Experience." *Anthropology & Humanism* 25(2): 120–30.

Weiss, Brad. 1996. *The Making and Unmaking of the Haya Lived World: Consumption, Commoditization, and Everyday Practice*. Durham: Duke University Press.

———. 2016. *Real Pigs: Shifting Values in the Field of Local Pork*. Durham: Duke University Press.

Welz, Gisela. 2015. *European Products: Making and Unmaking Heritage in Cyprus*. New York: Berghahn.

Index

www.ingramcontent.com/pod-product-compliance
Ingram Content Group UK Ltd.
Pitfield, Milton Keynes, MK11 3LW, UK
UKHW020847010226
467547UK00007B/22